Latin America:
An Interpretive History

EIGHTH EDITION

Latin America:

An Interpretive History

E. Bradford Burns
University of California, Los Angeles

Julie A. Charlip
Whitman College

Upper Saddle River, New Jersey

Library of Congress Cataloging-in-Publication Data

Burns, E. Bradford.

 Latin America: an interpretive history / E. Bradford Burns and Julie A. Charlip. —
8th ed.

    p. cm

 Includes bibliographical references and index.

 ISBN 0-13-193043-5

 1. Latin America—History. 2. Latin America—Social conditions. 3. Latin America—
Economic conditions. I.Charlip, Julie A., 1954- II. Title.

 F1410.B8   2007

 980—dc22   2006015083

Vice President/Editorial Director: Charlyce Jones-Owen
Executive Editor: Charles Cavaliere
Associate Editor: Emsal Hasan
Editorial Assistant: Maureen Diana
Senior Media Editor: Deborah O'Connell
Vice President/Director of Production and Manufacturing: Barbara Kittle
Senior Managing Editor: Joanne Riker
Production Liaison: Louise Rothman
Prepress and Manufacturing Manager: Nick Sklitsis
Prepress and Manufacturing Buyer: Benjamin Smith
Director of Marketing: Brandy Dawson
Assistant Marketing Manager: Emily Cleary
Cover Art: Jaime Colson, Merengue, 1937. Courtesy of Museo Bellapart, Dominican Republic
Director, Image Resource Center: Melinda Reo
Manager, Visual Research: Beth Brenzel
Cover Image Specialist: Karen Sanatar
Composition and Full Serice Project Management: Jodi Dowling/Techbooks
Printer/Binder: Courier Companies Inc.
Cover Printer: Courier Companies Inc.

Credits and acknowledgments borrowed from other sources and reproduced, with
permission, in this textbook appear on appropriate page within text.

Pearson Education LTD.
Pearson Education Australia PTY, Limited
Pearson Education Singapore, Pte. Ltd
Pearson Education North Asia Ltd
Pearson Education, Canada, Ltd
Pearson Educación de Mexico, S.A. de C.V.
Pearson Education—Japan
Pearson Education Malaysia Pte. Ltd

10 9 8 7 6 5 4 3
ISBN: 0-13-193043-5

For our students

CONTENTS

2 FROM CONQUEST TO EMPIRE 31

3 INDEPENDENCE 63

4 NEW NATIONS 87

5 THE EMERGENCE OF THE MODERN STATE   121

6 NEW ACTORS ON AN OLD STAGE   156

7 THE MEXICAN EXPLOSION   179

LIST OF MAPS

PREFACE

This edition of *Latin America: An Interpretive History* is, in many ways, the text that its readers have requested. I made major revisions in the seventh edition, and readers asked that I go even further in revising, not just updating, the original text by E. Bradford Burns. Therefore, the eighth edition gives greater prominence to my voice and to the work of recent scholars in ways that I believe harmonize with Professor Burns' original intent. The central paradigm still is that "poor people inhabit rich lands" because the elites have "tended to confuse their own well being and desires with those of the nation at large."

The strength of this text has always been its clear narrative, weaving together the story of an entire region, with coverage of broad themes and regional differences. I have endeavored to continue this pattern and follow in Professor Burns' formidable footsteps. However, I have also made substantial changes in organization and presentation.

One of the most significant changes is that the dependency paradigm plays a less obvious role in this edition. Latin American nations are, indeed, dependent in many ways, particularly in the global economy, and that relationship is fully discussed here. Dependency as a theory emerging from Latin America is also important and is given due attention. But the text also discusses alternative approaches to understanding Latin America's economic problems.

While trying to keep the text relatively "concise," I have also attempted to add material that would make a more complete package, especially for faculty teaching at schools with more limited resources. To that end, this edition contains statistical tables, and the document section has been expanded and converted into a separate booklet. There are, indeed, many wonderful websites with documents available, but websites come and go with alarming frequency, and it can be a burden for professors to locate documents. I hope that *Consider the Source* fills this lacuna.

In the seventh edition, I added a table, Statistics on the Nations of Latin America, drawn from the CIA *World Fact Book* of 2000. I have retained that data, along with a 2005 update, and moved them both to *Consider the Source* in hopes that students will engage with the data. I have also expanded the chart to include Canada, so that we can consider the Western Hemisphere as a whole.

I have revised "The Novel as History," not just to update the list of wonderful fiction available but also to change the tone of the essay: It is, of course, no longer such a novel idea. The new approach makes it clearer, I hope, that the essay is aimed at students. It is an invitation for them to try reading Latin American literature and to see it as a tool in understanding the region's history.

In the interest of providing more tools, I have added an essay, "*Testimonio*: A Rich and Complex Source." The essay introduces testimonio and the controversy about it and offers a bibliography of the genre. Despite its limitations, testimonio does offer another useful window onto the Latin American experience.

Finally, we have added color plates of Latin American art. The text, of necessity I believe, focuses a great deal on economic, social, and political issues. These images provide a view into the culture of Latin America as well.

ACKNOWLEDGMENTS

I owe a debt of thanks to the many colleagues and students who have taken the time to send me their feedback on the text. I am particularly grateful to the three readers who provided close reading and wonderful suggestions. My students in History 188, Modern Latin America, have asked questions that made me rethink aspects of the textbook. Charles Cavaliere at Prentice Hall has been patient and supportive. As always, I am most indebted to my husband, Charly Bloomquist, and my daughter, Delaney; they are my joy.

Julie A. Charlip
Walla Walla, Washington

CHAPTER 1

LAND AND PEOPLE

When Europeans first encountered the New World, they found a land unlike any they had ever seen. It was a lush tropical wonder, colored by brilliant plants and animals. Amerigo Vespucci marveled, "Sometimes I was so wonder-struck by the fragrant smells of the herbs and flowers and the savor of the fruits and the roots that I fancied myself near the Terrestrial Paradise."

As Spanish colonies, the New World offered wealth that other Europeans envied. The British priest Thomas Gage commented: "The streets of Christendom must not compare with those of Mexico City in breadth and cleanliness but especially in the riches of the shops that adorn them."

But the images of an earthly paradise and colonial splendor would fade over time. By the nineteenth century, Latin America would be considered "backward." In the twentieth century, the region would be described as "underdeveloped," "Third World," or simply "impoverished." In the twenty-first century, Latin America is the region of greatest inequality in the world.

What happened to the Garden of Eden? In 1972, E. Bradford Burns, the original author of this textbook, called the problem the enigma: "Poor people inhabit rich lands." And although in the ensuing years those lands have been exploited and subjected to substantial environmental degradation, they are still rich—and the majority of the people are still poor.

Latin America has moved from paradise to poverty as a result of historical patterns that have developed over the years. This book explores those patterns in an attempt to understand why the Latin America of the twenty-first century is still wrestling with issues it has faced throughout its history. We argue that the most destructive pattern has been the continuing tendency of the elites of the region to confuse their nations' well-being with their own. Earlier scholars, however, placed the blame on the region's climate, on racist characterizations of the populace, and on the size of the population.

THE LAND

In the 1490s, Christopher Columbus tried to convince himself, and his dis-
believing crew that the island of Cuba was actually a peninsula of China. In
reality, they had stumbled upon the unexpected: a region of such vastness
and geographical variety that, even today, not all of the territory is controlled
by the people who have so desperately tried to do so. It has been a land of
both opportunity and disaster. Geography is destiny until one has the technology to surmount it. The geographic attributes of Latin America have contributed to the region's economic organization and created challenges for
settlement and state building.

The original territory claimed by the kingdoms of the Iberian peninsula
included all of Central and South America, modern Mexico, many of the
islands off the coasts, as well as much of what is now the United States.
Contemporary Latin America is a huge region of a continent and a half,
stretching 7,000 miles southward from the Rio Grande to Cape Horn. Geo-
politically the region today encompasses eighteen Spanish-speaking republics,
Portuguese-speaking Brazil, and French-speaking Haiti, a total of approximately eight million square miles.

It is a region of geographic extremes. The Andes, the highest continuous mountain barrier on earth, spans 4,400 miles and has at least three dozen
peaks that are taller than Mount McKinley. The Amazon River has the greatest discharge volume, drainage basin, and length of navigable waterways on
the planet. Yet Latin America also contains the driest region on earth, the
Atacama Desert. Half of Latin America is forested, comprising one quarter
of the world's total forest area, which has led to its description as the "lungs
of the world."

In the U.S. press, Latin America often seems a tragic victim of its climate,
rocked by frequent earthquakes, volcanic eruptions, punishing hurricanes, and
deadly avalanches. Indeed, Latin America has more than its share of natural
disasters, a result of sitting atop five active tectonic plates—Caribbean, Cocos,
Nazca, Scotia, and South American. In addition, part of South America's Pacific
coast lies along the "ring of fire," the region where 80 percent of the seismic and
volcanic activity of the earth takes place. That we in the United States seem to
know so much about these events, however, says more about the limited media
portrayal of the region than it does about the frequency of climatic violence.

But climate has long been a factor in foreign views of the region. Most of
Latin America lies within the tropics, which prompted Europeans to speculate
that the hot, steamy climate made people lazy. It is true that a generous nature
provided natural abundance that made it possible for subsistence farmers to
support themselves, with no incentive to work in European-owned enterprises.
As many Latin Americans gradually lost access to the best lands and were
forced to eke out a living on poor soils or work on the large landholdings of
elites, it became clear that the climate was no drawback to hard work.

Latin America's Environmental Woes

Brazil's Amazon rain forest is a jungle the size of Western Europe that is known as "the lungs of the world." It can absorb greenhouse gases and is home to 10 percent of the world's fresh water and 30 percent of the world's plant and animal species. And from the founding of the capital, Brasilia, in 1960 until 1992, 160,000 square miles of rain forest disappeared—an area equal in size to the nation of Paraguay or to the five Central American nations. From 1990 to 2003, it was further deforested at the average rate of 6,240 square miles per year.

Environmental degradation is one of the most serious issues facing modern Latin America. The region encompasses some of the most endangered forest habitats on Earth, as well as the most rapid rates of deforestation. Coastal and marine areas are contaminated by land-based pollution, overexploitation of fisheries, the conversion of habitat to tourism, oil and gas extraction, refining, and transport. The region increasingly suffers from desertification, a process in which productive but dry land becomes unproductive desert. Desertification is caused by overcultivation, overgrazing, deforestation, and poor irrigation practices.

In addition, damage is inflicted by U.S.-organized programs for drug eradication. Colombia uses aerial fumigation, spraying toxic herbicides on regions where drugs are produced. The spraying contaminates everything—schools, houses, water, pastures, farms, and the workers who toil in the fields. Residues are left in the ground and water, and many areas are defoliated. In reaction, subsistence farmers move farther up steep hillsides or into the Amazon rain forest.

And that's just the rural areas.

Seventy-seven percent of Latin Americans live in urban areas, making it the most urbanized area in the "developing" world and as urban as the European Union. This change has occurred rapidly. In the 1950s, 60 percent of Latin Americans lived in the countryside. In 1960, for the first time more than 50 percent of the population was urban. The rapid influx of people strains urban water supplies and sanitation infrastructure.

São Paulo and Mexico City are teeming with more than eighteen million people. In Brazil, hundreds of thousands live in shantytowns that began as temporary housing in the 1950s migrations and have since evolved into permanent slums. In Mexico City, the inability of the government to adequately house and provide services to its millions was spotlighted when a 1985 earthquake destroyed flimsy housing and left many homeless. Only Cuba has been able to manage urbanization by placing controls on population movement, developing the countryside, and developing urban centers other than Havana.

Problems are exacerbated by the region's poverty and demands for job creation and economic development. In 2003, Brazil elected Luiz Inacio "Lula" da Silva, a candidate who pledged to help the country's poor. One year into his term, environmentalists accused him of sacrificing the Amazon to the effort to create jobs for the 53 million Brazilians who live on less than $1 a day.

Latin America has only one country, Uruguay, with no territory in the tropics. South America reaches its widest point, 3,200 miles, just a few degrees south of the equator, unlike North America, which narrows rapidly as it approaches the equator. However, the cold Pacific Ocean currents refresh much of the west coast of Latin America, and the altitudes of the mountains and highlands offer a wide range of temperatures that belie the latitude. For centuries, and certainly long before the Europeans arrived, many of the region's most advanced civilizations flourished in the mountain plateaus and valleys. Today many of Latin America's largest cities are in the mountains or on mountain plateaus: Mexico City, Guatemala City, Bogotá, Quito, La Paz, and São Paulo, to mention only a few. Much of Latin America's population, particularly in Middle America and along the west coast of South America, concentrates in the highland areas.

In Mexico and Central America, the highlands create a rugged backbone that runs through the center of most of the countries, leaving coastal plains on either side. Part of that mountain system emerges in the Greater Antilles to shape the geography of the major Caribbean islands. In South America, unlike Middle America, the mountains closely rim the Pacific coast, whereas the highlands skirt much of the Atlantic coast, making penetration into the flatter interior of the continent difficult. The Andes predominate: The world's longest continuous mountain barrier, it runs 4,400 miles down the west coast and fluctuates in width between 100 and 400 miles. Aconcagua, the highest mountain in the hemisphere, rises to a majestic 22,834 feet along the Chilean–Argentine

This turn-of-the-century photograph captures the drama of Chile's Aconcagua Valley in the towering Andes. (Library of Congress)

frontier. The formidable Andes have been a severe obstacle to exploration and settlement of the South American interior from the west. Along the east coast, the older Guiana and Brazilian Highlands average 2,600 feet in altitude and rarely reach 9,000 feet. Running southward from the Caribbean and frequently fronting on the ocean, they disappear in the extreme south of Brazil. Like the Andes, they too have inhibited penetration of the interior. The largest cities on the Atlantic side are all on the coast or, like São Paulo, within a very short distance of the ocean.

Four major river networks, the Magdalena, Orinoco, Amazon, and La Plata, flow into the Caribbean or Atlantic, providing access into the interior that is missing on the west coast. The Amazon ranks as one of the world's most impressive river systems. Aptly referred to in Portuguese as the "riversea," it is the largest river in volume in the world, exceeding that of the Mississippi fourteen times. In places, it is impossible to see from shore to shore; and over much of its course, the river averages 100 feet in depth. Running eastward from its source 18,000 feet up in the Andes, it is joined from both the north and south by more than 200 tributaries. Together this imposing river and its tributaries provide 25,000 miles of navigable water. Farther to the south, the Plata network flows through some of the world's richest soil, the Pampas, a vast flat area shared by Argentina, Uruguay, and Brazil. The river system includes the Uruguay, Paraguay, and Paraná rivers, but it gets its name from the Río de la Plata, a 180-mile-long estuary separating Uruguay and the Argentine province of Buenos Aires. The system drains a basin of more than 1.5 million square miles. Shallow in depth, it still provides a vital communication and transportation link between the Atlantic coast and the southern interior of the continent.

No single country better illustrates the kaleidoscopic variety of Latin American geography than Chile, that long, lean land clinging to the Pacific shore for 2,600 miles. One of the world's bleakest and most forbidding deserts in the north, the Atacama, gives way to rugged mountains with forests and alpine pastures. The Central Valley combines a Mediterranean climate with fertile plains, the heartland of Chile's agriculture and population. Moving southward, the traveler encounters dense, mixed forests; heavy rainfall; and a cold climate, warning of the glaciers and rugged coasts that lie beyond. Snow permanently covers much of Tierra del Fuego.

Yet, even with Chile's extremes from the desert to the snow, geographical differences are even wider in Bolivia, Brazil, Colombia, Mexico, and Peru, which alone encompasses eighty-four of the 104 ecological regions in the world and twenty-eight different climates. In fact, Latin America is the most geographically diverse area in the world. It includes seven distinct geographical zones: border, tropical highlands, lowland Pacific coast, lowland Atlantic coast, Amazon, highland and dry Southern Cone, and the temperate Southern Cone.

The United States–Mexico border is an area of arid or temperate climate, low population, and is the only place in the world where rich and poor countries abut. Because it is home to the manufacturing assembly industry (*maquiladora*), the region has a higher gross domestic product than the rest of

Latin America. To its south, the tropical highlands include the highlands of Central America and the Andean countries north of the Tropic of Capricorn. Access to the coast of this region is difficult, yet it is also an area of high population density, including most of the indigenous population of Latin America. Because of poor soil and high population, this is the poorest area in Latin America—even though the region includes the relatively high-income areas of Mexico City and Bogotá.

The lowland Pacific and Atlantic coasts are both tropical, although both have small dry areas. Although the highest population density of all Latin America is found on the Pacific coast, the Atlantic coast also has a large population. The income of the regions is about 20 percent higher than that of the tropical highlands, partly because of their advantageous position for international trade. But the lowlands are also areas that are prone to disease, and tropical soils present problems for successful agriculture.

Latin America's tropical beauty is on display in this 1911 photograph from Panama. (Library of Congress)

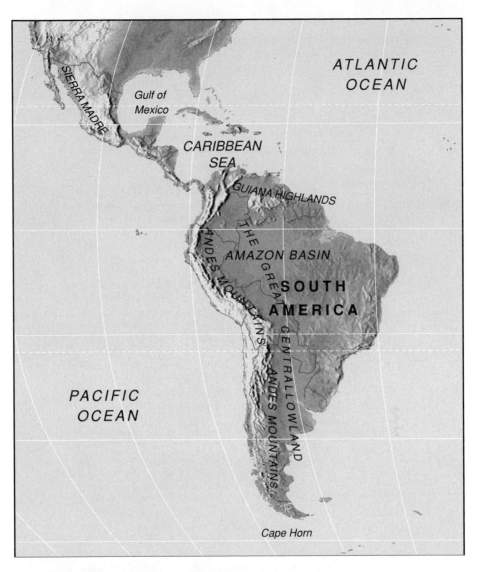

Map 1.1 Physical Map of Latin America

The Amazon zone has the lowest population density of Latin America. It boasts a higher gross domestic product than neighboring areas because absentee owners earn high rents from mining and from large plantations. These economic activities are taking a toll on the delicate ecology of the area. The dry Southern Cone has only a slightly higher population than the Amazon, but there is a high population density in the temperate Southern Cone. Both are high-income areas.

Environmental Issues by Country

Argentina	Environmental problems (urban and rural) typical of an industrializing economy such as deforestation, soil degradation, desertification, air pollution, and water pollution
Bolivia	The clearing of land for agricultural purposes and the international demand for tropical timber are contributing to deforestation; soil erosion from overgrazing and poor cultivation methods (including slash-and-burn agriculture); desertification; loss of biodiversity; industrial pollution of water supplies used for drinking and irrigation
Brazil	Deforestation, endangered Amazon Basin plant and animal habitat, illegal wildlife trade; air and water pollution in Rio de Janeiro, Sao Paulo, and several other large cities; land degradation and water pollution caused by improper mining activities; wetland degradation; severe oil spills
Chile	Widespread deforestation and mining threaten natural resources; air pollution from industrial and vehicle emissions; water pollution from raw sewage
Colombia	Deforestation; soil and water quality damage from overuse of pesticides; air pollution, especially in Bogotá, from vehicle emissions
Costa Rica	Deforestation and land use change, largely a result of the clearing of land for cattle ranching and agriculture; soil erosion; coastal marine pollution; fisheries protection; solid waste management; air pollution
Cuba	Air and water pollution; biodiversity loss; deforestation
Dominican Republic	Water shortages; soil eroding into the sea damages coral reefs; deforestation
Ecuador	Deforestation; soil erosion; desertification; water pollution; pollution from oil production wastes in ecologically sensitive areas of the Amazon Basin and Galapagos Islands
El Salvador	Deforestation; soil erosion; water pollution; contamination of soils from disposal of toxic wastes
Guatemala	Deforestation in the Petén rainforest; soil erosion; water pollution
Haiti	Extensive deforestation (much of the remaining forested land is being cleared for agriculture and used as fuel); soil erosion; inadequate supplies of potable water
Honduras	Urban population expanding; deforestation results from logging and the clearing of land for agricultural purposes; further land degradation and soil erosion hastened by uncontrolled development and improper land use practices such as farming of marginal lands; mining activities polluting Lago de Yojoa (the country's largest source of fresh water), as well as several rivers and streams, with heavy metals

Mexico	Scarcity of hazardous waste disposal facilities; rural to urban migration; natural fresh water resources scarce and polluted in north, inaccessible and poor quality in center and extreme southeast; raw sewage and industrial effluents polluting rivers in urban areas; deforestation; widespread erosion; desertification; deteriorating agricultural lands; serious air and water pollution in the national capital and urban centers along US-Mexico border; land subsidence in Valley of Mexico caused by groundwater depletion
Nicaragua	Deforestation; soil erosion; water pollution
Panama	Water pollution from agricultural runoff threatens fishery resources; deforestation of tropical rain forest; land degradation and soil erosion threatens siltation of Panama Canal; air pollution in urban areas; mining threatens natural resources
Paraguay	Deforestation; water pollution; inadequate means for waste disposal pose health risks for many urban residents; loss of wetlands
Peru	Deforestation (some the result of illegal logging); overgrazing of the slopes of the costa and sierra leading to soil erosion; desertification; air pollution in Lima; pollution of rivers and coastal waters from municipal and mining wastes
Uruguay	Water pollution from meat packing/tannery industry; inadequate solid/hazardous waste disposal
Venezuela	Sewage pollution of Lago de Valencia; oil and urban pollution of Lago de Maracaibo; deforestation; soil degradation; urban and industrial pollution, especially along the Caribbean coast; threat to the rainforest ecosystem from irresponsible mining operations

Source: Material drawn from Central Intelligence Agency, *The World Factbook, 2005,* http://www.cia.gov/cia/publications/factbook/

Latin Americans have always been aware of the significance of their environment. Visiting the harsh, arid interior of Northeastern Brazil for the first time, Euclydes da Cunha marveled in his *Rebellion in the Backlands (Os Sertões,* 1902) at how the land had shaped a different people and created a civilization that contrasted sharply with that of the coast:

Here was an absolute and radical break between the coastal cities and the clay huts of the interior, one that so disturbed the rhythm of our evolutionary development and which was so deplorable a stumbling block to national unity. They were in a strange country now, with other customs, other scenes, a different kind of people. Another language even, spoken with an original and picturesque drawl. They had, precisely, the feelings of going to war in another land. They felt that they were outside Brazil.

The variety of environment within countries has also been a trope in literature. Gabriel García Márquez grew up in Aracataca, the model for the fictional Macondo, a lush, steamy tropical zone. At fourteen, when he first went to Bogotá, he described it as "a remote and mournful city, where a cold drizzle had been falling since the beginning of the sixteenth century." He uses similar language in *One Hundred Years of Solitude* (1967) to describe Bogota's effects on Fernanda del Carpio: "Fernanda was a woman lost in the world. She had been born and raised in a city six hundred miles away [from Macondo], a gloomy city where on ghostly nights the coaches of the viceroys still rattled down cobbled streets."

Latin American films, too, often assign nature the role of a major protagonist. Certainly in the Argentine classic *Prisoners of the Earth* (*Prísioneros de la Tierra;* 1939), the forests and rivers of the northeast overpower the outsider. Nature even forces the local people to bend before her rather than conquer her. A schoolteacher exiled by a military dictatorship to the geographically remote and rugged Chilean south in the Chilean film *The Frontier* (*La Frontera;* 1991) quickly learns that the ocean, mountains, and elements dominate and shape the lives of the inhabitants. Nature thus enforces some characteristics on the people of Latin America. The towering Andes, the vast Amazon, the unbroken Pampas, the lush rain forests provide an impressive setting for an equally powerful human drama.

The numbers of humans in that drama has been an issue of great concern, especially in the context of Latin American development. In the 1960s, Latin America's annual birthrate of 2.8 percent made it the most rapidly growing area in the world. By the end of the twentieth century, the region's population growth rate had slowed to a low of 1.6 percent, closer to the world average of 1.5 percent. Half of that population is either Brazilian or Mexican. Despite concerns in the more developed world about Latin American population growth, the region is relatively underpopulated, with the exception of overcrowded El Salvador and Haiti. More than twice the size of Europe, the area has a smaller population than Europe. It occupies 15 percent of the world's land mass but contains only 9 percent of the world's population. That population has its roots in the people who came to the region from Asia, Europe, and Africa.

THE INDIGENOUS

Some 30,000 years ago, when there still existed a land bridge between Asia and North America, migrants crossed the Bering Strait in pursuit of game animals. Moving slowly southward, they dispersed throughout North and South America. Over the millennia, at an uneven rate, some advanced through hunting and fishing cultures to take up agriculture. At the same time, they fragmented into many cultural and linguistic groups, with up to

Population Density of Latin America and Selected European Countries, 2005

COUNTRY	LAND AREA (In square kilometers)	POPULATION	DENSITY
Netherlands	33,889	16,407,491	484
Belgium	30,278	10,364,388	342
El Salvador	20,720	6,704,932	324
Haiti	27,560	8,121,622	295
United Kingdom	241,590	60,441,457	250
Germany	349,223	82,431,390	236
Italy	294,020	58,103,033	198
Dominican Republic	48,380	8,950,034	185
Denmark	42,394	5,432,335	128
Poland	304,465	38,635,144	127
France	545,630	60,656,178	111
Hungary	92,340	10,006,835	108
Cuba	110,860	11,346,670	102
Austria	82,444	8,184,691	99
Costa Rica	50,660	4,016,173	79
Honduras	111,890	6,975,204	62
Mexico	1,923,040	106,202,903	55
Ecuador	276,840	13,363,593	48
Nicaragua	120,254	5,465,100	45
Colombia	1,038,700	42,954,279	41
Panama	75,990	3,039,150	40
Guatemala	108,430	14,655,189	29
Venezuela	882,050	25,375,281	27
Brazil	8,456,510	186,112,794	22
Peru	1,280,000	27,925,628	21
Chile	748,800	15,980,912	21
Paraguay	397,300	6,347,884	20
Uruguay	173,620	3,415,920	19
Argentina	2,736,690	39,537,943	14
Bolivia	1,084,390	8,857,870	8

Source: Data drawn from Central Intelligence Agency, *The World Factbook, 2005,* http://www.cia.gov/cia/publications/factbook/

2,200 different languages, although they maintained certain general physical features in common: straight black hair, dark eyes, copper-colored skin, and short stature.

The indigenous groups can best be understood by grouping them as nonsedentary, semi-sedentary, and sedentary societies. Nonsedentary societies were gathering and hunting groups that followed a seasonal cycle of moving through a delimited territory in search of food; they were found mostly in what is now the northern Mexico frontier, the Argentine Pampas, and the interior of Brazil. In semi-sedentary societies, hunting was still important, but they had also developed slash-and-burn agriculture, which shifted sites within their region. They populated much of Latin America and were often found on the fringes of fully sedentary peoples. Fully sedentary peoples had settled communities based on intensive agriculture, which provided enough of a surplus to support a hierarchical society with specialized classes. They were found in central Mexico, Guatemala, Ecuador, Peru, and Bolivia. The most advanced of these groups founded the impressive imperial societies.

Varied as the early American cultures were, a majority of them shared enough traits to permit a few generalizations. Family or clan units served as the basic social organization. All displayed a profound faith in supernatural forces that they believed shaped, influenced, and guided their lives. For that reason, the *shamans*, those intimate with the supernatural, played important roles. They provided the contact between the mortal and the immortal, between the human and the spirit, and they served as healers. In the more complex and highly stratified societies, there was a differentiation between the more extensive landholdings of the nobility and that of the commoners. But in all indigenous societies, land was provided to everyone on the basis of

A Miskito man in Nicaragua shows the continuing presence of indigenous populations. (Photograph by Julie A. Charlip)

membership in the community. Game roamed and ate off the land. Further, the land furnished fruits, berries, nuts, and roots. Tilling the soil produced other foods, such as corn and potatoes. Many artifacts, instruments, and implements were similar from Alaska to Cape Horn. For example, spears, bows and arrows, and clubs were the common weapons of warfare or for the hunt. Although these similarities are significant, the differences among the many cultures were enormous and impressive. By the end of the fifteenth century, between nine million and 100 million people inhabited the Western Hemisphere. Scholars still heatedly debate the figures, and one can find forceful arguments favoring each extreme.

Mistaking the New World for Asia, Christopher Columbus called the inhabitants he met "Indians." Exploration later indicated that the "Indians" belonged to myriad cultural groups, none of which had a word in their language that grouped together all the indigenous people of the New World. They were as differentiated as the ancestral tribes of Europe, and their identities were locally based. The most important indigenous groups were the Aztecs and the Mayas of Mexico and Central America; the Carib and the Arawak of the Caribbean area; the Chibcha of Colombia; the Inca of Ecuador, Peru, and Bolivia; the Araucanian of Chile; the Guaraní of Paraguay; and the Tupí of Brazil. Of these, the Aztec, Maya, and Inca exemplify the most complex cultural achievements, with fully sedentary and imperial societies.

Two distinct periods, the Classic and the Late, mark the history of Mayan civilization. During the Classic period, from the fourth to the tenth centuries, the Mayas lived in Guatemala; then they suddenly migrated to Yucatan, beginning in the Late period, which lasted until the Spanish conquest. The exodus baffles anthropologists, who have most often suggested that the exhaustion of the soil in Guatemala limited the corn harvests and forced the Mayas to move in order to survive. Corn provided the basis for the Mayan civilization, and the Mayan account of creation revolves around corn. The gods "began to talk about the creation and the making of our first mother and father; of yellow corn and of white corn they made their flesh; of cornmeal dough they made the arms and the legs of man," relates the *Popul Vuh*, the sacred book of the Mayas. All human activity and all religion centered on the planting, growing, and harvesting of corn. The Mayas dug an extensive network of canals and water-control ditches, which made intensive agriculture possible. These efficient agricultural methods produced corn surpluses and hence the leisure time available for a large priestly class to dedicate its talents to religion and scientific study.

Extraordinary intellectual achievements resulted. The Mayas progressed from the pictograph to the ideograph and thus invented a type of writing, the only Indians in the hemisphere to do so. Sophisticated in mathematics, they invented the zero and devised numeration by position. Astute observers of the heavens, they applied their mathematical skills to astronomy. Their careful studies of the heavens enabled them to predict eclipses, follow the path of the

The Mayan monument known as the Castillo at Chichén Itzá in the Yucatan is indicative of the sophisticated societies that pre-dated the Spanish conquest. (Library of Congress)

planet Venus, and prepare a calendar more accurate than that used in Europe. As the ruins of Copán, Tikal, Palenque, Chichén Itzá, Mayapán, and Uxmal testify, the Mayas built magnificent temples. One of the most striking features of that architecture is its extremely elaborate carving and sculpture.

To the west of the Mayas, another native civilization, the Aztec, expanded and flourished in the fifteenth century. The Aztec empire had its origins in the Mexica, a group that had migrated from the north in the early thirteenth century to the central valley of Mexico, where they conquered several prosperous and highly advanced city–states. Constant conquests gave prominence to the warriors, and, not surprisingly, among multiple divinities the god of war and the sun predominated. Propitiatiation of him, as well as of other gods, required human sacrifices. In 1325, they founded Tenochtitlán, their island capital, and from that religious and political center they radiated outward to absorb other cultures until they controlled all of Central Mexico. Their highly productive system of agriculture included the *chinampas*, floating gardens that made effective use of their lake location. The Aztecs devised the pictograph, an accurate calendar, an impressive architecture, and an elaborate and effective system of government.

Largest, oldest, and best organized of the Indian civilizations was the Incan, which flowered in the harsh environment of the Andes. By the early sixteenth century, the empire extended in all directions from Cuzco, regarded as the center of the universe. It stretched nearly 3,000 miles from Ecuador into Chile, and its maximum width measured 400 miles. Few empires have been more rigidly regimented or more highly centralized, a real miracle when one realizes that it was run without the benefit—or hindrance—of written accounts or records. The only accounting system was the *quipu*, cords upon which knots were made to indicate specific mathematical units. Scholars now believe the Incas wove a verbal code into the threads. Spanish chroniclers attested that the cords were used not just to record such mathematical data as censuses, inventories, and tribute records, but also for royal chronicles, records of sacred places and sacrifices, successions, postal messages, and criminal trials. The highly effective government rapidly assimilated newly conquered peoples into the empire. Entire populations were moved around the empire when security suggested the wisdom of such relocations. Every subject was required to speak Quechua, the language of the court. In weaving, pottery, medicine, and agriculture, the achievements of the Incans were magnificent. Challenged by stingy soil, they developed systems of drainage, terracing, and irrigation and learned the value of fertilizing their fields. They produced impressive food surpluses, stored by the state for lean years.

Many differences separated these three high indigenous civilizations, but at the same time some impressive similarities existed. Society was highly structured. The hierarchy of nobles, priests, warriors, artisans, farmers, and slaves was ordinarily inflexible, although occasionally some mobility did occur. At the pinnacle of that hierarchy stood the omnipotent emperor, the object of the greatest respect and veneration. The sixteenth-century chronicler Pedro de Cieza de León, in his own charming style, illustrated the awe in which the people held the Inca: "Thus the kings were so feared that, when they traveled over the provinces, and permitted a piece of the cloth to be raised which hung round their litter, so as to allow their vassals to behold them, there was such an outcry that the birds fell from the upper air where they were flying, insomuch that they could be caught in men's hands. All men so feared the king, that they did not dare to speak evil of his shadow."

Little or no distinction existed between civil and religious authority, so for all intents and purposes Church and State were one. The Incan and Aztec emperors were both regarded as representatives of the sun on earth and thus as deities, a position probably held by the rulers of the Mayan city–states as well. Royal judges impartially administered the laws of the empires and apparently enjoyed a reputation for fairness. The sixteenth-century chroniclers who saw the judicial systems functioning invariably praised them. Cieza de León, for one, noted, "It was felt to be certain that those who did evil would receive punishment without fail and that neither prayers nor bribes would avert it."

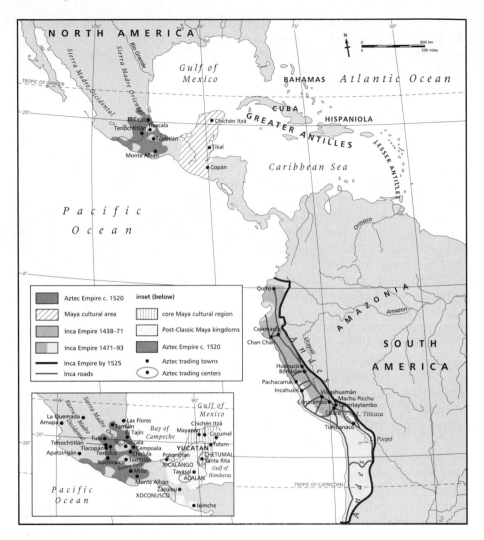

Map 1.2 Pre-Columbian America
Adapted from Spodek, Howard, *The World's History Combined*, 3rd ed. © 2006. Electronically reproduced by permission of Pearson Education, Inc., Upper Saddle River, NJ.

These civilizations rested on a firm rural base. Cities were rare, although a few existed with populations exceeding 100,000. They were centers of commerce, government, and religion. Eyewitness accounts as well as the ruins that remain leave no doubt that these cities were well-organized and contained impressive architecture. The sixteenth-century chronicles reveal that the cities astonished the first Spaniards who saw them. Bernal Díaz del Castillo, who accompanied Hernando Cortés into Tenochtitlán in 1519, gasped, "And when we saw all those cities and villages built in the water, and other great towns on dry land, and that straight and level causeway leading to Mexico [City], we were astounded. These great towns and cities and buildings rising from the water, all made of stone, seemed like an enchanted vision from the tale of Amadis. Indeed, some of our soldiers asked whether it was not a dream!"

The productivity of the land made possible an opulent court life and complex religious ceremonies. The vast majority of the population, however, worked in agriculture. The farmers grew corn, beans, squash, pumpkins, manioc root, and potatoes, as well as other crops. Communal lands were cultivated for the benefit of the state, religion, and community. The state thoroughly organized and directed the rural labor force. Advanced as these native civilizations were, however, not one developed the use of iron or used the wheel because they lacked draft animals to pull wheeled vehicles. However, the indigenous had learned to work gold, silver, copper, tin, and bronze. Artifacts that have survived in those metals testify to fine skills.

There is some disagreement among scholars about the roles that women played in these societies. In both the Inca and Aztec worlds, women primarily bore responsibility for domestic duties. The roles were so clearly defined among the Mexica that when a child was born, the midwife would give a girl a spindle, weaving shuttles, and a broom, whereas a boy would be given a shield and arrows. Many scholars now contend that these roles were different but not necessarily unequal; instead, they see gender complementarity, in which men and women formed equally important halves of the social order. For example, home was a sacred place, and ritual sweeping was related to religious practices. Childbirth was considered akin to battle; as one Nahuatl account described it, "Is this not a fatal time for us poor women? This is our kind of war."

In the Aztec empire, women also sold goods in the markets, where they often had supervisory positions; they were cloth makers and embroiderers, and they served as midwives. In Inca society, women took care of the home, but they also worked in agriculture. Their work tended to be seen not as private service for husbands but as a continuation of household and community. Here there was complementarity as well: men plowed, women sowed, and both harvested.

Although Mexica women in Central Mexico could not hold high political office, this was not the case at the fringes of the empire. Mixtec women inherited dynastic titles and frequently served as rulers. The same was true on the fringes of the Inca empire, for example, in the highlands of Ecuador. However, the complementary social positions and occasional positions of power do not imply political equality. In both empires, men held the highest positions of power.

The spectacular achievements of these sedentary farming cultures contrast sharply with the more elementary evolution of the gathering, hunting, and fishing cultures and semi-sedentary farming cultures among the Latin

American indigenous populations. The Tupí tribes, the single most important native element contributing to the early formation of Brazil, illustrate the status of the many intermediate farming cultures found throughout Latin America.

The Tupí tribes tended to be very loosely organized. The small, temporary villages, often surrounded by a crude wooden stockade, were, when possible, located along a river bank. The indigenous lived communally in large thatched huts in which they strung their hammocks in extended family or lineage groups of as many as 100 people. Most of the tribes had at least a nominal chief, although some seemed to recognize a leader only in time of war and a few seemed to have no concept of a leader. More often than not, the *shaman* was the most important and powerful tribal figure. He communed with the spirits, proffered advice, and prescribed medicines. The religions abounded with good and evil spirits.

The men spent considerable time preparing for and participating in tribal wars. They hunted monkeys, tapirs, armadillos, and birds. They also fished, trapping the fish with funnel-shaped baskets, poisoning the water and collecting the fish, or shooting the fish with arrows. They cleared away the forest to plant crops. Nearly every year during the dry season, the men cut down trees, bushes, and vines, waited until they had dried, and then burned them, a method used throughout Latin America, then as well as now. The burning destroyed the thin humus and the soil was quickly exhausted. Hence, it was constantly necessary to clear new land, and eventually the village moved in order to be near virgin soil. In general, although not exclusively, the women took charge of planting and harvesting crops and of collecting and preparing the food. Manioc was the principal cultivated crop. Maize, beans, yams, peppers, squash, sweet potatoes, tobacco, pineapples, and occasionally cotton were the other cultivated crops. Forest fruits were collected.

To the first Europeans who observed them, these people seemed to live an idyllic life. The tropics required little or no clothing. Generally nude, the Tupí developed the art of body ornamentation and painted elaborate and ornate geometric designs on themselves. Into their noses, lips, and ears they inserted stone and wooden artifacts. Feathers from the colorful forest birds provided an additional decorative touch. Their appearance prompted the Europeans to think of them as innocent children of nature. The first chronicler of Brazil, Pero Vaz de Caminha, marveled to the king of Portugal, "Sire, the innocence of Adam himself was not greater than these people's." As competition for land and resources increased, chroniclers would later tell quite a different tale, one in which the Indians emerged as wicked villains, brutes who desperately needed the civilizing hand of Europe.

The European romantics who thought they saw a utopia in native life obviously exaggerated. The indigenous by no means had led the perfect life. Misunderstanding, if not outright ignorance, has always characterized outsiders' perceptions of them. Far too often since the conquest, images of native peoples have erred at either extreme—the violent savage or the noble savage—rather than showing their humanity. It is through their own words that the indigenous can be seen as more fully human, as in this Nahuatl lament over the conquest: "Broken spears lie in the roads; we have torn our hair in our grief. . . . We have pounded our hands in despair against the adobe walls, for our inheritance, our city, is lost and dead."

The European

The Europeans who came to dominate Latin America came primarily from the Iberian peninsula, a land of as much contrast as the New World. Almost an island, the peninsula is bounded by the Bay of Biscay, Atlantic Ocean, Gulf of Cádiz, and the Mediterranean Sea. Half of its territory comprises arid tableland. But this *meseta* is bisected by one imposing mountain system—the Sierra da Estrela, Sierra de Gredos, and Sierra de Guadarrama—and circled

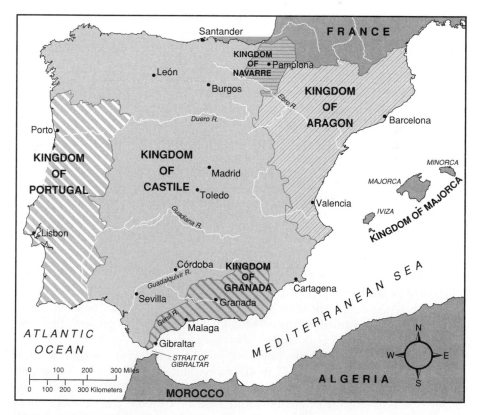

Map 1.3 Iberian Peninsula
http://www.fordham.edu/halsall/maps/1492spain.jpg

by another—the Cantabrian Cordillera, Ibera mountains and Sierra Morena, and Cordillera Bética. Spain is divided by the Pyrenees from the rest of Europe, and separated from Africa only by the Staits of Gibraltar. The varied climate ranges from the cold winters of the north to the subtropical sunshine of the south.

The region was also the crossroads of many peoples—Iberians, Celts, Phoenicians, Greeks, Carthaginians, Romans, Visigoths, and Muslims—and these cultures blended together. The most stable periods in this varied history were under Roman rule, from about 19 B.C.E. to the late fifth century, which was followed by rule by the Visigoths, who continued many Roman customs, during the sixth and seventh centuries. The Visigoths fell to the Muslims in the invasion of 711–720, which prompted similar laments to those of the Mexica: "Who can bear to relate such perils? Who can count such terrible disasters? Even if every limb were transformed into a tongue, it would be beyond human capability to describe the ruin of Spain and its many and great evils."

Muslim control of the peninsula was never complete, and even its dominance of the south waxed and waned, due in part to divisions between Berbers and Arabs within the Muslim community. Furthermore, although many Christians converted to Islam, the majority of the rural population was still Christian as late as 948, when Arab geographer Ibn Hawqal visited. In addition, Christian groups in the north continued to resist the Muslim forces. The Umayyad caliphate was successful at slowly conquering and ruling much of the south of Spain, raising Córdoba to a cultural center and ruling from 929 to 1031. Two subsequent caliphates, the Almoravid, a Berber group from North Africa (1086–1147), and the Almohad (1146–1220s), were able to maintain unity in al-Andalus, as the Muslims called their Iberian territories. But by the thirteenth century, the Christian groups from the north of the peninsula had gained strength. The crusade to retake the peninsula had begun in 732 at the Battle of Tours, and it would take until 1492, when Granada fell, to expel the Muslims from the peninsula.

Throughout the years of Muslim rule, Iberia was a land of three cultures: Muslim, Jewish and Christian. There were conflicts, but the eleventh century was considered a high point of cooperation between the Jewish and Muslim communities, resulting in a flourishing of culture. Caliph Al-Hakam II (961–976) is said to have founded a library of hundreds of thousands of volumes, something impossible to imagine in the rest of Europe at the time. One of the great contributions of Muslim Spain was the preservation and translation of classical philosophy.

Both Jews and Muslims, however, would suffer with the reunification of the peninsula under the Catholic monarchs, Isabella I of Castile and Ferdinand II of Aragón, who were married in 1479. In 1492, the monarchs ordered the expulsion of all Jews and Muslims unless they converted to Christianity. Catholicism became the official religion and served as a proto-nationalism: To be Spanish was to be Catholic.

But the Catholic Church in Spain was far from a monolithic entity. One split was between the secular and the regular clergy. The secular clergy were loosely organized and charged with administering to Christian populations. These were the worldly orders, concerned with the day-to-day lives of their flocks, and as a result they needed to find economic activities in that world to sustain them. The regular clergy were tightly organized into orders—Franciscan, Dominican, Augustinian—each with its separate rules and concerns. These clerics had largely withdrawn from the world to the solitude of monasteries and they were accorded higher status because they were seen as devoting their lives to God rather than to man. Members of the clergy served in government ministries, but the monarchs had the power of appointment of bishops. In fact, the Spanish Crown had more control over the Church than did any other monarchy in Europe. The two institutions were dependent upon one another, equal pillars of society.

Although 1492 is popularly referred to as the *reunification*, there is little accuracy in the term. The peninsula had always been a splintered entity, and the royal marriage did not create a territorial or administrative merger. Further, each kingdom was a loose confederation: Isabella's "Aragón" included Aragón, Catalonia, Valencia, Majorca, Sardinia, and Sicily, each autonomous in legal, administrative, and economic matters. There were still customs barriers between Aragón and Castile, the much larger region, which acquired the southern territories.

There were no Spaniards at this point, although the region was called Hispania starting in the Roman era. People identified with their region, such as Aragón or Catalonia, and more specifically with their city. This urban focus was so widespread that even in rural areas, people tended to live in nucleated towns and went out to their fields.

The social structure was divided most importantly along the lines of nobles and commoners, with the landed nobleman at the top. This hierarchy could be further subdivided by occupation, with professionals—trained for the Church, law, or medicine—ranking at the top. Next were merchants, who despite being lower ranking had the advantage of access to liquid assets and were worldly through their ties to long-distance trade. These households were staffed by a variety of servants and retainers. More plebian than merchants were the artisans, though many gathered substantial assets in large shops employing staffs of journeymen, apprentices, and slaves. And at the bottom of society were the farmers and herders, but even among them there was a division based on the size and success of agricultural enterprises.

At the center of Iberian life was the extended family, with cousins as closely tied as brothers. The head of the family was the patriarch, whose status was partly based on gender and partly on age. Women's positions, in turn, were dictated by the standing of their fathers and husbands. It was common for men to have sexual relationships outside of marriage, and the offspring were usually recognized and given help, although rarely were they included in the official family. The family might be viewed as a corporation, and it was desirable for nobles to have a son at court, a son in the clergy, and daughters who married into other noble families or wealthy merchant families.

Like most peoples, the Iberians believed their ways of life, customs, language, and religion were superior to all others. But they also lived in a region of great diversity, exposed to many different ethnic groups and beliefs. When they arrived in the New World, they brought with them both their prejudices and their familiarity with diversity.

THE AFRICAN

From the very beginning, some Africans from the Iberian Peninsula participated in the exploration and conquest of the Americas. The majority, however, came as slaves, with the first sent from Iberia as early as 1502. The slave trade brought people directly from Africa starting in Cuba in 1512 and in Brazil in 1538, continuing until the trade ended in Brazil in 1850 and in Cuba in 1866. During the course of three centuries, some three million slaves were sold into Spanish America and five million in Brazil.

Slaves came from West and Central Africa, a region that encompasses the Sahara Desert and its oases; the savanna immediately to the south, which is a semiarid grassland; and the tropical rain forest. The region's economies were based on agriculture—as in Eurasia and the Americas, Africans began plant domestication around 5000 B.C.E.—and featured both domestic and imported crops brought in through trade networks. Iron technology, begun circa 500 B.C.E. and spread by Bantu expansion, allowed the expansion of agriculture into formerly unavailable land. Early states (200–700 C.E.) in West and Central Africa, such as the Jenne, developed through trade within sub-Saharan Africa. From 700 to 1600 C.E., trans-Saharan trade with Arabs and Muslims led to the growth of Western and Central African states with stronger governments, more pronounced class stratification, and larger urban systems.

Around 700, the first Muslim traders established commerce between the northern savanna regions and their home bases north of the Sahara. By 900 C.E., trade between sub-Saharan Africa and the Muslim world was substantial and regular. The Muslim traders brought cloth, salt, steel swords, glass, and luxury goods in exchange for gold, slaves, ostrich feathers, fine leathers, decorative woods, and cola nuts. Gold had been mined in West Africa since 800 C.E. But with the advent of the Muslim trade, there was a larger market for the mineral, which led to greater production, the development of larger cities, and a more powerful elite, with greater class stratification and stronger governments. There was also some conversion to Islam, especially among merchants, because Islam provided a code of ethics

This woman in Bluefields, Nicaragua, is part of a substantial population that is of African descent. (Photograph by Julie A. Charlip)

leading to the trust necessary for long-distance trade. Although rulers and commoners sometimes followed suit, conversion was often only nominal, and traditional practices continued. A similar pattern would be seen with Christianity in the New World.

The more organized states of 700 to 1600 C.E. often included an opulent life at court, furnished by talented artisans, who provided bronze castings, carved wooden sculptures, ivory carving, cast gold, featherwork, and painted leather. Commoners were employed in public works projects, including royal tombs, walled palaces, mosques, irrigation and drainage systems, and great walls around cities.

Although most independent polities were small (comparable to city–states), there were three imperial societies: Ghana, Mali and Songhai. Ghana was an inland empire centered on the western portion of present-day Mali. It consisted of a number of chiefdoms joined together. Oral tradition says Ghana had twenty kings before the time of Muhammad circa 600 C.E. A powerful empire from 700–1100 C.E., it was destroyed by the Almoravids, and its fall led to the dispersal of the Soninke people. The kingdom of Mali, founded around 1200 C.E., was even larger and richer than Ghana. Centered on the city of Niani in the old Ghana empire, it incorporated all of Ghana and

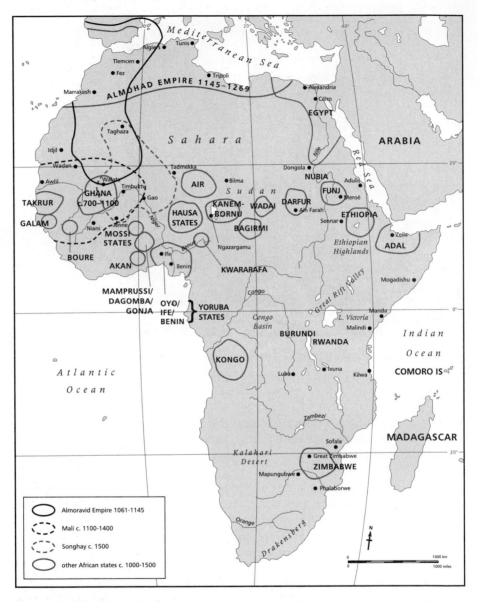

Map 1.4 African Kingdoms

Adapted from Spodek, Howard, *The World's History Combined*, 3rd ed. © 2006. Electronically reproduced by permission of Pearson Education, Inc., Upper Saddle River, NJ.

extended west to the Atlantic Ocean. In the process, Mali overextended its military, and in the 1400s its capital of Timbuktu was taken over by Tuareg nomads. The Songhai was once a part of the eastern Mali empire. Founded in 1350, the empire grew by 1515 to become the largest sub-Saharan empire, with more than one million people. Eventually weakened by internal dissension—the rich province of Hausaland was lost after a local ethnic group staged a revolt—the empire collapsed in 1590, conquered by Moroccan forces while the Songhai fought over the royal succession.

The development of large and complex polities came later to the forest than savanna. The rise of complexity parallels the rise of large-scale trade networks with the savanna kingdoms to the north. They probably traded with Ghana, leading to the rise of a wealthy merchant class, which gained power and led the forest communities. By 1200, the Ife and Benin states developed sophisticated royal courts with an extravagant bronze sculptural tradition.

River systems linked these African regions, connecting the western Sudan to the Atlantic. Mali was the center of political power from the thirteenth to the seventeenth centuries largely because of its location at the headwaters of the Niger, Senegal, and Gambia river systems, which united West Africa and provided a corridor that eventually added Hausa kingdoms; Yoruba states; and Nupe, Igala, and Benin kingdoms via river to the Atlantic. This maritime culture facilitated trade and coastal protection.

Repeated invasions by the Phoenicians, Greeks, Romans, and Arabs brought foreigners to Africa as early as 100 B.C.E. but the fall of the seaport of Ceuta on the Strait of Gibraltar to the Portuguese in 1415 C.E. heralded new European incursions. The Europeans were attracted by Africa's commercial potential—gold, ivory, cotton, and spices. However, African naval power protected the region against raids, with the result that trade had to be carried on peacefully and on African terms. For example, Afonso I, king of Kongo, seized a French ship and crew for trading illegally on the coast in 1525.

The Portuguese soon discovered that the Africans themselves were the continent's most valuable export. Between 1441 and 1443, the Portuguese began to transport Africans to Europe for sale. The majority of these slaves were purchased from African authorities, who responded to the growing demand. There was already a widespread practice of slavery in Africa, where land was held communally and slaves were the only form of private, revenue-producing property. Land was made available to whomever could work it, and Africans would purchase slaves to fill that purpose. In practicality, the slaves functioned much like tenants and hired workers in Europe. In 1659, Giacinto Brugiotti da Vetralla commented that Central African slaves were "slaves in name only." Such comments have led to the conclusion that slavery in Africa did not incorporate the brutality of slavery in the New World, a view that would seem to be confirmed by Olaudah Equiano, a slave from Nigeria, who recounted the horrors of the middle passage, noting, "I was now persuaded that I had gotten into a world of bad spirits."

African elites gladly participated in trade with Europeans, mostly for prestige and luxury items because European trade offered nothing that Africans did not produce. Africans manufactured sufficient steel and cloth, including beautiful varieties that Europeans said rivaled Italian manufacture and in such volume that rivaled Dutch production. Furthermore, although Africans did import European arms, they were of use primarily against fortifications, of which there were few. Warfare in Africa continued primarily with African weapons and for African political reasons.

The majority of Africans who came to the Americas came from three large cultural zones. The region that provided the majority of the first wave of slaves was Upper Guinea, ranging from the Senegal River to modern Liberia, where the Mande language family dominated. Next was Lower Guinea, ranging from the Ivory Coast to Camaroon, where Akan and Aja languages were predominant. The third primary area was Central Africa, including the Angola coast, Kongo, the Costa de Mina, present-day Benin, and stretching inland as far as modern Zaire, where Bantu was the dominate family of languages.

Although there was great diversity within these regions and language families—ranging from eight ethnic identities in Upper Guinea to twenty-seven in Central Africa—there was also enough commonality to help build a new culture in the Americas. Though the designs differed, the various cultures had traditions of making cloth, which they draped and wrapped around their bodies; and pottery making, basket weaving, and rhythmic drumming were part of the musical tradition.

Most important, the Africans also brought their religious beliefs to the New World. Many of the slaves from Upper Guinea were Muslims, but the majority of Africans who came to the New World had spiritist beliefs. In this belief system, there is a material and an otherworld, where people go when they die. Some gifted people, known as diviners, could pass between the two worlds, receiving revelations from the other world and communicating them to people in the material world. These belief systems continued in the New World as separate systems alongside Catholicism. There was also a mixing of Catholic and African elements that developed into Santería in Cuba, candomblé in Brazil, and vudún in Haiti.

Africans could be found in all parts of Latin America and formed a large part of the population. They quickly became and remained the major work force in the Caribbean and in Brazil. Their presence dominated the plantations on which they worked, and their influence spread quickly to the "big house," where African women served as cooks, wet nurses, and companions to the woman of the house, while black children romped with white children.

Male slaves outnumbered female slaves by a ratio of almost two to one. One explanation has been that large landowners preferred men because they considered them better field hands and hence more profitable. However, African slave-owning societies preferred to own women, who had the primary responsibility for agriculture and who could be integrated into kin groups as concubines or wives. As a result, prices for women were higher than they were for men. Nonetheless, women in the New World often worked in the fields, in addition to performing domestic service. Their owners discouraged large-scale reproduction as uneconomical. Thus, the Latin American slave system was seldom self-sustaining and required constant replacement through the slave trade. This imbalance made it particularly difficult to continue West African family organization, which was based on a large extended household and polygamy.

African influence also permeated the cities, where slaves worked as domestic servants, peddlers, mechanics, and artisans. In the sixteenth century, blacks outnumbered whites in Lima, Mexico City, and Salvador da Bahia, the three principal cities of the Western Hemisphere. The sex ratio among slaves seems to have been more equal in the cities, where women played particularly active roles as domestic servants, street vendors, prostitutes, and mistresses. The urban records seem to indicate that more freedwomen than freedmen existed. The city apparently offered African women more opportunity to change their status, partly because of their skills as vendors and their appeal as prostitutes and mistresses.

Africans were valued not simply for unskilled labor but for their fine artisanal skills, especially because, unlike the indigenous, they were skilled in iron work. Visitors to the Caribbean and Brazil remarked on the diversity of skills mastered and practiced by the Africans. They were masons, carpenters, smiths, lithographers, sculptors, artists, locksmiths, cabinetmakers, jewelers, and cobblers. Around the plantations and in the cities, these crafts people, artisans, and mechanics became an indispensable ingredient in New World society.

The Africans also were important as cowboys, particularly on the plains of Venezuela, Brazil, and Argentina. Slaves from the Senegambia area were particularly skilled with horses and cattle, and Angolans were noted for cattle raising. In Potosí and Nueva Granada, most of the supervisory positions were held by slaves. Africans also dominated the workforce in the copper mines of Venezuela.

Slaves continued to focus on their original nations, and, particularly in urban areas, they elected kings and queens with great ceremony, celebrated traditional festivals, and formed mutual aid societies. Whatever cultural differences Africans may have had, they also were able to organize multiethnic runaway slave communities, known variously as *palenques* or *cumbes* in Spanish America and *quilombos* in Brazil. The most famous quilombo, Palmares, located in Alagoas, lasted roughly from 1630–1697; it included as many as 5,000 African slaves from different African regions, who spoke different languages, but who were united in the community. There were six attempts to conquer Palmares between 1680 and 1686, and the final assault was won only after a bitterly fought forty-four-day siege. Quilombos, in fact, were so established as communities that they competed with Brazilian farms and stores to sell supplies in the Rio de Janeiro area.

That the African presence remained and was not entirely subsumed by the dominant culture is made clear in this description of a marketplace in Rio in the 1870s by Adèle Toussaint-Samson, a French traveler: "the large 'Minas' negresses, with their headdress in the shape of a muslin turban, with their faces full of scars and seams, having a chemise and a skirt with ruffles as their clothing, are squatted on mats, near their fruits and vegetables; at their sides are their boys and girls, in complete nudity." In the 1870s, with the slave trade long over, such visible elements of African traditions were still being passed down by Afro-Brazilians.

MESTIZAJE AND THE CREATION OF NEW PEOPLE

The three peoples of the Americas came together in sometimes violent and sometimes consensual ways. Through their interactions, they created new groups of people: *mestizos*, a mixture of indigenous and European; *mulatto*, mixing African and European; and *zambo*, the joining of indigenous and African. The Iberians developed an extensive vocabulary in an attempt to describe the exact mixture of races. Iberians were already concerned with purity of blood, shunning any trace of Muslim or Jewish heritage. These concerns would be magnified with colonial race mixture, or *mestizaje*. Although originally the term referred specifically to indigenous-European mixtures, it came to be used more broadly to refer to all "race" mixtures, which produced a variety of darker skinned people, known generally as *castas*.

Mestizaje would prove to be an extraordinarily complex issue. To Iberians, mixture was generally viewed as contamination. Yet at other times miscegenation was actually encouraged in order to facilitate economic relations with indigenous people or to hasten assimilation. Indigenous peoples would sometimes reject *mestizos* for abandoning the indigenous side of the equation. Independence leader Simón Bolívar used the concept of mestizaje to argue that Spain's colonial subjects were not Spanish and should be independent, whereas Cuba's José Martí argued that the new nations should be faithful to their own creative mestizaje rather than adopt foreign ideals.

Many nineteenth-century elites hoped mestizaje would whiten their populations, leading to greater progress. However, elites also echoed the theories of the Frenchmen Count Joseph Arthur Gobineau and Gustave Le Bon, who argued that people of mixed race "always inherited the most negative characteristics of the blended races." In practice, nineteenth-century nation-building efforts often used mestizaje to deny the continued presence of indigenous people.

Twentieth-century Latin Americans would ponder the meaning of mestizaje, what it included from each group and what resulted. In Mexico in 1925, José Vasconcelos lauded the *mestizo* as "the cosmic race," although by 1944, he dismissed the concept as "one of my silly notions." In Andean countries, the *mestizo* was often disparagingly referred to as a *cholo*, a marginalized figure rejected by both whites and the indigenous. Brazilians would

Labels for Miscegenation in Eighteenth-Century New Spain

1. Spaniard and Indian beget mestizo
2. Mestizo and Spanish woman beget castizo
3. Castizo woman and Spaniard beget Spaniard
4. Spanish woman and Negro beget mulatto
5. Spaniard and mulatto woman beget morisco
6. Morisco woman and Spaniard beget albino
7. Spaniard and albino woman beget torna atrás
8. Indian and torna atrás woman beget lobo
9. Lobo and Indian woman beget zambaigo
10. Zambaigo and Indian woman beget cambujo
11. Cambujo and mulatto woman beget albarazado
12. Albarazado and mulatto woman beget barcino
13. Barcino and mulatto woman beget coyote
14. Coyote woman and Indian beget chamison
15. Chamiso woman and mestizo beget coyote mestizo
16. Coyote mestizo and mulatto woman beget ahí te estás

Source: Magnus Mörner, *Race Mixture in the History of Latin America*
(Boston, MA: Little, Brown, 1967), 58.

Labels for Miscegenation in Eighteenth-Century Peru

1. Spaniard and Indian woman beget mestizo
2. Spaniard and mestizo woman beget cuarterón de mestizo
3. Spaniard and cuarteróna de mestizo beget quinterón
4. Spaniard and quinterona de mestizo beget Spaniard or requinterón de mestizo
5. Spaniard and Negress beget mulatto
6. Spaniard and mulatto woman beget quarterón de mulato
7. Spaniard and cuarteróna de mulato beget quinterón
8. Spaniard and quinterona de mulato beget requinterón

Source: Magnus Mörner, *Race Mixture in the History of Latin America*
(Boston, MA: Little, Brown, 1967), 58–59.

sometimes point to race mixture (*mestiçagem* in Portuguese) as supposed proof that racism did not exist in their country. Brazilian sociologist and anthropologist Gilberto Freyre heralded miscegenation as the essence of national identity and a successful adaptation to the tropics in his seminal *Casa*

Grande e Senzala (*The Mansions and the Shanties*), which was wildly popular when it appeared in 1933 and frankly addressed issues of sexuality.

In fact, sexuality was at the heart of this view, exemplified by Brazilian novelist Jorge Amado's contention that racial problems could only be solved by "the mixture of blood." He contended, "No other solution exists, only this one which is born from love." Nonetheless, by the late twentieth century, the cult of mestizaje had been transformed to cynicism, summed up deftly in one of the "187 Reasons Why Mexicans Can't Cross the Border" by performance artists Guillermo Gómez-Peña and Roberto Sifuentes—"because we're still waiting to be cosmic."

In the twenty-first century, mestizaje is frequently recast as hybridity, a notion more conceptual than racial, a postmodern pastiche of cultures past and present. Hybridity may be new as an analytical concept, but the reality on which it is based is as old as the conquest that brought these people together. Each contributed to the formation of unique civilizations on the basis of mixture and conflict among the three. Overlaying these societies were powerful institutions that were imported from the Iberian Peninsula and adapted to local circumstances.

RECOMMENDED READINGS

Barton, Simon. *A History of Spain*. Hampshire, England: Palgrave Macmillan, 2004.

Gallup, John Luke, Alejandro Gaviria, and Eduardo Lora. *Is Geography Destiny? Lessons from Latin America*. Palo Alto, CA: Stanford University Press, 2003.

Lockhart, James, and Stuart B. Schwartz. *Early Latin America: A History of Colonial America and Brazil*. Cambridge: Cambridge University Press, 1983.

Miller, Mary Grace. *Rise and Fall of the Cosmic Race: The Cult of Mestizaje in Latin America*. Austin: University of Texas Press, 2004.

Naro, Nancy Priscilla. *A Slave's Place, A Master's World: Fashioning Dependency in Rural Brazil*. London: Continuum, 2000.

Thornton, John. *Africa and Africans in the Making of the Atlantic World, 1400–1800*. Cambridge: Cambridge University Press, 1998.

Topik, Steven. "Historical Perspectives on Latin American Underdevelopment," *The History Teacher*, Vol. 20, No. 4. (1987), 545–560.

Sweet, James H. *Recreating Africa: Culture, Kinship, and Religion in the African—Portuguese World, 1441–1770*. Chapel Hill: University of North Carolina Press, 2003.

CHAPTER 2

FROM CONQUEST TO EMPIRE

The exploits of dashing *conquistadores* roving in search of "God, gold, and glory" stir the imagination. Childhood stories portray clever Christopher Columbus as the great adventurer, or fearless Hernando Cortes, who supposedly defeated an entire empire with but a handful of men. But the "true story," to borrow from the account by Bernál Díaz de Castillo, is more complicated and far more intriguing. It is a story about human beings, not gods or primitives, who fought to gain or maintain position in a changing world. What were the motives and methods of the Iberians who sailed to the New World and the indigenous people who greeted and fought them? How were the Iberians able to maintain these colonies for more than 300 years?

EUROPEAN EXPLORATION

The encounter of New and Old Worlds was prompted by profound changes occurring in Europe in the late 1400s. The population had finally rebounded after one-third of the populace succumbed to the Black Death, a plague that spread throughout Europe beginning in 1347. The increasing, and increasingly urbanized, population provided a larger market and greater incentives for trade. The resolution of struggles among nobles, including the Hundred Years' War and the War of the Roses, led to consolidation of larger kingdoms, financed by merchants, who hoped the kings would create stability for local markets and help relaunch foreign trade.

Their goals were furthered by new shipbuilding techniques, which allowed ships to travel longer distances, and new navigation equipment that made travel more accurate. In addition, the invention of movable type led to the increase in knowledge. The second book ever printed, after the Bible, was *Marco Polo's Travels*. Published in 1477, the book told travel tales from

200 years earlier and it piqued a renewed interest in Asian goods. Merchants dreamed of breaking the Arab and Italian monopolies of trade with Asia, thereby sharing the lucrative profits from the spices, precious stones, pearls, dyes, silks, tapestries, porcelains, and rugs coveted by wealthy Europeans. The products were available via overland routes, but these were controlled by the Ottoman Empire, which conquered Constantinople in 1453. Iberian merchants sought a route that would cut out the middle man, a water route that would take them to the East.

Portugal led the quest for those new trade routes and became, for a time, Europe's foremost sea power, which was due in part to its fortunate location on the westernmost tip of continental Europe. Most of the sparse population, which was less than 1 million in the fifteenth century, inhabited the coastal area, facing the great, gray, open sea and nearby Africa. The Portuguese initiated their overseas expansion in Africa in 1415 with the conquest of strategic Ceuta, guardian of the opening to the Mediterranean.

The first to appreciate fully that the ocean was not a barrier but a vast highway of commerce was Prince Henry (1394–1460), who was known as "the Navigator" to English writers, although he was a confirmed landlubber. Listening to the expert advice of his day, he defined Portugal's policy of exploration, comprising systematic voyages outward, each based on intelligence collected from former voyagers and each traveling beyond its predecessors. In 1488, Bartolomeu Dias rounded the Cape of Good Hope and pointed the way to a water route to India. With Dias's success, the Portuguese were not interested in the suggestions made by Christopher Columbus, who argued that a quicker route to the East could be obtained by sailing west.

Cristobal Colón, as the Spanish called him, embodied many of the interests of his time. One of many Genoese living in Seville, he first went to sea as a young man, serving as a trader or clerk. A Genoese mercantile firm sent him to Portugal, where he learned maritime mapmaking. He went on to live on Madeira as the agent of a Genoese firm trading sugar. He traveled the coast of Africa, learning the gold trade and observing the slave trade as well. By the time he approached Spain, he was well acquainted with Italian trade, Portuguese navigation and settlement, and trade in sugar, gold and slaves.

The story of Columbus is filled with myths, such as his supposedly novel idea that the world was round and that Queen Isabel pawned her jewels to finance the mission. In reality, Columbus did not need to convince any educated person that the world was round—Artistotle observed circa 300 B.C.E. that Earth cast a round shadow on the moon. The queen did not offer her jewels—in fact, the crown offered little more than recognition, the granting of 10 percent of the bounty encountered and the title Admiral of the Ocean Seas. The crown did arrange for two ships for Columbus, provided by the city of Palos as repayment of its debt to the crown. Columbus was financed primarily by Genoese merchants in Seville. He rounded up a crew and headed off in the belief that Asia was but 2,400 miles away. In actuality, the distance is 16,000 miles, with an unexpected, intervening land mass.

News from Columbus that he had reached India by sailing west in 1492 momentarily disturbed the Portuguese. Unlike Portugal, Spain had earned little reputation for maritime prowess. In the last quarter of the fifteenth century, some Spanish expeditions plied the African coast, and one of them laid Spanish claims to the Canary Islands. Most Spanish energy, however, had been expended internally on the struggle to expel the Moors and on the effort of unification. Columbus's timing was fortuitous; the energy, talent, and drive that previously had gone into the reconquest, or *reconquista*, that holy and political campaign allying cross and sword for eight centuries, were invested immediately in overseas expansion.

The return of Columbus from his first voyage intensified rivalry between Spain and Portugal, both of which sought to guard their sea lanes. War threatened until diplomacy triumphed. At Tordesillas in 1494, representatives of the two monarchs agreed to divide the world. An imaginary line running pole to pole 370 leagues west of the Cape Verde Islands gave Portugal everything discovered for 180 degrees east and Spain everything for 180 degrees west. Within the half of the world reserved for Portugal, Vasco da Gama discovered the long sought after water route to India. His protracted voyage in 1497–1499 joined East and West by sea for the first time. Although subsequent voyages by Columbus in 1493–1496, 1498–1500, and 1502–1504 suggested the extent of the lands he had found, they also proved that in fact he had not reached India.

Portugal for the moment monopolized the only sea lanes to India, and that monopoly promised to enrich the realm. The cargo that Vasco da Gama brought back to Lisbon repaid sixty times over the original cost of the expedition, enriching Portugal. Pedro Alvares Cabral set sail in 1500 to follow up da Gama's exploit, but the fleet veered off course, landing in Brazil, which later was found to fall within the half of the world allocated to Portugal. Along the coasts of South America, Africa, and Asia, the Portuguese eagerly established their commercial empire, whereas the Spanish concentrated more on colonization.

PATTERNS OF CONQUEST

The explorers who arrived after Columbus were not soldiers of the crown. In fact, Spain had no standing army and instead had recruited men to fight throughout the reconquista. The conquest of the New World was primarily a private venture. At first, commercial companies with a few investors hired employees to explore. Soon these companies were replaced by a company of men who outfitted themselves and who would be paid with a share of the wealth they found. Some of the crew were retainers or slaves of their backers, and their shares went to their employers. Most, however, were free agents who borrowed money or bought supplies on credit. They were primarily literate commoners, lower ranking professionals and marginal *hidalgos* (noblemen), lower ranking nobility, all taking a chance to acquire wealth and prestige. Many of the adventurers had never before handled a sword. For example, among the men who accompanied Francisco Pizarro to conquer the Inca empire were twelve notaries and twenty-four artisans, including smiths, tailors, and carpenters.

These private undertakings were formalized by a contract, known as a *capitulación*, signed between the monarch and the aspiring conquistador, who was given the title of *adelantado*. Those contracts introduced European capitalism, as it had taken shape by the early sixteenth century, into the Americas. The adelantados by no means wandered around the Americas unchecked by the monarchs. Royal officials accompanied all the private expeditions to ensure respect for the crown's interests and fulfillment of the capitulación.

The Spanish conquest proceeded as a relay system: After establishing a base in one area, the adventurers would explore farther and create new settlements. From the first settlements on the island of Hispaniola (later Haiti and the Dominican Republic), explorers moved on to Cuba, to Mexico, and then to Guatemala. The Spanish learned that there were many separate indigenous peoples; although some of them would rush to fight the Spanish, others would seek to aid them. The conquistadors would seize the *cacique*, the term for the community leader among the Taino/Arawak people on the islands, which the Spaniards erroneously used throughout the Americas. They would induce the leader to force his people to submit. The first Spaniards to arrive would divide the goods, leaving little for the later arrivals who followed to seek their fortune. Latecomers would then move on in search of new conquests, frequently egged on by both Spaniards and indigenous who spoke of El Dorado, the mythical golden city that lay beyond.

Hernando Cortes became perhaps the most famous conquistador, but he started out as a marginal nobleman, a notary who fled to the New World after a narrow escape from a jealous husband. He was only 19 years old when he arrived in Hispaniola in 1504, where, with the help of kinship connections from his native Estremadura, he acquired an *encomienda*. The encomienda was an institution borrowed from the reconquista, whose forces had been paid by giving them control over a group of laborers. Cortes was rewarded with a second encomienda after serving as Diego Velasquez's clerk during an expedition to Cuba. Velasquez became governor of Cuba and appointed Cortes as chief magistrate of Santiago. In 1519, Velasquez chose Cortes to lead an expedition in the governor's name to search for the Aztec empire. But he then reconsidered, fearing that the ambitious and headstrong Cortes would not be loyal. Velazquez's fears were well-founded: Hearing he was to be replaced, Cortes took off early with 600 men, sixteen horses, eleven ships, and some artillery and headed north.

It took Cortes two years to defeat the Aztec empire. After first trying to convince him to leave, the central city–states of the Aztec empire fought valiantly against the invaders. But Cortes was aided primarily by thousands of indigenous people who were subjected to the Aztec imperial yoke. Indeed, these communities at times skillfully manipulated the Spanish into attacking their traditional indigenous enemies. Similarly, the illegitimate and modestly prepared Francisco Pizarro, after three attempts, finally completed his conquest of the Inca empire in 1535, aided by a rivalry between two claimants to the Inca crown, which had already divided the empire and provided the conqueror with thousands of indigenous allies.

The Spanish pattern of exploration and settlement changed after 1521, the year not only of Cortes's triumph but also that of the circumnavigation of the globe, which was begun by Ferdinand Magellan in 1519 and was successfully concluded by Juan Sebastián del Cano. He proved that Asia could be reached by sailing west, but his expedition around South America also proved that the westward passage was longer and more difficult than the African route used by the Portuguese. But at the same time, Spain realized it did not need the route to India. Conquered Mexico revealed that the New World held far more wealth in the form of the coveted gold and silver than the Spaniards could hope to reap from trade with Asia. Instead of viewing the New World as a mere way station en route to Asia, the Spanish made America their center of attention.

The rest of the New World civilizations fell rapidly to the Spanish: Within half a century after Columbus's discovery, Spanish adelantados had explored and conquered or claimed the territory from approximately 40 degrees north—Oregon, Colorado, and the Carolinas—to 40 degrees south—mid-Chile and Argentina—with the exception of the Brazilian coast. Reflecting the Spanish preference for urban living, by 1550 the settlers had already founded all of Latin America's major cities: Havana, 1519; Mexico City, 1521; Quito, 1534; Lima, 1535; Buenos Aires, 1536 (refounded in 1580); Asunción, 1537; Bogotá, 1538; and Santiago, 1541.

Meanwhile, the Portuguese largely ignored Brazil from its discovery in 1500 until 1532. Feeling pressured by Spanish and French interests, the crown authorized Martim Afonso de Sousa to found the first town, São Vicente, near present-day Santos. But the Portuguese followed the patterns they had established in Africa, focusing more on trading forts than on colonization.

Legend has given the conquistadores glory for the conquest, but in reality they ended their lives with far less prestige. Columbus was returned to Spain in chains, accused of misgovernment. He spent the last months before his death trying to gain money and honors that he claimed he had been promised. Cortes, too, died in Spain complaining that his power had been preempted by the viceroy and arguing with the audiencia over the outrageous size of his encomienda. Pizarro was assassinated by the followers of his former partner, Diego de Almagro, who felt that Almagro had been cheated out of his share of the wealth. Despite their achievements and outsized reputations, they were never significant in the establishment of stable, long-lasting colonies. In fact, their supposed feats of derring-do would not have been possible without the much more prosaic role of the merchants, who advanced the money and supplies to finance such expeditions and support the colonies. One merchant, Hernando de Castro, complained in 1520 that because of the power struggle between "this Cortes" and Cuban Governor Velasquez, "it is clearly no time to do business." And business was at the center of the conquest and colonization.

COLONIAL ECONOMY

Expeditions to the New World were economic enterprises for both the crown and the conquistadores. Spain operated under an economic system known as mercantilism, which held that national wealth and power was built by controlling trade and gathering bullion. The goal was for the empire to sell more than it bought, keeping bullion in the kingdom's coffers. The adventurers who headed to the New World were equally motivated by wealth. As Bernál Diaz, chronicler of the Aztec conquest, commented: "We came here to serve God and also to get rich."

The Americas at first frustrated the Iberians. The Taino/Arawak people of the Caribbean and the Tupí of the Brazilian coast showed no interest in transoceanic trade. The Portuguese contented themselves for three decades with exporting the brazilwood found growing close to the coast. The Spaniards lacked even that product to stimulate commerce in the Caribbean.

With little trade in sight, the Iberians focused on the search for a single item: gold. It offered three attractive advantages: easy shipment, imperishability, and high value. As Columbus wrote, "O, most excellent gold! Who has gold has a treasure with which he gets what he wants, imposes his will on the world and even helps souls to paradise." The Portuguese encountered little of it in Brazil, but the Spaniards came into limited but tantalizing contact with the prized metal almost at once, as the Taino displayed some golden ornaments. The Taino also spoke of gold on various Caribbean islands, causing the Spaniards to begin a feverish search for deposits. The Spanish forced the indigenous people to bring in quotas of gold; if they failed, the Spaniards cut off their hands. Nonetheless, only modest amounts of gold were found. Between 1501 and 1519, the Caribbean produced approximately 8 million pesos of gold.

The principal source of gold in Spanish America was New Granada (Colombia), which by 1600 had exported more than four million ounces of gold. Most of that gold came from placer deposits worked by slave labor. Production of gold in New Granada grew steadily, with eighteenth-century production nearly tripling that of the sixteenth. In total, it supplied Spain with about thirty million ounces of gold.

Gold discoveries in Brazil came late in the colonial period. The hardy *bandeirantes* (explorers) found gold for the first time in 1695 in the interior of Minas Gerais; other rich strikes occurred in 1721 in Mato Grosso and in 1726 in Goiás. Such discoveries were incentives to open the vast southern interior of Brazil to settlement. Each discovery precipitated a wild rush of humanity from abroad and within Brazil eager to seek their fortunes. The boom not only caused notable population growth in eighteenth-century Brazil but also caused a population shift from the older sugar-producing region of the Northeast to the newly opened regions of the Southeast. Gold production mounted there until 1760, when a decline set in. During the eighteenth century, Brazil produced thirty-two million ounces of gold, a majority of the world's gold supply.

Most of Spain's wealth, however, came not from gold but from silver, discovered after the conquest of Mexico and Peru. Spaniards found silver in Mexico at Taxco in 1534 and in Zacatecas in 1546. Other strikes followed at Guanajuato (1550) and San Luis Potosí (1592). In the sixteenth century, Mexico shipped more than thirty-five million pesos worth of precious metals to Spain, becoming Spanish America's leading producer toward the end of the seventeenth century. The single richest mine, however, was discovered in 1545 at Potosí, a remote area in mountainous Upper Peru (later Bolivia), one of the richest silver mines the world was ever to see. Collectively, these mines produced some 100,000 tons of silver during the colonial period. The crown carefully collected their *quinto,* or one fifth, of the precious metals, employing large bureaucracies to oversee their interests.

Mining exemplified the region's dependence on exports. The crowns were hungry for gold and silver, but more than that, they were hungry for wealth. In areas without gold and silver, Iberians and their descendants searched for other exportable goods. They sent to Iberia—and on to Europe—the rich purplish-blue dye made from the indigo plant and the deep red dye, *cochineal,* made from the insects feeding on nopal cactuses. The hides of New World cattle made fine leather goods. Cacao beans fed the new desire for chocolate, sweetened by New World sugar. Success depended on the resources provided by geography and by perhaps the greatest wealth of the colonies—the labor force to produce the goods.

In search of a workable labor system, Spaniards first looked to their own traditions. Seeing the conquest of the New World as a continuation of their reconquest of the Iberian peninsula, they transferred the *encomienda,* or entrustment. Once used for the control and exploitation of the Moors, the adelantados employed it in the Americas to Christianize and exploit the indigenous. The institution required the Spanish *encomendero* to instruct the indigenous entrusted to him in Christianity and European civilization and to defend and protect them. In return he could demand tribute and labor.

The crown hesitated to approve the transfer of the encomienda to the Caribbean. After all, the monarchs had just unified Spain and were in the process of strengthening their powers in the peninsula. They were reluctant therefore to nourish in the New World a class of encomenderos who could impose their will between the monarchs and their new indigenous subjects. It smacked too much of feudalism for royal tastes, prompting Isabel in 1501 to order the governor of the Indies to free the indigenous. When that experiment resulted in the flight of indigenous from estates and their refusal to work for the Spaniards, the queen changed her mind.

In 1503, by royal *cédula* (edict), Isabel legalized and institutionalized the encomienda in the New World. The cédula expressed concern about the welfare of the indigenous subjects and admonished the Spaniards to treat them well, but it also sanctioned a labor system that would permit many abuses. In 1513, King Ferdinand promulgated the Laws of Burgos, the first general code for the government and instruction of the indigenous. It called for fair, humane treatment, a policy that royal officers found difficult to enforce. Charles V tried to abolish the encomienda in 1519, but by then it was too firmly entrenched to be summarily eradicated. The encomenderos refused to acknowledge the abolition, and royal officials did not enforce the law.

The encomienda system spread rapidly and was most effective among sedentary indigenous populations accustomed to participating in indigenous draft rotary labor systems, which had built and maintained communal structures and provided labor for indigenous nobility. Such systems had existed among the Aztecs (*coatequitl*) and the Inca (*mita*). In many regions, indigenous people continued to live in their own villages, sending a portion of workers to labor on Spanish lands. Where no such indigenous base presented itself, the Spaniards simply could not establish the encomienda. This was apparent when Zacatecas with its rich silver deposits, was discovered, in 1547. The indigenous people of the north, such as the Chichimec, were mostly nonsedentary. They had no basic, coherent unit of organization on which to build, no cacique to seize, no tradition of tribute and rotary draft labor. At best, the Spanish could try to enslave them, but their high mortality rate made them a poor investment as slaves.

Because nothing could be done without labor, the encomiendas were highly prized. Whereas Cortes's encomiendas numbered 100,000, latecomers were less fortunate. For example, Bartolomé García wrote plaintively to the Crown that in Paraguay he had been given in encomienda only sixteen Guaraní workers, located some eighty leagues away, "from where one can get no service." Where there were semi-sedentary people—Tucumán, Paraguay, Chile north of the Bío Bío River—the Spaniards were able to devise a modified encomienda system. The Spaniards had to integrate with the indigenous people and become their leaders, in essence, to position themselves as the cacique and create a local unit via the kinship group. Here, miscegenation played an important role. A classic example of how this system worked was in Paraguay, where Spanish settlers allied themselves with the Guaraní and helped them fight their traditional enemies, the Guaycuru. Because Spanish women were not eager to come to the fringe areas, Spaniards married or, more commonly, cohabited with Guaraní women, forming kinship ties. Much of what passed for an encomienda, consisting largely of personal service and agricultural work by women, was no more than this extended kinship pattern.

Perhaps one in fifty of the Spaniards who came to the colonies were awarded encomiendas. As immigration to the central areas soared, there was growing pressure to redistribute the encomienda. While practical pressures fractured the institution, it was also under suspicion at court, a circumstance that was due in part to Church reports that encomenderos violated their entrustment by mistreating the indigenous.

One of the most vocal defenders of the indigenous was Bartolomé de las Casas, a Dominican missionary and later bishop. His persuasive arguments at court contributed to Pope Paul III's 1537 bull declaring that the indigenous were fully capable of receiving the faith of Christ—that is, they possessed souls and should not be deprived of their liberty and property. It was partly on that basis, though certainly also because of political concerns regarding encomendero power, that Charles then promulgated the New Laws in 1542, which forbade the enslavement of the indigenous, their compulsory personal service, the granting of new encomiendas, and the inheritance of existing encomiendas. The colonists protested vehemently: Rebellion threatened Mexico, and in Peru encomenderos rose up to defy the law. Once again under extreme pressure, the monarch modified some of the laws and revoked others. The encomienda continued for some time in parts of the sprawling American empire, but after the mid-sixteenth century the institution waned, more because of demographic than moral pressures.

Replacing the encomienda was the *repartimiento*, the temporary allotment of indigenous workers for a given task. It is significant that under this institution royal authorities controlled and parceled out the workers. The Spanish colonist in need of laborers applied to a royal official explaining both the work to be done, the time it would take to complete, and the specific number of indigenous it would require to do it. In theory, the crown officials looked after the welfare of the workers to ensure fair payment and satisfactory working conditions; in practice, abuse of the repartimiento system abounded. Planters and miners constantly badgered royal officials to bend the system to better fit local needs. The institution flourished in the last half of the sixteenth century and in the first half of the seventeenth.

In addition to furnishing an agricultural labor force, the repartimiento system also provided the major share of the workers for the mines in South America. In the Viceroyalty of Peru, the *mita* at Potosí became particularly burdensome. All adult male Quechua and Aymara were subject to serve in the mita for one year out of every seven. Far from his home, the miner worked under the most dangerous conditions and earned a wage that did not suffice for half of his own and his family's expenses.

As in Spanish America, landowners in Brazil relied in part (during the sixteenth century along the coast and for several more centuries in the interior and in the north) on the indigenous as a source of labor. Some employed indigenous labor from the *aldeias*, the villages. The crown and the religious orders tried to concentrate the nomadic peoples into villages, first organized and administered by the religious orders but after 1757 administered by the crown. Protected within the village, they were introduced to Christianity and European civilization. In return, they gave a portion of their labor to the Church and State. This part of the aldeia system resembled the encomienda. In addition, planters could apply to the aldeia administrators for paid indigenous workers to perform a specific task for a specified period of time. In this respect, the aldeia system approximated the repartimiento. The aldeia system included only a small percentage of Brazil's indigenous people. The rest of the indigenous planters hunted, with limited success, to enslave them.

The existence of a sedentary indigenous workforce was one of the key differences between labor organization in Brazil and in Spanish America. Because the Tupí either died off or fled to remote areas, the Portuguese followed the pattern they had used on the island of Madeira—African slaves. Africans offered the added benefit of immunity to European diseases because of the many years of contact between the regions. By the end of the sixteenth century, Africa furnished most of the productive labor in Brazil and the West Indies. Brazil alone received nearly 40 percent of the Atlantic slave trade, six times more than reached the United States.

Although the vast majority of slaves worked in sugar production first in Brazil, and eventually in Cuba and Haiti, slaves were not limited to these areas. Slaves served throughout Latin America as the backbone of the skilled labor force. They worked as artisans, muleteers, herdsmen, and skilled labor at the mines. By 1570, there were more blacks than Spaniards in Peru and there were at least 120,000 slaves in Mexico from 1519 to 1650. Because they were expensive, however, miners in Spanish America sought to limit the use of Africans to skilled labor.

In the highland areas of Spanish America, some settled indigenous populations survived, and colonists competed for the scarce labor, prompting colonists to offer wages. As early as 1546 at the mines of Zacatecas, indigenous workers were paid wages to lure them to the relatively remote northern region. Wage labor systems spread beyond mining areas as the repartimiento system became more cumbersome, breaking down under favoritism and bribery.

Regardless of the labor system, one pattern remained the same: Masses of indigenous and African workers toiled for the benefit of a small number of European elites and their descendants—called creoles (*criollos*) in Spanish America and *mazombos* in Brazil—who always constituted a small minority of the population, even with the demographic collapse of the indigenous world.

The crown approved the creation of a large wage-earning class as a progressive step. To the monarch it seemed to verify the assimilation and Europeanization of the indigenous. However, employers wanted to keep the wages low and keep the workforce from moving on in search of better jobs. Some tried to convert contract wage labor into debt peonage, tying the indigenous and their descendants to the landowner by debt. The employers made deceptively friendly loans to the workers, who were to repay with their labor. However, the wages often did not suffice to liquidate the debt, which fathers passed on to their sons. But the very labor scarcity that prompted debt peonage also provided workers with some maneuverability. When possible, workers gravitated toward employers who promised better salaries or working conditions. Many workers had no qualms about accepting a loan from one employer, then moving on to another. Without a strong military or police force, fleeing workers were virtually impossible to catch—especially when they could flee to unoccupied lands.

Initially, land was abundant and Spaniards were more concerned about acquiring the labor to work it for them. However, competition for land intensified as more Spaniards immigrated to the New World, the indigenous population recovered from the initial demographic collapse after the conquest, and lucrative markets for agricultural products developed both abroad and in the colonies. Ownership of land became a basis for wealth and prestige and conveyed power. From the beginning, the adelantados distributed land among their followers as a reward for services rendered. The officers received large shares of land as well as grants of workers, whereas the common men received smaller shares of land but usually were not granted an encomienda.

In 1532, when Martim Afonso founded São Vicente, he distributed the land with a lavish hand to his followers, establishing a pattern of land distribution quite contrary to the prevailing custom in Portugal. Since 1375, the Portuguese kings had sparingly parceled out the *sesmaria*, traditional land grants, so that no one person received more than could be effectively cultivated. Aware of the immensity of the territory in front of him, Afonso ignored such a precaution. As a consequence, the good coastal land was quickly divided into immense sugar plantations, and not many more decades elapsed before the huge sesmarias for cattle ranches in the interior put much of the backlands under claims as well.

Over time, many of the original grants of land grew to gigantic proportions. The more astute landowners bought out their neighbors or simply encroached upon other lands. The declining indigenous population freed more land, which the Iberians rapidly monopolized. A series of legal devices favored the Spaniard in acquiring land: the *congregación, denuncia,* and *composición.* The congregación concentrated the indigenous in villages and thereby opened land for seizure; the denuncia required the indigenous to show legal claim and title to their property—a legality for which their ancient laws had not prepared them—and failure to do so meant that the land could be seized; the composición was a means of claiming land through legal surveys, a concept once again for which the indigenous had little preparation. By these, as well as by other means, the Spanish landowners steadily pushed the remaining indigenous up the mountainsides and onto the arid soils of the marginal lands.

For their part, the Portuguese monarchs were critical of the inefficiency of the large *fazendas* and belatedly tried to reverse the course by promulgating decrees to limit the size of these estates. One of the viceroys late in the eighteenth century, the Marquis of Lavradio, complained bitterly that the huge estates, which were poorly managed and often only partially cultivated, retarded the development of Brazil. He pointed to the unused fields held by their owners as symbols of prestige, whereas, at the same time, he noted that farmers petitioned him for land to till. Some of the regions imported food that they were perfectly capable of producing themselves. Nonetheless, the *latifundia* that originated at the birth of the colony remained as dominant a characteristic of Brazil as it did of Spanish America.

Some of the haciendas and fazendas achieved princely proportions. There were instances of haciendas in Mexico exceeding one million acres. In Brazil, the ranch of Diaz d'Avila by all accounts surpassed most European states in size. The Luso-Brazilians quickly developed the prototype of the plantation economy, thanks to the ready and profitable market they found in Europe for sugar, a crop that grew well along the coast. By 1550, Pernambuco, the richest and most important of the sixteenth-century captaincies, produced enough sugar in its fifty mills to annually load forty or fifty ships for Europe. The Brazilian sugar plantations flourished during the second half of the sixteenth century and the first half of the seventeenth century. The economic pattern of a single crop for international trade, known as monoculture, was fastened onto Brazil early. In Spanish America, for many years the haciendas produced only for local markets. One of their chief responsibilities was to feed the mining towns. Only as the eighteenth century neared did the haciendas enter into international trade on a scale comparable to that of the Brazilian plantations.

The type of life exemplified by the hacienda or fazenda often has been termed feudal, a term that carries a strong emotional overtone connoting exploitation. Certainly, the classical feudalism of medieval society did not appear in the New World. Weak though his power might have been in some of the remoter areas, the king never relinquished the prerogatives of sovereignty to the landlords. Royal law prevailed. Neither does the self-sufficient manorial system properly describe the large estates because, for all of their self-sufficiency, they were closely tied by their major cash crop to the capitalistic economy. Perhaps the *patrimonialism* defined by Max Weber comes closest to describing the system. Under patrimonialism, the landowner exerts authority over his followers as one aspect of his property ownership.

Those who live on his land fall under his control. He uses armed force arbitrarily to enforce his authority within the bounds of his estate. With such authority, he administers his estate in a highly personal manner. Finally he controls all trade between his estate and the outside world. Through that trade, he participates in the capitalistic marketplace.

The plantations, ranches, and mines provided a rich and varied source of income for the Iberian monarchs, capitalists, and merchants. Sugar, tobacco, cacao, indigo, woods, cotton, gold, silver, diamonds, and hides were among the natural products that American colonies offered the Old World. The Iberian Peninsula depended on the New World for its prosperity. Both Lisbon and Madrid relied heavily on its raw products for their foreign trade. For example, for many years the products of Brazil constituted approximately two thirds of Portugal's export trade.

Iberian settlers searched for any means of making money, but they were restricted by more than geographical constraints. They were also subject to the desires of European markets and were restricted by Iberian controls over trade. Often just one or a small number of products sold abroad dictated the course of colonial prosperity. If a product sold well, an entire region prospered; if not, stagnation and misery prevailed.

The Iberians did not achieve notable efficiency in the exploitation of those natural products with which a generous nature endowed their lands. With little competition and cheap labor, there was no incentive to overcome old-fashioned, inefficient methods. The case of sugar is an excellent example. The Portuguese held almost a monopoly on sugar production for well over a century. Between 1650 and 1715, the Dutch, English, and French increased production of sugar in the Caribbean; they were efficient and organized, had new equipment and extensive financial resources, and they enjoyed a geographic position closer to the European markets. As a result, the sugar economies of Portugal's European rivals prospered, while the economy of the traditional producer languished. With quick and large profits as its goal, the economy of Latin America was largely speculative and hence subject to wide variations. The patrimonial system of land and labor contributed to economic fluctuations and inefficiency. In sum, the economy of Latin America was not geared to its own best interests but to the making of immediate profits for the Iberian metropolises and for a small, New World planter-trader elite, who were almost exclusively of European origin.

The wealth of the New World would be worth nothing without the European goods that it could buy. Spaniards disdained such indigenous products as maize and instead insisted on their familiar wheat, olive oil, and wine. International merchants were generally based in Mexico City and Lima and were the junior partners of merchants in Seville and Cádiz, which had a monopoly on Spanish trade. As the regional and local economies grew and became more complex, more junior partners were assigned to regional capitals. Their goal was generally to make enough money to return to Spain and live well. However, they also invested in mines and estates, which gave them local investments and, eventually, incentive to remain in the colonies.

The Spanish fleet system shipped all goods between Spain and the colonies, starting in the 1520s. There were two fleets a year, one to New Spain and one to Cartagena and Panama. The system was successful in protecting its shipments, with only two losses: one to Sir Francis Drake in 1572 and the other to the Dutch in 1628. The weather was a more serious threat.

Simultaneously, there was tremendous contraband trade among the colonies and with other countries. The vast territory and limited number of officials made it impossible for Spain to fully control colonial trade. Ships would put in at the many uncontrolled coves, or would claim to be in distress, which gave them the legal right to put in to port at other locations. It is impossible to know the extent of contraband, but some scholars estimate that as much as two-thirds of all trade in the region was conducted illegally.

Although foreign trade was the motor of activity, the growth of mining centers led to local demand for food and goods, providing a market of lower income Spaniards and indigenous who could not buy expensive imported goods. Local entrepreneurs served the new markets in myriad ways: carting, livestock, roadbuilding, processing of imported goods, and through the creation of *obrajes*, or workshops, for local manufacture. *Tratantes*, dealers in locally produced goods, did not share the status of the merchants linked to international commerce, but they managed a lucrative business. Nonetheless, most of the colonial world was a subsistence economy, operating outside all but the local markets in surplus goods and artisanry.

THE CONQUERED PEOPLES

It is impossible to know how many people inhabited the Americas when Columbus arrived. Scholars' estimates range from 9 million to a high of 100 million persons. It is clear, however, that after the arrival of the Spanish, the indigenous died in precipitous numbers. Even discounting the actual conquest years, tribute records in New Spain show a decline of some 80 percent just from 1548–1595. In coastal areas and in the Caribbean Islands, estimates have ranged closer to 100 percent, although recent work on the continuity of Taino culture challenges the idea of complete indigenous elimination.

Regardless of the exact numbers, clearly this population decline was one of the greatest demographic disasters in history. Although indigenous people certainly were killed by Spanish warfare and brutality, the greatest cause of indigenous death was disease. Because the Americas had been isolated from contact with Europe and Africa, the inhabitants had no immunities to diseases such as plague, smallpox and typhus; even influenza and measles claimed lives in the colonies. They died in such great numbers that one German missionary commented in 1699, "The Indians die so easily that the bare look and smell of a Spaniard causes them to give up the ghost."

The deaths devastated the indigenous world. Often people who were weakened by one disease ended up dying from a secondary infection. So many fell ill that they were unable to nurse and feed each other. There was also an enormous psychological toll as survivors saw people around them die by the thousands. In attempts to control the population, Spanish priests gathered the remaining people into newly formed villages, where disease spread even more rapidly.

Yet, some areas remained relatively unscathed, especially remote highland areas. And as contact between groups increased, the indigenous gradually developed immunities to Spanish diseases. After a steep decline throughout the sixteenth century, the indigenous population rebounded and grew.

The extent to which the indigenous world changed depended on the extent of Spanish contact, which in turn depended on the mineral wealth and economic potential of a region. Initially there was little contact between most indigenous and Spaniards, with indigenous leaders serving as intermediaries between the groups. Eventually there was greater individual contact, especially as both populations grew and an increasingly complex economy and society drew the two worlds together. The process was quite slow, even in the zones of greatest contact. For example, in what is now Central Mexico, it was not until 1650–1800 that many indigenous communities exhibited such signs of intercultural mixing as full bilingualism. As late as the Mexican Revolution in 1910, revolutionary leader Emiliano Zapata found it necessary to give speeches in Nahuatl, and non-Spanish-speaking populations are still significant today.

Indigenous communities displayed remarkable cultural resilience. To the extent possible, they were selective about what to incorporate and what to ignore; for example, Spanish tools were frequently adopted though indigenous styles of dress were maintained. The indigenous were not without resources—they used their internal unity, as well as intergroup conflict, to set the terms of interaction with the Spaniards.

Among the tools of resistance were petitions, lawsuits, and rebellions. Local rebellion was endemic to colonial Latin America; sometimes it was widespread, threatening entire regions, although more frequently it was restricted to the village level. The two main patterns can be seen in resistance to conquest taking place in various locations over a roughly fifty-year period, and later reaction to changes in established relationships, particularly in the late colonial period.

The indigenous were best equipped to withstand the conquest wars because such wars were a part of the pre-Columbian past. The physical destruction and political consequences fell heaviest on indigenous elites above the city–state level. Provincial chieftains quickly lost their authority, and indigenous cities lost their preeminence as centers of native life. The cities built on old indigenous cities became Spanish centers; and indigenous life, with the exception of the indigenous intermediaries, moved entirely to the countryside and rural towns and villages.

The ethnic unities that supported state organization declined, and native priests at all levels came systematically under attack: Lands that had been worked for their benefit were confiscated and redistributed; indigenous priests were killed, brought to trial, or harried into secrecy. The result was turmoil; but part of the turmoil enabled the lower classes and oppressed indigenous groups to free themselves from their previous bonds. Some indigenous commoners eagerly denounced arbitrary acts and pagan habits of their nobles. Some towns and hamlets of landless farmers that had been attached to indigenous noble estates declared their independence.

The majority of the natives did not suffer a fall from social eminence because they had been commoners to begin with. Indeed, some may argue that the new rulers were less demanding and less divine. There was an increasing blurring of class lines, with the breakdown of sumptuary laws, which had stipulated that only indigenous nobility could possess cacao or consume alcoholic beverages. There was a growing business in the production of *pulque*, an alcoholic drink made by fermenting cactus juice, and the establishment of taverns and inns. What had once been a custom reserved for ritual celebration became a common public practice.

New Spanish crops and especially the introduction of livestock changed the countryside, but there was enough land so that indigenous still held their own until late in the colonial period. They now had to contend with stray cattle from the Spanish ranches wandering into subsistence plots and causing damage. In addition, the Spanish tried to monopolize trade, breaking up the old, indigenous commercial networks. The indigenous were able to trade, but not to dominate the old trade patterns as they had in the past.

The indigenous came to view the crown as their protector, and indeed, the crown's attitude was that the indigenous needed protection: They were seen as *"niños con barbos,"* children with beards. Royal officials helped establish the corporate rights of indigenous villages, hoping to practice protective segregation. They thought they would protect the indigenous from the worst features of nonindigenous ways and allow the best features to be formally and carefully introduced.

COLONIAL ADMINISTRATION

Spain and Portugal ruled their American empires for more than three centuries, a remarkable longevity that places them among the great imperial powers of all time. They owed that success to quite different concepts of imperial organization. The Spanish colonial administration was relatively well organized, the hierarchical ranks were well-defined, and the chain of command was easy to recognize. The Portuguese empire was loosely organized and the institutions more transitory. The two monarchies used different colonial systems, partly because of their own histories and partly because of the material conditions they encountered.

In both countries, the monarch was the State. He ruled as the supreme earthly patriarch in the well-established hierarchy of God, King, and Father, as envisioned in St. Augustine's concept of Christian monarchy. The mystique and tradition of the monarchy gave the institution such force that no one questioned the king's right to rule or refused his loyalty to the crown. The monarch possessed all power, and from the throne all power emanated. As such, it was the crown that legitimated all colonial arrangements.

However, the great distance between the Iberian peninsula and the New World and the slowness of communication and travel worked to confer considerable local autonomy on officials in the New World. In practice it meant that the kings could only hope to dictate the broad outlines of policy, leaving much of the interpretation and implementation to colonial and local officials *Obedezco pero no cumplo* ("I obey but I do not fulfill") became the accepted way for New World officials to manifest their loyalty to the Spanish crown while bending the laws to suit local situations. The philosophy of acknowledging the king's authority without enforcing his will—as common a practice in Brazil as it was in Spanish America—accounts, at least in part, for the longevity of the empires. It permitted a certain flexibility in the laws that could accommodate many interests, the monarch's as well as the colonist's. As the third governor general of Brazil, Mem de Sa, confided to the king, "This land ought not and cannot be ruled by the laws and customs of Portugal; if Your Highness was not quick to pardon, it would be difficult to colonize Brazil."

To keep their royal officials and their subjects in check, the Iberian monarchs sent to the New World officials of unquestioned loyalty. At best, they suspected that the colonies increased in everyone "the spirit of ambition and the relaxation of virtues." For that reason they hesitated to appoint many Americans to the highest colonial posts. They frankly suspected their loyalty. But as the empires matured, Americans increasingly held influential ecclesiastical, military, and political positions. Despite royal frowns, Iberian officials married into distinguished American families, providing a link between the local and the Iberian elite. The crown's check on these officials was the *visita*, an on-the-spot investigation to which all subordinates could be subjected. And at the end of all terms of office, each administrator could expect a *juicio de residencia*, a judicial inquiry into his public behavior.

Considering the size of the American colonies and the handful of royal officials, almost all of whom resided in the most populous cities, the extent of Iberian control over the colonies was remarkable. It must be concluded then that the crowns maintained their authority and control principally through the power of legitimacy or hegemony. The Americans accepted the system, rarely questioned it, and seldom challenged it. Popular uprisings, mostly motivated by economic discontent, broke out periodically, but the populace reacted to specific grievances rather than adhering to any philosophical current advocating change. For their part, the American elites, feeling they had more to gain through cooperation with the crown, lent their considerable authority to the maintenance of the imperial system.

The Spanish crown was assisted in administration of the colonies by the Council of the Indies (*Consejo de Indias*), which was not formed until 1524. By contrast, the *Casa de Contratacion* (*House of Trade*), which was in charge of colonial commerce, was founded in 1503. The Council comprised a group of ministers, named by the king, who controlled legislative, executive, and judicial decisions regarding the colonies. Like the king, however, the Council was an ocean away from the territories it sought to govern.

The king's principal representative in the New World was the viceroy. Columbus bore the title of viceroy of any new lands he might discover when he left Spain in 1492, and the various conquistadores served as governors of the territories they conquered. The administrative skills of the conquistadores varied considerably, and their self-interest made them questionable representatives of the crown. In 1535, the crown appointed Antonio de Mendoza, a member of one of Spain's foremost families and a trusted diplomat of Charles V, as the first viceroy of New Spain. Amid great pomp, he arrived in Mexico City and immediately tried to restrict the authority of the adelantados and encomenderos while he strengthened and centralized the king's power in the New World. By the time he left Mexico in 1551, he had imposed law and order, humbled the landowning class, and exalted the royal powers. In short, he consolidated the conquest of New Spain. Peru became the second viceroyalty. The first viceroy arrived in 1543 to find chaos, rivalries, and civil war disrupting Spanish South America. Not until the able administration of the fifth viceroy, Francisco de Toledo (1569–1581), was the king's authority firmly imposed on his unruly South American subjects. Like Mendoza, his major achievement was the consolidation of Spanish rule.

The *audiencia* was the highest royal court and consultative council in the New World. As such, it had wide-ranging powers to make political and administrative decisions as well as serving as final arbiter for civil and criminal complaints. The first audiencias were established in Santo Domingo, 1511; Mexico City, 1527; Panama City, 1535; Lima, 1542; and Guatemala, 1543. In the eighteenth century, fourteen such bodies functioned. The number of *oidores*, or judges, sitting on the audiencia varied. In the sixteenth century, their number fluctuated between three and four, but later it expanded to as many as fifteen. Because the tenure of the oidores exceeded that of the viceroy and overlapped each other, the oidores provided continuity to royal administration.

Captaincies-general were the major subdivisions of the viceroyalties. Theoretically, the captains-general were subordinate to the viceroys, but in practice they communicated directly with Madrid and paid only the most formal homage to the viceroys. Ranking beneath them were the governors, *corregidores*, and *alcaldes mayors*, the chief administrators of municipalities. Within their localities, these minor officials possessed executive, judicial authority, and limited legislative powers.

Municipal government, known as the *cabildo* or *ayuntamiento*, initially provided the major opportunity for the creole, the American-born white, to hold office and to exercise some political power during the early colonial period. By the middle of the eighteenth century, the creoles also held all but the highest government offices. As in Brazil, the town council governed not only the town itself but also the surrounding countryside, thus in some instances exercising power over vast areas. Property-owning citizens at first elected the *regidores*, the town councilmen, although later increasing numbers purchased or inherited the office.

Parallel to the creole cabildos were indigenous cabildos; in some regions they disappeared relatively quickly, merging into the creole cabildos. In other regions, they lasted until independence or the early national period. Especially in the early years, the Spaniards relied on indigenous leadership to collect tribute or to organize the workforce for public works. In essence, royal administration of the colonies rested on a handful of royal officials who oversaw Spanish settlers, and later creoles, and indigenous who actually produced the wealth.

For much of the colonial period, Spanish America was divided into only two viceroyalties—the Viceroyalty of Mexico, including all of modern Central America, and the Viceroyalty of Peru, encompassing all of Spanish South America. However, as the late colonial period saw the reorientation of trade to the Atlantic coast and the rising importance of the port at Buenos Aires, the crown created two new viceroyalties—New Granada, including modern Colombia, Venezuela, and Ecuador, and La Plata, encompassing parts of modern Chile, Argentina, Bolivia, and Uruguay.

The new viceroyalties signal the importance of trade in shaping government entities. From the earliest colonial days, merchants constituted a small but important class. They united into *consulados* and obtained formidable privileges and prerogatives. The crown authorized the first such trade association for Mexico in 1592; the merchants of Lima received permission for one in 1613. Thereafter, the consulado spread to other parts of Spain's American empire, a significant indicator of increasing trade with the metropolis. Together with the consulados in Seville and Cádiz, they exercised a monopoly over the trade and commerce of Spanish America.

Although Brazil emerged as Portugal's most valuable overseas possession, until the nineteenth century it was governed by no special laws or institutions that would have distinguished it as a separate, distinct, or privileged entity within the larger empire. From 1532–1534, in order to colonize Brazil without reaching into the royal coffers, the Portuguese monarch distributed Brazil in the form of large captaincies to twelve donataries who were to enjoy broad powers in return for colonizing the American domains. By 1548, John III reversed that decision and began to reassert his authority. In 1549, a central

Map 2.1 Viceroyalties in the Colonial Americas, 1776
Source: Craig, Albert M.; Graham, William A.; Kagan, Donald; Ozment, Steven M.; Turner, Frank M. *Heritage of World Civilizations Combined,* 7th ed. © 2006. Electronically reproduced by permission of Pearson Education, Inc., Upper Saddle River, NJ.

government under a governor-general began to bring some order. In 1646, the king elevated Brazil to the status of a principality, and thereafter the heir to the throne was known as the Prince of Brazil. After 1720, all the chiefs of government of Brazil bore the title of viceroy, and Brazil was in effect a viceroyalty thereafter.

Portugal was well into the sixteenth century before the rulers made any distinction between home and overseas affairs. Never did the crown authorize a special body to handle exclusively Brazilian matters. A variety of administrative organs that exercised a combination of consultative, executive, judicial, and fiscal functions assisted the king in ruling his domains. One of the most important was the Overseas Council (*Conselho Ultramarino*) created by John IV in 1642. It was the evolutionary result of considerable experience. The president, secretary, and three councilors of the Overseas Council usually had served in the colonies. The council divided itself into standing committees to treat the various military, administrative, judicial, and ecclesiastical matters. As its primary duty, it advised the king.

Other governmental organs continued to have dual metropolitan and colonial responsibilities. In Portugal, a Treasury Council (*Conselho da Fazenda*) administered public finances and the treasury. A Board of Conscience and Religious Orders (*Mesa de Consciência e Ordens*) established in 1532 advised the crown on indigenous matters. Finally the *Casa da Suplicacão* served as a supreme court for many colonial judicial disputes. A royal secretary or secretary of state, who after 1736 bore the title of Minister of Navy and Overseas, also assisted the monarchs in their imperial rule. These ministers became increasingly important in the second half of the eighteenth century.

In Brazil, representatives of the royal government administered the colony. At the apex stood the governor-general, who, after 1720, was called the viceroy. His effectiveness depended largely on his own strengths and weaknesses. Those viceroys who were vigorous exerted considerable influence over the colony. Those who were weak found themselves practically unable to control the capital city and their powers eroded by ambitious bishops and subordinate bureaucrats.

Salvador da Bahia, a splendid port, served as the first seat of the central government of Brazil. Prompted by foreign threat to the south of the colony, in 1763 the seat of the viceroyalty was moved southward to Rio de Janeiro. Foreign threats to the northeastern sugar coast ended after the defeat and expulsion of the Dutch in 1654. However, by the end of the seventeenth century, Portuguese America faced a growing threat from the Spanish in the Plata region. In 1680, the Portuguese founded the settlement of Colônia do Sacramento on the left bank of the Rio de la Plata, across from Buenos Aires. The Spanish challenge to Portuguese claims to the region caused a century and a half of intense rivalry and frequent warfare along the Plata.

The governors-general and later the viceroys depended on a growing bureaucracy to administer the colony, oversee its military preparedness, dispense the king's justice, and collect taxes. Of greatest importance was the High Court (*Relação*), first established in Bahia in 1609. A second was established in Rio de Janeiro in 1751. These courts primarily had judicial responsibilities: They functioned as the highest law tribunals in Brazil from which there was limited appeal to the Casa de Suplicação in Lisbon. Tax questions and the supervision of the treasury were the responsibility of another bureau, the Board of Revenue (*Junta do Fazenda*).

The nation we know today as Brazil was divided during most of the colonial period into two states. The state of Brazil was by far the more important of the two, but another impoverished colony existed in the far north, the state of Maranhão. The northern state never developed the vitality of the southern one and heavily depended on Lisbon. The king appointed a governor-general and a chief justice after the state was established in 1621. A slow growth and a scanty population negated the need for a high court and none was ever authorized. In 1751, the capital was transferred from São Luis to Belém, which was a smaller though increasingly more active port that for some time had been the effective center of the state. In recognition of the growing importance of the Amazon, the king created in 1755 the Captaincy of São José do Rio Negro (the present-day Amazonas), subordinate to the Captaincy of Pará.

Captaincies were the principal territorial subdivisions of the two states. Representatives and appointees of the king, the governors or captains-general of those captaincies carried out the same responsibilities on a regional level as the governor-general or viceroy did on a broader scale. Here, as in so many instances, theory and practice diverged. Distance, the varying effectiveness of personalities, political intrigue, and vagueness of the law often meant that the governor-general was only first among equals and sometimes unable to exert any authority in the captaincies. In truth, the governor-general and his later successor, the viceroy, never exercised the same degree of control or authority as their counterparts in Spanish America.

The municipal government was the one with which most Brazilians came into contact and the only one in which they participated to any degree. Governing much more than the town and its environs, the municipality extended into the countryside. In sparsely settled Brazil, the municipalities contained hundreds and often thousands of square miles. The most important institution of local government was the *senado da câmara*, the municipal council. A restricted suffrage of the *homens bons*, the propertied class, elected two justices of the peace, three aldermen, and a procurator to office every three years. The senado frequently served as the first arena for the struggles between the *mazombos*, the whites born in Brazil, and the *reinóis*, the whites born in Portugal. Portuguese officials, occupying all levels of government except the municipal, enforced the law of the empire; their point of view was global. The mazombos on the municipal councils cared only for the local scene; their vision was Brazilian.

The Catholic Church

Perhaps even more important than the governmental organization was the Church. Ferdinand and Isabel were the Catholic monarchs, and they took their position seriously. The monarchs defended the faith within their realms, in return for which the Pope conferred royal patronage upon the crown by bulls to the Spanish monarchs in 1501 and 1508 and to the Portuguese monarchs temporarily in 1515 and permanently in 1551. That royal patronage permitted the Iberian monarchs to exercise power over the Church in their empires in all but purely spiritual matters. They collected the tithe and decided how it should be spent; appointed (and at times recalled) the bishops, priests, and other ecclesiastical officials; authorized the construction of new churches; determined the boundaries of the bishoprics; and approved and transmitted papal messages—or refused to. The royal patronage meant that the state dominated the Church, but conversely, it allowed the Church to pervade the state. If the king and his ministers had a final say in Church matters, it is equally true that clerics often occupied the top administrative posts in governments. Churchmen often served as ministers, captains-general, viceroys, and even regents. Cardinal Henry, after all, ruled the Portuguese empire in the sixteenth century.

Columbus's instructions stated, "the King and Queen, having more regard for the augmentation of the faith than for any other utility, desire nothing other than to augment the Christian religion and to bring divine worship to many simple nations." Accordingly, twelve friars accompanied Columbus on his second voyage to the New World. Conversion was essential not only to give the indigenous the true faith and eternal salvation but also to make them loyal subjects to Their Most Catholic Majesties. To be Portuguese or to be Spanish was to be Roman Catholic. Religion served as a proto-nationalism as the Catholic monarchs used faith to measure citizenship, starting with the expulsion of Jews and Muslims. Iberians were born, reared, married, and buried Catholics, and the Church touched every aspect of their lives.

A religious people, the indigenous did not need to be convinced of the existence of deities. Indigenous people were polytheistic and accustomed to adding the gods of conquerors to their pantheon of gods. After all, the god of the conqueror must clearly be stronger; the symbol for conquest in Nahuatl, the language of the Aztec empire, was the burning temple. A more difficult problem was Catholic insistence on monotheism, and the proliferation of Latin American saints days can be attributed to the linking of Catholic saints with local deities. Much to the priests' chagrin, indigenous idols could often be found behind the Catholic altars. Each village had its own saint and *cofradia*, or lay brotherhood, devoted to festivals and commemoration of the saint. These celebrations, entwined with precolonial beliefs, became an important part of indigenous life. The survival of pre-Columbian religious beliefs, however, did not diminish the important place that Catholicism came to occupy.

Like the government, Church structure was hierarchical and territorial, with archbishops located in the viceregal capitals. Below them were bishops in the other major cities, followed by clergy in cathedral chapters and urban parishes. At the bottom of the ecclesiastical structure were the priests in the countryside, instructing the indigenous in encomienda villages. These were

The Catholic Church, one of the most important institutions of colonial Latin America, was central to the goal of turning the indigenous into Spanish subjects. The magnificent cathedral in the Zocalo of Mexico City was built on the ruins of an Aztec temple. (Library of Congress)

the most recent arrivals, those with the least training and no connections. Like the encomienda, the rural parish was erected directly on the indigenous provincial unit. The priests used the authority of the caciques to get churches built and to get the indigenous to attend services. They also relied on the *fiscal*, an indigenous leader who served as a Church officer and recruited sacristans and singers to participate in Church functions.

Priests behaved in the same way as other immigrants to the New World. They used ties of kinship and region to build their power bases, and they married their female relatives off to encomenderos, miners, and wealthy merchants. Their economic base was built on the pious donations given to them, which they used to buy income-producing property and to build elaborate churches. Elites tended to join the regular orders—Franciscans, Dominicans, Augustinians—whereas those of lower rank became the secular priests. Not tied to an order, they participated in society much like any other Spaniard—they looked for ways to make money.

Perhaps the relations between Church and State were not always perfect examples of harmony, but they were sufficiently tranquil to allow the
Church to grow wealthy in the New World. Tithes, the sale of papal indul-
gences, and parochial fees provided a small share of the Church's income.
The legacy furnished the principal source of wealth. In their wills, the afflu-
ent were expected to leave at least part of their wealth to the Church. As a
result, the Church accumulated vast estates, quickly becoming the largest
landowner in the New World. The Church also became an important lender,
and ecclesiastical coffers grew with fees and interest rates on loans. Church
wealth was by no means evenly distributed. In cities such as Lima, Salvador
da Bahia, Ouro Prêto, Quito, Antigua, and Mexico City, ostentatiously imposing
churches crowded one another, whereas "shocking poverty" characterized
hundreds of humble parish churches dotting the countryside. While some of
the higher clergy lived on incomes surpassing those of many of the sovereign
princes of Germany, impoverished clerics administered to the needs of the
faithful in remote villages.

The wealth reinforced the conservative inclinations of the Iberian
Church. It was not from the masses that the Church drew its leadership.
Generally the sons of the wealthy and/or noble became bishops and archbishops, positions in the New World that were dominated by the European-
born. Thus, the highest ranks of the clergy, like those in the civil service, were
associated with and filled by the elite. In wealth, power, prestige, and monopoly of education, the Roman Catholic Church by the end of the eighteenth century ranked as an omnipotent institution in the Western
Hemisphere. Its influence weighed heavily, not only in the social and religious life of the community but in politics and economics as well.

The relationship between the Church and the indigenous was a complicated one. Initially, the clergy were responsible for evangelizing, converting
the indigenous to Christianity. Their initial level of success is questionable; for
example, the Nahuatl expression for baptism was to pour water over one's
head—descriptive but not indicative of much understanding. A few clergymen, such as Bernardo de Sahagún, labored to understand the indigenous by
teaching their leaders Spanish and Latin while simultaneously learning the
native languages. Few went as far as Sahagún, who with indigenous assistance compiled a multivolume compendium of native history and tradition,
the Historia general de las cosas de Nueva España.

Some clergy took seriously their role as protectors of the indigenous, a
position exemplified by Antonio de Montesinos and Bartolomé de las Casas.
In 1511, Montesinos chided parishioners in Santo Domingo with a sermon
written by the three Dominicans in the parish. Calling himself "the voice of
Christ crying in the wilderness of this island," he denounced colonists' abuse
of the indigenous and demanded, "Are they not men? Do they not have
rational souls? Are you not bound to love them as you love yourselves? Don't
you understand this? Don't you feel this? . . . Be sure that in your present

Europeans who had never set foot in the New World imagined the conquest as particularly bloodthirsty, a view that fueled the "Black Legend" of Spanish cruelty. This engraving by Theodore de Bry shows conquerers torturing the indigenous with fire, amputations, and hangings. (Library of Congress)

state you can no more be saved than the Moors or Turks, who do not have and do not want the faith of Jesus Christ." He was joined in his cause by Las Casas, once an encomendero himself, who became the most famous supporter of the indigenous cause. His *Brevísima Relación De La Destrucción De Las Indias* (Short Account of the Destruction of the Indies) detailed, with some exaggeration and hearsay, the abuses of the Spaniards. The work was widely read in Europe and contributed to the "Black Legend," the idea that the Spanish conquest was somehow more brutal than conquests in other parts of the world. This conquest, though brutal, was certainly not more so than the many conquests that characterized European history; the motivation for the critique had more to do with European jealousy of Spanish wealth than with reality.

Although many priests undoubtedly helped the indigenous, most clergy believed in the hierarchical social system that put the indigenous and African slaves at the bottom of society. The indigenous served as a workforce for the Church, as well as for secular society, tilling Church lands and building local churches and opulent urban cathedrals. Some clergymen were also guilty of abuse of native populations, as evidenced by many indigenous petitions to the crown.

Perhaps most importantly from the Spanish point of view, the clergy upheld the social order from the pulpit, where they preached resignation. If God had made them poor, it would be a sin to question why. Poverty was to have its reward in the next life. It was a message not just for the indigenous, but for the lower ranks of Spanish and mestizo society as well. The messages of passivity and acceptance legitimated a hierarchical society.

The Church maintained a careful vigil over that society. Alleged backsliders, especially Jewish converts, the New Christians, could expect to account for themselves before the Inquisition. Philip II authorized the establishment of the Holy Office in Spanish America in 1569, and it began to operate in Lima in 1570, in Mexico City in 1571, and in Cartagena in 1610. It is significant that he exempted the indigenous from the jurisdiction of the Inquisition "because of their ignorance and their weak minds." The Inquisition served more of a political than a religious end in its vigilant efforts to purge and purify society in order to make it unified and loyal. The considerable power of the Inquisition lasted until the last half of the eighteenth century. As an institution it was never established in Brazil, but it operated there through the bishops and visitations from Inquisitors.

The Church was also responsible for much of the culture in the Spanish colonial world. While the Church censored books, it also educated Americans and fostered most of the serious scholarship in the New World. Because Church members composed a large share of the educated of the colonies, it was from their ranks that most of the teachers came. The Church exercised a virtual monopoly over education. Monasteries housed the first schools and taught reading, writing, arithmetic, and Catholic doctrine. The Spanish monarch encouraged the founding of universities in the New World, granting the first charters in 1551 to the University of Mexico and the University of San Marcos in Lima. The clergy occupied most of the chairs. Before Harvard opened its doors in 1636, a dozen Spanish-American universities, drawing on medieval Spanish models, offered a wide variety of courses in law, medicine, theology, and the arts, most of them taught in Latin. The universities made one major concession to the New World: They taught theological students indigenous languages for their future benefit and effectiveness.

The Church also offered women an alternative to family life, a choice they did not always make voluntarily. Patriarchs sometimes placed their daughters in convents to guard their virginity or to prevent marriage. A marriage could mean a huge dowry of land, property, or capital, which the father preferred to pass on intact to a son. On the other hand, widows often retired to a convent from which they administered their wealth, estates, and property. A religious life by no means meant one dominated exclusively by prayer and meditation. Neither were nunneries necessarily dreary houses of silence, service, and abnegation. Through the religious orders, women operated schools, hospitals, and orphanages. In some convents, the nuns, attended by their servants,

The Virgin de Guadalupe

The melding of Catholic and indigenous tradition is perhaps most effectively embodied in the Mexican veneration of the Virgin of Guadalupe. According to legend, an indigenous man named Juan Diego was crossing the hill of Tepeyac on December 9, 1531, when a beautiful, dark-skinned woman appeared to him. She instructed Juan Diego to tell the bishop, Juan de Zumarraga, that she "ardently wish[es] and greatly desire[s] that they build my temple for me here, where I will reveal . . . all my love, my compassion, my aid, and my protection."

Virgin Mary, statue, taken during Festival of the Virgin of Guadalupe, 12 December, Mexico City, Mexico, Central America. (Mireille Vautier, Picture Desk, Inc./Kobal Collection)

Juan Diego followed her instructions, but Bishop Zumarraga was skeptical and demanded proof. The disconsolate man returned to see the Virgin, who instructed him to go to the top of the hill and gather flowers. The hill had been barren, but the amazed man found the hilltop in bloom. He gathered the flowers in his cloak and brought them to the bishop on December 12. When he opened his cloak to show the bishop the out-of-season flowers, they spilled out and left an image of the Virgin on the lining of the cloak.

Convinced and repentant, the bishop ordered the construction of the church. Conveniently, the very spot where the dark Virgin appeared was the site of a temple to the indigenous goddess Tonantzin, whose temple Zumarraga had ordered destroyed. Tonantzin had been an earth goddess, mother of gods, and protector of humanity.

Similarly, the Virgin de Guadalupe Tepeyac is seen as a protector, especially of the poor and oppressed. She is distinguished from the Spanish Virgin de Guadalupe de Estremadura by her location at what had been an indigenous holy site, and in her appearance. Because she is dark skinned, *morena*, she provided a link with Catholicism for the indigenous.

The original church was replaced by a larger one in 1709, and a new basilica was dedicated at the site in 1976. Juan Diego's mantle is preserved and on display at the shrine, which draws thousands of devout Catholics each year, especially on December 12.

entertained, read secular literature, played musical instruments, sang, prepared epicurean delights, and enjoyed a lively and comfortable life.

One of the most remarkable intellectuals of the colonial period was a nun, Sor Juana Inés de la Cruz (1651–1695), whose talent earned her fame in New Spain during her lifetime and whose complex and brilliant poetry ensured her an exalted place in literature. A favorite of the viceregal court, she chose to enter the convent in order to pursue the kind of intellectual life that was not open to women in secular society. At the convent of San Jerónimo she had her own library and study, where she conducted *tertulias*, literary salons. Though she became famous for her poetry, she was equally interested in philosophy and natural science. With a change in the viceregal and bishopric hierarchy, she fell from favor and came under attack for her worldly studies and the antipatriarchal tone of some of her writing. Under pressure from the hierarchy, she sold her extensive library of some 4,000 volumes, as well as her musical and scientific instruments. She died in 1695 after contracting the plague while nursing her sick sisters.

Colonial Society

Legally and socially, the Spanish colonies were divided into two worlds: the *república de indios*, Republic of Indians, and the *república de españoles*, Republic of Spaniards. The separation of the two worlds was never complete, and race mixture blurred the boundaries as time went by. The issue of racial purity was a sensitive one to Spaniards already biased against the impurity of Jewish or Muslim heritage. Although Spanish men mixed freely with indigenous and African women, they tried to maintain strict control over Spanish women to maintain a pure Spanish lineage. These concerns reinforced the Iberian tradition of the patriarchal family, sanctified by religion and serving as a model for the organization of society and polity.

During the early decades of conquest and colonization, more European males than females arrived in the New World. Thirty women were allowed on Columbus's third voyage in 1498, and in 1527 the crown licensed brothels in Puerto Rico and Santo Domingo "because there is need for it in order to avoid worse harm." In the later conquests, Spanish women sometimes fought alongside the men. Doña Isabel de Guevara participated in the conquest of the region of La Plata in the 1530s. In seeking an encomienda years later, Doña Isabel recounted, "The men became so weak that all the tasks fell on the poor women, washing the clothes as well as nursing the men, preparing them the little food there was, keeping them clean, standing guard, patrolling the fires, loading the crossbows when the Indians came sometimes to do battle, even firing the cannon, and arousing the soldiers who were capable of fighting, shouting the alarm through the camp, acting as sergeants and putting the soldiers in order. . . . [O]ur contributions were such that if it had not been for us, all would have perished; and were it not for the men's reputation, I could truthfully write you much more and give them as the witnesses."

The paucity of Spanish women led many men to turn to indigenous women. From the beginning, the conquerors regarded indigenous women as part of the conquest, and rape was common. Indigenous men would frequently hide women from the Spaniards in the Caribbean islands. Other indigenous groups gave women to the Spaniards to cement alliances. The conquest of women is in many ways a metaphor for the conquest of the New World itself—the conquest of virgin territory. The most famous example of Spanish conquest of indigenous women is the story of Malintzin, known by the Spanish as Doña Marina or Malinche, a term that in Mexico has come to mean traitor. Malintzin was a Mayan woman who had been sold into slavery before she was given as a gift to Hernando Cortes. Because she could speak Nahuatl, the language of the Aztecs, she became Cortes's translator. She bore Cortes a son, but within a few years he married her off to one of his men, Juan de Jaramillo.

To increase stability in the colonies, the crown insisted that married men bring their wives to the New World and encouraged the export of eligible young women to marry off in the colonies. By the 1540s, there was one Spanish woman for each seven or eight men. As in Spain, marriages were arranged to benefit family wealth and position. Marriage linked encomenderos, miners, government officials, and merchants.

In this patriarchal organization, the male head of the family dominated the household and its businesses: In rural Brazil, that included plantation, slaves, and tenants. Although males of the household liberally expanded the basic family unit through their sexual escapades to include hosts of mestizo and mulatto children, the Iberian woman was expected to live a pure life of seclusion. Ideal models were set for the behavior of the women of the patriarch's family, who were destined either for matrimony or religious orders. They were to remain virgins until their marriage and to live separated from all men except their fathers, husbands, and sons. A high value was placed on their duties as wives and mothers, and control over their sexuality was essential to guarantee that the Iberian elites remained of pure blood. Although women of other economic strata could not follow such an elitist model, they were certainly influenced by it.

Despite the patriarchal bias, Iberian women enjoyed more freedoms than their European sisters. Women retained their family names when married and both maternal and paternal surnames were passed to the children. Women owned half the property of their marriages and inherited equally with their brothers. Widows were frequently executors of men's wills and guardians of their children, and their freedom often resulted in great societal pressure for them to remarry. Sometimes the women would choose instead to retreat to convents as *beatas*, holy women, though not technically nuns. In the New World, women took on new roles: They were left in charge of encomiendas when their husbands traveled and proved to be sharp businesswomen. Some wealthy women were active in the business world, investing in real estate or manufacturing. They sometimes bought and sold slaves and took a direct role in the administration of their properties.

Whereas elite Iberian and creole women were expected to stay mostly in the home, lower-class women, of necessity, participated in many occupations. Women of the middle sectors tried to work in their homes, by renting rooms or taking in sewing. But lower-class women were very much in the public view, working as spinners, producers and sellers of brandy (*aguardiente*), bakers, healers (*curanderas*), midwives, seamstresses, potters, candlemakers, innkeepers, and landladies. They dominated the local market, selling food, produce, and handicrafts, and frequently worked as domestics in the homes of the upper classes.

Women's roles were clearly linked to the issue of economic class and occupation, which in turn was coupled with race and ethnicity. The Spanish and Portuguese occupied the top tier of the social hierarchy in the New World. Below them came their descendants, of pure Iberian blood but born in the colonies—the creoles of Spanish America and the *mazombos* of Brazil. Together they constituted a small minority, precariously balanced above the darker masses. At the base of society was the mass of darker people, especially the indigenous people and the Africans, and the increasing number of *castas*, the people of mixed race. The latter groups would eventually push for their place in the hierarchy, challenging Iberian hegemony.

In sum, the colonial period in Latin America was formative, with greater significance than for the North American colonies. It began a century earlier, and by 1550 every major city in the region had been founded. Although the Spaniards had transplanted institutions from the Old World to the New World, they were forced to modify them to fit local circumstances, frequently building on the indigenous structures. During 300 years of imperial rule, patterns emerged that would resonate throughout the modern period: It was a hierarchical society, led by the small, white elite that dominated the poor, darker masses. Political, economic and social power was in the hands of a few, buttressed by the validation of a hierarchical Church. The economy was characterized by large landholdings and low-paid workers, with a dependence on exports, making the region disproportionately affected by foreign affairs. And it would be foreign affairs that would impel the colonies to become nations.

RECOMMENDED READINGS

Lockhart, James, and Stuart B. Schwartz. *Early Latin America: A History of Colonial Spanish America and Brazil*. Cambridge: Cambridge University Press, 1983.

———, and Enrique Otte, eds. *Letters and People of the Spanish Indies, Sixteenth Century*. Cambridge: Cambridge University Press, 1976.

Powers, Karen Vieira. *Women in the Crucible of Conquest: The Gendered Genesis of Spanish American Society, 1500–1600*. Albuquerque: University of New Mexico Press, 2005.

Restall, Matthew. *Seven Myths of the Spanish Conquest*. New York. Oxford University Press, 2003.

———. *The Maya World: Yucatec Culture and Society, 1550–1850*. Stanford, CA: Stanford University Press, 1997.

Terraciano, Kevin. *The Mixtecs of Colonial Oaxaca: Ñudzahui History, Sixteenth Through Eighteenth Centuries*. Stanford, CA: Stanford University Press, 2001.

CHAPTER 3

INDEPENDENCE

Spain and Portugal managed to hold on to their sprawling overseas possessions for more than 300 years, an empire of impressive duration. But it is, perhaps, inevitable that distant subjects one day recognize first that they are capable of standing alone, and subsequently that they need their independence to flourish economically and politically. As Spain fought European wars, Latin Americans found themselves at times experiencing the wealth of free trade and at others successfully handling their own military defense. They came to see themselves as the true rulers of their lands, and a feeling of inferiority before the Iberian-born gave way to a feeling of equality and then to superiority. A greater appreciation of and pride in the regions where Latin Americans were born and raised gave rise to feelings of nativism, a group consciousness attributing supreme value to the land of one's birth and pledging unswerving dedication to it. Spain tried to gain better control of the colonies, but those attempts did more to provoke than to contain their colonies. The result was the struggle for independence.

With the exception of Haiti and the struggle in Mexico, it was the creole and mazombo elites who directed the movements toward independence. But these elite leaders relied on the darker and poorer masses to win the wars. The majority populations had their own reasons for fighting, which were often at odds with the leadership, and the independence wars were simultaneously civil wars.

The major historical questions for consideration during this period, encompassing the end of the eighteenth century and the opening of the nineteenth, are why the Latin Americans pursued independence, how they achieved it, and what they intended to do with it. Who benefited and who lost as a result of the political change from colony to nation? And finally, why did independence affirm rather than change the basic patterns of society?

A New Sense of Self

Before the end of the first century of Iberian colonization, the inhabitants of the New World began to reflect on themselves, their surroundings, and their relations to the rest of the world. They spoke and wrote for the first time in introspective terms. Juan de Cárdenas, although born in Spain, testified in his *Problemas y Secretas Maravillosos de las Indias* (The Marvelous Problems and Secrets of the Indies), published in 1591, that in Mexico the creole surpasses the *peninsular* (the Iberian) in wit and intelligence. Evincing a strong devotion to New Spain, Bernardo de Balbuena penned his *La Grandeza Mexicana* (The Grandeur of Mexico) in 1604 in praise of all things Mexican. He implied that for beauty, interest, and charm, life in Mexico City equaled—or surpassed—most Spanish cities. In 1618, Ambrósio Fernandes Brandão made the first attempt to define or interpret Brazil in his *Diálogos das Grandezas do Brasil* (Dialogues of the Greatness of Brazil). In doing so, he exhibited his devotion to the colony, chiding those Portuguese who came to Brazil solely to exploit it and return wealthy to the peninsula. Poets, historians, and essayists reflected on the natural beauty of a generous nature. They took up with renewed vigor the theme extolled in the early sixteenth century that the New World was an earthly paradise.

These nativist attitudes were given further impetus by Enlightenment philosophers who viewed the Americas as inferior to Europe. The denigration of all things American was most pointedly expressed in the *Histoire philosophique et politique des établissements et du commerce des Européens dans les deux Indes* (Philosophic and Political History of the Establishment of European Commerce in the Indies), which first appeared in 1770 and again in some fifty editions during the next thirty years. The *Histoire's* contributors included such prominent philosophes as Denis Diderot. Americans were not only dismissed as less intelligent than Europeans, but even less virile: "The men there are less strong, less courageous, without beard or hair: degenerate in all signs of manhood. . . . The indifference of the males toward that other sex to which Nature has entrusted the place of reproduction suggests an organic imperfection, a sort of infancy of the people of America similar to that of the individuals in our continent who have not reached the age of puberty."

Latin Americans leaped to their own defense. Juan Vicente de Güemes Pacheco y Padilla, the creole son of the former viceroy of New Spain, insisted that American men were "extremely inclined to engage in sex." On a more lofty note, Francisco Javier Clavijero likened the ancient Mexican world to the classical societies of Greece and Rome in his four-volume history of New Spain, *Storia antica del Messico*, in 1780–1781. The popular work was disseminated widely and in several languages. Juan José de Eguiara y Eguren, rector of the University of Mexico, showed that the subsequent inhabitants of New Spain were equally erudite by publishing the *Bibliotheca mexicana* (1755), a compendium of scholarly works.

At the same time, parts of Enlightenment thought appealed to New World intellectuals. The eighteenth century was a time of intellectual ferment in Europe, and those ideas were disseminated to Spain and the colonies. Americans were particularly interested in rationalism and scientific study of nature and economy. The works of René Descartes and Isaac Newton quickly entered the university curriculum. John Locke's conceptions of individual property rights dovetailed nicely with Adam Smith's liberal ideas of free trade and an unfettered market. American elites discussed the new ideas at *tertulias*, social gatherings in their homes, whereas the masses frequented cafes, where newspapers were read aloud and events discussed.

The revolution in scientific and economic ideas led to the formation of Economic Societies of the Friends of the Country (*Sociedades Económicas de Amigos del País*), which had developed in Spain and spread to the New World by the 1780s. In general, the societies showed a strong tendency to emphasize the natural and physical sciences, agriculture, commerce, and education, as well as to give some attention to political and social questions. Portuguese America had not a single university, but its counterpart of the Spanish economic societies was the six literary and scientific academies established between 1724 and 1794 in Salvador and Rio de Janeiro. Each had a short but apparently active life.

The printing presses in Spanish America—Lisbon rigidly prohibited the setting up of a press in its American possessions—contributed significantly to spreading ideas. Among their many publications numbered several outstanding newspapers, all fonts of enlightened ideas and nativism. Their pages were replete with references to, quotations from, and translations of the major authors of the European Enlightenment.

For Latin Americans, the Enlightenment ideas that were most important focused on reason and the belief in progress. The political ideas were of less importance, with many believing that increased liberty could be accomplished within the Spanish system rather than calling for independence. Indeed, the Spanish crown had become more liberal under the Bourbons; and Spaniards, too, looked forward to modernization and progress within the royal structure.

The Bourbons, a French dynasty, had come to the Spanish throne in 1714, after a long War of Succession that followed the death of the last Habsburg heir in 1700. On acceding to the throne, the new Bourbon leaders found a bankrupted kingdom, overextended in European affairs, with an inefficient system of colonial administration. The new leaders aimed to change all that.

THE BOURBON REFORMS

The sense of nativism took root in fertile ground when the crown enacted a series of laws that have become known as the Bourbon reforms. By the mid-eighteenth century, the Bourbons faced increased interest in their colonies on the part of other European monarchs, along with a hefty bill for the costs of participation in the Seven Years' War (1756–1763). Charles III (1759–1788) determined to reform the imperial structure, with the goal of increasing administrative efficiency, political control, and profits. The power of the Council of the Indies waned as the ministers of the king took over many of its former duties. In the eighteenth century, the chief responsibility for the government of Spanish America rested in the hands of the Minister of the Indies. The Casa de Contratación also felt the weight of Bourbon reforms: The king's ministers absorbed so many of its powers that it became useless and was abolished in 1790.

The Bourbon kings infused a more liberal economic spirit into the empire, which at first blush would appear to favor colonial economic welfare, although the intent was to strengthen Spain by liberalizing trade, expanding agriculture, and reviving mining. However, the crown also set up a more efficient tax administration, which made sure that colonists actually paid their taxes. In the eighteenth century, Cádiz lost its old commercial monopoly when the king permitted other Spanish ports to trade with the Americas. The fleet system gradually disappeared. After 1740, Spanish ships commonly rounded Cape Horn to trade with Peru and slowly abandoned the old isthmian trade route. In the 1770s, Charles lifted the restrictions on intercolonial commerce.

The most radical innovation was the establishment of the intendancy system, an administrative unit used by the Bourbons in France and copied by their relatives in Spain. The intendants, royal officials of Spanish birth, with extensive judicial, administrative, and financial powers, supplanted the numerous governors, corregidores, and alcaldes mayores in the hope that a more efficient and uniform administration would increase the king's revenue and end bureaucratic abuses and corruption. In financial affairs, the intendants reported directly to the crown. In religious, judicial, and administrative matters, they were subject to the viceroy and were to respect his military prerogatives. In 1764, Cuba became the first intendancy, and by 1790 the system extended to all the Spanish American colonies.

The new system infuriated the creoles, who were accustomed to holding all but the highest government offices. Creole families owned most of the rural estates, provided nearly all parish priests, and dominated the lower reaches of imperial government, particularly as secretaries and petty administrators. As the colonial viceroys brought fewer people with them, creoles filled out their entourages. The creoles not only dominated the cabildos, but they also held the majority in the audiencias.

However, creoles were denied the highest positions, which remained in the hands of the Iberian born. Of the 170 viceroys, only four were creoles—and they were the sons of Spanish officials. Of the 602 captains-general, governors, and presidents in Spanish America, only fourteen had been creoles; of the 606 bishops and archbishops, 105 were born in the New World. Such preference aroused bitter resentment among the creoles. The gap was made greater by the appointment of the intendants, all peninsulars, who formed a new layer of political power between the creoles and the crown. As Bolívar stated in 1815, "The hatred that the Peninsular has inspired in us is greater than the ocean which separates us."

The Iberian suspicion of the New World elite in effect questioned both their ability and their loyalty. One Portuguese high official remarked of Brazil, "That country increases in everyone the spirit of ambition and the relaxation of virtues." A distinguished Chilean, advising the king that all would be better served if the crown would make use of the creoles, concluded, "The status of the creoles has thus become an enigma: [T]hey are neither foreigners nor nationals . . . and are honorable but hopeless, loyal but disinherited."

Further, the New World inhabitants resented the flow of wealth into the pockets of the peninsulars and reinóis who came to the Americas to exploit the wealth only to return to Iberia to spend their hastily gained riches. By the end of the colonial period, most of the merchants who dominated foreign trade were still peninsulares. A visitador to New Spain, José de Gálvez, expressed to the crown an oft-repeated creole grievance: "Spaniards not only don't allow us to share the government of our country, but they carry away all our money."

As another reform measure, in the 1760s Charles III created a colonial militia with creole officers in order to defend the increasingly important distant fringes of the empire. The idea was to transfer the cost of defense of the colonies to the Americans. Initially, the militias were almost fictional and served little purpose other than to give titles to miners and merchants. The granting of military commissions to the creoles afforded them a new prestige. Usually the high ranks were reserved for—or bought by—wealthy members of the local aristocracy. Hence, a close identification developed between high military rank and the upper class. Further, the creole officers enjoyed a most practical advantage, the *fuero militar*, a special military privilege, that exempted them from civil law. In effect, it established the military as a special class above the law, the results of which would be increasingly disruptive for Latin American society. For the middle and lower classes, militia service was frequently seen in a more negative light, as they were called away from their shops and work to train, parade, and occasionally fight. Whereas the upper classes could pay for substitutes, the middle and lower classes lacked the funds for such an option.

Obviously, the points of view of the Iberian and the American varied. The first came to the New World with a metropolitan outlook. He saw the empire as a unit that catered to the well-being of the European center. The latter had a regional bias. His prestige, power, and wealth rested on his mines and lands. His political base was the municipal government, whose limited authority and responsibility reinforced his parochial outlook. In short, he thought mainly in terms of his region and ignored the wider imperial views.

Portuguese mercantilism was never as effective as that of its neighbor, particularly before 1750. Attempts were made sporadically to organize annual fleets protected by men-of-war to and from Brazil, but the highly decentralized

Portuguese trade patterns and a shortage of merchant and war ships caused difficulties. Between the mid-seventeenth and mid-eighteenth centuries, the crown partially succeeded in instituting a fleet system for the protection of Brazilian shipping. Still, it never functioned as well as the Spanish convoys. Economic companies fared little better. The crown licensed four. In general they were unpopular with the residents of Brazil and the merchants, both in Portugal and Brazil. The Brazilians criticized them for abusing their monopolies and raising prices with impunity. The merchants disapproved of the monopolies, which eliminated them from much trade, and accused the companies of charging outlandish freight rates. All sides bombarded the companies with charges of inefficiency. Nonetheless, crown monopolies—such as brazilwood, salt, tobacco, slaves, and diamonds—flourished.

Royal control over Brazil tightened during the eighteenth century. The plantations produced their major crops for export, demand dictated incomes, and incomes regulated production. Though Lisbon encouraged the capitalist trends toward higher production, it continued to prevent direct trade with European markets, much to the increasing frustration of the Brazilian elites. Their desire to enter the capitalist marketplace of the North Atlantic, along with the imperial, mercantilist, and monopolistic policies of the Portuguese crown, charted a course of conflict that prompted the exercise of greater royal control.

The absolutist tendencies noticeable during the reign of John V (1706–1750) were realized under the Marquis of Pombal, who ruled through the weak Joseph I (1750–1777). Pombal hoped to strengthen his economically moribund country through fuller utilization of its colonies. To better exploit Brazil, he centralized its government. He incorporated the state of Maranhão into Brazil in 1772. He dissolved the remaining hereditary captaincies, with one minor exception, and brought them under direct royal control and tried to restrict the independence of municipal governments. To fortify royal authority, Pombal expelled the Jesuits from the empire in 1759. He accused the order of challenging the secular government and of interposing itself between the king and his indigenous subjects. Some 600 Jesuits were forced to leave Brazil. In 1767, Charles III followed suit, expelling some 2,200 Jesuits from Spanish America.

The Temptations of Trade

In the late colonial period, there was a new orientation in the colonies toward the Atlantic coast. In response, Spain created two new viceroyalties in 1776. New Granada included modern Colombia, Venezuela, and Ecuador; La Plata encompassed parts of modern Chile, Argentina, Bolivia, and Uruguay. La Plata became important as a route between the Peruvian silver mines and Atlantic ports, and an increased demand for hides brought prosperity to the region. Venezuela rose in importance as a wheat producer for Cartagena, where the fleet was supplied, and as a cacao producer. Cuba followed Brazil's lead and between 1750 and 1770, the island converted to a sugar economy, with exports leaping from a mere 300 tons a year to 10,000 tons.

The privileged classes in the New World were most interested in the reform of commerce and trade. The American merchants and planters chafed under crown monopolies and restrictions. They were especially unhappy about reforms that increased Spanish economic power. The pressures of the British and French on the Iberian monarchs for greater trade with their American empires, burgeoning European contraband in the Americas, and the more liberal commercial code promulgated by Spain in 1778 brought Latin America into ever closer contact with Europe's more dynamic economies.

Physiocrat doctrine—the ideas that wealth derived from nature (agriculture and mining) and multiplied under minimal governmental direction—gained support among Brazilian intellectuals. They spoke out in favor of reducing or abolishing taxes and duties and soon were advocating a greater freedom of trade. From Bahia, João Rodrigues de Brito boldly called for full liberty for the Brazilian farmers to grow whatever crops they wanted, to construct whatever works or factories were necessary for the good of their crops, to sell in any place, by any means, and through whatever agent they wished to choose without heavy taxes or burdensome bureaucracy, to sell to the highest bidder, and to sell their products at any time when it best suited them.

Similar complaints and demands reverberated throughout the Spanish-American empire. Chileans wanted to break down their economic isolation. Reflecting on the potential wealth of Chile and the lingering poverty of its inhabitants, José de Cos Iriberri, a contemporary of the Bahian Rodrigues de Brito, concluded, "Crops cannot yield wealth unless they are produced in quantity and obtain a good price; and for this they need sound methods of cultivation, large consumption, and access to foreign markets." Manuel de Salas agreed and insisted that free trade was the natural means to wealth. And Anselmo de La Cruz asked a question being heard with greater frequency throughout the colonies: "What better method could be adopted to develop the agriculture, industry, and trade of our kingdom than to allow it to export its natural products to all the nations of the world without exception?"

As the American colonies grew in population and activity, and as Spain became increasingly involved in European wars in the eighteenth century, breaches appeared in the mercantilist walls that Spain had carefully constructed around its American empire. British merchants audaciously assailed those walls and when and where possible widened the breaches. During the Seven Years' War, the Caribbean became a zone of military occupation. Havana was then the third largest city in the New World, smaller than Mexico City and Lima but larger than New York and Boston. When the island was taken by the British in 1762, Havana was opened to free trade. In ten months, more than 1,000 ships entered the port, compared with 1,500 ships in the preceding ten years. When the British left, the desire for more free trade remained.

For their part, the Spanish Bourbons tried hard to introduce economic reforms that would reinforce Spain's monopolistic economic control. They authorized and encouraged a series of monopolistic companies. The Guipúzcoa Company in Venezuela best illustrates the effects of these monopolies and the protests they elicited from a jealous native merchant class. By the end of the seventeenth century, Venezuela exported a variety of natural products, most important of which were tobacco, cacao, and salt, to Spain, Spanish America, and some foreign islands in the Caribbean. This trade expanded to England, France, and the British colonies during the early years of the eighteenth century. A small, prosperous, and increasingly influential merchant class emerged. The liberator of northern South America, Simón Bolívar, descended from one of the most successful of these merchant families. The creation of the Guipúzcoa Company in 1728, designed to ensure that Venezuela stayed within the imperial markets and to eliminate trade with foreigners, evoked sharp protest from the merchants. They complained that the company infringed upon their interests, threatened their economic well-being, shut off their profitable trade with other Europeans, and failed to supply all their needs. Spain, after all, they quickly pointed out, could not absorb all of Venezuela's agricultural exports, whereas an eager market in the West Indies and northern Europe offered to buy them. Finally, exasperated with

Simón Bolivar (1783–1830) is often considered the father of the South American independence movements. (Library of Congress)

the monopoly and discouraged from expecting any results from their complaints, the merchants fostered an armed revolt against the company in 1749, a revolt that took Spain four years to quell.

The struggle against the company was both armed and verbal, and it fostered a hostile feeling toward the crown, which was committed to support the unpopular company. The friction between the local merchants, business people, landowners, and population on the one hand, and the Guipúzcoa Company and crown on the other, continued throughout the rest of the century. The merchants' belief that freer trade would fatten their profits was more than satisfactorily proven when Spain, after 1779, entered the war against England with the consequent interruption caused by the English fleet in the trade between Venezuela and Spain. The merchants took immediate advantage of the situation to trade directly and openly with the English islands in the Caribbean. Their profits soared.

Two new institutions organized the protests and activities of the disaffected Venezuelans. The Consulado de Caracas, established in 1793, brought together merchants and plantation owners, and it soon became a focal point for local dissatisfaction and agitation. Then in 1797 the merchants formed a militia company to protect the coast from foreign attack. That responsibility intensified their nativism, or, at that stage, patriotism. Nurtured by such local institutions, the complaints against the monopoly, burdensome taxes, and restrictions mounted in direct proportion to the increasing popularity of the idea of free trade. As one merchant expressed it, "Commerce ought to be as free as air." One of the results of these intensifying complaints was the series of armed uprisings in 1795, 1797, and 1799. Great Britain continued to encourage these and other protests against Spain's system of commercial monopoly. Clearly, English interests coincided with those of the creole elite, who thought in terms of free trade.

Economic dissatisfaction extended beyond the narrow confines of the colonial elite. Many popular elements protested the burdensome taxes and expressed hope for improvements. Popular songs at the end of the eighteenth century expressed those economic protests:

All our rights
We see usurped
And with taxes and tributes
We are bent down.
If anyone wants to know
Why I go shirtless
It's because the taxes
Of the king denude me.
With much enthusiasm
The Intendents aid the Tyrant
To drink the blood
Of the American people.

EARLY WARNING SIGNS

The majority of the colonial population probably understood and appreciated the economic motivations for independence more than they did the political ones. Popular antitax demonstrations rocked many cities in both Spanish and Portuguese America in the eighteenth century. Indigenous communities protested the *reparto* system, which forced them to buy goods from creoles and peninsulars. There were more than sixty revolts in the Andes alone during the 1770s. Most of these, however, were locally based and focused on local problems, without a larger vision of change in society. However, oppressive economic conditions helped to spark two potentially serious popular uprisings, the Tupac Amaru Revolt in Peru in 1780 and the Comunero Revolt in New Granada (Colombia) in 1781, and to foment the Bahian Conspiracy in Brazil in 1798.

The Tupac Amaru Revolt, which began near Cuzco in November 1780, was sparked primarily by the raising of the *alcabala*, or sales tax, to 4 percent in 1772 and to 6 percent in 1776. José Gabriel Condorcanqui Noguera, a mestizo who also held the title of indigenous curaca, tried to move both the indigenous and the creoles to rise against the Spanish. As he spoke against forced labor and invoked images of the ancient Inca empire, indigenous people responded en masse, attacking white towns. Because whites were barely 8 percent of the Peruvian population, the alarmed creoles joined the Spanish in brutally quelling the revolt in 1781. Although Tupac Amaru was captured and killed in 1781, the uprisings that he inspired continued until 1783. The movement spread across thousands of square miles and ended with the deaths of tens of thousands of people. The crown recognized that it needed to address the cause of the uprising. A special junta created by the viceroy of Peru concluded that the reparto was the central concern for the indigenous community. The crown abolished the reparto and established a special audiencia to hear indigenous complaints. It is important to note, however, that not all the indigenous followed Tupac Amaru's lead. At least twenty indigenous leaders stayed loyal to the crown. Their decisions were locally based, sometimes hinging on rivalries among individuals, villages, and ethnic groups.

The Comunero Revolt in New Granada (Colombia) in 1781 was also a protest against a tax increase as well as burdensome monopolies. Creoles and mestizos in New Granada rose up to nullify unpopular Spanish laws, and the revolt spread spontaneously through New Granada. There were riots in Socorro in March, and by late May the rebellion had spread throughout the Eastern Cordillera, with 20,000 armed protesters marching on Bogotá. Faced with the growing success of the rebels, the Spanish authorities capitulated to their demands for economic reforms. However, once the comuneros dispersed, satisfied with their apparent success, the viceroy abrogated former agreements and arrested the leaders, who were executed in 1782 and 1783.

Across the continent in Bahia, another popular conspiracy, this one against the Portuguese metropolis, came to a head in 1798. It exemplified the spread of the ideas of the Enlightenment among the masses, which, in this case, thought in terms of economic, social, and political reforms, even of independence. The conspirators were from the popular classes: soldiers, artisans, mechanics, workers, and so large a number of tailors that the movement sometimes bears the title of the "Conspiracy of the Tailors." All were young (under thirty years old), and all were mulattos. The conspirators spoke in vague but eloquent terms of free trade, which they felt would bring prosperity to their port, and of equality for all men without distinctions of race or color. They denounced excessive taxation and oppressive restrictions. Regional elites did not support their cause, however, and four mulatto leaders were executed.

INTERNATIONAL EXAMPLES

The turmoil of the late eighteenth century was, of course, not felt only in Spanish America. The New World colonies to the north chafed under similar economic and political controls exerted by Great Britain. The Spanish crown, however, felt so sure of its colonies that it did not see a threat in supporting the thirteen colonies in their struggle; Spanish support had more to do, however, with animosity to the British than with support of independence. Nonetheless, Spain was a signatory to the 1783 Treaty of Paris, which made the United States independent.

The ideas of the North American independence movement were no secret in Spain and its colonies. Newspapers published translated versions of the work of Thomas Paine and reported on the English colonial struggle. Although Latin Americans found many of the ideas appealing, they still tended to believe that their concerns could be worked out within the monarchy, especially as Spanish thought included some liberalizing and enlightened aims.

The French Revolution of 1789 at first seemed to broaden the ideas of U.S. independence. Many were impressed by the French idea that citizens should be politically active and that through action they could make change. But as the revolution moved further left, it became too radical for even the most liberal thinkers in Spanish America.

The greatest repercussions of the French Revolution were felt in Saint Domingue, the French colony that occupied the western third of the island of Hispaniola. Sugar profits had soared in the eighteenth century as French planters exploited the good soil of the island, adopted the latest techniques for growing and grinding the cane, and imported ever larger numbers of African slaves to work the land and to process the crops. The motherland smiled with satisfaction on its rich Caribbean treasure. A multiracial society had developed, a divided society, which by 1789 counted 40,000 whites and half a million blacks with approximately 25,000 mulattos. The Code Noir, promulgated in 1685, regulated slavery. Theoretically it provided some protection to the black slave, facilitated manumission, and admitted the freed slave to full rights in society. In reality, the European code but slightly ameliorated the slave's dreadful state. In general, slavery on the lucrative plantations was harsh. To meet the demand for sugar, the plantation owner callously overworked his slaves, and to reduce overhead he frequently underfed them. An astonishingly high death rate testified to the brutality of the system.

The distant French revolutionary cry of "Liberty, equality, fraternity" echoed in the Caribbean in 1789. Each segment of the tense colony interpreted it differently. The white planters demanded and received from the Paris National Assembly a large measure of local autonomy. Then the Assembly extended the vote to all free persons, a move favoring the mulattos. The planters' demand for the repeal of that law precipitated a struggle between them and the mulattos.

Then, on August 22, 1791, the slaves demanded their own liberty and rebelled in northern Saint Domingue. More than 100,000 arose under the leadership of the educated slave Toussaint L'Ouverture, son of African slave parents. In pursuit of his goal of liberating his fellow slaves, he fought for the following decade against, depending on the time and circumstances, the French, British, Spaniards, and various mulatto groups. Victory rewarded his extraordinary leadership and the courage of the slaves. By 1801, L'Ouverture commanded the entire island of Hispaniola.

Meanwhile, the chaos of the French revolution had yielded to the control of Napoleon, who took power in 1799. In 1801, Napoleon resolved to intervene to return the island to its former role as a profitable sugar producer. A huge army invaded Saint Domingue and the French induced L'Ouverture to a meeting only to seize him treacherously. Imprisoned in Europe, he died in 1803. His two lieutenants, Jean-Jacques Dessalines and Henri Christophe, took up the leadership. A combination of the slaves' strength and yellow fever defeated the massive French effort. On January 1, 1804, Dessalines proclaimed the independence of the western part of Hispaniola, giving it the name of Haiti.

The surviving French planters fled to Cuba, Mexico, and Venezuela. They brought with them their horror stories of rampaging slaves, burning sugar fields, and bloody struggle. Haiti's independence was a potent symbol. For the exploited slaves of the New World, it represented hope. For the creole elites, it was a chilling example of what they had always feared—that the dark masses would rise up against the tiny white elite. If that was the cost of independence, it was too high a price to pay.

Latin American elites were deeply shaken by the slave uprising that won Haiti its independence from France. Haitian leader Toussaint L'Ouverture is pictured here in a military uniform with epaulettes, protecting a black woman and her two children while confronting a white man. (Library of Congress)

IMPETUS FROM THE OUTSIDE

Latin America watched in horror as the French revolution devolved into the Jacobin terror. In 1793, Spain joined Britain in war against the French Republic, which ended in defeat for Spain. In humiliating treaties of 1795 and 1796, Spain was forced to ally with France, becoming an enemy of the British. Spain had been economically sound at the beginning of the war; by the end, the bankrupt crown confiscated Church property, raised taxes, and even taxed the nobility, all highly unpopular measures.

In 1799, Napoleon's coup ended the revolution. That same year, future Latin American independence leader Francisco de Miranda commented, "We have before our eyes two great examples, the American and the French Revolutions. Let us prudently imitate the first and carefully shun the second."

But more war was in store for Europe. In 1802, Napoleon became first consul for life, and he was crowned emperor in 1804. Although his troops failed to retake Haiti, he set out to bring Europe under his control. Because of the treaties, Spain was forced to fight on the side of the French in the ensuing Napoleonic Wars. In 1805, Britain defeated the Spanish navy at Trafalgar, and in 1806 a French blockade destroyed Spain's economy. In 1807, Spanish authorities gave Napoleon permission to cross Spain and conquer Portugal. The Portuguese royal family, the Braganzas, however, did not fall prisoner to the conquering French armies. Prince-Regent John packed the government aboard a fleet and under the protecting guns of English men-of-war sailed from Lisbon for Rio de Janeiro just as the French reached the outskirts of the capital. The transfer of a European crown to one of its colonies was unique. The Braganzas were the only European royalty to visit their possessions in the New World during the colonial period. They set up their court among the surprised but delighted Brazilians and ruled the empire from Rio de Janeiro for thirteen years.

After seizing control of the Portuguese metropolis, Napoleon immediately turned his attention to Spain. Spanish opponents of Charles IV forced him to resign in favor of his son, Ferdinand VII. Bonaparte invited the regents to France to discuss the issue of the dispute over the crown. There he forced both to abdicate and put them in jail, then appointed his brother, Joseph, as king.

The Spanish people rose up against the French forces on May 2, 1808, a battle immortalized by the painter Francisco Goya. The Spaniards formed local juntas to rule in the name of the king under the principle that in his absence, sovereignty resided in the people, who bore the responsibility to defend the nation. It soon became clear that the Spaniards needed unity to defeat the French, and the regional juntas gave way to the *Junta Suprema Central y Gubernativa de España e Indias* (Supreme Central Governing Committee of Spain and the Indies).

Spanish Americans reacted with equal repugnance to the French usurper. Various juntas appeared in the New World to govern in Ferdinand's name. In effect, this step toward self-government constituted an irreparable break with Spain. By abducting the king, Napoleon had broken the major link between Spain and the Americas. The break once made was widened by the many grievances of the Latin Americans against Spain.

Most of Latin America achieved its independence during a period of two decades, between the proud declaration of Haiti's independence in 1804 and the Spanish defeat at Ayacucho, Peru, in 1824. Nearly 20 million inhabitants of Latin America severed their allegiance to France or to the Iberian monarchs. Every class and condition of people in Latin America participated at one time or another, at one place or another, in the protracted movement. But the slave uprising in Haiti proved to be unique. Most of the independence movements were led by creole elites.

ELITIST REVOLTS

Between 1808 and 1810, Spaniards and Americans together formed juntas to rule in the name of the deposed king. Most agreed that their differences with the Crown could be resolved and they hoped to remain within the Spanish monarchy. But then the Spanish resistance lost more ground to the French forces—Seville fell, and the Junta Central fled first to Cádiz and then to the Isle of León, the only Spanish territory still free from French control. The junta appointed a new Council of Regency to rule and then dissolved itself. In the colonies, more radical creoles took the reigns and ousted the Europeans. In 1810, the movements for independence began simultaneously in opposite ends of South America, Venezuela and Argentina. The struggle for Spanish America's independence fell into three rather well-defined periods: the initial thrust and expansion of the movement between 1810 and 1814, the faltering of the patriotic armies and the resurgence of royalist domination from 1814 to 1816, and the consummation of independence between 1817 and 1826.

In Venezuela from 1808–1810, the captaincy general was run by Vicente Emparán, the Spanish governor of Cumaná province. But in 1810 it was clear that Spanish forces were losing to the French. Venezuela's local elites—both Americans and Spaniards—ousted Emparán and appointed a *Junta Conservadora de los Derechos de Fernando VII* (Supreme Junta to Conserve the Rights of Fernando VII) to rule in his place. The junta, however, asserted, "Venezuela has declared its independence, neither from the *Madre Patria*, nor from the sovereign, but from the [Council of] Regency, whose legitimacy remains in question in Spain itself." Such claims have been dismissed by some scholars as "false monarchism," a claim to rule in the name of the king only as a pretense for the goal of independence. Others argue that some creole elites sincerely intended to remain within the monarchy until circumstances made it appear that such a goal was not within reach.

The new junta was viewed with some suspicion by the elites of Caracas, mostly entrepreneurs, who had formed their own Junta Suprema. They suspected that the new junta was merely a creation of the merchants of Cádiz, whose interests collided with those of Venezuelan exporters. Opinion was divided throughout the territory, with some supporting the Supreme Junta of Caracas and others supporting the Council of Regency in Cádiz. Alliances were not always what one might expect. A mostly Spanish junta in Cumaná province supported not the Regency in Spain but the junta of Caracas. But the town of Barcelona, seeking autonomy from Cumaná, created its own junta and recognized both the Junta Suprema de Caracas and the Council of Regency in Cádiz.

In a move to unite the area, the Caracas Junta called for elections to a congress to determine the region's future. The elections were indirect—locally chosen electors would then elect the deputies to the *Cuerpo Conservador de los Derechos de D. Fernando VII en las provincial de Venezuela* (Body to Conserve the Rights of D. Fernando VII in the provinces of Venezuela). Voting was restricted to free males ages twenty-five years and older with at least 2,000 pesos in movable property. But before elections could be held, the council in Cádiz attempted to control the region by sending Captain General Fernando Miyares, former governor of Maracaibo, to take control. Cádiz also decreed an end to Venezuela's free trade, arguing that because Great Britain and Spain were not at war, such emergency measures were not necessary. The junta of Caracas refused to obey, and Cádiz sent troops based in Cuba and Puerto Rico, which blockaded Venezuela. The Americans found themselves in the rather odd position of fighting against Spanish control, which was asserted by those who did not even have control of the kingdom headed by Joseph Bonaparte.

Younger, more radical Venezuelans rose up to challenge the Caracas leadership, which consisted of politically moderate merchants and hacendados. The radicals, with the exception of wealthy aristocrat Simón Bolívar, were generally middle class, including lawyers, notaries, journalists, small merchants, and lower ranking officials. When news of a Spanish massacre in Quito reached Caracas, the radicals started a riot, which was mostly peopled by blacks and castas. The terrified moderates on the Junta Suprema de Caracas were more frightened by the thought of social disorder than by continued Spanish dominance. They responded by exiling radical leaders and barring the return of revolutionary Francisco Miranda, who was in Britain. They also sent armed forces to subdue the city of Coro, but they were defeated by the radicals, who convinced the authorities to let Miranda return. With his leadership, they immediately began to press for independence.

The congress elected in 1811, however, had been chosen by property owners and was dominated by moderates. They appointed a new regime, a weak triumvirate to rule in the interests of the elites. Property requirements were imposed to vote or hold office, a national guard was established to regulate slaves, and new vagrancy laws took aim at the *llaneros*, the cowboys of the grasslands whose free lifestyle was seen by the urban elites as chaos. The radicals did not object to the new rules because they shared the same social and economic interests as the moderates. Despite their use of the dark masses, the radicals' sole issue was independence from Spain, not social and political change within the Americas.

The next year was spent in bloody battle as the royalists continued to fight against the so-called "First Republic." Because the white population of the region was only 22 percent, both royalists and rebels counted on the support of the blacks and castas. Venezuela descended into chaos, and both sides encouraged racial warfare. The Spanish regime collapsed in August 1813, and Bolívar formed the "Second Republic," which was little more than a military dictatorship. Bolívar's victory was fragile and temporary. He faced the challenge of José Tomás Boves, a lower class trader from Asturias who had lived in the llanos. He organized a cavalry of llaneros, many of them pardos and blacks, and promised them the lands of white republicans. His forces drove Bolívar from Venezuela, and whites fled in fear of the "dark hordes." Both peninsulars and creoles were relieved when a Spanish army arrived in April 1815. By then, one-fifth of the population, some 80,000 people, had died.

Events unfolded differently in Río de la Plata, which had been drawn into the Napoleonic Wars in 1806, when Buenos Aires was attacked by the British. The viceroy, the Marquis of Sobremonte, had fled, but the local militia gathered under the leadership of Santiago Liniers, a French officer who was serving in the Spanish forces. The *porteños* (residents of the port city of Buenos Aires), defeated the invaders, and Liniers was named temporary viceroy. The American forces were also successful against a second invasion attempted by the British in 1807.

When news of Joseph Bonaparte's ascension to the throne reached Buenos Aires in July 1808, Liniers and the provincial intendants proclaimed their loyalty to Ferdinand. In September, they recognized the junta central in Seville, which claimed to rule in the name of the king and the people. In November, Liniers opened Buenos Aires to free trade, and trade with the now-allied British provided enough customs revenue to pay an 8,000-member militia.

In January 1809, the peninsulars plotted to depose Liniers, who they saw as too friendly to the creoles. Cornelio Saavedra, the creole militia leader who defended Liniers, characterized the Spaniards as men who, seeing the loss of Spain in Europe, "proposed the idea of forming another Spain in America in which they and the many whom they hoped would emigrate from Europe would continue to rule and dominate."

The creoles successfully came to Liniers' defense, but in August 1809 the junta in Spain sent a new viceroy, Balthasar de Cisneros. Cisneros put an end to free trade and tried to reduce the size of the militia. The peninsulars expected that Cisneros would restore their old influence, whereas the creoles struggled for supremacy by keeping control of the militia, which far outnumbered the Spanish garrison.

With the news in 1810 that the French had conquered Seville and set the junta central on the run to Cádiz, the creoles saw their opening. The creole militia rose up in May and demanded a *cabildo abierto*, an open town meeting— that is, open to the urban elite. The elites tried to impose a conservative junta, but they capitulated when threatened by the creole-controlled militia.

The new junta was divided evenly between military leaders, who mostly came from the elites, and intellectuals, who were generally from the middle class. The creoles in charge drove the peninsulares from office, arrested, exiled, and executed them. A Committee of Public Safety was formed to catch counterrevolutionaries, who were summarily executed.

The leaders of the May revolution, however, were in for a surprise. The provinces outside of Buenos Aires saw the uprising as a local matter. Leaders in the Banda Oriental (Uruguay), Paraguay, and Upper Peru (Bolivia) felt no unity with the porteños. The interior of the region was largely conservative, based on the large haciendas that were worked by mestizos and indigenous, who were involved in patron–peon relationships. The provincial area of Buenos Aires was the wide open pampas, where there was a great deal of unclaimed land and the freedom offered by the mobile society of the gaucho. Neither region had any desire to be dominated by the port city, which was a commercial and bureaucratic center. Furthermore, the port wanted free trade, whereas the Andean provinces of Salta, Tucumán, Jujuy, and Catamarca, which produced food, livestock, and pack animals for the silver mines of Upper Peru, had begun to industrialize and required protection for the fledgling sugar, textile, and transport equipment factories. Mendoza, San Juan, and La Rioja in the far west, though mostly an area of subsistence agriculture, could sell wine and brandy, if protected.

The Buenos Aires junta tried to take the other regions by force, but a year later only a small territory was under their control. Political power was in the hands of a triumvirate headed by Bernardino Rivadavia, whose program called for a constitutional monarchy, the formation of a maritime insurance company and new meat-salting plants, and the colonization of the interior by Europeans.

The colonization plans further antagonized the provinces, whereas urban Buenos Aires was unhappy with the idea of constitutional monarchy. The triumvirate was brought down in 1812 by forces led by José de San Martín. San Martín was born in Río de la Plata and was sent to Spain to train as a soldier, reaching the rank of lieutenant colonel. He left Spain for London, where he met Venezuelan Francisco Miranda before returning to Buenos Aires. In 1814, San Martín was named commander of the Army of the North, and Rio de la Plata's independence seemed momentarily safe.

While the colonies fought over which path to take, changes were also occurring in Spain. The Regency had called for a *côrtes*, a parliament, and elections were held in the colonies to send representatives. The Côrtes decided that it was the repository of nation sovereignty and created a government that consisted of the Regency as executive, a judiciary, and a legislative branch, which would dominate. When the Regency objected, its members were arrested and the Côrtes appointed a new Regency.

The cortes was divided on several issues: Spanish liberals wanted a modern constitutional monarchy, whereas conservatives wanted absolutism. Neither group wanted the Americans to have autonomy. After much debate, the cortes produced a constitution in 1812. It did not give the Americas full equality, but it did provide them with equal representation in the legislative branch. It recognized mestizos and the indigenous as citizens, but continued black slavery. Most important, it restricted the power of the king and made the legislative branch the most powerful.

After the defeat of Napoleon, Ferdinand VII was returned to the throne in 1814. He had no intention of reigning as a constitutional monarch and abolished the cortes and the constitution. He persecuted the liberals who had usurped his authority and determined to take control of the colonies by dispatching a large army to South America in 1815. By 1816, independence movements had been crushed everywhere but Buenos Aires and Paraguay. Movements had not even begun yet in Peru, Central America, Cuba, or Puerto Rico. Not only were prospects of independence defeated, but there seemed little hope for improved relations with Spain. Ferdinand's retaliatory measures, however, fueled new resentments and led to renewed fighting in the colonies.

In Buenos Aires, independence leaders called a congress in Tucumán in 1816 and wisely made overtures to the provinces. The same year, Bolívar, who had been in exile, returned to Venezuela. He took Angostura in 1817 and organized a new army with the help of José Antonio Páez.

San Martín organized forces in Río de la Plata, along with the Chilean exile Bernardo O'Higgins, to liberate Chile in 1817 and 1818. In a truly amazing feat, San Martín's army of 5,000 crossed the Andes over six different passes, including several that were more than 10,000 feet high. Bolívar borrowed San Martín's strategy and crossed the Andes in the north to free New Granada in 1819. The Spanish forces were on the run, and they were desperately in need of reinforcements. But none would come.

In Spain, rebellions against Ferdinand's absolutism began in 1814. The monarch struggled to control the peninsula while holding on to his far-flung empire. In 1819, he began massing forces at Cádiz to send to the colonies. But there were problems: Many of Spain's ships were not seaworthy, and there was no money for repairs. Even worse, the troops became restless, amid wretched conditions, shortages of food and clothing, and the spread of disease. Junior officers complained, and on January 1, 1820, they were led in mutiny by Lieutenant Colonel Rafael del Riego. Riego had been a loyal Spanish officer who fought for Ferdinand and was even imprisoned in France. Not only did the troops refuse to go to the Americas, but Riego also demanded the restoration of the 1812 constitution. Ferdinand had no choice but to capitulate.

Royalist forces continued to fight in the colonies, and bloody battles continued, but without reinforcements the royalists were doomed. The

Americans triumphed in Venezuela in 1822 and in Ecuador in 1823. That same year, the forces of San Martín and Bolívar converged on Peru, and the decisive battle of Ayacucho in 1824, under the leadership of Antonio José de Sucre, effectively ended the war.

POPULAR REVOLUTION IN MEXICO

New Spain initially started on the same path as the rest of Spanish America. Taking advantage of the political vacuum in Spain in 1808, the creoles maneuvered to form a local junta to govern the viceroyalty, a move calculated to shift political power from the Spaniards to the Mexican elite. Alarmed by the maneuvering, the peninsulars feared the loss of their traditional, preferred positions. They acted swiftly to form their own junta and thus shoved the creoles aside. The creoles plotted to seize power and enlisted the help of Father Miguel Hidalgo, the parish priest of the small town of Dolores. In September 1810, the peninsulars discovered the plan and jailed the leaders. The wife of one leader, Josefa Ortiz de Dominguez, got word to Hidalgo, who on September 16, 1810, rang the church bells to summon the mostly mestizo and indigenous parishioners.

But Hidalgo's ideas were different from the other creole leaders. Well educated, and profoundly influenced by the Enlightenment, Hidalgo professed advanced social ideas. He believed that the Church had a social mission to perform and a duty to improve the lot of the downtrodden. Personally, he bore numerous grievances against the peninsulars and the Spanish government—he had been educated by the Jesuits until their expulsion in 1767, and he had been investigated by the Inquisition on charges of mismanaging funds while he was the rector of the College of San Nicolás Obispo in Valladolid.

When his parishioners gathered, Hidalgo exhorted them to rise up and reclaim the land stolen from them 300 years before: "Long live Ferdinand VII! Long live America! Down with bad government! Death to the Spaniards!" Hidalgo's words fell on fertile ground. The town of Dolores was a mere ten miles from Guanajuato, making it dependent on the mining economy. In 1809, an unusually dry summer had decreased maize production, ruining many small farmers. Food prices had quadrupled, and miners couldn't feed the mules needed in mining, leading to layoffs of mine workers.

Hidalgo had unleashed new forces. Unlike the creoles who simply wanted to substitute themselves for the peninsulars in power, the mestizo and indigenous masses desired far-reaching social and economic changes. There were 600 people gathered in Dolores; as they marched toward Guanajuato, the numbers swelled to 25,000. At Guanajuato, the intendant, the local militia, the peninsulars, and some creoles barricaded themselves in the granary, leaving the city defenseless. The lower classes of Guanajuato joined the insurgents and burned and pillaged the city. By the time the mob reached Mexico City, it numbered 60,000 to 80,000, and in their rampage they made no distinction between creole and peninsular. With energies released after three centuries of repression, the indigenous and mestizos struck out at all they hated. The creoles became as frightened as the peninsulars, and the two rival factions united before the threat from the masses.

Hidalgo did little to discipline the people under him. Indeed, his control of them proved minimal. His ideas were disorganized, vague, and at times contradictory. While voicing his loyalty to Ferdinand, he denounced the abuses of the viceregal government—later he declared Mexico free and independent. He threatened the peninsulars with death, and he abolished slavery. Poised before Mexico City, he hesitated then ordered a withdrawal, an action that cost him much of the allegiance of the masses. The Spanish army regained its confidence and struck out in pursuit of the ragtag rebels. Once captured, the royalists tried Hidalgo before a nine-member panel that included six creoles. In mid-1811, ten months after the Grito de Dolores, a firing squad executed him. His severed head was mounted on the wall of the granary at Guanajuato, a clear warning to others.

Nonetheless, Hidalgo's banner was taken up by another parish priest, José Maria Morelos. Morelos came from a poor mestizo family and worked as a mule driver; through great personal effort he became a priest, always assigned to the poorest, backwoods parishes, where poor indios and mestizos labored. He had joined Hidalgo's movement, but after Hidalgo's death he determined that undisciplined hordes were not the answer. He trimmed the forces, organized them into a more disciplined force, and tried to appeal to the creoles while still carrying Hidalgo's banner of social reform. He defined his program: establish the independence of Mexico; create a republican government in which the Mexican people would participate with the exclusion of the wealthy nobility and entrenched officeholders; abolish slavery; affirm the equality of all people; terminate the special privileges of the Church as well as the compulsory tithe; and partition the large estates so that all farmers could own land. At Chilpancingo, he declared that Mexico's sovereignty resided in the people, who could alter the government according to their will. He called forth pride in the Mexican—not in the Spanish—past. His program contained the seeds of a real social, economic, and political revolution and thereby repulsed peninsular and creole alike. He ably led his small, disciplined army in central Mexico for more than four years. In 1815, the Spaniards captured and executed him. The royalists immediately gained the ascendancy in Mexico and dashed the hopes of the mestizos and indigenous for social and economic changes. New Spain returned momentarily to its colonial slumbers.

When independence was won it Mexico, it was under conservative leadership, a reaction to Ferdinand's acceptance of the liberal 1812 constitution. The peninsulars and creoles in New Spain rejected Spanish liberalism just as they had earlier turned away from Mexican liberalism. In their re-action to the events in Spain, they decided to free themselves and chart their own destiny. They were joined by the Church hierarchy, who feared the loss of property and secular restrictions if the liberals in control of Spain had their way. The peninsulars and creoles selected a pompous creole army officer, Augustín de Iturbide, who had fought against Hidalgo and Morelos, first as their instrument to effect independence and then as their emperor. The most conservative forces of New Spain ushered in Mexican independence in 1821. They advocated neither social nor eco-nomic changes. They sought to preserve—or enhance if possible—their privileges. The only innovation was political: a creole emperor replaced the Spanish king, which was symbolic of the wider replacement of the penin-sulars by the creoles in government. The events harmonized little with the concepts of Hidalgo and Morelos but suited creole desires. The Mexican struggle for independence began as a major social, economic, and political revolution but ended as a conservative coup d'etat. The only immediate victors were the creole elite.

THE BRAZILIAN EXCEPTION

Portuguese America achieved its independence during the same tumultuous years. Brazil entered into nationhood almost bloodlessly, and following the trend evident in Spanish America, the mazombos clamored for the positions of the reinóis, although their ascendancy was more gradual than that of the creoles. The difference lay in the way Brazil achieved its independence.

Under the guidance of John VI, Brazil's position within the Portuguese empire improved rapidly. He opened the ports to world trade, authorized and encouraged industry, and raised Brazil's status to that of a kingdom, the equal of Portugal itself. Rio de Janeiro changed from a quiet viceregal capi-tal to the thriving center of a far-flung world empire. The psychological im-pact on Brazilians was momentous. Foreigners who knew Brazil during the first decade of the monarch's residence there commented on the beneficial effect the presence of the crown exercised on the spirit of Brazilians. Ignacio José de Macedo typified the optimism of his fellow Brazilians when he pre-dicted, "The unexpected transference of the Monarchy brought a brilliant dawn to these dark horizons, as spectacular as that on the day of its discov-ery. The new day of regeneration, an omen of brighter destinies, will bring long centuries of prosperity and glory."

When the royal court returned to Lisbon in 1821, after thirteen years of residence in Brazil, John left behind the Braganza heir, Prince Pedro, as re-gent. The young prince took up his duties with enthusiasm, only to find him-self caught between two powerful and opposing forces. On the one side, the newly convened parliament, the Côrtes, in Lisbon, annoyed with and jealous of the importance Brazil had assumed within the empire during the previous

Map 3.1 Latin America in 1830

Source: Craig, Albert M.; Graham, William A.; Kagan, Donald; Ozment, Steven M.; Turner, Frank M. *Heritage of World Civilizations Combined,* 7th ed. © 2006. Electronically reproduced by permission of Pearson Education, Inc., Upper Saddle River, NJ.

decade and a half, sought to reduce Brazil to its previous colonial sub-servience; on the other, Brazilian patriots thought in terms of national inde-pendence. As the Côrtes made obvious its intent to strip Brazil of previous privileges as well as to restrict the authority of its prince-regent, Pedro listened more attentively to the mazombo views. He appointed the learned and nationalistic mazombo José Bonifácio de Andrada e Silva to his cabinet, making him the first Brazilian to hold such a high post. Bonifácio was instrumental in persuading Pedro to defy the humiliating orders of the Côrtes and to heed mazombo opinion, which refused to allow Lisbon to dictate policies for Brazil.

Princess Leopoldina, although Austrian by birth, had dedicated her energies and devotion to Brazil after she arrived in Rio de Janeiro in 1817 to marry Pedro. She too urged him to defy Portugal. She wrote him as he traveled to São Paulo in September 1822: "Brazil under your guidance will be a great country. Brazil wants you as its monarch. . . . Pedro, this is the most important moment of your life. . . . You have the support of all Brazil." On September 7, 1822, convinced of the strength of Brazilian nationalism, Pedro declared the independence of Latin America's largest nation, and several months later in a splendid ceremony he was crowned "Constitutional Emperor and Perpetual Defender of Brazil."

The evolutionary course upon which Brazil embarked provided a stability and unity that no other former viceroyalty of the New World could boast. Contrary to the contractual political experiences of Spanish America, an unbroken patriarchal continuity, hereditary governance, flowed in Brazil. Similar to that of Spanish America, Brazilian independence affected and benefited only the elite. Like the elites everywhere, the Brazilians rushed to embrace foreign ideas and to continue, even to deepen, the colonial dependency on exports.

Inevitably, Latin American independence was characterized by continuity more than by change. The creole elites expanded their already dominant position in Latin American society. Although they had courted the masses, they had no intention of sharing wealth and power with them. For the majority, there was little difference between colonialism and early nationhood.

RECOMMENDED READINGS

Archer, Christon I., ed. *The Wars of Independence in Spanish America*. Wilmington, DE: Scholarly Resources, 2000.

Kinsbruner, Jay. *Independence in Spanish America: Civil Wars, Revolutions, and Underdevelopment*. Rev. ed. Albuquerque: University of New Mexico Press, 2000.

Lynch, John. *The Spanish–American Revolutions, 1808–1826*. 2nd ed. New York: Norton, 1986.

———. *Latin America Between Colony and Nation: Selected Essays*. Houndmills, Basingstoke, Hampshire [England] and New York: Palgrave Macmillan, 2001.

Rodriguez O., Jaime E. *The Independence of Spanish America*. Cambridge: Cambridge University Press, 1998.

CHAPTER 4

NEW NATIONS

Most of Latin America had gained independence by the end of the first quarter of the nineteenth century. The protracted struggle elevated to power a small, privileged elite who, with few exceptions, enjoyed many benefits from the Spanish and Portuguese colonial systems and reaped even greater rewards during the early decades of nationhood. The independence of the new nations proved almost at once to be nominal because the ruling elites became economically subservient to Great Britain. The impetus to build a nation-state came from "above." In the apt judgment of Cuban independence leader José Martí, the elites created "theoretical republics." They tended to confuse their own well-being and desires with those of the nation at large, an erroneous identification as they represented less than 5 percent of the total population. That minority set the course upon which Latin America has continued to the present.

In any examination of the decades immediately following independence, fundamental questions arise: How do people create new governments, and what types of government should they forge? How does economic poverty influence the exercise of sovereignty? Should past social patterns be abandoned or enhanced? These and other questions challenged the new nations and their citizens.

MONARCHY OR REPUBLIC?

Who would govern and how they would govern were fundamental questions facing the newly independent Latin Americans. They were questions previously unasked. For centuries all authority and power had been concentrated in the Iberian kings, who ruled the New World in accordance with an ancient body of laws and customs. For nearly three centuries, the inhabitants of the New World had accepted their rule, and the monarchies provided their own hereditary continuity. The declarations of independence created a novel political vacuum. Latin Americans experienced anguish, bloodshed, and chaos in their uncertain and contradictory efforts to fill this vacuum.

Brazil alone easily resolved the questions, mainly because of the presence of the royal family in Portuguese America. On hand to lend legitimacy to the rapid, peaceful political transition of Brazil from viceroyalty to kingdom to empire were first King John VI and then his son, Prince Pedro, heir to the throne, who severed the ties between Portugal and Brazil and wore the new imperial crown. The mazombo elite supported the concept of royal rule and thereby avoided the acrimonious debates between republicans and monarchists that split much of Spanish America. Obviously facilitating their decision was the convenient presence of a sympathetic prince, a Braganza who had declared Brazil's independence. By his birth and inheritance as well as through the concurrence of the Brazilian elite, Pedro's position and power were at once legitimate. As a Braganza, he inherited his authority. Historical precedent strengthened his position. The throne legitimately occupied by a Braganza proved to be the perfect unifier of the new and immense empire.

Although there was a genuine consensus as to who would rule, the question remained open as to how he should rule. The emperor and the elite agreed that there should be a constitution, but the contents and limits of that projected document sparked a debate that generated the first major crisis in the Brazilian empire. Elections were held for an assembly that would exercise both constituent and legislative functions. The group that convened on May 3, 1823, comprising lawyers, judges, priests, military officers, doctors, landowners, and public officials, clearly represented the privileged classes of the realm. They came from the ranks of the old landed aristocracy and the new urban elite, two groups that remained interlinked. Almost at once, the legislature and the executive clashed, each suspicious that the other infringed on its prerogatives. Furthermore, the legislators manifested rabid anti-Portuguese sentiments and thus by implication a hostility to the young emperor born in Lisbon. Convinced that the assembly not only lacked discipline but also scattered the seeds of revolution, Pedro dissolved it.

Despite the dissolution, Pedro intended to keep his word and rule under a constitution. He appointed a committee of ten Brazilians to write the document and then submitted it to the municipal councils throughout Brazil for their ratification. After most of them signified their approval, Pedro promulgated the new constitution on March 25, 1824. It provided for a highly centralized government with a vigorous executive. Although power was divided among four branches—executive, legislative, judiciary, and moderative—the lion's share rested in the hands of the emperor. Assisted by a Council of State and a ministry, the emperor exercised the functions of chief executive, a role enhanced by the novel moderative power, which made him responsible for the maintenance of the independence of the nation as well as the equilibrium and harmony of the other powers and the twenty provinces.

The emperor was given and was expected to use broad powers to ensure harmony in a far-flung empire whose wide geographic and human diversity challenged the existence of the State. In the last analysis, the crown was the one pervasive, national institution that could and did represent all Brazilians. The General Assembly was divided into a senate, whose members were appointed by the emperor for life, and a chamber of deputies periodically and indirectly elected by a highly restricted suffrage. The constitution afforded broad individual freedom and equality before the law. Proof of the viability of the constitution lay in its longevity: it lasted sixty-five years, until the monarchy fell in 1889. It has proven to be Brazil's most durable constitution and one of Latin America's longest lived.

The Brazilians gradually took control of their own government. At first, Pedro disappointed them by surrounding himself with Portuguese advisers, ministers, and prelates. The Brazilians had their independence but were tacitly barred from exercising the highest offices in their own empire. The mazombos accused the young emperor of paying more attention to affairs in the former metropolis than to those of the new empire. As the Brazilians demanded access to the highest offices of their land, the currents of anti-Portuguese sentiments swelled. Pedro's failure to understand those nationalistic sentiments and to appoint Brazilians to top positions was a primary cause of the discontent leading to his abdication in 1831. After his departure for Europe, members of the elite with their roots firmly in the plantation economy replaced the Portuguese-born who monopolized the high posts of the First Empire. In 1840, when Pedro II ascended the throne, a Brazilian—for the adolescent emperor had been born and raised in the New World—even occupied that exalted position. Thus, the mazombo ascendancy was much more gradual than the creole. It began in 1808 when the royal court arrived in Rio de Janeiro and reached its climax in 1840 when a Brazilian-born emperor took the scepter.

Unlike Brazil, Spanish America experienced a difficult transfer and legitimation of power. The question of what form the new governments should take absorbed considerable energy and aroused heated debates, particularly over the issue of republic versus monarchy. Monarchy harmonized with the past and with the hierarchical, aristocratic structure of Spanish American society. However, a desire to repudiate at least the outward symbols of the Spanish past, an infatuation with the political doctrines of the Enlightenment, and the successful example of the United States strengthened the arguments of the partisans for a republic. Only in Mexico did the monarchists carry the day, but, unable to persuade a European prince to accept the new Mexican scepter, the creoles crowned one of their own, Augustín de Iturbide, whose brief reign lasted from May of 1822 until February 1823. Still, because Mexico at that time included the territory from Oregon to Panama, it meant that together with Brazil, a majority of Latin America in late 1822 and early 1823 fell under monarchical sway.

Iturbide's reign was not a happy one, largely because he was trying to satisfy conflicting groups with the scant resources of an economy hard hit by the independence wars. To reassure the merchants and capitalists, he cut taxes, which led to a decline in the revenue needed to maintain the army. To pay the army, which was crucial to uphold a government that had not yet achieved hegemony, he issued paper money, which led to inflation. He then took foreign loans that the government could not repay and demanded forced loans from the elites and from the Church, alienating his strongest supporters. With growing political unrest, Iturbide closed Congress, which alienated his political allies. The final straw came when there were no funds to fight the Spanish royalist troops still holding out at the fortress of Veracruz. Iturbide responded to the complaints of the Mexican force's commander, Antonio Lopez de Santa Anna, by firing him. Santa Anna then led a coup against Iturbide. The army banished Iturbide in early 1823, abolished the empire, and helped to establish a liberal, federal republic. With that, the principle of republicanism triumphed, at least as an ideal, throughout Spanish America. Nonetheless, some would continue to argue the case for monarchy, and, in fact, Mexico experimented with it once again in the 1860s.

Mexicans repeatedly turned to the leadership of Antonio Lopez de Santa Anna, shown here during the war with the United States (1846–1848). Santa Anna served as president eleven times between 1830 and 1855. (Library of Congress)

The Age of Anarchy in Mexico Heads of State, 1822–1855

1822–1823	Emperor Agustín de Iturbide
1824–1829	Guadalupe Victoria (Felix Fernández)
1829	Vicente Guerrero
1829	José María Bocanegra (Interim)
1829	Pedro Vélez, Luis Quintanar, Lucas Alamán (Triumvirate)
1830–1832	Anastasio Bustamante
1832	Melchor Múzquiz (Interim)
1832–1833	Manuel Gómez Pedraza
1833–1835	Antonio López de Santa Anna
1835–1836	Miguel Barragán
1836–1837	José Justo Corro
1837–1839	Anastasio Bustamante (Acting)
1839	Antonio López de Santa Anna (Acting)
1839	Nicolás Bravo
1839–1841	Anastasio Bustamante (Acting)
1841	Javíer Echeverría
1841–1842	Antonio López de Santa Anna (Acting)
1842	Anastasio Bustamante (Acting)
1842–1843	Nicolás Bravo
1842	Anastasio Bustamante (Acting)
1843	Antonio López de Santa Anna (Acting)
1843–1844	Valentín Canalizo
1844	Antonio López de Santa Anna (Acting)
1844–1846	José Joaquín Herrera
1846	Mariano Paredes y Arrillaga
1846	Nicolás Bravo (Acting)
1846	Mariano Salas
1846–1847	Valentín Gómez Farías (Acting)
1847	Antonio López de Santa Anna (Acting)
1847	Pedro María Anaya
1847–1848	Manuel de la Peña y Peña
1847	Antonio López de Santa Anna (Acting)
1848–1851	José Joaquín Herrera (Interim)
1851–1853	Mariano Arista
1853	Juan Bautista Ceballos (Interim)
1853	Manuel María Lombardini
1853–1855	Antonio López de Santa Anna (Acting)
1855	Martín Carréra

Source: http://www.mexconnect.com/mex_/history/presidents.html

SHAPING THE NEW REPUBLICS

Although most of Spanish America opted for republics rather than monarchies, the question of who should rule was still a thorny one. The immediate answer was to turn the reins of authority over to independence heroes, and therefore the first chiefs of state in many lands were the very men who had declared and fought for the independence of these nations. The Latin Americans found it more difficult to select successors to the independence heroes, most of whom were turned out of office as their popularity faded and people found that war heroes did not necessarily make great statesmen. Efforts to fill presidential chairs unleashed bitter power struggles, which were conducive to despotism among various factions of the elite.

Latin Americans also debated how the new polities should be organized, with the key debate between federalism and centralism. Those opposed to change preferred centralism, which echoed the strong central control of the Spanish monarchy. But a host of local rivalries, and the apparent successful example of North American federalism, combined to persuade many Latin American leaders that regional autonomy was preferable. Federalism also drew the support of local and regional leaders who wanted to maintain their power. Further, most of the population identified with their immediate region, the *patria chica*, or small country, rather than the abstract idea of the nation. The patria chica had deep roots in the pre-Columbian past, when indigenous identity was based on the city-state, and in the Spanish history of identifying with their provinces.

The federalist and centralist factions became aligned with two main political currents that dominated Latin American politics during the nineteenth century—liberalism and conservativism. In some ways, it is difficult to specify the differences between the two political views. As one Mexican textbook put it, "The Liberals were long-haired young lawyers with modest incomes; whereas most of the Conservatives were prosperous members of the church or army, middle-aged and older, and regularly groomed at the barbershop."

Generally, Liberals looked to the United States as a model, whereas Conservatives looked to Europe's constitutional monarchies. Liberals favored a wider form of democracy, and Conservatives wanted more limited participation, fearing that openness would lead to chaos. Both wanted to see the economic transformation of their countries, but they debated how to go about it, with Conservatives reluctant to let go of such colonial institutions as forced labor. Neither group wished to cede control to the masses.

One issue on which Liberals and Conservatives consistently disagreed was the role that the Catholic Church would play in the new nations. The Church was the one colonial institution to survive independence, and it enjoyed great popular support. In addition, as a result of efficient organization, able administration, and the generosity of the pious, the Church continued to amass riches. At the end of the eighteenth century, the Church controlled as much as 80 percent of the land in some provinces of New Spain. That, however, constituted only part of the Church's wealth. Although rural estates and urban properties of the Church accounted for half the total value of the nation's real estate, the Church's real wealth accrued from mortgages and the impressive sums of interest collected.

Church power came not just from its wealth. The clergy, one of the best-educated segments of society, enjoyed tremendous prestige, particularly among the masses, which often made a mere suggestion carry the weight of a command. The clerics regularly entered politics, held high offices in the new governments, or endorsed political candidates. The clergy exerted its influence within the educational system; in almost all of the new countries they monopolized education from the primary school through the university. Further, the masses had more contact with the Church than with officials of the new State. In addition to Sunday services, people looked to the priests for all the most important events of their lives: baptism of their babies, marriage ceremonies, last rites, and burial in a Church graveyard.

Criticism of the Church centered not on religion itself but rather on the secular power and influence of the institution and its servants. Liberals believed that the very existence of the State was threatened by the Church's temporal powers and argued for lay teaching; secularization of the cemeteries; civil marriage; the establishment of a civil register for births, marriages, and deaths; and State control over religious patronage, just as the crown had once been authorized to name and remove Church hierarchy. The debates between Liberals and Conservatives, particularly about the Church, would come to dominate the first fifty years of political life.

Initially, Liberal ideas held sway, and they were reflected in the emphasis on elections. In the first flush of freedom, most of the new nations granted broad suffrage rights. Free, independent men were given the right to vote, which included the indigenous and free blacks. In Buenos Aires, an 1821 law established universal male suffrage. Peru's 1823 constitution gave voting rights to all Peruvian men who were married or over twenty-five years old and who were literate property owners, or had a profession or trade, or worked in a "useful industry." In addition, the literacy requirement was postponed until 1840—presumably the new State hoped to provide education—and later the indigenous and mestizos were exempted from that requirement. Not all of Latin America followed suit. For example, Chile's 1833 constitution only gave the vote to literate men who satisfied property or income requirements. Most regions provided indirect elections, with voters choosing an electoral college or voting for a legislature that in turn selected senators and presidents.

Elections for all levels of government were routinely held, indicating that it was an important aspect of legitimation. Even those who resorted to violence to attain power also took the electoral route, sometimes using violence to guarantee a victory. Political contenders worked to mobilize voters to support them, which usually meant appealing to specific, local interests. The concept of citizen—the abstract idea of a member of the national polity—had not yet taken root. Latin Americans still thought in terms of the *pueblos* (towns), the *comunidades* (communities), and the *vecino*, literally neighbor, or a resident of a particular place. But most Latin Americans simply did not go to the polls. Voter turnout was usually below 5 percent, and, sometimes, it was even as low as .02 percent. There were rare exceptions, such as the 20 percent voter turnout in Mexico in 1851. Elites lamented "the lack of civic spirit," and electoral campaigns often were aimed more at voter turnout than at assuring a particular outcome. There are several explanations for the lack of interest in voting: Voting and representation were new, abstract ideas; there was frequently violence at the polls; and people trusted their leaders to take care of business for them. The idea of placing trust in a leader, whether local or national, would become the bedrock for the *caudillos*, the strongmen who brought stability to the young nations.

Voting rights tended to become more restricted throughout the nineteenth century, as the elites wrote and rewrote their constitutions. The most popular models were the North American and French constitutions as well as the Spanish Constitution of 1812, considered in the early nineteenth century as a splendid example of liberal thought. The Latin Americans promulgated and abandoned constitutions with numbing regularity. It has been estimated that in the century and a half after independence, they wrote between 180 and 190 of them, a large percentage of which were adopted during the chaotic period before 1850. Venezuela holds the record with twenty-two constitutions since 1811. Four major Latin American nations have a somewhat more stable constitutional record. Brazil's constitution, promulgated in 1824, lasted until 1889. After several attempts, Chile adopted a constitution in 1833 that remained in force until 1925. Argentina's constitution of 1853 survived until 1949 and was put into force again in 1956. Mexico promulgated a constitution in 1857 that remained the basic document until 1917.

Generally the constitutions invested the chief executive with paramount powers so that both in theory and in practice he exercised far greater authority than the other branches of government, which were invariably subservient to his will. In that respect, the Latin Americans reverted to their experience of the past. The presidents played the omnipotent role of past kings. By the mid-nineteenth century, all the Latin American governments shared at least three general characteristics: strong executives, a high degree of centralization, and restricted suffrage.

It has sometimes been imagined that the majority of the Latin American population, illiterate and rural, was left out of this nation-building process. Undoubtedly, for many people that was true, especially in areas that were relatively untouched by the independence wars. In some parts of Central America, it was months after independence before people learned that they were no longer part of the Spanish empire. But in regions where there had been a great deal of fighting, the masses were already mobilized around the Enlightenment rhetoric of the independence project. Would-be national leaders had to contend with politicized populations. The process of State building occurred not just at the national level but in all regions.

And the direction that the new leaders took was not uncontested in the communities.

The central government sought to control municipal governance and to construct it as a unit of the new nation, but the municipal inhabitants saw the local government as embedded in local traditions and concerns. From the national point of view, municipal governments were units charged with carrying out State and national laws, administering justice, policing the population, collecting taxes, organizing local militias, and providing information to the national level. They were funded in the same manner as local colonial administration—land rentals, taxes paid by vendors on market days, fines, and a head tax. The income paid for administrative costs, public works, schools (where they existed), and religious celebrations, usually of the local patron saints. In this way, the elites sought to create new national identities by drawing on local ones. But the outlook for the majority remained local, and even when expected to behave as national citizens serving on town councils, they frequently spoke in the name of the traditional community. They also transformed traditional community organizations to meet the new demands of independence. For example, the *cofradía*, or religious brotherhood, grew to be not just a religious organization but one that provided for community well-being, as a location of community organizing, and as a landholder.

In the countryside, the indigenous and mestizo lower classes struggled with creole and mestizo elites over control of property, particularly over municipal boundaries and the continued existence of community land. Local communities also fought against national programs that would adversely affect them. For example, the people of the Mexican state of Guerrero supported the overthrow of President Anastasio Bustamante because his government failed to protect local cotton growers and weavers from foreign imports. Throughout the 1840s, when Mexico was ruled by centralists, the people of Guerrero rebelled against increased taxes and the decrease in the number and autonomy of municipalities; they were aware of divisions at the national level, and they used that opportunity to press their demands. The lower classes were usually most successful in strongly federalist areas, which were usually areas where there had been combat in the independence wars. In centralist areas, where there had been little fighting for independence, the lower classes tended to lose out to the elites.

Rural people learned to work the new systems to their advantage whenever possible. For example, indigenous people in Peru when in land disputes with estate owners emphasized that under an 1828 law, they had become individual proprietors. But when it came to taxation, they spoke of communal land because the law still provided for a different level of taxation for the indigenous. In some areas, the indigenous joined with mestizos and formed a *campesino* identity, rather than an indigenous one. (Campesino is often translated as "peasant," but that term has questionable implications about relationship to land and markets. In general, Latin Americans use the term to refer to rural people who work primarily in subsistence agriculture and sometimes to refer to lower-income country people in general). At times, popular groups sought the protection offered by Conservatives, at others the freedoms promised by Liberals.

The struggles of the early republics should not, then, be seen merely as the rivalries between elites. The masses were not simply dragged into battles that did not affect them. The majority of people acted in their own self-interest in attempts to maintain autonomy and preserve their rights and privileges.

THREATS TO THE NATIONS

The new nations were fragile constructions, and their leaders faced multiple threats to their continued existence. From the start, the new leaders feared that Spain or Portugal, alone or in union with other European governments, might try to recapture the former colonies in the New World. The conservative monarchies of Russia, Austria, and Prussia formed the Holy Alliance, which numbered among its goals the eradication of representative government in Europe and the prevention of its spread to areas where it was previously unknown. The Alliance boldly intervened in a number of European nations to dampen the fires of liberalism. At one time, it seemed possible that the Holy Alliance might help Spain in an effort to reassert its authority over its former American colonies. The possibility alarmed their rival, England, which was interested in Latin American markets, as well as the United States, which was concerned about Russian settlement advancing down the western coast of North America.

The English urged the United States to join in a statement discouraging foreign colonization of the Americas. Instead, an independent-minded President James Monroe in 1823 issued what became known as the Monroe Doctrine, which declared that the Americas were no longer open to European colonization and that the United States would regard any intervention of a European power in the Americas as an unfriendly act against the United States. Most Latin American elites welcomed the possibility of help from their northern neighbors as they took their first shaky steps as new nations. However, they found the doctrine to be empty rhetoric: The United States did not come to the aid of Latin American countries until the end of the nineteenth century.

Latin American fears of European intervention were not unfounded. Spain invaded Mexico and Central America in 1829 and 1832. France and Great Britain also intervened in the New World. The French occupied Veracruz, Mexico, in 1838 to force Mexico to pay alleged debts; and they blockaded Buenos Aires in 1838–1840 and again in 1845–1848, this time in

The new Latin American nations recruited the indigenous to man their armies. This 1868 photograph shows a Peruvian soldier and his wife. (Library of Congress)

conjunction with the British, to discipline Argentine dictator Manuel de Rosas. During the 1860s, Spain made war on Peru, seizing one of its guano-producing islands, and bombarded the Chilean port of Valparaíso.

The most brazen European intervention occurred in Mexico during the 1860s. Responding to the grandiose schemes of Napoleon III, a French army in 1862 landed in Mexico under the pretense of collecting debts. They marched into central Mexico and left the hapless Maximilian of Austria on a shaky throne dependent on French military support. The French remained until 1866, tired of fighting the troops commanded by Benito Juárez, chastised by an unhappy U.S. government and increasingly concerned about competition in Europe as Otto von Bismarck unified Germany. These examples show that Latin American anxieties over European intervention were well-founded.

But it was not only the Europeans that the new countries had to fear. Although in 1823 the United States claimed to be Latin America's defender, by 1846 the United States had become an aggressor in its westward march. The conflict began as a dispute about the western boundary of Texas, which had just been annexed by the United States. The boundary had always been the Nueces River, but Texans and the United States now claimed the boundary was the Río Bravo (or Río Grande as it was called in the United States). The result was a disastrous war in which the better armed and trained U.S. forces pushed all the way to Mexico City. In the Treaty of Guadalupe Hidalgo, which ended the war of North American Invasion (known in the U.S. as the Mevican-American war), the United States won the huge California and New Mexico territories.

The threats to the new Latin American nations were by no means all external. The unity of the new nations proved to be extremely fragile, and the forces that shattered it more often than not were internal. Geography provided one major obstacle to unity and the creation of the nation-state. Vast tracts of nearly empty expanse, impenetrable jungles, mountain barriers, and lonely deserts separated and isolated population pockets among which communication was tardy and difficult, and transportation was often nonexistent or at best hazardous and slow. The rainy season halted all communication and transportation in many regions. Such poor communications and transportation complicated the exchange of goods, services, and ideas on a national basis. It was easier and cheaper to ship a ton of goods from Guayaquil, Ecuador, to New York City via the Straits of Magellan than to send it 200 miles overland to the capital, Quito. Rio de Janeiro could import flour and wheat more economically from England than from Argentina. Likewise the inhabitants of northern Brazil found it easier to import from Europe than to buy the same product from southern Brazil, despite the fact that sailing vessels connected Brazil's littoral population nuclei. Most of the population lived within easy reach of the coast.

To penetrate the interior, the Brazilians relied on inland waterways, in some areas generously supplied by the Amazon and Plata networks, or cattle trails. A journey from Rio de Janiero to Cuiabá, capital of the interior province of Mato Grosso, took eight months in the 1820s. The situation was comparable in Spanish America. The trip from Veracruz, Mexico's principal port, to Mexico City, a distance of slightly less than 300 miles over the nation's best and most used highway, took about four days of arduous travel when Frances Calderón de la Barca made the journey under the most favorable conditions in 1839. She described the road as "infamous, a succession of holes and rocks." In the 1820s a journey from Buenos Aires to Mendoza, approximately 950 miles inland at the foothills of the Andes, took a month by ox cart or two weeks by carriage, although a government courier in an emergency could make the trip in five days on horseback.

Distance, difficult geography, slow communication and transportation, and local rivalries, in part spurred by isolation, encouraged the growth of a regionalism hostile to national unity. Experiments with federalism intensified that regionalism and reinforced the loyalty to the patria chica. As a result, soon after independence the former territories of the Spanish viceroyalties disintegrated. None splintered more than the Viceroyalty of New Spain. In 1823, Central America, the former Kingdom of Guatemala, seceded. In turn, in 1838–1839, the United Provinces of Central America broke into five republics. Texas left the Mexican union in 1836, and after the war of 1846–1848 the United States won California, Arizona, and New Mexico. Gran Colombia failed to maintain the former unity of the Viceroyalty of New Granada: Venezuela left the union in 1829 and Ecuador followed the next year. Chile and Bolivia felt no loyalty to Lima, and consequently the Viceroyalty of Peru disbanded even before the independence period was over. In a similar fashion, Paraguay, Uruguay, and part of Bolivia denied the authority of Buenos Aires, thus spelling the end of the Viceroyalty of La Plata. By 1840, the four monolithic Spanish viceroyalties had split, giving rise to all of the Spanish-speaking republics of the New World except Cuba, which remained a Spanish colony until 1898, and Panama, which split from Colombia in 1903. In both cases, the new nations' fate was tied to the emergence of a new, aggressive North American imperialism in the late nineteenth and early twentieth centuries.

None of the eighteen new nations had clearly defined frontiers with its neighbors, a problem destined to cause war, bloodshed, and ill will. In some cases, commercial rivalries added to the difficulties. Further, the rapid multiplication of new nations raised hemispheric trade barriers, which in turn complicated and intensified those rivalries. In short, former colonial regional rivalries took on a nationalistic tone after independence. The resultant suspicion and distrust among the eighteen countries accelerated the tensions felt within the new societies. On occasion, these tensions gave rise to war, as neighbor fought neighbor in the hope of gaining a trade advantage, greater security, or additional territory.

Argentina and Brazil struggled in the Cisplatine War (1825–1828) over possession of Uruguay and in an exhausted stalemate agreed to make the disputed territory independent; Chile attacked Peru and Bolivia in 1836 to prevent the federation of the two neighbors, and during the War of the Pacific (1879–1883) the three fought for possession of the nitrate deposits of the Atacama Desert. Chile won and expanded northward at the expense of both Peru and Bolivia. The Dominican Republic battled Haiti in 1844 to regain its independence. Throughout the nineteenth century, the five Central American republics challenged each other repeatedly on the battlefield. This catalog of conflicts is only representative, not inclusive.

The wars constituted another arena in which local identities and roles intersected with the national project envisioned by elites. For example, autonomous campesino guerrilla bands organized to protect their villages in Peru from Chilean invaders. They were particularly opposed to leadership in northern Peru that took a conciliatory approach to the invading Chileans. Thus, local indigenous groups envisioned themselves as fighting for the nation in contrast to abandonment by the northern leadership.

The major conflict of the century pitted tiny, landlocked Paraguay against the Triple Alliance—Argentina, Brazil, and Uruguay—in a clash of imperialistic pretensions in the strategic La Plata basin, which was but one phase in a continuing struggle to maintain the balance of power there. It took the allies five years, 1865–1870, to subdue Paraguay. That war solved two difficult problems that had troubled the region since independence: First, it definitively opened the Plata River network to international commerce and travel, a major concern of Brazil, which wanted to use the rivers to communicate with several of its interior provinces. Second, it freed the small nations of Uruguay and Paraguay from further direct intervention from Argentina and Brazil, which came to understand the importance of the independence of the two small Platine countries as buffer zones. The two large nations might try to sway one or both of the small nations to its side, but neither Brazil nor Argentina physically intervened again.

Relations between the new nations and the Roman Catholic Church created tensions of another sort. The Latin American chiefs of state claimed the right to exercise national patronage as heirs of the former royal patronage. The Pope in turn announced that the patronage had reverted back to the papacy, its original source, with the declarations of independence. In their open sympathy with the Spanish monarchy, the popes had antagonized the Latin American governments. In 1824, Pope Leo XII had issued an encyclical to archbishops and bishops in America to support Ferdinand VII. This confirmed to Latin American leaders that the Vatican was in league with the Holy Alliance. The new governments in turn expelled a number of ranking clerics who refused to swear allegiance to the new State.

Out of consideration for the feelings of Madrid, the Vatican for a long time refused to recognize the new American nations, much to the chagrin of their governments, which were fearful that the discontent of the American Catholics with their isolation might endanger independence. Rome began to change its attitude toward the Latin American nations in 1826, when the Pope announced his willingness to receive American representatives strictly as ecclesiastical delegates, in no way implying political recognition. The next year the Roman pontiff began to approve candidates presented by the American governments. With the death of Ferdinand VII in 1833, the Pope no longer felt any Spanish constraints on his policy in the New World. In 1835, the Vatican recognized New Granada (Colombia) and the following year accredited to Bogotá the first papal nuncio. The recognition of New Granada

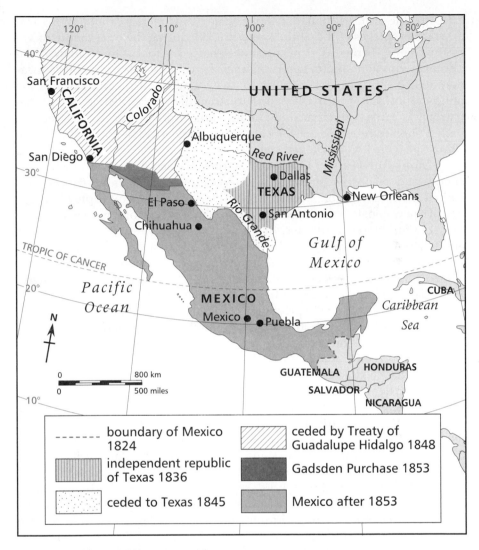

Map 4.1 Mexico, 1824–1853

Adapted from Spodek Howard, *The World's History Combined*, 3rd ed. © 2006. Electronically reproduced by permission of Pearson Education, Inc., Upper Saddle River, NJ.

signified the end both of the problem over political recognition and of Spanish influence over the Vatican's diplomacy in and relations with Spanish America.

The struggles between Liberals and Conservatives sometimes became violent as well. Mexico, in particular, suffered from the conflict over the question of the proper place of the Church within the new nations. The early constitutions established Roman Catholicism as the national religion but endorsed the principle of national patronage. The Liberals campaigned to reduce the privileges of the Church, and in 1833, during the brief tenure of Valentín Gómez Farías as chief of state, enacted reforms to secularize the California missions and to confiscate their funds, to secularize public education, to abolish compulsory tithes, to give members of religious orders the option of retracting their vows, and to strengthen the principle of national patronage. Santa Anna removed Gómez Farías from power in 1834 and annulled these reforms. Under the succeeding Conservative governments, the Church regained its privileged status.

During the years of Conservative rule, Mexico expended much of its energy and resources fighting Texas secession, French intervention, and United States expansion. The end result was Mexican bankruptcy and the rise of a new generation of Liberals, the most prominent of whom was Benito Juárez, a full-blooded Zapotec. In the Plan of Ayutla issued in 1854, Juárez and fellow Liberals called for the overthrow of Santa Anna and a new constitution. They came to power the following year but were repeatedly challenged. Of all the issues at stake, the issue of Church power predominated.

The Mexican Liberals initiated their reforms in 1855 with the Ley Juárez, which restricted the privileges of military and ecclesiastical courts by abolishing the *fueros*, their jurisdiction in purely civil cases. In 1856, the Ley Lerdo required all corporations to sell their lands; the intention of this law was to divest the Church of all its property not strictly devoted to religious purposes. It also attacked indigenous communal lands, which were to be divided and privatized.

The new constitution promulgated in 1857 incorporated both the Ley Juárez and the Ley Lerdo and went on to nullify compulsory observance of religious vows and to secularize education. The Conservatives and the Church denounced the new laws and constitution. Pope Pius declared, "We raise our Pontifical voice in apostolic liberty . . ., to condemn, to reprove, and to declare null and void the said decrees and everything else that the civil authority has done in scorn of ecclesiastical authority and of this Holy See." The clergy and military united to defend their privileges and attacked the Liberals, initiating the bloody War of the Reform of 1858–1861. The bold challenge to the Liberal government unleashed an avalanche of anticlerical laws upon the Church: the nationalization of cemeteries, civil marriage, abolition of tithes, nationalization of all real property of the Church, separation of Church and State, suppression of all monasteries, and the prohibition of novitiates in nunneries.

Defeated on the battlefields, the Conservatives resolved to seek foreign intervention rather than accept the triumph of Juárez. Their desires coincided with the ambitions of Napoleon III, who intervened in 1862 supposedly to force Mexico to pay its debts. At the invitation of the Conservatives, Napoleon helped reinstitute monarchy by naming Austrian Archduke Maximilian to the throne. Maximilian arrived in 1864, and much to the annoyance of the Conservatives, he turned out to have liberal views; he accepted the religious reforms. To oppose the French intervention and monarchical restoration, the Liberals took up arms again. Napoleon found it necessary to commit 34,000 regular troops to support the unsteady throne of Maximilian. Even so, the monarchy never extended its authority over more than a fraction of Mexican territory and never enjoyed the support of more than a minority of the Mexican population. The French withdrawal in 1866 condemned the monarchy to immediate extinction. The next year the Liberal army captured and shot Maximilian. Juárez returned to Mexico City and the Herculean task of rebuilding a ravaged Mexico. The Church had lost considerable wealth, prestige, and power during its prolonged struggle with the State, but the battles were by no means over. They flared up later and extended well into the twentieth century.

Mexico represents an extreme in the Church–State struggles that added much to the tensions of nineteenth-century Latin America. Although such bitter warfare did not characterize the entire hemisphere, no new nation entirely escaped the conflict.

ECONOMIC INSTABILITY

Economic freedom had been one of the main concerns of the creole elites who fought for independence. But the destruction caused by the wars was devastating, particularly in Mexico, Venezuela, and Gran Colombia. Mining and manufacturing suffered the most during the decades after independence. With some mines flooded and machinery destroyed during the fighting, the labor system in flux, and investments lacking, the production of the once-fabled mines plummeted. The decline continued steadily in Mexico and Peru until mid-century. The Bolivian mines did not revive until around 1875. It would take substantial investment to refurbish these industries, but capital vanished along with the Spaniards who fled at the end of the wars.

Great Britain was waiting in the wings. Foreign Secretary George Canning mused in 1824, "Spanish America is free, and if we do not mismanage our affairs sadly, she is English." As soon as Portugal and Spain fell to Napoleon, eager British merchants began to move in large numbers into Latin America to capture the markets they had so long craved. The British immediately sold more to Latin America than anyone else and almost monopolized the imports into certain countries.

The British government successfully wrested from the Latin Americans agreements and treaties favorable to its merchants, traders, and bankers. Brazil's experience was classic. The new empire provided the English merchants and manufacturers with their most lucrative Latin American market. Exports to Brazil in 1825 equaled those sold to the rest of South America and

Mexico combined and totaled half those sent to the United States. Naturally the British wanted to keep their Brazilian market. In exchange for arranging Portugal's recognition of Brazilian independence in 1825, London exacted a highly advantageous commercial treaty from Pedro I. It limited the duty placed on English imports to 15 percent and bound Brazil not to concede a lower tariff to any other nation. The treaty thereby assured British manufacturers domination over the Brazilian market and postponed any Brazilian efforts to industrialize.

London supplied most of the loans and investments to the new nations. Already by 1822, four Latin American loans had been floated. In 1824 there were five more, and the following year an additional five. Foreign investors had particular interests in these economies. During the first half of the century, Europe had entered a period of rapid population growth and accelerated industrialization and urbanization. They needed raw products: food for the urban centers and materials for the factories. In turn, they sought markets in which to sell growing industrial surpluses. Latin America exported the raw materials required in Europe and imported the manufactured goods pouring in from distant factories.

Between 1800 and 1850, world trade tripled, and Latin America participated in that growth. While two or three ships a year had handled trade between Chile and England from 1815 to 1820, more than 300 carried Chilean exports to England in 1847. The value of exports leaving Buenos Aires nearly tripled from 1825 to 1850. The sector of the economy that recovered most quickly after the wars was agriculture, and Europe provided a ready market. The sale of agrarian products provided the basis for any prosperity that Latin America enjoyed in the decades before 1850.

Trade was facilitated by improved international transportation. Faster sailing vessels and the introduction of the steamship, which was being used successfully in North Atlantic crossings in the 1830s, were responsible. The steamships appeared in the waters of Brazil and of Chile, in 1819 and in 1822, respectively. In 1840, the British chartered the Royal Mail Steam Packet Company to provide regular twice monthly steamship service to the entire Caribbean area. That same year, the Pacific Steam Navigation Company initiated steamship service along the western coast of South America. For the Atlantic coast, the Royal Mail Steam Packet from England to Brazil began service in 1851. At the same time, the United States expanded its international steamship service, which reached Latin America in 1847 with the foundation of the Pacific Mail Company. These improved communication and transportation systems further meshed the economies of Latin America with those of the United States and Europe and most particularly with that of Great Britain.

In order to produce the goods for export, Latin American elites needed to control land and labor. But the labor question was not as easily resolved as in the colonial period. Commitments had been made in order to mobilize the masses during the war, and to some extent, those promises had to be kept. During the independence struggle, creoles had used the metaphor of slavery to discuss their colonial plight. Bolívar told his troops in 1824, "You are going to complete the greatest task that heaven has been able to entrust to man—that of saving the entire world from slavery." The independence leader, of course, was speaking metaphorically about colonial subjects as slaves. However, this rhetoric was adopted by the real Latin American slaves. When Ecuadoran slave Angela Batallas appealed to the new nation for her freedom, she said, "I do not believe that meritorious members of a republic that . . . have given all necessary proofs of liberalism, employing their arms and heroically risking their lives to liberate us from the Spanish yoke, would want to pledge to keep me in servitude." She even appealed directly to Bolívar who, despite his elitism, had commented, "It seems to me madness that a revolution for freedom expects to maintain slavery."

The madness, however, did not immediately end. Although all of the new nations ended the African slave trade and freed children born to slaves, abolition came more slowly. Only Central America, Chile, and Mexico abolished slavery in the 1820s and by midcentury many Latin American blacks were still enslaved. Indigenous tribute also lingered, not ending legally until 1854 in Peru, 1857 in Ecuador, and 1874 in Bolivia.

Enforcement of the laws was uneven at best. As usual, resourceful landowners found a variety of ways of observing the letter of the law while changing only slightly the patterns of labor employment. They developed systems of apprenticeship and debt peonage to that end. In some relatively isolated areas, such as Chiapas, debt peonage was fairly successful in tying workers to haciendas via inheritable debt arrangements. But in much of Latin America, inadequate police forces and transportation systems simply made it impossible to find or return workers.

Abolition of Slavery

Argentina	1813
Colombia	1821
Chile	1823
Central America	1824
Mexico	1829
Bolivia	1831
Uruguay	1842
Ecuador	1851
Colombia	1852
Venezuela, Peru	1854
Paraguay	1870
Cuba	1886
Brazil	1888

Most large estates survived intact from the turmoil of the independence period. In fact, many multiplied in size during those turbulent years. In northern Mexico, the Sanchez Navarro family, by a combination of astute business practices and shrewd political maneuvering, managed to preserve everything it had amassed during the colonial period. The power base the family chiefs had built in the state of Coahuila enabled them to expand significantly during the early decades of Mexican independence. Their landholdings reached a maximum between 1840 and 1848, consisting of seventeen haciendas that encompassed more than 16 million acres, the largest latifundia ever to have existed in Mexico. In Argentina, the Anchorena family, wealthy merchants in Buenos Aires, began to invest in ranches in 1818. Four decades later, they boasted of being the largest landowners in the country with 1.6 million prime, amply watered acres.

Indeed, the times proved to be exceptionally propitious for the landlords to extend their holdings. The governments put the lands of the Church, indigenous communities, and public domain on the market, as in Mexico with the Ley Lerdo. From the old *ejidos,* common land belonging to a village, the new governments authorized small plots for subsistence, while hacendados and fazendeiros added to their already large landholdings. By 1830 in Argentina, approximately 21 million acres of public land had been acquired by 500 individuals.

Meanwhile, the rapid consolidation of large but often inefficient estates raised serious social and economic questions, which were rarely addressed. In Mexico, shortly after independence, Francisco Severo Maldonado, for one, warned that national prosperity required widespread land ownership. He advocated the establishment of a bank to buy land from those who owned large, unused parcels and to sell it "at the lowest possible price" to those without land. One observer of Brazil's economy, Sebastião Ferreira Soares, concluded in 1860 that if Brazil's economy were to develop, it would require that uncultivated land be put in the hands of people who would work it. An editorial in the Buenos Aires newspaper *El Rio de La Plata,* September 1, 1869, lamented, "The huge fortunes have the unfortunate tendency to grow even larger, and their owners possess vast tracts of land which lie fallow and abandoned. Their greed for land does not equal their ability to use it intelligently or actively."

One inevitable result of agrarian mismanagement was the increase in the price of basic foodstuffs. In 1856, the leading newspaper of Brazil's vast Northeast, *Diário de Pernambuco,* sharply condemned large landholdings as a barrier to development. Their owners withheld land from use or cultivated the land inefficiently, resulting in scarce and expensive foodstuffs. Better use of the land, the newspaper editorialized, would provide more and cheaper food for local markets as well as more exports. At the same time in the southern province of Rio de Janiero, a region undergoing a boom in coffee production for export, Ferreira Soares came to similar conclusions about the distortion of the economy through land misuse and export orientation. He observed with alarm the rapid extension of the export sector accompanied by declining production of food for internal consumption, a trend he documented with convincing statistical evidence. He noted that foods that had been exported from Rio de Janeiro as late as 1850 were being imported a decade later. Prices of basic foodstuffs—beans, corn, flour—rose accordingly.

Despite the occasional criticism, there was unlikely to be any change in economic organization. It was the landed gentry who controlled the Latin American governments. The chiefs of state owned large agricultural estates or were intimately connected with the landowning class. Representatives of that privileged class filled the legislatures. The voting requirements of property ownership and/or literacy almost restricted the franchise to that class. The courts represented them—from the ranks of the elite came the lawyers and judges—and usually decided cases in their favor.

The elites tended to romanticize the large estate, one useful means of enhancing their ideology. No one better idealized the mid-nineteenth century hacienda than Jorge Isaacs in his highly acclaimed novel *Maria* (1867). The author created a patriarchal estate in the Cauca Valley of Colombia that served as a model: orderly, hierarchical, harmonious, the novel's well-run estate centered on the comfortable "big house" and patriarchal authority, which extended from the doting family to the devoted slaves. "Father" always knew best in that patrilineal setting. The novel's extreme popularity arose mainly from the ideal but tragic romance it depicted, although it must also have come from its appealing portrait of the idyllic country life in which people and nature intertwined, in which social roles were well-defined and unquestionably accepted, and in which alienation apparently was unknown. This vision complemented a system that doubtless seemed less perfect to the *campesinos* than it did to the elites.

Prosperity, however, was elusive. Unsettled conditions during the early decades of the national period inhibited economic growth. Foreign and domestic wars damaged infrastructure, interrupted trade, and frightened off wary investors. The chronic political instability so characteristic of most of the new countries did not provide the proper climate for development. Politics rather than economics absorbed most of the attention and energy of the new nations. At the same time, the quality of public administration deteriorated. Many trained public administrators departed with the defeated Spanish armies or returned to Lisbon with John's court. Recruitment was seldom based on talent; rather, positions in the civil service came as a political reward, and the frequent changes of government hindered the training of a new professional civil service. The national treasuries lay bare. Public financing was precarious and the fiscal irresponsibility of the governments notorious. By 1850, the Latin American governments had defaulted on most of their loans, and no new investment would come into the region for some twenty years.

But the economic problems did not induce Latin American elites to rethink their economic policies. Just as they were captivated by foreign political ideologies that bore little relevance to local conditions, the Latin American elite also showed a penchant for economic doctrines more suitable to an industrializing Europe than underdeveloped Latin America. Adam Smith mesmerized many Latin American intellectuals, who embraced free trade as a solution to their nations' economic problems. Of course, Smith was writing about England in 1776, at a time when the country enjoyed the natural protection of being the world's only industrialized power. But, in the words of Mexico's *El Observador* in 1830, the country needed "absolute and general freedom of commerce" to promote prosperity.

In reaction to the former mercantilism they had deplored, the Latin Americans adopted policies of economic liberalism that they associated with the triumph of the Enlightenment but that bore no relation to the requirements of Latin America. Consistently modest tariffs deprived the new governments of sorely needed incomes and facilitated the flood of European manufactured articles inundating the New World, to the detriment of local industrialization. Mexico, for example, opened its ports in 1821 to all foreign goods at a uniform tariff of 25 percent ad valorem. Artisan manufacturing immediately declined. A petition to the national government in 1822 from Guadalajara for protection blamed the Liberal tariff for putting 2,000 artisans in that city alone out of work.

The elites were also taken with the ideas of David Ricardo, who argued that each country should emphasize its comparative advantage. For example, perhaps both England and Spain could produce wine and textiles. Nature, however, gave Spain much greater endowments for wine production, making it able to produce a higher quality product at a lower cost. Similarly, Ricardo argued, the already industrialized English could produce higher quality and lower priced textiles. Each should focus on its strengths, and each would do well. There are, of course, several problems with this theory. The comparative advantage of Latin America was in primary products, which England wanted to buy at the lowest possible cost. Those products were then transformed into finished products and sold back to Latin America at a higher price. Furthermore, Latin America could become as strong a manufacturer as England with the proper protections for its industry, the path that the United States took. But the elites, who were getting rich via mining and farming, followed Ricardo uncritically.

In catering to the caprices of an unpredictable market shaped by their trading partners, the Latin Americans encouraged the growth of a reflex economy, little different than the previous colonial economy. The economic cycle of boom and bust repeatedly reoccurred in all regions of Latin America, condemning most of the area to the periphery of international capitalism. Peru was one of the most successful countries in Latin America as a participant in the growing export trade. But it, too, would display the classic boom-and-bust pattern.

The source of Peru's wealth was enormous deposits of guano, bird droppings, found off the coast on the Chinchas, Ballestras, Lobos, Macabi, and Guanape islands. Peru's guano was particularly attractive because of its high nitrate content, due to the diet of fish consumed by the birds and to the coastal weather conditions. The Humboldt Current brings cold water from Antarctica to the Equator, which mixes with the warm air on the coast and prevents rainfall. The hot air bakes the droppings, keeping the nitrates from evaporating.

Guano was in great demand as fertilizer in Europe and the United Sates, and Peru quickly capitalized on the product. Exports went from zero in 1840 to 350,000 tons a year by the 1850s, constituting 60 percent of the country's exports. It has been estimated that during the guano boom, 1840–1880, more than 20 million tons of guano was exported, creating $2 billion in profits. By the 1880s, however, the boom was over. First, Peru lost important guano territories to Chile in the War of the Pacific. Then, guano lost its appeal as the market switched to nitrates as fertilizer. Chile, having won the Atacama Desert from Peru, cornered the market on nitrates and began its own boom—and eventual bust—cycle.

CONTROL BY CAUDILLOS

The violence, tension, and economic uncertainties during and after the struggles for independence gave rise to the rule of the *caudillo,* or strong leader. The caudillos were an assorted lot. Some were popinjays who sported splendiferous uniforms and adopted sonorous titles; others lived ascetic lives, hidden from public view and attired in somber suits. All radiated mystique and charisma. They rose in the vacuum of power left by the departure of Spanish authority. Most originally were military leaders who were the only ones capable of maintaining order in a society that had become armed and militarized in the wars. They ruled by virtue of their personal authority, not by institutional legitimacy. The majority of the caudillos faithfully represented the elites and thus at least paid lip service to the ideology of progress. Those caudillos often spouted language drawn from the ideologues of the Enlightenment.

Advocating a selective Europeanization while cautious not to disturb well-established institutions, they enjoyed the support of the elites. In truth, these caudillos offered a continuation of the patterns of the past: large landed estates, servile-labor systems, export-oriented economies, and highly centralized political power. Since all power, all authority emanated from the caudillo, he played, in short, the role of the "king." In practice, however, he exercised more control over his "subjects" than the Spanish monarchs ever dared. The caudillos shared power with no one. As one remarked, "I neither want nor like ministers who think. I want only ministers who can write, because the only one who can think am I, and the only one who does think am I." Neither convictions nor principles necessarily guided the caudillo. He favored expediency, an ideological irresponsibility in which his will and whim were supreme. To rule, the caudillo employed force with impunity. Nor did his measures stop with imprisonment, confiscation, or exile. He could and did impose the death penalty as he saw fit. The general lack of restraints on his power permitted him to tax and spend as he pleased, a situation conducive to financial abuse, if not outright dishonesty.

To balance the picture, it should be noted that many of the "elite" caudillos bestowed some benefits on the nations they governed. Those disturbed by the chaos of the early decades of independence welcomed the order and stability characteristic of *caudillismo*. The early caudillos unified some of the nations, and there can be no doubt that their great strength in several notable cases prevented a national disintegration. Later caudillos liked to cast themselves as modernizers and in that role bequeathed material improvements to the nations they governed. They built roads and imposing government buildings, lay railroad tracks, strung telegraph wires, and renovated ports. They even built schools with the intention of propagating their own virtues in them.

Although the caudillos did not have to be concerned about public opinion—for all intents and purposes it did not exist—they did seek the support of at least three groups, individually or in combination, to buttress their personal power: the rural aristocracy, the Roman Catholic Church, and the army. The early caudillos were more often than not members of or related to the rural landowning class, men notable for their desire to preserve their class's prestige, wealth, and power and for their opposition to land reform, extension of the suffrage, and popular government. The caudillos usually represented these interests. Despite the fact that they ruled from the capital cities (although they might spend long periods of time on their estates), they tended to suppress the influence of the more liberal urban elements. The Church as an institution was a conservative force suspicious of reforms and usually in open conflict with the Liberals. Church leaders, with a few notable exceptions, rallied to endorse any caudillo who respected and protected Church interests and property.

The army, the only truly national institution, immediately emerged as a political force. Its strength revealed the weakness of the political institutions. In many countries it was the dominant political force and has so remained. Since few of the republics developed satisfactory means to select or alter governments, palace coups—in which the military always had a role—became the customary means to affect political shifts throughout the nineteenth century. The military then exercised the dual role of guaranteeing order on one hand and changing governments on the other. No caudillo or president would willfully alienate the military. Consequently, officers enjoyed generous salaries and rapid promotions.

The Latin American armies became and have remained top-heavy with brass. Thus, armies not only retarded the growth of democracy through their political meddling but also slowed down economic growth by absorbing a lion's share of the national budgets. They spent the capital needed for investment. On the average, prior to 1850, the military received more than 50 percent of the national budgets. Mexico provided one of the most shocking examples: Between 1821 and 1845 the military budget exceeded the total income of the government on fourteen occasions. Caudillos often arose from the ranks of the army; thus they understood and commanded the major institution for maintaining order and power. Chile was the first, and for a long time the only, Spanish-speaking nation to restrict the army to its proper role of defending the nation from foreign attack. After 1831 and until the civil war of 1891, the army kept out of Chilean politics. Few other nations could boast of a similarly well behaved military.

A few caudillos, however, championed the life styles and needs of the dispossessed majority and can be considered "popular" or "folk" caudillos. A highly complex group, they shared some of the characteristics of the elite caudillos, but two major distinctions marked them as unique. They refused to accept unconditionally the elites' ideology of progress, exhibiting a preference for the American experience with its Indo–Afro–Iberian ingredients and, consequently, a greater suspicion of the post-Enlightenment European model. Further, they claimed to serve the folk rather than the elite.

The folk expected their leader to represent and strengthen their unity, personify their values, and increase their harmony; in short, to be as one with the people he led. Their caudillo recognized and understood the folk's distinctive way of life and acted in harmony with it. In the eyes of the people, he inculcated the local, regional, or national values— traditional values—with which most of the people felt comfortable. He was a natural, charismatic leader of the majority, who found in him an adviser, a guide, a protector, and a patriarch in whom they entrusted their interests. They surrendered power to him; he incarnated authority. In his discussion of leadership and folk, José Carlos Mariátegui ascribed to the leader the roles of "interpreter and trustee." Mariátegui concluded, "His policy is no longer determined by his personal judgment but by a group of collective interests and requirements." The leader seemingly arose from and blended with his physical and human environment. Thus identified with Latin America, he contrasted sharply with the Europeanized leaders imposed by the elites.

Juan Bautista Alberdi, probably more than anyone else in the nineteenth century, studied the psychology of the relationship of popular caudillos with the masses, and he concluded that the people regarded a popular caudillo as "guardian of their traditions," the defender of their way of life. He insisted that such leaders constituted "the will of the popular masses. . . . the immediate organ and arm of the people . . . the caudillos are democracy." If the folk obeyed unreservedly those popular leaders, the caudillos in turn bore the obligation to protect and to provide for the welfare of the people. The ruled and the ruler were responsible to and for each other, a personal relationship challenged in the nineteenth century by the more impersonal capitalist concept that a growing gross national product would best provide for all.

The popularity of those caudillos is undeniable. Their governments rested on a base of folk culture, drew support and inspiration from the folk, and expressed, however vaguely, their style. Under the leadership of such caudillos, the masses apparently felt far more identification with government than they ever did under the imported political solutions advocated by the intellectuals and the elite. On many occasions, the folk displayed support of their caudillos by fighting tenaciously to protect them from the Europeanized elites or foreign invaders. Few in number at the national level, the folk or populist caudillos had disappeared by 1870. But during the first half of the nineteenth century, these few leaders showed the possibility of a different kind of leadership and development.

The Argentine gaucho, the cowboy of the pampas, became the symbol of backwardness for such Europeanized elites as Domingo Faustino Sarmiento. In his 1845 *Facundo: Civilization and Barbarism,* Sarmiento launched a thinly veiled attack against caudillo Juan Manuel de Rosas and a direct critique of the culture of the Argentine countryside. (Library of Congress)

One of the most controversial folk caudillos was Juan Manuel de Rosas, who enjoyed the support of the Argentine gauchos from 1829 until his exile in 1852. He appeared in Argentine history at the exact moment that Argentina, submerged in anarchy, threatened to split apart. The old viceroyalty of La Plata had disintegrated in the early nineteenth century and Argentina itself dissolved into squabbling regions. Sharpest was the rivalry between Buenos Aires, in which the port and coastal province grew prosperous through trade with Europe, while the interior provinces were impoverished and wracked by civil wars.

Buenos Aires elites advocated a centralized government—which it fully expected to dominate—whereas the interior provinces favored a federalized one that would prevent the hegemony of the port. The bitter struggle between Buenos Aires and the interior delayed Argentine unification until Rosas strode onto the political stage. He had lived and worked in *gaucho* country before being elected governor of Buenos Aires in 1829, and he judiciously pursued the federalist idea of a pastoral economy, based on the simple premise that whatever complemented the life of the interior's cattle-herding people benefited society. Understandably, the cattle breeders and the hide and meat producers supported Rosas because his economic inclinations favored them. Indeed, he was one of them—he owned extensive estancias, and his cousins were the Anchorenas, the largest landowners in Argentina. In his full exercise of political control, however, the caudillo acted as a centralist. Suspicious of Europe, he defied on occasion both England and France, deflecting their economic penetration of Argentina.

The Argentine masses were convinced that Rosas had their interests at heart and governed for their benefit. It would appear that the gauchos enjoyed an access to land, freedom of movement, greater economic alternatives, and better living conditions during the Rosas period than at any time afterward. To stimulate occupation of the land, in 1840 Rosas initiated a program to distribute land to soldiers. Nonetheless, there was no large-scale redistribution of land under Rosas, and vagrancy laws were initiated towards the end of his rule. But the masses—both the rural gauchos and urban blacks and mulattos—demonstrated their identification with and loyalty to Rosas by their willingness to fight for him for nearly a quarter of a century. Their caudillo suffered defeat and exile only when the elites enlisted the Brazilian and Uruguayan armies to unite with them to overthrow him. Defeated at the Battle of Monte Caseros, Rosas left Argentina for a European exile. The fall of Rosas in 1852 opened the door to the promulgation of a liberal constitution, the growth of capitalism, a flurry of land speculation, and the commercial expansion of the cattle industry on an unprecedented scale. Argentina merged with the capitalist world and intensified its dependency in the process.

An intriguing example of the caudillos who preferred local models to imported ones is Rafael Carrera, who governed Guatemala from 1839 until his death in 1865. At least half indigenous, Carrera negated many of the Enlightenment reforms applied by previous Liberal governments and ruled, at least in part, for the benefit of the indigenous, the vast majority of the Guatemalans. The elites regarded him as a barbarian; the indigenous exalted him as their savior.

Carrera led the indigenous revolt of 1838–1839. Among the many changes that popular rebellion represented was the refusal of the indigenous to countenance any further exploitation and destruction through Europeanization. They wished to be left alone by the elites of Guatemala City so that they could live unmolested according to the dictates of their own culture. They rejected Europeanizing education, culture, economy, and laws that would integrate them into a capitalist economy centered in Europe. They chose instead to withdraw, to isolate themselves; and withdrawal was, and remains, a common reaction of the indigenous to the Europeans. But, in regions where the elites depended on those indigenous for labor and taxes, withdrawal signified rebellion. Carrera understood the indigenous position, he sympathized with their desires, and he rose to power on their strength. As Carrera wrote in his memoirs, "When attempts are made suddenly to attack and change the customs of the people, it provokes in them such emotion that, no matter how sound the intention of those who seek to change their traditional ways and institutions, they rise in protest."

During the generation in which Rafael Carrera dominated Guatemala, he respected the native cultures, protected the indigenous as much as was possible, and sought to incorporate them into his government. His modest successes in those efforts assume greater significance when compared with the disastrous conditions suffered by the indigenous majority during the decades of liberal, Europeanized governments that preceded and followed the Carrera period. That popular caudillo, totally unschooled in foreign theories, was a practical man who knew Guatemala and its peoples well. He had traveled and lived in many parts of the nation, always among the humble folk whom he understood. He learned from and drew upon his Guatemalan experiences, a marked contrast to the elites seduced by European experiences and theories. Carrera appreciated the indigenous opposition to the Europeanization process imposed by the Liberals. He regarded it as his principal duty to allow "the people to return to their customs, their habits, and their particular manner of living." The government, he affirmed, had the obligation of representing the majority of the people and of offering "a living example of virtue, equity, prudence, and justice." Those principles seem to have guided much of his long administration.

While Carrera repudiated the radical ideas of the Liberals, he never rejected change. He believed it must come slowly and within the particular social context, a change acceptable to the people and not forced on them. The president held that the art of governing well sprang from the "formation of a government of the people and for the people." Accordingly, the government officially abandoned the Liberals' goal to incorporate the indigenous into Western civilization. One could even argue that under Carrera the government was "Indianized." Indigenous and particularly mestizos, all of relatively humble classes, participated directly in the government, holding, in addition to the presidency of course, such exalted offices as the vice presidency, the heads of ministries, governorships, and high military ranks. The army became nearly an indigenous institution. The Carrera government was unique to Latin America for encouraging the political ascendancy of the once-conquered race.

To lift some of the economic burden from the impoverished majority, President Carrera reduced taxes on foodstuffs and abolished the head tax. Further, he excused the indigenous from contributing to the loans the government levied from time to time to meet fiscal emergencies. By removing many of the taxes on the indigenous, which were paid in the official currency circulating in Europeanized Guatemala, the government lessened the need for the indigenous population to enter the monetary economy, thus reducing the pressure on them to work on the estates. The indigenous, then, could devote that time and energy to their own agricultural and community needs.

Of all the efforts made on behalf of the indigenous, none surpassed those affecting the protection of indigenous lands, the return of land to indigenous communities, and the settlement of land disputes in their favor. The government declared in 1845 that all who worked unclaimed lands should receive them. What was even more unusual was that it enforced the decree. It was decided in 1848 and again in the following year that all pueblos without ejidos were to be granted them without cost, and, if population exceeded available lands, then lands elsewhere were to be made available to any persons who voluntarily decided to move to take advantage of them. In 1851, Carrera decreed that "the Indians are not to be dispossessed of their communal lands on any pretext of selling them," a decree strengthened a few months later by prohibiting the divestment of any pueblos of their lands for any reason.

Carrera thus spoke forcefully and effectively to the most pressing problem of Latin America: the concentration of land in the hands of the elite and the need for the rural masses to have land to cultivate. Those decades witnessed increasing agrarian diversification. The intent was not so much to increase exports as to ensure a plentiful supply of food in the marketplace at prices the people could afford. From the evidence at hand it would seem that the quality of life for the indigenous majority improved during the Carrera years. The characteristics marking the Carrera experience as unique in Indo-America are the respect the government extended to indigenous cultures and the reluctance to push the indigenous population into Europeanizing themselves.

The indigenous victory under Carrera proved to be as transitory as the gauchos' under Rosas. The death of Carrera in 1865 reinvigorated the elites' effort to wield power, and they succeeded under the leadership of another and different type of caudillo, Justo Rufino Barrios (1873–1885). Positivist in orientation, President Barrios duly emphasized order and material progress. Under the liberal reforms of the Barrios period, capitalism made its definitive entry into Guatemala, which meant large-scale exportation of coffee with all the attendant consequences for the agrarian economy.

During the period when Carrera governed Guatemala, Bolivia, another overwhelmingly indigenous country, witnessed the singular leadership of its own popular caudillo, Manuel Belzú. He played an extremely complex role combining the forces of populism, nationalism, and revolution in ways that would not be used again in Latin America for more than half a century. He built an effective power base of campesino and urban-artisan support, which brought him to the presidency in 1848 and sustained him until he peacefully left the presidential palace in 1855. As dispossessed and impoverished as their counterparts throughout Latin America, the artisans and campesinos rallied to Belzú probably because his novel rhetoric spoke directly to their needs and certainly because of a series of wildly popular actions he took. He encouraged the organization of the first modest labor unions, ended some free-trade practices, terminated some odious monopolies, abolished slavery, permitted the landless indigenous to take over lands they worked for the latifundista elite, and praised the indigenous past. Often vague and frequently unsuccessful, his varied programs nonetheless won popular support. To his credit, Belzú seemed to have understood the basic problems bedeviling Bolivia: foreign penetration and manipulation of the economy and the alienation of the indigenous land.

Under the intriguing title "To Civilize Oneself in Order to Die of Hunger," a series of articles in a weekly La Paz newspaper in 1852 highlighted a vigorous campaign denouncing free trade and favoring protectionism. The paper argued that free trade deprived Bolivian workers of jobs while enriching foreigners and importers. It advocated "protectionism" as a means to promote local industry and thereby benefit the working class, goals that had the obvious support of the president. Indeed, free trade bore some responsibility for the nation's poor agricultural performance. A chronic imbalance of trade between 1825 and 1846 had cost Bolivia nearly 15 million pesos, much of which was spent to import food the country was perfectly capable of producing. La Paz, for example, imported beef, mutton, and potatoes, among other foods. The local producers might deserve protection from cheaper imports, but protective tariffs alone would not necessarily raise the efficiency of the notoriously inefficient latifundia.

Although taking no legal steps to reform the land structures, Belzú never opposed the indigenous occupation of their former community lands. Landlords, fearful of the restive indigenous masses, found it prudent to move to the safer confines of the cities, thus abandoning their estates, which the indigenous promptly occupied. Two major consequences of the de facto land reforms were the greater supplies of food entering the marketplaces and the drop in food prices. Belzú further delighted the campesinos by relieving them of some taxes.

If rhetoric were the measure of government, Belzú's administration stood as revolutionary. These examples from his public speeches serve as a yardstick:

> Comrades, an insensitive throng of aristocrats has become arbiter of your wealth and your destiny; they exploit you ceaselessly and you do not observe it; they cheat you constantly and you don't sense it; they accumulate huge fortunes with your labor and blood and you are unaware of it. They divide the land, honors, jobs and privileges among themselves, leaving you only with misery, disgrace, and work, and you keep quiet. How long will you sleep? Wake up once and for all! The time has come to ask the aristocrats to show their titles and to investigate the basis for private property. Aren't you equal to other Bolivians? Aren't all people equal? Why do only a few enjoy the conditions of intellectual, moral and material development and not all of you?

> Companions, private property is the principal source of most offenses and crimes in Bolivia; it is the cause of the permanent struggle among Bolivians; it is the basis of our present selfishness eternally condemned by universal morals. No more property! No more property owners! No more inheritances! Down with the aristocrats! Land for everyone; enough of the exploitation of man. . . . Aren't you also Bolivians? Haven't you been born to equality in this privileged land?

For the great mass of dispossessed campesinos, Belzú's heady words did not fall on idle ears. Some seized the estates, and where the landlords resisted, the followers of Belzú attacked and defeated them.

The identification of the folk with President Belzú established the harmony and integration between caudillo and people that conferred sweeping power on the former. The president cultivated that identification. From the balcony of the presidential palace, Belzú assured his listeners, "I am one of you, poor and humble, a disinherited son of the people. For that reason, the aristocrats and the rich hate me and are ashamed to be under my authority." The president frequently reminded his followers that all power originated in the people who had conferred it on him. He simply acted on behalf of the people and their interests. Belzú correctly claimed that new elements of order and stability supported his government: "The popular masses have made themselves heard and played their role spontaneously; they have put down rebellions and fought for the constitutional government. The rise to power of this formidable force is a social reality of undeniable transcendence."

In the last analysis, Belzú was too Europeanized to feel comfortable for long as a folk caudillo, for he insisted on codifying his government within the confines of a Europeanized constitution. His political reforms and Constitution of 1851 reduced the presidential term to a specific period and prohibited reelection. Elections in 1855, classified by one Bolivian historian as "the cleanest ever held," brought a constitutional end to the Belzú presidency, awarding the office to the president's preferred candidate—his illegitimate son, Jorge Córdoba—a man unequal to the tumultuous task. In August of 1855, at the height of his power, Belzú stepped down, unwilling to follow the well-established precedent of *continuismo*, turned over the presidency to his elected successor, and temporarily left Bolivia. To the indigenous masses, he remained their "tata Belzú," friend and protector, whose short, unique government had benefited them.

The indigenous had every reason to be apprehensive of the electoral process in which they had played no role. With Belzú in Europe, the old elites quickly seized power. At the same time, they took possession of their former lands and returned the campesinos to subservience. In the years that followed, the indigenous often revolted with cries of "Viva Belzú!" on their lips, but as the elites became increasingly integrated into international trade and consequently strengthened, they were not about to repeat the previous political errors that had permitted a popular caudillo to govern. When, for example, the Huaichu of Lake Titicaca rebelled in 1869 to regain communal lands, President Mariano Melgarejo dispatched the army to massacre them.

The populist caudillos constitute an intriguing chapter in nineteenth-century Latin American history. They appeared and disappeared within a sixty-year period. Yet, in 1850, three folk caudillos ruled at the same time: Carrera, Belzú, and Rosas. Two of those nations had large indigenous populations with well-defined cultures, while the Argentine gauchos boasted an equally well-defined folk culture. The popular caudillos identified with the majority and vice versa. In all three cases, foreign investments were comparatively low or practically nonexistent; the governments and majority expressed strong views against foreigners and shunned foreign influences. At the same time, land became available for the majority and pressures on the peasants diminished. Subsistence agriculture dominated export agriculture. More food was available for popular consumption.

Although those folk governments obviously appealed to large elements of society that had been customarily neglected, we cannot lose sight of the fact that they were few in number and had disappeared by 1870. The elites succeeded in imposing their will on the folk and on Latin America. Nonetheless, those few folk governments serve as useful reminders of possible alternatives to the Europeanized governments that the elites imposed. If, indeed, the people enjoyed a more satisfactory quality of life under the folk caudillos, those governments then suggest possible roads to development that were denigrated or ignored after 1870.

CHANGE AND CONTINUITY

The continuity between the thirty years after independence and the colonial period is remarkable. Economic changes were few. Agriculture and the large estate retained their prominence, and the new nations became as subservient to British economic policies as they once had been to those of Spain and Portugal. The wars of independence had shaken and weakened some of the foundation stones of society, but the edifice stood pretty much intact. A small, privileged elite ruled over muted although sometimes restless masses. Fewer than one in ten Latin Americans could read and fewer than one in twenty earned enough to live in even modest comfort. Land remained the principal source of wealth, prestige, and power, and the few owned much of the land.

There were also, however, some significant changes. The first and most obvious was the transmission of power from the Iberians to the creole and mazombo elites. Political power no longer emanated from Europe; it had a local source. The second was the emergence of the military in Spanish America as an important political institution destined to play a decisive role in Latin American history. The military were the elite's only guarantee of order, and initially it provided prestigious employment for some sons of the rich as well as a means of upward mobility for ambitious plebeians. Early in the national period, the Liberals challenged the status of the military, thus alienating the officers and driving them into the welcoming embrace of the Conservatives. The remarkable early stability of both Brazil and Chile can be explained in part by the close identification and harmony between Conservatives and the military.

Some of the changes masked continuity. For example, the formal categories regarding race divisions and noble birth were eliminated. But the reality remained: a small, mostly white, group of elites maintained control over wealth, power, and the lives of darker masses. Elites were still concerned with *calidad,* but quality was no longer as limited to racial and hereditary considerations. Quality now referred to respectability, which was earned by family background, the organization and location of one's household, formal training and education, occupation, economic resources, and perceived color. At the other extreme were *pleybeyos,* or plebeians, those who were basically coarse and common. Other terms that were used for this increasingly binary division were *gente alta,* literally high people, and *gente baja,* low people, and *gente decente,* decent people, versus *gente de pueblo,* common people. The majority were also referred to as *las masas* (the masses) and *las clases populares* (the popular classes). The desire of the *gente alta* to maintain their position could be seen in the change in constitutions and laws that narrowed suffrage rights as well as continued attempts to control land and labor.

The change was summed up in a Mexican folk expression: "Same horse, different rider."

RECOMMENDED READINGS

Blanchard, Peter. "The Language of Liberation: Slave Voices in the Wars of Independence," *Hispanic American Historical Review*, 82:3, 499–523.

Guardino, Peter. *Peasants, Politics, and the Formation of Mexico's National State: Guerrero, 1800–1857*. Stanford, CA: Stanford University Press, 1996.

Gootenberg, Paul. *Imagining Development: Economic Ideas in Peru's "Fictitious Prosperity" of Guano, 1840–1880*. Berkeley: University of California Press, 1993.

Mallon, Florencia E. *Peasant and Nation: The Making of Postcolonial Mexico and Peru*. Berkeley: University of California Press, 1995.

Voss, Stuart F. *Latin America in the Middle Period, 1750–1920*. Wilmington, DE: Scholarly Resources, 2002.

Wasserman, Mark. *Everyday Life and Politics in Nineteenth Century Mexico: Men, Women, and War*. Albuquerque: University of New Mexico Press, 2000.

CHAPTER 5

THE EMERGENCE OF THE MODERN STATE

By the late nineteenth century, the chaos of the early independence years gave way to the emergence of a new political stability and economic prosperity. Foreign threats had diminished, the republican principle had triumphed everywhere but in Brazil, and centralized government had been gradually accepted. Nationalism became a better defined force as more and more citizens in the various states expressed greater pride in their homeland, appreciated its uniqueness, and sought its progress. Feuding elites realized that they would profit most from stable governments that would encourage foreign investment and trade. Positivist ideology dominated government circles and complemented foreign investment and capitalist expansion. However, whereas elites overcame many of their earlier divisions to concentrate on the national project of "progress," large numbers of the population felt marginalized and threatened by the changes. They responded with protests and at times violence.

Although political change and instability marked the first fifty years of nationhood, economic and social innovations as well as political stability characterized Latin America in the late nineteenth and early twentieth centuries. An accelerating prosperity—at least for the favored classes—encouraged material growth and attracted a wave of immigrants, particularly to Argentina, Brazil, and Chile. The combination of stability and prosperity helped to accelerate three trends: industrialization, urbanization, and modernization, which in turn threatened to alter some of the established patterns inherited from the colonial past.

But to understand the successes, failures, and challenges of this period, the historian must question the type of economic growth that occurred and who benefited from it. Did Latin America's new-found wealth help the masses of working people? Did they have a voice in the changes made by the elites?

121

POLITICAL STABILITY

The conflict among elites that characterized the early national period gave way to agreement on a new economic project: the large-scale export of primary products and the import of foreign capital and manufactured goods, accompanied by limited industrialization. This new economic order required political order as well—without political stability, foreigners would not invest in Latin America.

With civil disorder on the wane, the chiefs of state consolidated and extended their authority. They governed supremely with few if any checks from the congresses and the courts, which they customarily dominated. In some cases, they selected their own successors, who were assured of impressive electoral victories. Nonetheless, a greater respect for legal forms prevailed, and some caudillos even appeared to be more legally conscious and circumspect than their predecessors. They paid more lip service to constitutional formalities and some even showed an occasional indication of heeding the constitution. In somber frock coats, representatives of the elite discussed and debated the political issues of the day.

The term *elite* can be hard to define. First, one must recognize that no single elite existed in any of the Latin American nations. Rather, a plurality of elites combined in various ways to dominate each nation. At best, elite is a shorthand expression signifying those in social, economic, and political control. The elites used their economic power, prestige and education to exert authority over a society whose formal institutions were of European inspiration. They made the major decisions affecting the economic and political life of their nations.

The earlier political division between conservativism and liberalism prevailed. The Liberals often flirted with federalist schemes, maintained a theoretical interest in the rights of man, demanded an end to the Church's temporal powers, embraced laissez-faire economic doctrine, and professed a willingness to experiment with new ideas and methods. The Conservatives, on the other hand, lauded centralism, defended a hierarchical society, approved the privileges and prerogatives of the Church, and felt more comfortable with a controlled or regulated economic system. However, neither political division expressed any desire to tamper with the major land, labor, and social systems. Nor did either party become seriously concerned with extending the suffrage; in fact, suffrage rights were more limited later in the nineteenth century than in the first chaotic years after independence. Consequently, on many fundamental issues the two major political divisions harmonized rather than diverged. In Brazil, the Visconde de Albuquerque wryly remarked, "There is nothing quite so much like a Conservative as a Liberal in office." More distinctive than party labels were the personalities. The individual, rather than a vague catalog of political ideas, attracted or repelled support. The politician as a man and as a leader exercised far more strength than did the more abstract institution, the party.

Two countries were unusual in achieving political stability early in the century: Brazil and Chile. Brazil had enjoyed stability during the First Empire (1822–1831); but during the regency established after the abdication of Pedro I, regional forces threatened the empire. One province after another, from the far north to the far south, rebelled against the government in Rio de Janeiro. To save national unity, the Brazilians proclaimed the young Pedro II emperor in 1840, four years before he was legally of age to ascend the throne. As expected, the monarchy, the only truly effective national institution in Brazil, provided the ideal instrument to impose unity on the disintegrating nation. Brazil's nearly disastrous experiment with federalism ended when Pedro II reimposed a high degree of centralism on the nation. In 1847, the emperor created the post of President of the Council of Ministers, and a type of parliamentary system developed. The emperor saw to it that the two political parties, Liberals and Conservatives, alternated in power.

The fall of a Liberal ministry in 1868 divided the political history of the Second Empire. The Liberals blamed the heavy hand of the emperor for their loss of power; in their opinion it was nothing short of a coup d'etat. As a result, the next year the Liberals issued a reform manifesto. If enacted, their federalist program would have weakened the government in Rio de Janeiro. At the same time, the Federal Republican Party emerged, and in a December 1870 manifesto denounced the monarchy and called for a federal republic. By 1870, significant structural change had been proposed, including the abolition of slavery, substitution of a republic for a monarchy and federalism for centralism, and the expansion of the political base.

The foundations of the monarchy slowly weakened. In the early 1870s, a Church–Crown conflict alienated conservatives allied with the Church. The dispute began when the Bishop of Olinda carried out a papal order, unapproved by the emperor, to expel Masons from the lay brotherhoods of the Roman Catholic Church. Pedro II ordered the bishop to remove the penalty. His refusal to comply directly challenged the emperor. The government arrested and jailed the churchman along with another bishop, and the royal courts found both guilty of disobeying civil law. The situation worsened in 1888 with the manumission of the slaves without any compensation to the owners, causing an important sector of the landowning class to abandon the emperor. Emancipation had been brought about largely by urban groups who did not identify closely with the monarchy, which they felt did not represent their interests. They viewed the aging emperor as a symbol of the past, anathema to the modernization they preached. It was among these urban groups that republican doctrine spread. That doctrine, as well as the urban mentality, also pervaded the army officer corps. Pedro had ignored the military officers, an increasingly restless group in the 1880s. In them, the disgruntled clergy, landowners, and urban dwellers, as well as the coffee planters, found their instrument for political change. The republican cause won many military converts, particularly among the junior officers who equated a republic with progress and modernization. The fate of the monarchy was sealed when the principal military leader, Marshal Deodoro da Fonseca, switched his allegiance and proclaimed in favor of a republic. Under his leadership on November 15, 1889, the army overthrew the monarchy and declared Brazil to be a republic. The old emperor abdicated and, like his father before him, sailed into European exile. The transition was bloodless. A new constitution, presidential, federal, democratic, and republican, was promulgated on February 24, 1891.

Chile reached stability even earlier. By 1830, a small and powerful landowning class had consolidated quickly in the relatively small geographic area of central Chile, hemmed in by the arid Atacama Desert to the north and the unconquered Mapuches to the south. From the ranks of the relatively homogenous Conservative elites emerged one of Chile's most skillful leaders of the nineteenth century, Diego Portales. Through his force and efficiency, he imposed Conservative rule in 1830, and it lasted until 1861. Although he never served as president, he held various ministerial portfolios and ruled behind the scenes until his assassination in 1837. Portales was concerned with power, discipline, stability, and order, not social or economic reforms. In sharp contrast to the rest of Spanish America, he succeeded in subordinating the army to a civilian government, thereby removing the military from nineteenth-century politics. He also framed the Constitution of 1833, which lasted until 1925.

Presidential mandates in Chile lasted five years and could be renewed for an additional five years. Three conservative leaders each held the office for ten years, enforcing the remarkable stability imposed by Portales. Manuel Montt, who served from 1851 to 1861, accepted a moderate, José Joaquín Pérez, to succeed him. The thirty years, 1861–1891, were a period of Liberal rule tempered by Conservative opposition, in direct contrast to the preceding three decades. The major reforms enacted by the Liberals indicated the direction and degree of change they advocated: private liberty of worship in houses and schools, the establishment of cemeteries for non-Catholics, the abolition of the privileged Church courts, civil marriage, freedom of the press, no reelection of the president, a modification of the electoral reform law to substitute a literacy test for property qualifications, greater autonomy for municipal governments, and the power of congress to override a presidential veto. As is obvious, none of these altered the power structure in Chile, none attempted to shift the social and economic imbalance of the country. Chile's record of stability and order encouraged economic prosperity and material progress.

Argentina and Mexico experienced far greater difficulty than did Chile and Brazil in their search for political stability. After Rosas fell in 1852, the city and province of Buenos Aires refused to adhere to the new Argentine union, fearing that they would have to surrender too much power. The old struggle between the port and the provinces continued until 1862, when the prestigious and powerful governor of Buenos Aires, Bartolomé Mitre, was able to impose his will on the entire nation. His force and ability reunited the nation. A succession of strong and able presidents, each of whom served for six years, followed him. These presidents wielded almost total power. In 1880, the thorny question of the city and province of Buenos Aires was finally solved. New legislation separated the city from the province, federalized the city, and declared it the national capital, a role it had previously played. The rich province then went on its own way with a new capital, La Plata. Meanwhile, the nation was investing the energy once given to political struggles into economic growth. In 1879–1880, General Julio Roca led a war that became known as the Conquest of the Desert, although it really constituted the conquest of the Araucanians. With the invention of the repeating rifle, the Argentines were able to finally succeed in overpowering the nonsedentary Indians who had daunted their Spanish forefathers by using the same pattern of annihilation carried out on the United States plains. For his efforts, Roca went on to become president.

Mexico's search for stability was one of the most difficult in Latin America, complicated by questions of federalism and the position of the Church in the new nation. The bloodshed and drama that began in 1810 lasted well over half a century and exhausted the nation. Finally a mestizo strongman, Porfirio Díaz, who had risen through the military ranks to become general and in the process had fought against Santa Anna, the French, and Maximilian, brought peace to Mexico in 1876—an iron peace, as it turned out. For the next thirty-four years, he imposed a conservative, centralized government on Mexico while ruling under the liberal, federal Constitution of 1857. His government brought order and stability to a degree unknown since the colonial period.

The strength and political longevity of Díaz rested on the powerful supporting alliances he created. The Church, the army, foreign capitalists, and the great landowners found it beneficial to back his regime, and they reaped substantial material rewards for their allegiance. On the other hand, the wily Díaz manipulated them at will for his own ends; for example, he promoted potential rivals to positions that required they relocate, undermining any chance of building a local power base. Under his guidance, Mexico made outstanding material progress and witnessed a prosperity surpassing the best years of colonial mining. The supporting alliance that Díaz formed proved to be the most effective combination of forces to promote political stability. To varying degrees the chiefs of states of other nations made use of similar combinations to buttress their power. The two key groups obviously were the army and the landowners.

In country after country in the late nineteenth century, Latin American elites followed the Argentine and Mexican patterns. They realized that years of political in-fighting had done nothing for the country and little for their personal wealth. Latin America offered investment opportunities for the wealth of Great Britain's expanding industry. But foreigners were not eager to invest in countries where governments changed hands on an annual basis and the security of investments could not be guaranteed. Latin American elites cast aside their political differences in the interests of economic unity. The political unity that resulted was in the interest of a stability that would attract foreign investment.

In some ways, the masses lost more than they gained with the new stability. The chaos of the first fifty years frequently gave people room to maneuver. With stability, however, came greater State control, which was enhanced by the latest technology. News of an uprising could be sent to the capital by telegraph, and the government could respond by sending troops on the train.

POSITIVISM AND PROGRESS

Latin American elites looked longingly at the material progress being made in Great Britain, France, Germany, and the United States. Many of them had mastered French, the second language of the elite, and a few had knowledge of English or German, which gave them direct access to information and literature from the nations whose progress impressed them. The newspapers carried full accounts of what was happening in the leading nations of the Western world, and the programs of the learned societies featured discussions of the technical advances of the industrializing nations. Many members of the elite traveled abroad and were exposed to the innovations firsthand. They returned to their quieter capitals in the New World with nostalgia for Paris and the irrepressible desire to mimic everything they had seen there. Of course, the imports bore testimony of the manufacturing skill and ingenuity of those technically advanced societies to larger segments of the population.

The elites closely followed the intellectual trends of Europe. In fact, they could more readily discuss the novels of Émile Zola or Gustave Flaubert than those of Jorge Isaacs or Machado de Assis, and they paused to admire European painters while they ignored the canvases of their compatriots. Not surprisingly, some members of the elite became knowledgeable about the new philosophy of positivism, formulated in Europe during the second quarter of the nineteenth century by French philosopher and sociologist Auguste Comte. They eventually imported it into Latin America, where governments warmly welcomed it.

Many of the ideas on progress that the Latin Americans extracted from the Enlightenment, Charles Darwin, Herbert Spencer, as well as from other sources, seemed to converge in Comte's positivism. Comte maintained that societies could advance through scientific, rational processes. He defined three stages of social development: the theological, characterized by belief in the supernatural; the metaphysical, a belief in ideas as reality; and the positive stage, in which phenomena are explained by observation, hypothesis, and experimentation. Outward manifestations of progress—railroads and industrialization were prime examples—assumed great importance in positivism and emphatically so among the Latin Americans, whether they acknowledged Comte or not.

With its emphasis on material growth and well-being, positivism ideally suited the trends of the second half of the century. It favored a capitalist mentality, regarding private wealth as sacred. Indeed, private accumulation of wealth was a sign of progress as well as an instrument for progress. Because of the weakness of domestic, private institutions, the State had to assume the role of directing progress. Deferring to the role of the State over the individual, positivism complemented the patriarchal experience of the Latin Americans. Of course, to promote capitalism and to direct progress, the State, according to positivist doctrine, had to maintain order and impose stability. With its special emphasis on order and progress, positivism reached the height of its influence between 1880 and 1900. It became an official doctrine of the Díaz regime in Mexico; some of his principal ministers, who fittingly were known as *científicos,* had imbibed deeply of Comte's doctrines and tried to offer a scientific solution to the problems of organizing national life. As Mexico's Nobel prize winning poet Octavio Paz would later reflect, "Positivism offered the social hierarchies a new justification. Inequalities were now explained, not by race or inheritance or religion, but by science."

In Venezuela, President Antonio Guzmán Blanco governed directly or indirectly from 1870 to 1888 under the influence of positivism. First he imposed order and then set out in pursuit of elusive progress. Order meant the consolidation of the past and admitted minimal social change, whereas progress signified the adoption of the outward manifestations of European civilization. Dreaming of Paris, Guzmán Blanco laid out wide boulevards for Caracas and constructed an opera house as well as a pantheon for national heroes. New railroads and expanded port facilities speeded Venezuela's exports to European markets to pay for the material progress.

Positivism also attracted many adherents in Brazil, particularly among the new graduates of the technical and military schools, members of the fledgling middle class. They favored the abolition of slavery, the establishment of a republic (albeit not a democratic one), and the separation of Church and State, changes that did occur in Brazil between 1888 and 1891. Material progress absorbed much of their concern. The flag of the Brazilian republic, created in 1889, bears to the present the positivist motto "Order and Progress."

Where political stability and economic prosperity existed, notable material progress occurred. It is not surprising that Brazil and Chile were among the first Latin American nations to experiment with the inventions and innovations correlated with progress offered by Europe and the United States. The steam engine made an early appearance in these two nations. In 1815, Bahia boasted its first steam-driven sugar mill. By 1852 there were 144 in operation. Similar technological changes took place throughout Latin America, albeit more slowly in the smaller countries.

None of the innovations had more impact than the railroads. Its steel rails had the potential of linking formerly divided territories. Penetrating distant regions, the railroads tapped new sources of economic prosperity. Bulky and perishable products could be rushed over long distances to eager markets. Just as important, troops could be sent on the railroad, bringing State power to the most distant corners. Railroad expansion was supported by such government incentives as the duty-free entry of materials and equipment, interest guarantees, and land grants. British capital readily responded and dominated rail construction. Britain supplied technicians and engineers as well and then sold English coal to the railroad companies to run the steam engines.

Cuba can boast of the first railroad in Latin America. The line from Havana to Güines, approximately thirty miles, began operation in 1838. Argentina's railroad era began in 1857 with the inauguration of a seven-mile line, and by 1914 Argentina boasted the most extensive railroad network in Latin America and the eighth largest in the world. In total, South America's railroad mileage grew from 2,000 miles in 1870 to 59,000 in 1900.

Along the newly laid rail lines, at rail junctions and at railheads sprang up villages and towns. Older settlements took on a new life. The railroad brought the countryside and the city into closer contact, and as a result the isolated and paternalistic patterns of plantation and hacienda life were challenged as never before. The railroads opened new markets for the incipient industries of the large cities and brought into the hinterlands a greater variety of goods than those populations had hitherto seen. Railroads thus helped to promote the fledgling industries. They also provided some amusement during their early years. When the railroad finally reached Guatemala City in the 1880s, it became a custom for the capital's inhabitants of all social levels to congregate at the railroad station for the semiweekly arrivals and departures of the train. On those occasions, the national band played in the plaza in front of the station for the further entertainment of the crowd.

But the railroad was also disruptive, as can be clearly seen in the case of Mexico. When Porfirio Díaz took power in 1876, only 400 miles of track had been laid. By the end of his regime in 1910, there were approximately 15,000 miles of rail. Speculators bought land along the railroad routes, frequently driving the indigenous from their landholdings. The indigenous, however, did not passively acquiesce as the railroad came through their lands. There were fifty-five agrarian rebellions from 1877 to 1884, many of them so significant that they required the deployment of federal troops to

No technology had a greater impact on Latin America than the railroad. The train, like the one pictured here in Mexico circa 1884, created markets and strengthened the state, which could now send troops to formerly remote areas. (Library of Congress)

suppress them. Of those, fifty took place within forty kilometers of a railroad route, and thirty-two of them took place within twenty kilometers.

But the elites were more concerned with the prosperity that the railroads fueled. A national market was created as products could be moved even from the most distant regions. The railroads tapped new minerals for export. Whereas Mexico before the railroads had sold only silver abroad, the railroads made it possible to export zinc, lead, and copper, intensifying the flow of Mexico's natural resources to the industrialized nations. It is noteworthy that Mexican exports increased eight and one-half times between 1877 and 1910, coinciding with the period of intensive railroad construction. U.S. interests completed the line linking the border with Mexico City so that in May of 1880 it was possible to travel by rail from Chicago to Mexico City for the first time.

Although railroads perfectly illustrated Latin America's urge to progress, they exerted an ironic negative influence on development. They deepened Latin America's dependency, strengthened the neocolonial institutions, and impoverished the governments. The primary explanation for those adverse effects lay in the fact that more often than not foreigners built and owned them and did so where they would best complement the North Atlantic economies rather than Latin America's. In Argentina, as but one example, English-financed, -built, -equipped, and -administered railroads

Railways in Latin America, 1913

COUNTRY	NUMBER OF COMPANIES	LENGTH (in kilometers)	TRACK PER 1,000 POPULATION (in kilometers)
Argentina	18	31,859	4.3
Bolivia	2	1,284	0.7
Brazil	15	24,737	1.0
Chile	10	8,069	2.4
Colombia	11	1,061	0.2
Costa Rica	1	878	2.5
Cuba	6	3,752	1.6
Dominican Republic	2	644	0.9
Ecuador	2	1,049	0.6
El Salvador	1	320	0.3
Guatemala	1	987	0.6
Haiti		180	0.1
Honduras	6	241	0.4
Mexico	13	25,600	1.8
Nicaragua	1	322	0.6
Panama	4	479	1.4
Paraguay	1	410	0.7
Peru	9	2,970	0.7
Puerto Rico	3	408	0.4
Uruguay	10	2,576	2.3
Venezuela	4	1,020	0.4
Latin America		83,246	1.4
Australia		31,327	6.9
Canada		49,549	6.5
New Zealand		4,587	4.3

Source: Victor Bulmer-Thomas, *The Economic History of Latin America Since Independence*, 2nd ed., New York, NY: Cambridge University Press, 2003, 105.

carried the resources of the rich pampas to the port of Buenos Aires for their inevitable export. As this example aptly suggests, the railroads served export markets by lowering transportation costs of bulky items, incorporating new regions into commercial agriculture, and opening up new lands and mines to exploitation. More often than not, the railroads expanded and strengthened the latifundia wherever the rails reached because they often conferred considerable value on lands once considered marginal. Whereas previously campesinos had been tolerated on that marginal land, its new value caused the landlords first to push the campesinos off the land and then to incorporate them into the estate's labor force. Commercial agriculture, much of it destined for export, replaced subsistence agriculture, and the numbers and size of small landholdings declined.

Bolivia provided a sobering example of the contribution of railroads both to the dependency on a single export and to the reduction of food production for local markets. By the end of the nineteenth century, rails connecting the highlands with Pacific ports accelerated tin ore exports. The rail cars descended the Andes loaded with the ore. In order to fill the otherwise empty cars on their return, the trains carried agricultural products imported from Peru, Chile, and the United States. The importation of food wrought havoc on the agrarian economy of the fertile Santa Cruz region, depriving it of its national market. Production declined sharply. Bolivia became locked into a double dependency status: dependent on foreign markets for its single export and on foreign producers for a part of its food supply.

Costa Rica illustrated in a slightly different but even more disastrous way the effects of railroads on the economy of a small nation. To market larger quantities of coffee and thus earn the money to modernize, the government encouraged the construction of a railroad (1870–1890) that stretched from the highlands, where the coffee grew, to Puerto Limón for shipment abroad. The onerous loans overburdened the treasury as the government paid outrageous interest rates to unscrupulous foreign money lenders. Further, the government bestowed on Chief Engineer Minor Keith 800,000 acres, land that fronted on the railroad and later became the center of the plantations of the United Fruit Company. Meanwhile, the railroad remained in foreign hands. British investors also controlled the ports, mines, electric lighting, major public works, and foreign commerce as well as the principal domestic marketplaces. In short, Costa Rica surrendered all its economic independence and mortgaged its future before 1890 to obtain some of the physical aspects of modernization.

Most of the other Latin American governments also contracted heavy debts to pay for their railroads. Those debts often led to foreign complications and always to some sacrifice of economic independence. One brazen example of foreign intervention triggered by railroad funding occurred in Venezuela. In 1903, German gunboats appeared off the coast to force the government to pay 1.4 million pounds sterling for loans associated with railroad building.

With the outsized importance of the railroad to Latin America in the nineteenth century, it should not be surprising that it became a key actor in fiction of the era. In Clorinda Matto de Turner's *Birds Without a Nest* (1889), the railroad serves to transport people from the primitive countryside to modern Lima. En route, the train is derailed when it collides with a herd of cows that refuse to move from the track, an apt metaphor for the struggle between rural tradition and urban modernity. Another sign of the times is that the train is righted by Mr. Smith, the engineer from the United States. The railroad was the central actor in Argentine Ricardo Güiraldes's short story, "Rosaura," the tale of a provincial young woman who is wooed and abandoned by a Europeanized young man from the city. Güiraldes characterizes the railroad's impact on the town:

> The soul of Lobos was simple and primitive as a red bloom. Lobos thought, loved, lived, in its own way. Then came the parallel infinities of swift rails, and the train, marching armored to indifference from horizon to horizon, from stranger to stranger, brushed its passing plume over the settlement. Lobos fell ill of that poison.

The telegraph had a more subtle impact, but it, too, furthered the communications revolution in Latin America. The telegraph contributed to national unity—at least among the elites—and helped to bring neighboring nations closer together. Both Chile and Brazil began service over short lines in 1852. In 1866, a cable connected Buenos Aires and Montevideo; and the following year the United States opened cable communication with Cuba. Other countries followed suit. Transatlantic cables put Latin America in instantaneous communication with Europe. Pedro II dictated the first message to be cabled from Brazil to Europe in 1874. Significantly, Rio de Janeiro was linked to Europe by cable long before it could communicate by telegraph with other parts of its own empire.

International communication was also enhanced by the increasing number of international steamship lines serving Latin America, putting the region in direct and regular contact with the principal ports of Europe and the United States. Sailings became increasingly frequent, ships carried more cargo, and service improved. The major ports underwent renovation with the addition of new and larger warehouses, faster loading and unloading machinery, larger and sturdier wharfs, and the dredging of deeper channels.

Clearly not all of Latin America shared fully in the progress. One astonished visitor to the highlands of Ecuador and to Quito in 1885 gasped, "The country does not know the meaning of the words progress and prosperity." At that time, the only communication between Quito, the capital high in the Andes, and Guayaquil, the Pacific port, was still by mule path, a route impassable during six months of the year because of the rainy season. Under optimum conditions, it was possible to make the journey in eight or nine days over the same route in use for centuries. As a port, Guayaquil was in contact with the world and showed signs of modernization long before the isolated capital did. The public streetcar, gas lighting, and other amenities reached Guayaquil years before they could be seen in the capital. Not until the end of the first decade of the twentieth century did a railroad link Guayaquil with Quito. The 227-mile railroad climb from the port to the capital took two days. The slower growth of Ecuador was not unique; it characterized many of the nations that lagged behind the leadership of Argentina, Brazil, Chile, and Mexico.

The concern with improved transportation and communication symbolized the dedication to progress. To a large extent, material advances measured modernization: How many miles of railroads, how much horsepower generated by steam engines, how many tons handled per hour in the ports, how many miles of telegraph wires? The higher the number given in response to these questions, the greater the progress the nation could claim. In their satisfaction with these material advances, the elites seemed oblivious of another aspect of modernization: The very steamships, railroads, and ports tied them and their nations ever more tightly to a handful of industrialized nations in Western Europe and North America, which bought their raw products and provided manufactured goods in return.

They failed to see the significance of the fact that many of the railroads did not link the principal cities of their nations but rather ran from the plantations or mines directly to the ports, subordinating the goal of national unification to the interests of the industrial nations for agricultural products and minerals. As the amount of loans increased to pay for the new material progress, the governments had to budget ever greater sums to pay interest rates. As foreign investment rose, the outflow of profit remittances multiplied. Increasingly, the voices of foreign investors and bankers spoke with greater authority in making economic decisions for the host countries. Local economic options diminished. In short, progress as it took shape in nineteenth-century Latin America adversely prioritized the needs and desires of a tiny Latin American elite and its foreign economic partners.

ECONOMIC PROSPERITY

The elite pursuit of progress had economic prosperity as the goal, and they were not disappointed. Thanks to loans, investments, and rising exports, a growing economy characterized parts of Latin America during the last half of the nineteenth century. That growth came from the consolidation of the export economy.

The demands of the industrialized nations for raw products rose impressively throughout the second half of the nineteenth century. Not only was there a rapidly increasing number of consumers in Western Europe and the United States, but also their per capita purchasing power was ever greater. The United States emerged as the principal industrialized nation of the world and as the foremost consumer of Latin America's exports. As the industrial centers bought more agricultural and mineral products from Latin America, the region's trade underwent a dramatic expansion. Plantation owners and miners produced larger amounts of grain, coffee, sugar, cotton, cacao, bananas, livestock, copper, silver, tin, lead, zinc, and nitrates for export. The natural products—such as palm oils, nuts, woods, rubber, and medicinal plants—also found a ready market abroad, and their exportation

Export Commodity Concentration Ratios, 1913

COUNTRY	FIRST PRODUCT	PERCENTAGE	SECOND PRODUCT	PERCENTAGE	TOTAL
Argentina	Maize	22.5	Wheat	20.7	43.2
Bolivia	Tin	72.3	Silver	4.3	76.6
Brazil	Coffee	62.3	Rubber	15.9	78.2
Chile	Nitrates	71.3	Copper	7.0	78.3
Colombia	Coffee	37.2	Gold	20.4	57.6
Costa Rica	Bananas	50.9	Coffee	35.2	86.1
Cuba	Sugar	72.0	Tobacco	19.5	91.5
Dominican Republic	Cacao	39.2	Sugar	34.8	74.0
Ecuador	Cacao	64.1	Coffee	5.4	69.5
El Salvador	Coffee	79.6	Precious metals	15.9	95.5
Guatemala	Coffee	84.8	Bananas	5.7	90.5
Haiti	Coffee	64.0	Cacao	6.8	70.8
Honduras	Bananas	50.1	Precious metals	25.9	76.0
Mexico	Silver	30.3	Copper	10.3	40.6
Nicaragua	Coffee	64.9	Precious metals	13.8	78.7
Panama	Bananas	65.0	Coconuts	7.0	72.0
Paraguay	Yerba mate	32.1	Tobacco	15.8	47.9
Peru	Copper	22.0	Sugar	15.4	37.4
Puerto Rico	Sugar	47.0	Coffee	19.0	66.0
Uruguay	Wool	42.0	Meat	24.0	66.0
Venezuela	Coffee	52.0	Cacao	21.4	73.4

Source: Victor Bulmer-Thomas, *The Economic History of Latin America Since Independence*, 2nd ed., New York, NY: Cambridge University Press, 2003, 58.

rose sharply. Similar to well-established patterns of the colonial past, the export sector of the economy remained the most active, the dynamic focus of investment, technological improvement, official concern, and demand for labor. More often than not, foreigners, with their own agendas, dominated that sector.

In order to focus on growing exports, the elites tried to monopolize the land. They had two goals: to transfer land from subsistence to export crops and to entice the campesinos to leave their small plots of land and work for the large estates. To that end, most Latin American governments adopted laws aimed at divesting indigenous communities of their land, as well as legislation to force campesinos to leave their small subsistence plots and labor on the large estates.

The success of such measures was mixed, depending to a great extent on the strength of the State and its local units of control. Where force was strong, the elites triumphed. In many places, however, the folk were able to continue manipulating the system. One of the most successful governments was the Díaz regime in Mexico. Legislation to commercialize land had been passed during the Reform administrations in the 1850s, but the laws could not be enforced because of the War of the Reform and French intervention and occupation. Díaz's rule, and his *Guardia Rural* (rural guard), made enforcement possible. By 1894, 20 percent of Mexico's land had changed hands. By the early twentieth century, most rural villages had lost their ejidos. And by 1910, half of all rural Mexicans lived and worked on haciendas.

Workers were more frequently tied to the haciendas by debt peonage, which had been tried with much less success during the colonial and early national eras. Peons would be given cash advances but were required to work until they were repaid. They often were paid in scrip rather than money, usable only at the *tienda de raya,* or hacienda store. Workers were charged exorbitant prices and routinely cheated on their payments. If the worker died, his debts passed to his children. Debt peonage in Mexico was particularly successful on the henequen plantations of the Yucatan and the lumber camps of Chiapas. B. Traven, the German novelist who captured the reality of Mexico in the early twentieth century in such classics as *The Treasure of the Sierra Madre,* wrote in *The Rebellion of the Hanged* about men who escaped from floggings in Yucatan only to descend into the hell of the Chiapas mahogany camps, where workers were hanged by the trees for days, exposed to the elements and the animals.

In many regions, however, elite measures failed dismally. Nicaraguan legislators adopted laws attempting to control labor in 1835, 1841, 1843, 1847, 1853, 1859, 1862, 1869, 1876, 1879, 1880, 1881, 1883, 1886, 1892, 1894, 1898, 1899, 1901, 1903, 1904, 1906, 1908, 1919, and 1923, and the issue was addressed in the constitutions of 1905 and 1911. The plethora of laws is clear testament to their futility. Workers routinely accepted cash advances at coffee haciendas then ran off to other haciendas. In the coffee-growing region of Carazo, hacendados complained that the local authorities were incapable of tracking down the rebellious workers.

The Nicaraguans concluded that the best way to keep a steady workforce nearby was to provide them with small plots of land—just enough to provide subsistence, but not enough to prevent campesinos from needing the extra income of harvest work.

Foreign observers marveled at the rapid rate of increase of Latin American trade in the last half of the nineteenth century. By 1890, Latin America's foreign commerce exceeded $1 billion per year and had increased roughly 43 percent between 1870 and 1884. By comparison, during the same period British trade increased by 27.2 percent. The five principal areas engaged in foreign commerce were Brazil, Argentina, Cuba, Chile, and Mexico, which together accounted for more than three-quarters of Latin America's trade. With the exception of Argentina, they exported more than they imported. Trade statistics for the individual nations were impressive. Argentine exports jumped sevenfold between 1853 and 1873 and doubled again by 1893.

Mexican exports quadrupled between 1877 and 1900. The smaller nations benefited too. Exports of coffee from Costa Rica increased fourfold between 1855 and 1915.

A number of inventions, among them the railroad, barbed wire, the canning process, and the refrigerator ship, facilitated the exploitation of Argentina's hitherto untamed pampas, potentially one of the world's most fertile regions. The sailing of the first primitive refrigerator ship from Buenos Aires to Europe in 1876 changed the course of Argentine economic history.

Annual Average Export Growth and Export Purchasing Power Growth, 1850–1870, 1870–1890, 1890–1912 (in Percentages)

	1850–1870		1870–1890		1890–1912	
COUNTRY	EXPORT GROWTH	EXPORT PURCHASING POWER GROWTH	EXPORT GROWTH	EXPORT PURCHASING POWER GROWTH	EXPORT GROWTH	EXPORT PURCHASING POWER GROWTH
Argentina	4.9	4.1	6.7	8.2	6.7	5.4
Bolivia	2.8	2.0	2.3	3.8	2.5	1.2
Brazil	4.3	3.5	2.5	4.0	4.3	3.0
Chile	4.6	3.8	3.3	4.8	5.0	3.7
Colombia	7.8	7.0	0.5	2.0	2.4	1.1
Costa Rica	4.7	3.9	5.6	7.1	0.5	−0.8
Cuba	3.5	2.7	2.3	3.9	2.4	1.1
Dominican Republic	4.5	3.7	5.1	6.6	5.9	4.6
Ecuador	4.9	4.1	1.7	3.2	3.9	2.6
El Salvador	5.7	4.9	2.0	3.5	2.6	1.3
Guatemala	3.2	2.4	6.9	8.4	1.1	−0.2
Haiti	2.5	1.7	3.3	4.8	−1.0	−2.3
Honduras	−0.5	−1.3	14.8	16.3	−0.3	1.6
Mexico	−0.7	−1.5	4.4	5.9	5.2	3.9
Nicaragua	0.8	0	6.1	7.6	2.3	1.0
Paraguay	4.4	3.6	6.0	7.5	2.2	0.9
Peru	6.4	5.6	−4.9	−3.4	6.9	5.6
Puerto Rico	0.1	−0.7	1.8	3.3	7.6	6.3
Uruguay	3.1	2.3	3.7	5.2	3.4	2.1
Venezuela	4.6	3.8	2.4	3.9	1.2	−0.1
Latin America	4.5	3.7	2.7	4.2	4.5	3.2

Source: Victor Bulmer-Thomas, *The Economic History of Latin America Since Independence,* 2nd ed., New York, NY: Cambridge University Press, 2003, 64.

The successful voyage proved that chilled and frozen beef could be sold in lucrative European markets. Measures were taken at once to improve the quality of the beef. By 1900, 278 refrigerator ships sailed between Great Britain and Argentina. During the decade of the 1870s, Argentina also made its first wheat shipments to Europe, a modest 21 tons in 1876. In 1900, wheat exports reached 2,250,000 tons. This extraordinary economic boom made Argentina the most prosperous nation in Latin America.

Chile offers an excellent but by no means exceptional example of the development of a mineral-exporting economy. Already in the first decades of independence, it exported increasing amounts of silver and copper. By midcentury, Chile enjoyed a well-balanced program of exports divided between various minerals and agricultural products. That diversification ended after 1878 when the new nitrate exports grew increasingly important until, within a few years, they dominated the export sector. Dependent on the world's need for nitrates, the Chilean economy declined or prospered according to demand and price for one product. The vulnerability of the economy was obvious.

Most governmental leaders paid far more attention to the international economy than to the national, domestic economy. The export sector of the Latin American economy grew more rapidly than the domestic sector, and income from foreign trade contributed an unusually high percentage of the gross national product. Foreign trade emphatically did not mean commerce among the Latin American nations. They were strangers in each other's marketplaces, frequently competitors producing the same export products. Their economies complemented the demands of the distant major capitalistic economies in Western Europe and the United States.

Mounting foreign investments also characterized the Latin American economy in the second of the nineteenth century. Europe generously sent capital, technology, and technicians to Latin America to assure the increased agricultural and mineral production its factories and urban populations required. The more pronounced stability of Latin America engendered greater confidence and generosity among foreign investors. The politicians of Latin America discovered the advantages of foreign investment. It created new wealth, which caudillos, politicians, and elite alike enjoyed. In a pattern established throughout the hemisphere, Porfirio Díaz meticulously paid off Mexico's foreign debts and decreed laws favorable to foreign investors. Foreign investment poured into Mexico. As investments rose, profit remittances flowed out of Latin America. The foreign capitalists might have invested in part to obtain the raw products they needed, but they also expected a rich return in the form of profits, interest payments, patent fees, and commissions.

To handle the new flow of money, banks, both national and foreign, sprang up with amazing rapidity in the major Latin American cities. Only one bank existed in Brazil in 1845, but in the following twelve years, twelve new banks were founded. Similar patterns were followed in the rest of the region. The banks facilitated international trade and investment, but the majority of people continued to borrow small amounts from individuals in their own communities.

Direct and Portfolio Investment in Latin America, 1914

COUNTRY	PUBLIC EXTERNAL DEBT			DIRECT FOREIGN INVESTMENT		
	MILLIONS OF U.S. DOLLARS	UNITED KINGDOM %	UNITED STATES %	MILLIONS OF U.S. DOLLARS	UNITED KINGDOM %	UNITED STATES %
Argentina	784	50.8	2.4	3,217	46.7	1.2
Bolivia	15	0	20.0	44	38.6	4.5
Brazil	717	83.4	0.7	1,196	50.9	4.2
Chile	174	73.6	0.6	494	43.1	45.5
Colombia	23	69.6	21.7	54	57.4	38.9
Costa Rica	17	47.1	0	44	6.8	93.2
Cuba	85	58.8	41.2	386	44.0	56.0
Dominican Republic	5	0	100	11	0	100
Ecuador	1	100	0	40	72.5	22.5
El Salvador	4	100	0	15	40.0	46.7
Guatemala	7	100	0	92	47.8	39.1
Haiti	1	0	100	10	10	100
Honduras	26	0	61.5	16	0	93.8
Mexico	152	92.1	7.9	1,177	54.0	46.0
Nicaragua	6	50.0	0	6	33.0	67.0
Panama	5	0	100	23	0	100
Paraguay	4	100	0	23	78.3	21.7
Peru	17	47.1	11.8	180	67.2	32.2
Puerto Rico	44					
Uruguay	120	75.0	0	355	43.4	0
Venezuela	21	47.6	0	145	20.7	26.2
Latin America	**2,229**	**67.8**	**13.8**	**7,569**	**47.4**	**18.4**
Agriculture				255	4.7	93.7
Mining				530	19.1	78.3
Oil				140	2.9	97.1
Railways				2,342	71.2	13.0
Public utilities				914	59.7	13.9
Manufacturing				562	14.8	3.0
Trade				485	0.4	7.0
Other and undistributed by sector				2,341	50.0	5.2

Source: Victor Bulmer-Thomas, *The Economic History of Latin America Since Independence*, 2nd ed., New York, NY: Cambridge University Press, 2003, 102.

By the eve of World War I, foreign investments totaled $8.5 billion. The English invested the heaviest, $5 billion, or 20 percent of British overseas investment. The French were second with $1.7 billion, followed very closely by the United States with $1.6 billion. Germany was fourth with somewhat less than $1 billion. The largest share of the money went to Argentina, Brazil, and Mexico, and the most popular investments were railroads, public utilities, and mining. British investments predominated in South America; those of U.S. capitalists dominated in Mexico and the Caribbean area.

With sources of capital, markets, and headquarters abroad, the foreign investors and business people identified neither with their host countries nor with local needs. Their ability to direct capital investment, their hostility to tariffs, and their preference for free-trade policies exerted an unfavorable influence on Latin America's economic development.

MODEST INDUSTRIALIZATION

During the second half of the century, the larger and more stable nations began to industrialize in order to meet growing internal demands for manufactured goods, to develop more balanced economies, and to protect the national economies from extremes of fluctuation in international trade. Some farsighted statesmen believed that without such industrialization the Latin Americans would be doomed to economic dependency and backwardness. The Chilean Manuel Camilo Vial, Minister of Finance during the administration of Manuel Bulnes (1841–1851), preached, "Any nation in which agriculture dominates everything, in which slavery or feudalism shows its odious face, follows the march of humanity among the stragglers....That future threatens us also, if we do not promote industry with a firm hand and a constant will." The governments raised tariffs, particularly during the final decades of the century, to encourage and protect the new industries and from time to time promulgated other legislation such as tax incentives and permission to import machinery duty free to give further impetus to the process. Industrialization grew gradually in the last decades of the nineteenth century, despite such disadvantages as limited capital, unskilled labor, low labor productivity, lack of coal, limited markets, and a mentality emphasizing the continued reliance on the exploitation of mineral and agricultural possibilities.

The burgeoning cities provided a ready labor supply for the new industrialization. Women—and all too many children—worked in the factories. Women had always played a major role in agriculture. While traveling in Central America in the midnineteenth century, William V. Wells observed, "I have always found the women of the lower classes in Central America simple, kind-hearted, and hospitable, generally performing the most laborious part of the work, and never tiring under their ceaseless tasks. They are truly the hewers of wood and drawers of water." In the second half of the century, increasing numbers of women tended the new industrial machinery, working the same long hours as men but for lower wages.

In the beginning, industrialization was primarily concerned with the processing of natural products for local consumption or export. Flour mills, sugar refineries, meat-packaging plants, tanning factories, lumber mills, wineries, and breweries developed wherever the requisite resources were at hand. Then service industries appeared: gas and electric utilities, repair shops and foundries, and construction enterprises. Finally, protected industries began to manufacture other goods for home consumption, principally, textiles and processed food.

In Brazil, the textile industry was by far the most important. The nine cotton mills in 1865 multiplied into 100 before the fall of the empire. The new republican government that came to power in 1889 visualized an industrial expansion for the nation. Symbolic of their ambitions, the Republicans changed the name of the Ministry of Agriculture to the Ministry of Industry. As further encouragement, they promulgated a protective tariff in 1890, raising to 60 percent the duty on 300 items, principally textiles and food products, which competed with nationally produced goods. Conversely, they lowered the duty on primary goods used in national manufacturing. Fundamental to any industrialization, the government established four new engineering schools in the 1890s.

The Argentine government began to turn its attention seriously to the encouragement of industrialization during the 1870s. In 1876, it enacted a high protective tariff. Industrialization concentrated in and around Buenos Aires, which by 1889 counted some 400 industrial establishments employing approximately 11,000 workers. During the last decade of the century, larger factories appeared and industry began to penetrate other regions, although Buenos Aires would always remain the focal point. The census of 1895 listed the number of factories and workshops as 23,000 with 170,000 employees (small workshops employing fewer than ten workers were by far the most common); the next census, 1914, raised the number of factories and workshops to 49,000 and the number of employees to 410,000. By that time, Argentina manufactured 37 percent of the processed foods its inhabitants consumed, 17 percent of the clothing they wore, and 12 percent of the metals and machinery they used.

Under Porfirio Díaz, Mexicans also used their success in export production to invest in manufacturing. By 1902, there were 5,500 manufacturing interests in Mexico. The most important industries were iron and steel, developed with a combination of foreign and domestic finance. New industries included production of cement, textiles, cigarettes, soap, bricks, furniture, flour, and beer, including José Schneider's 1890 founding of the Cerveceria Cuahtemoc, which produced Carta Blanca. Industrial production tripled during the Porfiriato, and the value of manufacturing rose by 6 percent a year. Despite these increases, manufacturing was still dwarfed by production of primary products, and industrial labor did not exceed 15 percent of the nation's workforce.

The most progress in manufacturing took place in Argentina, Brazil, Chile, Mexico and Peru. Among the five nations, domestic production of consumer goods reached from 50 to 80 percent. However, the goods were largely of low quality, protected by tariffs, and no progress was made towards the creation of manufactured goods for export.

PROGRESS ON THE PERIPHERY

Few parts of Latin America were left untouched by the drive for progress of the late nineteenth century. Even areas that had been poor backwaters in the colonial period followed the same patterns as the rest of the region by orienting their economies and polities to the export market. The small Central American nation of Nicaragua is one example.

As early as 1835, the Nicaraguan government tried to promote exports by giving ten-year tax exemptions to the production of indigo, cochineal, and coffee. It soon became clear that the most likely success was coffee production on Nicaragua's fertile highlands. By 1846, the government exempted coffee planters, their families, and workers from military service and exempted coffee farms from taxes. Production was encouraged in 1858 by allowing the growers to import duty-free goods equivalent to the value of the coffee they exported. The government undertook transportation and communications improvements, with an eye toward the coffee market. The first telegraph lines were established in 1876, and in 1882, underwater telegraph lines connected Nicaragua to the world's major cities; by 1890, there were 2,478 kilometers of telegraph lines, and by 1905 there were 4,330 kilometers. Construction of the railroad, Ferrocarril del Pacífico de Nicaragua, began in Corinto in 1878, and by 1886, it had reached the port of Momotombo on Lake Nicaragua. By 1909, there were 275 kilometers of track. Furthermore, coffee planters were not charged for shipping their produce on the government-owned railroads. Clearly, Nicaragua's economic and political leaders were interested in developing the economy and, starting in the midnineteenth century, saw coffee as the way to do it. Both the conservative governments (1862–1903) and the liberal government of José Santos Zelaya (1893–1909) threw their support behind the new export commodity.

Nicaraguan farmers responded to the incentives provided by the government and the market: 26 million trees were in production by 1892. Exports rose from 4.5 million pounds in 1880 to 11.3 million by 1890. From 1904–1924, coffee exports averaged 23 million pounds a year. In 1871, coffee represented only 10 percent of the value of Nicaragua's exports, in fourth place behind indigo, rubber, and gold. By the 1880s, coffee had become the country's most important export, and in 1890, coffee constituted at least 60 percent of exports.

The larger producers of cacao, indigo, and sugar quickly turned to coffee production. They sought more land to bring into cultivation, and elites in government responded with laws intended to commercialize property. A small proportion of nationally owned land was sold to large growers, and a small percentage of municipal ejidos and indigenous communal land ended up in coffee production. However, despite decrees in 1877 and 1881 that authorized the sale of communal lands, municipal governments continued to receive large tracts of land from the federal government for use as ejidos. And they gave small plots of land in the ejidos to small farmers, most of whom continued to produce subsistence crops. The donation of small plots of land continued apace, and rental plots were available at nominal fees well into the twentieth century.

By providing small plots of land, the government guaranteed a seasonal workforce for the large coffee estates that formed. Coffee requires minimal upkeep during the year, but during the harvest there are massive labor demands. The government adopted a multitude of vagrancy laws and requirements that Nicaraguans work in the harvests; most of the laws were flouted with regularity as workers ran off to competitors. The easiest solution was to provide them with land that enabled them to grow food for subsistence, with the lure of the nearby haciendas for seasonal labor to earn the needed additional income.

As large coffee farms spread across most of the countryside, they were joined by an even greater number of small and medium-sized coffee farms. These smaller farmers produced significant amounts of coffee and became an important part of the coffee economy, lending legitimacy to the economic

Coffee became one of Latin America's most important exports in the late nineteenth century. This stereographic image of Nicaraguan women sorting coffee in 1903 also shows how images of Latin America were exported as something exotic for foreign customers. (Library of Congress)

and political system. Men who owned even relatively small farms had the right to vote, and they participated in heated municipal and regional elections. They also made use of the legal system to protect their rights.

The various indigenous communities of Nicaragua responded differently to the new commercial incentives. In Carazo, some Indians who had produced sugar in the early national period easily switched to coffee and joined the Hispanized, or *ladino*, world. In parts of neighboring Masaya, they lost their lands and largely became a workforce for the powerful interests in the old colonial capital of Granada. In the northern province of Matagalpa, where coffee production came relatively late, many indigenous communities were more successful in keeping their land and indigenous identity.

Similar patterns appeared in Guatemala and El Salvador, where small farmers were created alongside the huge plantations and where some indigenous communities managed to hold onto their lands into the twentieth century. Some profited, others lost, but few were untouched by the spread of the export economy and the growth of government institutions that accompanied it.

THE GROWTH OF CITIES

Although most of the population remained in the countryside, the export economies of the late nineteenth century fostered the growth of cities. For purposes of definition, most of the Latin American nations classify as urban those localities that have some type of local government and a population of at least 1,000 to 2,000 inhabitants.

The cities played ever more important roles in each nation. The government and administrative apparatus, commerce, and industry were located in the cities. Increasingly, they served as hubs of complex transportation and communications networks. Further, they provided important recreational, cultural, and educational services. Rapid urban growth resulted from the arrival of greater numbers of foreign immigrants, a constantly increasing population (Latin America counted 60 million inhabitants in 1900), and an attraction the city exerted over many rural dwellers. Promises of better jobs and a more pleasant life lured thousands each year from the countryside to the city, a road that became increasingly more heavily trodden. On the other hand, even where that promise was lacking, the grinding poverty and modernization of the countryside pushed many desperate folk into urban areas.

But cities failed to play the role they might have in encouraging national development. The urban facade of modernization deceived. The high concentration of land in a few hands dictated the function of cities just as it molded other aspects of life. The export-oriented economy encouraged the prosperity of a few ports, a transportation system focusing on them, the expenditure of export wealth to beautify the capital city, and the concentration of absentee landlords in the capital to be near the center of power. The capital and the ports (in the case of Argentina, for example, the capital is also the principal port) absorbed the wealth of the export economy. The large estates, overreliance on an export economy, and the resultant dependency help to explain why only one or two major "modern" cities dominated each Latin American nation and why urban modernity remained little more than a facade.

Urban culture with its capitalist-consumer imprint imposed a particular mentality on many city dwellers, which in turn shaped an outlook differing from that of most of the rural inhabitants. In an urban environment, traditional relationships tended to bend under necessity or examples of newer ones. In very general terms, the more intimate living conditions of the city and the greater familiarity of the city dwellers with foreign cultures exposed them to different ideas and alternative values. Many read newspapers and participated in public events. They were aware of changes the world was undergoing; they knew of the opportunities open to the trained and the talented and were willing to strive for those opportunities. Consequently they laid plans for the future, and, exerting every effort to realize those plans, they worked to shape their own destinies. The educational opportunities, varied careers, and job possibilities afforded by the city encouraged them to aspire toward upward mobility.

The statistics on Latin America's urban boom are impressive. Argentina's urban population doubled between 1869 and 1914, when 53 percent of Argentines lived in cities, 25 percent of them in Buenos Aires alone. Brazil witnessed similar urban growth. Between 1890 and 1914, the government created approximately 500 new municipalities. From 1890–1920, Recife and Rio de Janeiro doubled in size; São Paulo increased eightfold, making it one of the fastest growing cities in the world. In 1910, the distinguished British diplomat and author James Bryce described São Paulo, a city then approaching half a million, as "the briskest and most progressive place in all Brazil.... The alert faces, and the air of stir and movement, as well as handsome public buildings, rising on all hands, with a large, well-planted public garden in the middle of the city, give the impression of energy and progress."

The reality of urban living, however, condemned many in the lower classes to grinding poverty. Brazilian novelist Aluísio Azevedo captured the urban reality in his novel, *The Slum*, published in 1890. He described the growth of the slum as "a brutal and exuberant world." "And on the muddy ground covered with puddles, in the sultry humidity, a living world, a human community, began to wriggle, to seethe, to grow spontaneously in that quagmire, multiplying like larvae in a dung heap." It was an environment in which employment opportunities failed to keep up with the numbers of potential workers, and in which women labored as washerwomen, domestics, and prostitutes.

For the elites, however, the cities offered delights. By the beginning of the twentieth century, nearly all the capitals and many of the largest cities boasted electricity, telephones, streetcar service, covered sewers, paved streets, ornamental parks, and new buildings reflecting French architectural influence. Nurtured in an increasingly prosperous urban environment, intellectual activity flourished. Some of Latin America's most prestigious newspapers were founded: *El Mercurio* in Chile and the *Jornal do Commércio* in Brazil, both in 1827; *El Comercio* in Peru in 1839; and *La Prensa* in 1869 and *La Nación* in 1870 in Buenos Aires. Starting with the University of Chile in 1843, the major universities of Latin America began to publish reviews, journals, annuals, and books, an activity that further stimulated intellectual development. Romanticism, with its individuality, emotional intensity, and glorification of nature, held sway in literary circles for much of the nineteenth century. José Mármol of Argentina, Jorge Isaacs of Colombia, and José de Alencar of Brazil were masters of the romantic novel. Excesses in romanticism prompted literary experiments by 1880 in modernism and realism, already in vogue in Europe. The brilliant Nicaraguan poet Rubén Darío helped to introduce modernism into Latin America, and by the end of the century he dominated the field of poetry. Critics considered him one of the most original and influential poetic voices of his time.

Under the sway of realism, urban writers depicted and denounced the injustices they observed in their society. Clorinda Matto de Turner wrote the first significant novel, *Aves sin Nido* (*Birds Without a Nest*, 1889), protesting the abysmal conditions under which the Quechua and Aymara of Peru lived. She saw the indigenous as victims of iniquitous institutions, not least of which in her opinion was the Church. With two notable exceptions, Latin American culture aped European trends, particularly those set in Paris. The exceptions were Ricardo Palma, whose original *"tradiciones peruanas,"* delightful historical anecdotes of Peru, recreated with wit and imagination his country's past, and Argentine José Hernández, foremost of the gaucho poets and creator *of Martín Fierro,* a true American epic, picturing life among Argentina's rugged cowboys.

Education continued to be a privilege of the elite. Overwhelming numbers of the masses remained illiterate. In Brazil, the illiteracy rate never dropped below 85 percent in the nineteenth century. Argentina dedicated much of the nation's budget to improving education. As a result, literacy in Argentina rose from 22 percent in 1869 to 65 percent in 1914, an enviable record throughout most of Latin America, where the illiteracy rate ranged from 40 to 90 percent during the second half of the nineteenth century. It was always much higher in the countryside than in the city and higher among women than men. A marked contrast existed between the well-educated few and the ignorant many, most of whom could not attend the new schools because they had to work. The children of the elite, however, seldom set foot in a public school. Their parents hired tutors or sent them to private schools for a typically classical education. Such segregation further removed the future leaders from national realities.

The modernizing elites began to worry that they could not progress as long as mothers—at least elite mothers—lacked the skills to teach their sons to be good citizens. Mexican journalist Florencio del Castillo declared in 1856, "The most effective way to better the moral condition of the land is to educate women." Just as women served as transmitters of Spanish culture during the colonial era, educated women were now to pass on the republican, progressive values so important to Latin American modernization. In Argentina, Juan Bautista Alberdi and Domingo Faustino Sarmiento included women in their vision of an educated, progressive country.

Of course, conservatives worried that education would encourage women to leave their traditional roles, and the idea of their education was not immediately accepted. It took more than just the enlightened attitudes of men like Sarmiento to win expanded education for women. Many women, particularly from the middle class, campaigned for educational opportunities. They founded journals and editorialized about the need for education. An article in the Brazilian journal *O Sexo Femenino* contended: "It is to you [men] that is owed our inadequacy; we have intelligence equal to yours, and if your pride has triumphed it is because our intelligence has been left unused. From this day we wish to improve our minds; and for better or worse we will transmit our ideas in the press, and to this end we have *O Sexo Femenino*; a journal absolutely dedicated to our sex and written only by us."

As educational opportunities for women improved, so did employment. Because girls and boys were usually taught in separate schools, women were trained to teach the girls. As schools later became coeducational, women were considered the most appropriate teachers of young children in primary schools. Normal schools were founded to train teachers for this role.

The bringing together of women in schools and producing journals gave impetus to an early feminist movement, which was concerned not only with basic education but also with the opening of higher education and the professions to women. Their actions were not taken lightly by the men at the top. Mexico's Minister of State Justo Sierra made the Porfirian attitude toward female education quite clear: "The educated woman will be truly one for the home: she will be the companion and collaborator of man in the formation of the family. You [women] are called upon to form souls, to sustain the soul of your husband; for this reason, we educate you ... to continue the perpetual creation of the nation. *Niña querida*, do not turn feminist in our midst."

Chile pioneered in offering professional education to women. A special governmental decree in 1877 permitted women to receive professional degrees, and in 1886 Eloisa Díaz became the first woman in all of Latin America to receive a medical degree. In 1892, Matilde Throup graduated from the law school in Santiago and became the first female lawyer in Latin America. The Brazilian government opened professional schools to women in 1879.

Women also became activists in the antislavery movements in Cuba and Brazil. Much like women in the United States, their focus on lack of freedom for blacks led them to see the limits on their own freedom. As the slaves were freed in Brazil in 1889, one journal proclaimed, "once more we

[women] ask equal rights, freedom of action, and autonomy in the home."
The demands, however, remained unmet.

SUPERFICIAL MODERNIZATION

During the second half of the nineteenth century, new forces appeared that
challenged the social, economic, and political institutions deeply rooted
in the colonial past. Urbanization, industrialization, and modernization
formed a trinity menacing to tradition. Once introduced, these mutually
supporting forces could not be arrested. The center of political, economic,
and social life, once located on the plantations and haciendas, shifted gradually but irreversibly to the cities.

By the beginning of the twentieth century, some of the Latin American
countries—certainly Argentina, Brazil, Chile, and Mexico—conveyed at least
the outward appearance of having adopted the patterns and modes of the
most progressive European nations and of the United States. Their constitutions embodied the noblest principles of Western political thought. Their

Street cars and European-style architecture are among the signs of modernity in
the Plaza de la Constitución, in Montevideo, Uruguay photographed between
1880 and 1900. (Library of Congress)

governmental apparatus followed the most progressive models of the day. Political stability replaced chaos. Expanding transportation and communication infrastructures permitted the governments to control a larger area of their nations than they ever had before. New industries existed. An ever larger banking network facilitated and encouraged commerce. Society was more diversified than at any previous time. In the capitals and the largest cities, the architecture of the new buildings duplicated the latest styles of Paris: In how many Latin American cities do the local citizens proudly point to the opera house and claim it to be a replica of the Paris Opera? To the extent that some of the Latin American states formally resembled the leading nations of the Western world, which they consciously accepted as their models of modernity, it is possible to conclude that those nations qualified as modern. However, many would argue that such modernity was only a veneer. It added a cosmetic touch to tenacious institutions while failing to effect the changes implied by the concept. Modernization in Latin America lacked real substance.

The superficiality of modernization guaranteed the continued domination of the past. The rural aristocracy still enjoyed power, their estates remained huge and generally inefficient, and their control over their workers was complete. The latifundia actually grew rather than diminished in size during the nineteenth century, at the expense of indigenous communities and their traditional landholdings, the properties confiscated from the Church, and the public domain.

By early 1888, slavery had been abolished. Still, former slaves and their descendants occupied one of the lowest rungs of the social and economic ladder. The doors to education, opportunity, and mobility remained tightly closed to them except in the rarest instances. The indigenous fared no better. Debt servitude of one or another variety characterized part of the labor market. It would have been foolish to have expected the law to intervene to restrict such abuses as the making, enforcing, and judging of the laws rested in the hands of the landowners and their sympathizers.

The wealthiest and most powerful class in Latin America in general was white or near white in complexion. Heirs of the creoles and mazombos, they enjoyed age-old economic advantages, to which, after independence, they added political power. The group that surrounded Porfirio Díaz spoke of themselves, symbolically enough, as the "New Creoles."

Rural tradition comfortably allied itself with the invigorated capitalism of nineteenth-century Latin America. Positivism even provided a handy ideological umbrella for the two. Like so much of the economic and political thought in Latin America then and since, it recognized no incompatibility in the imposition of capitalist industrialization on a traditional rural base. With its emphasis on order and hierarchy, positivism assured the elites their venerable privileges, relative prosperity, selective progress, and held out promise of the same to the restless middle sectors. There was little promise, however, for the lower class majority.

But social inequality, paternalistic rule, privilege, and dependency clearly were incompatible with the new trends started during the last half of the century. The Chilean intellectual Miguel Cruchago Montt pointed out in his *Estudio sobre la organización económica y la hacienda pública de Chile* (Study of Chile's Economic Organization and Public Finances), published in 1878, that the colonial past dominated the present and frustrated development. The past could no longer exist unchallenged once Latin Americans began to think in terms of national development.

At the opening of the twentieth century, the Colombian Rafael Uribe stated that the basic economic question concerned the quality of life of the "people": "Are they able to satisfy their basic needs?" The reality was they could not. A majority of the Latin Americans were no better off at the dawn of the twentieth century than they had been a century earlier. In fact, a persuasive argument can be made that they were worse off. The negative response to Uribe's question foretold conflict.

THE POPULAR CHALLENGE

The Latin American nations marched toward progress to a tune played by the elites but not without discordant chords sounded by large numbers of the humble classes. For the majority of Latin Americans, progress was proving to mean increased concentration of lands in the hands of ever fewer owners; falling per capita food production with corollary rising food imports; greater impoverishment; less to eat; more vulnerability to the whims of an impersonal international market; uneven growth; increased unemployment and underemployment; social, economic, and political marginalization; and greater power in the hands of the privileged few. Ironically, the more the folk cultures were forced to integrate into world commerce, the fewer the material benefits they reaped. But poverty through progress must be understood in more than the material terms of declining wages, purchasing power, or nutritional levels. Traditional ways of life and the cultural arrangements they embodied were destroyed along with the indigenous villages. A tragic spiritual and cultural impoverishment accompanied the physical poverty.

The impoverished majority both bore the burden of the inequitable institutional structure and paid for the modernization enjoyed by the privileged. The deprivation, repression, and cultural attack of the majority by the minority created tensions that frequently gave rise to violence. The poor protested their increasing misfortunes as modernization increased. For their own part, the privileged were determined to modernize and to maintain the order required to do so. They freely used whatever force was necessary to accomplish both. Consequently, the imposition of progress stirred social disorder.

Indigenous rebellions flared up from Mexico to Chile. The indigenous refused to surrender their remaining lands quietly as the large estates intensified their encroachment. The arrival of the railroads, which accelerated those encroachments, spawned greater violence. Doubtless the major indigenous rebellion in terms of length, carnage, and significance in the Americas of the nineteenth century was the Caste War of Yucatan between the Mayas and the peninsula's whites and mestizos.

In the years after Mexico declared its independence, the sugar and henequen plantations had expanded to threaten the corn cultures of the Mayas by incorporating their lands into the latifundia and by impressing the Indians into service as debt peons. The Maya fought for their land and freedom. They defended their world. On the other side, the Yucatan elite professed that they fought for "the holy cause of order, humanity, and civilization." Much of the bloodiest fighting occurred during the period from 1847 to 1855, but the war lingered on until the early twentieth century. During those decades, the Mayas of eastern and southern Yucatan governed themselves.

Free from white domination, the Mayan rebels took the name of Cruzob, turned their backs on the white world, and developed their own culture, a synthesis of their Mayan inheritance and Spanish influences. The Cruzob retained their knowledge of agriculture and village and family organization from the pre-Columbian past. Unique to the Cruzob was the development of their own religion, based largely on their interpretation of Christianity. Unlike other syncretic regions of Latin America, it developed without dependence on the sporadic participation of Roman Catholic priests (to perform baptisms, marriages, or an occasional mass) and free from the critical eye of the white master. Incorporating the indigenous folkways, it strengthened the Cruzob and provided a spiritual base for independence other indigenous people lacked. What was notable about the Cruzob was the emergence of a viable indigenous alternative to Europeanization. Although infused with Spanish contributions, it bore a strong resemblance to the pre-Columbian Mayan society. Reviving their indigenous culture by repudiating "foreign" domination and substituting their own values for "foreign" ones, the Cruzob revitalized their society. They became masters of their own land again.

Powerful forces at work in the closing decades of the nineteenth century overwhelmed the Cruzob. The poor soil of Yucatan, exhausted under corn cultivation, no longer yielded sufficient food. Disease reduced the Mayan ranks faster than battle did. At the same time, Mexico, increasingly stable under Porfirio Díaz, showed less tolerance for the Cruzob and more determination to subdue them in order to exploit Yucatan. A treaty between Mexico and Great Britain closed British Honduras to the Cruzob, thus cutting off their single source of modern weapons and ammunition. Finally, the expanding wagon trails and railroads from northern Yucatan, which accompanied the spread of the prosperous henequen plantations, penetrated the Cruzob territory. A growing market for forest woods even sent the whites into the seemingly impenetrable forest redoubts of the Cruzob. Consequently a declining Cruzob population and relentless Mexican pressures brought to an end the Mayan independence of half a century. The long and tenacious resistance testified to the indigenous preference, a rejection of the modernization preferred by the elites.

The indigenous were not the only rebels. In Brazil, where slavery lingered after midcentury, the slaves vigorously protested their servitude. Sober members of the elites regarded the slave as "a volcano that constantly threatens society, a mine ready to explode," as one nineteenth-century intellectual phrased it in his study of Brazilian slavery. Foreign visitors also sensed the tensions created by slave society. Prince Adalbert of Prussia visited one large, well run plantation, which he praised as a model. After noting the seemingly friendly relations between master and slaves, he revealed, "The loaded guns and pistols hanging up in his [the master's] bedroom, however, showed that he had not entire confidence in them [the slaves] and indeed, he had more than once been obliged to face them with his loaded guns." The decade of the 1880s, just prior to emancipation, witnessed mounting slave resistance. The slaves fled the plantations, killed the masters, and burned fields and buildings. One fiery Afro-Brazilian abolitionist leader, Luis Gonzaga de Pinto Gama, declared, "Every slave who kills his master, no matter what the circumstances might be, kills in self-defense." He also preached the "right of insurrection." Once freed, African Americans throughout the Americas protested their poverty and the institutions that they felt perpetuated their problems. For example, Panama City seethed with racial tensions during the decades from 1850 to 1880. The African American, urban masses resented their depressed conditions and used violence—robberies, fires, rioting—as a means of protest. Many referred to the situation as a "race war," exacerbated by an economic reality in which the poor were black and the rich were white.

Rural rebellions abounded, signifying still other challenges to the elite institutions and commitment to modernization. More often than not, the ideology behind those rebellions was vague and contradictory. Somehow, the rebels hoped to save their lands, improve their standards of living, and share in the exercise of power. Two popular revolts, one in Brazil, another in Argentina, illustrate the motives, the violence, and the repression.

The Quebra-Quilo Revolt, which took place from late 1874 to early 1875, ranked high in significance because the subsistence farmers of Brazil's interior northeast succeeded in checking the government's new modernization drive (which was underway in 1871 but ineffectual by 1875). The causes of that revolt were not unique: new taxes and the threat smallholders felt from the large landowners absorbing their farms, complicated by the imposition of the metric system with the requirement of fees for official alteration and authentication of weights. A journalist covering the revolt called it "the direct consequence of the suffering and deprivation... of the working classes of the interior," whereas a participant claimed, "The fruit of the soil belongs to the people and tax ought not be paid on it." As riots multiplied in the marketplaces, the municipal and provincial authorities feared the "forces of Barbarism" were poised to sweep across the northeast. The campesinos were unusually successful. They ignored the new taxes, destroyed the new weights and measures, and burned official records and archives (thus protecting their informal title to the land by reducing to ashes the legal documentation). The subsistence farmers in most cases had taken physical possession and worked the land over the generations without title. They faced possible eviction by anyone who could show the proper paper authenticating legal ownership. By destroying the records, they removed evidence—the local notarial registers of land, for example—from use in judicial proceedings, thereby putting themselves on equal legal footing with the local landed elite. Momentarily, then, the sporadic riots that constituted the revolt achieved their goals, while temporarily frustrating the penetration of the elites into their region.

In Argentina, revolts shook the province of Santa Fe in 1893. Small farmers there protested a tax on wheat to pay for the government's innovations, including railroads, that seemed to favor the large landowners. Furthermore, they resented the fact that immigrants received land and preferential treatment denied the locals. In the meantime, social disorder rose dramatically in the Argentine province of Tucumán between 1876 and 1895. During those two decades, the number of arrests, ones involving mostly illiterate workers, jumped from under 2,000 per year to over 17,000, while the total population merely doubled during the same period.

Popular protest also assumed forms other than rebellion. Banditry and millenarian movements flourished in the nineteenth century. Thanks to the conceptual framework offered by E. J. Hobsbawm, it is possible with many cautions to consider banditry as a form of social protest and millenarianism as a type of popular revolution.

Religious in content, advocating a radical change in the world, millenarianism profoundly and totally rejects the present while expressing a passionate hope for a happier future. Those faithful to such ideas believe the world will come to a sudden, apocalyptic end but are vague about how this will happen and about the details of the new society that will replace the old. Although political revolutionaries also advocate a new society, they diverge from millenarianism because revolutionaries plan for and express ideas about how society will be remade. Millenarianists, on the other hand, expect the change to take place through divine intervention according to God's will and plan. Their duty is to prepare themselves for the new world. Obviously people hoping for a new and better life are expressing a form of dissatisfaction with the life they currently lead. Although they do not want confrontation, events may frequently force violence.

Brazil witnessed a remarkable array of millenarian movements. Doubt-less the best known took place in the dry, impoverished backlands of the state of Bahia where the mystic Antônio the Counselor gathered the faithful between 1893 and 1897. Thousands flocked to his settlement at Canudos to listen to the Counselor preach. They stayed to establish a flourishing agrar-ian community. He alienated the government by advising his adherents not to pay taxes. Furthermore, his patriarchal ideas smacked of monarchism to the recently established republican government in Rio de Janeiro. The Church authorities denounced him, resenting his influence over the masses. The local landlords disliked him because he siphoned off the rural workers and stalemated the expansion of their fazendas. Those powerful enemies de-cided to arrest Antônio and scatter the settlers at Canudos. However, they failed to consider the strength and determination of his followers. It took four military campaigns, all the modern armaments the Brazilian army could muster, and countless lives to suppress the millenarian movement. The final campaign directed by the minister of war himself devastated the settlement at Canudos house by house. The people refused to surrender. The epic struggle inspired Euclydes da Cunha's 1902 masterpiece, *Rebellion in the Backlands.*

Messianic movements flourished among the Andean people after the conquest. They yearned for a return to an order, basically the traditional Incan one destroyed by the Spanish conquest, that would benefit them rather than the outsider. Exemplary of such movements in the nineteenth century was one that occurred among the Bolivian people of Curuyaqui in 1891 and 1892. An individual called Tumpa, known as "the supreme being," appeared in the community announcing his mission "to liberate them from the whites." Under his prophetic new system, Tumpa promised that the whites would work for the indigenous. His followers took up arms as urged by the mes-sianic leader; the whites fled to the cities, and the army arrived to brutally crush the uprising. The carnage disproved at least two of Tumpa's prophe-cies: first, that only water would issue forth from the soldier's guns, and sec-ond, that anyone who did die for the cause would return to life in three days.

Northwestern Mexico was the scene of the miracle cures of Teresa Urrea, referred to by hundreds of thousands of devotees as Teresita or the Saint of Cabora. In 1889, after a severe psychological shock, she lapsed into a comatose state. Considered dead, she regained life just prior to her burial. She reported having spoken to the Blessed Virgin, who conferred on her the power to cure. By 1891, pilgrims flooded Cabora seeking her help. Teresita's compassion for the poor earned her the devotion of the masses and the suspicion of the Díaz government. The Yaqui and Mayo confided in her and unburdened their suf-ferings before her. Believing she enjoyed influence with God, they pressed her for help and advice. In 1890, the Tarahumara mountain village of Tomochic adopted Teresita as their saint, placing a statue of her in their Church. The vil-lage began to modify its Roman Catholicism to a more indigenous religion focused on the Saint of Cabora. The next year Tomochic rebelled against the government and requested Teresita to interpret God's will to them. The government reacted immediately and harshly, but it still took several armed expeditions to quell the rebellion. The village was destroyed, and not a man or boy over thirteen years of age survived the slaughter. In mid-May of 1892, a group of approximately two hundred Mayo attacked the town of Navojoa shouting, "Viva la Santa de Cabora!" Considering her a dangerous agitator of the masses, the Díaz government exiled Teresa Urrea to the United States. Teresita, herself opposed to violence, had served more as a figurehead, a catalyst, a remarkable charismatic personality, whose compassion gave unity of expression to the miserable masses of northwestern Mexico.

Banditry attracted the desperate, those who had lost out in the system whether they were the poor or members of the impoverished gentry. Whatever else banditry might have signified, it was as much a means of protesting injustice or righting wrongs as it was of equalizing wealth or taking political revenge. Although unsympathetic to banditry, the Brazilian jurist of the mid-nineteenth century, Tavares Bastos, realized that the bandits often were victims of the State who, no longer confiding in its laws, made their own justice.

Bandits roamed the Brazilian interior in the nineteenth century, particularly the impoverished northeast, where many won the admiration of the poor and the respect of the wealthy, who not infrequently co-opted them and utilized their services. Some scholarship correlates the rise of banditry in the late nineteenth century with the breakdown of the patriarchal order in the countryside. Brazilian popular poetry abounds with tales of the bandit hero. A well-known poem sung at the beginning of the twentieth century related the history of Antônio Silvino, who became a bandit in 1896 to avenge an injustice: His father was slain by a police official who went unpunished by the government. Others relate the adventures of Josuíno Brilhante, also seemingly forced into banditry to avenge injustices against his family. He assaulted the rich and distributed their goods and money among the poor, boasting that he never robbed for himself.

Banditry characterized much of Spanish America as well. Mexican banditry flourished, and interestingly enough, regions that produced bandits, such as Chalco-Río Frío, eastern Morelos, and northwestern Puebla, spawned agrarian revolutionaries before the century ended, providing further evidence of the social dimension banditry could assume on occasion. Peru offers numerous examples of peasant bandits. In his study of them, Enrique López Albujar described banditry as "a protest, a rebellion, a deviation, or a simple means of subsistence." He concluded that nineteenth-century Peruvian banditry produced an array of folk heroes because those bandits corrected injustices, robbed to help the poor, and protested social and economic inequities. For their part, Chilean officials tended to lump together indigenous and bandits of the rugged Andes as "criminals." They also routinely complained that local populations supported the bandits, thus facilitating their antiestablishment activities.

The motives and activities of the bandits varied widely, but at least in part they could be explained as protests against the wrongs of society as they viewed it. Because of their strength and because they often opposed the elites and official institutions, they received the support, indeed the admiration, of large numbers of the humble classes, who often hid them, lied to the authorities to protect them, guided them through strange terrain, and fed them. To the poor, the bandits were caudillos who by default helped them to sustain their folk cultures and deflect modernization.

The folk by no means rejected change simply to preserve the past unaltered. Rather, they wished to mediate change over a longer period of time. They opposed those changes imposed by the elites that they judged harmful or potentially threatening. They perceived the threat that the export economy and the capitalist mentality promoting it posed to their remaining lands and to their control over their own labor. The elites showed little patience and less tolerance with folk preferences, caution, and concerns. They dealt severely with any protest and thus further raised the level of violence. In the last analysis the elites triumphed. After all, they controlled the police, the militia, and the military. Furthermore, the popular protests tended to be local and uncoordinated. Thus, despite the frequency of such protests, the elites imposed their will and their brand of progress. The triumph of that progress set the course for twentieth-century history in Latin America. It bequeathed a legacy of mass poverty and continued conflict.

RECOMMENDED READINGS

Bulmer-Thomas, Victor. *The Economic History of Latin America Since Independence*, 2nd ed. New York, NY: Cambridge University Press, 2003.

Burns, E. Bradford. *The Poverty of Progress: Latin America in the Nineteenth Century*. Berkeley: University of California Press, 1980.

Charlip, Julie A. *Cultivating Coffee: The Farmers of Carazo, Nicaragua, 1880–1930*. Athens: Ohio University Press, 2003.

Hobsbawm, Eric. *Bandits*. 4th ed. New York: New Press, 2000.

Lauria Santiago, Aldo. *An Agrarian Republic: Commercial Agriculture and the Politics of Peasant Communities in El Salvador, 1823–1914*. Pittsburgh, PA: University of Pittsburgh Press, 1999.

Levine, Robert M. *Vale of tears: Revisiting the Canudos Massacre in Northeastern Brazil, 1893–1897*. Berkeley: University of California Press, 1992.

Reed, Nelson A. *The Caste War of the Yucatan*. Stanford, CA: Stanford University Press, 2001.

Topik, Steven C., and Allen Wells, eds. *The Second Conquest of Latin America: Coffee, Henequen, and Oil During the Export Boom, 1850–1930*. Austin: University of Texas Press, 1998.

CHAPTER 6

NEW ACTORS ON AN OLD STAGE

As Latin America approached its independence centennial, two trends, one of external and the other of internal origin, emerged with greater clarity. The first was the emergence of the United States as a major world power. Motivated by economic interests, U.S. leaders adopted a philosophy of Manifest Destiny, justifying aggression by claims of concern about security and by blatantly racist attitudes toward Latin America. The second trend was the emergence of two new significant population groups within Latin America: a small middle class, which aspired to the wealth of the elites via the path of progress shown by the United States, and the working class, which sought to improve its lot more through European examples of labor unions, introduced by the flood of immigrants to such countries as Brazil and Argentina. Together, the United States and the Latin American middle sectors helped to shape Latin American history during the twentieth century. What were their motivations and goals? How would they influence the flow of history?

THE PRESENCE OF THE UNITED STATES

Foreign influence, especially Great Britain's, shaped much of the historical course of Latin America during the nineteenth century. At first, Great Britain had no serious rivals to its economic domination of the region. But as the United States grew stronger, its capitalists and politicians were determined to spread across the North American continent and to dominate the Caribbean. By the early twentieth century, the United States had succeeded in doing both and was well on its way to replacing Britain's century-long domination of Latin America. Concerns for security and desires for trade shaped U.S. attitudes and policies toward Latin America. Obviously the United States and Latin America shared the same geography, the Western Hemisphere, thus being neighbors, in a certain romantic sense, even though much of the United States was closer to Europe than it was to most of South America.

Despite the tough talk of the Monroe Doctrine in 1823, the United States was not at the time a world power, and Washington officials ignored the proclamation for decades. Meanwhile, European powers intervened in Latin America at will: The British reoccupied the Falkland Islands despite vigorous Argentine protests, the French intervened in Mexico and the Plata area, and the French and British blockaded Buenos Aires, all without the United States reminding the European interlopers of the content or intention of Monroe's statement. Only when the British and French maneuvered to

United States Relations with Latin America

1823	Monroe Doctrine declares Western hemisphere closed to European recolonization and pledges that attacks against Latin America would be viewed as attack against United States.
1835–1845	Anglo-American settlers in Texas revolt against Mexico, establish independent nation, and finally join United States.
1845	John L. O'Sullivan, editor of *Democratic Review*, coins phrase "Manifest Destiny," belief by many in United States that the country's westward expansion was ordained by God.
1846–1848	War of North American Invasion (known in United States as Mexican-American War).
1848	Treaty of Guadalupe Hidalgo cedes northern half of Mexico to United States.
1850	United States and Great Britain agree in Clayton-Bulwer Treaty that neither power will build a Nicaraguan canal without the other's approval. No Nicaraguan participates in the treaty.
1853	Gadsden Purchase from Mexico gives United States territory for a railroad route across southern Arizona and New Mexico.
1854	American diplomats issue Ostend Manifesto, urging acquisition of Cuba from Spain by force if necessary.
1855	U.S. filibuster William Walker and mercenaries help Nicaraguan Liberals defeat Conservative rivals, only to turn on their allies. Walker declares himself president and rules for two years, with U.S. recognition.
1857	U.S. entrepreneur Cornelius Vanderbilt funds war against Walker, who disrupts Vanderbilt's steamship business.
1860	British forces capture Walker and turn him over to Honduras, where he is shot by firing squad.
1865	United States mobilizes troops along Mexican border to threaten French occupying army.
1889	First Inter-American Conference held in Washington, D.C.
1895	United States forces Great Britain into arbitration in boundary dispute with Venezuela. In one of its first acts of "gunboat diplomacy," the United States sends the *U.S.S Wachusett* to Guatemala to defend North American lives and property.

1898–1902	United States invades Cuba as independence forces are close to defeating Spain. United States occupies Cuba and takes control of Puerto Rico, Guam, and the Philippines.
1898	United States intervenes in Nicaragua.
1899	United States intervenes in Nicaragua.
1899	United Fruit Company (UFCO) formed, buys seven independent companies in Honduras.
1901	Great Britain cedes right to build a Central American canal to United States in Hay-Pauncefote Treaty. Again, no Nicaraguan participates in negotiations.
1901	United States threatens not to end occupation of Cuba unless new constitution includes Platt Amendment, giving United States right to intervene in Cuba.
1903	Theodore Roosevelt sends gunboats to Panama to prevent Colombia from fighting region's independence movement. United States is rewarded with the Hay-Bunau-Varilla Treaty, giving United States sovereignty "in perpetuity" in Panama Canal Zone. United States intervenes in Honduras and Dominican Republic.
1904	Theodore Roosevelt issues his Corollary to the Monroe Doctrine, declaring United States to be policeman of the Caribbean. United States forces place Dominican Republic under a customs receivership.
1905	United States Marines land in Honduras.
1906–1909	U.S. forces occupy Cuba.
1909–1913	William Howard Taft promotes "Dollar Diplomacy," aimed at creating stability abroad to promote U.S. business interests.
1909–1910	U.S. forces help Nicaraguan Conservatives overthrow José Santos Zelaya.
1912–1925	U.S. Marines intervene in Nicaragua.
1912	U.S. Army forces land in Cuba, Panama, and Honduras.
1914	Panama Canal opens.
1914	U.S. Navy fights rebels in Dominican Republic. U.S. Army invades Haiti. U.S. forces shell and then occupy Vera Cruz, Mexico.
1915–1934	U.S. Marines intervene in Haiti.
1916	Pancho Villa raids Columbus, New Mexico. U.S. forces invade Dominican Republic.
1916–1917	U.S. Expeditionary Force under Gen. John J. "Black Jack" Pershing unsuccessfully pursues Pancho Villa in northern Mexico.
1916–1924	U.S. Marines occupy Dominican Republic.
1917–1922	U.S. forces invade and occupy Cuba.
1918	U.S. army lands in Panama to protect United Fruit plantations.
1918–1919	United States intervenes in Mexico.
1919	U.S. Marines land in Honduras during presidential campaign.
1920–1921	U.S. troops support a coup in Guatemala.
1921	United States intervenes in Costa Rica and Panama.
1924	U.S. Army intervenes in Honduras during elections.
1925	U.S. Army lands in Panama during a general strike.
1926–1933	U.S. Marines occupy Nicaragua and fight nationalistic forces of Augusto César Sandino.

thwart the union of Texas with the United States did President John Tyler invoke the principles of the doctrine in 1842 to warn the Europeans to keep out of hemispheric affairs. Indeed, as later used, the doctrine provided a handy shield for North American expansion, well underway by the mid-1840s. As President James Polk gazed westward toward California, he notified the Europeans that his country opposed any transfer of territory in the New World from one European state to another or from a nation of the Western Hemisphere to a European nation. However, by his interpretation the Monroe Doctrine did not prohibit territorial changes among the nations of this hemisphere. Such an interpretation complemented the annexation of Texas by the United States in 1845 and of Arizona, New Mexico, and California in 1848. Expansionist sentiment rose to a fever pitch as the stars and stripes fluttered across the continent toward the Pacific Ocean. An editorial in the influential *De Bow's Commercial Review* in 1848 expressed the ebullient mood of a confident nation:

> The North Americans will spread out far beyond their present bounds. They will encroach again and again upon their neighbors. New territories will be planted, declare their independence, and be annexed. We have New Mexico and California! We will have Old Mexico and Cuba!

The editorial reflected the era's dominant theme: *manifest destiny*, an expression coined in 1845 by John L. O'Sullivan, editor of the *Democratic Review*. The term meant that the United States, as a result of Anglo-Saxon superiority, was destined to absorb its neighbors. As O'Sullivan put it: "This continent is for white people, and not only the continent but the islands adjacent, and the Negro must be kept in slavery."

Initial U.S. expansionist efforts were deeply entwined with the issue of slavery, both in the United States and in Latin America. O'Sullivan's brother-in-law was Cristobal Madán, a Cuban planter who served as leader of the annexationist lobby in New York in 1845. Madán represented the Cuban planters who wanted to join the United States as a slave state. Slave owners in the United States south looked longingly at Cuba, Mexico, and Central America as potential slave states.

Great Britain served as the major check on U.S. expansion southward into Middle America and the Caribbean during the midnineteenth century. The best the United States could arrange at the time was an agreement in 1850, the Clayton-Bulwer Treaty, in which both nations promised not to occupy, fortify, colonize, or otherwise exercise domination over Central America. Specifically, neither country would seek to build an interoceanic canal. The treaty temporarily checked the territorial expansion of both nations into troubled and tempting republics that otherwise stood helpless before the two aggressive Anglo-Saxon powers. Significantly, no representatives of the targeted Latin American nations were a party to the treaty. At about the same time the attention of the United States focused inward once again, as a divided nation girded itself for internal strife.

While civil war rent the United States, several European nations pursued their own adventures in the New World. Spain reannexed the Dominican Republic and fought Peru and Chile. France intervened in Mexico. Only after it became apparent that the North was winning the U.S. Civil War and was determined to oppose European ventures in the Western Hemisphere did Spain depart from the Dominican Republic and return the Chincha Islands to Peru. When Napoleon III hesitated to withdraw French forces from Mexico, the government in Washington dispatched a large army to the Mexican border to help the French emperor make up his mind. Once these European threats to Latin America had ended, the United States seemed content to ignore the region, at least for the moment, while the nation concentrated its energies on reconstruction, railroad building, and industrialization.

But the rapid industrial growth of the post-Civil War years eventually prompted United States business people and leaders to search for new markets, and none seemed more promising than Latin America, long the domain of European trade. One of the most remarkable secretaries of state, James G. Blaine, understanding the need for friendship and cooperation among the nations of the hemisphere, sought to stimulate more intimate commercial relations as a logical means to solidify the inter-American community. The United States had long appreciated the strategic importance of Latin America but had been slow to develop its trade relations with the huge area. During the second half of the nineteenth century, North American commerce with and investments in Latin America rose gradually. In the vigorous industrial age that had begun in the United States, Secretary of State Blaine envisioned a fraternal hemispheric trade in which the United States supplied the manufactured goods and Latin America the raw products. With that idea in mind, he presided over the first Inter-American Conference, held in Washington in 1889–1890. Although cordiality characterized the sessions, it became increasingly obvious that the Latin Americans were less interested in placing orders for the new industrial products than they were in containing the expansion of an ambitious neighbor by obtaining a promise of respect for the sovereignty of their nations. The times augured ill for such a promise. In fact, at that very moment, a rising tide of sentiment favoring expansion once again swept the United States.

Others in the United States realized as Blaine did that Latin America contained great wealth and potential, but unlike the secretary of state they showed less subtlety in coveting it. In the eyes of many, the Latin Americans appeared too slow in fulfilling the destiny that nature had charted for the area. A growing number of U.S. citizens thought that Latin America needed a dose of "Protestant virtues and Yankee know-how" to turn potential into reality. The Reverend Josiah Strong summed up much of the opinion of his fellow countrymen in his influential book *Our Country,* published in 1885, when he wrote, "Having developed peculiarly aggressive traits calculated to impress its institutions upon mankind, [the United States] will spread itself over the earth. If I read not amiss, this powerful race will move down Central and South America, out upon the islands of the sea, over upon Africa and beyond. And can anyone doubt that the result of this competition of races will be the 'survival of the fittest'?" Imbued with the Spencerian and Darwinian philosophy popular at the time, the good reverend spoke with the enthusiasm, confidence, and arrogance of his generation.

Other powerful voices soon echoed his views. Senator Henry Cabot Lodge spoke of "our rightful supremacy in the Western Hemisphere." Naval officer, historian, and strategist Alfred T. Mahan lobbied for a bigger and better navy—preferably able to quickly cross the continent and protect both coasts. Senator Albert J. Beveridge put his faith in a still more potent force: "God has marked the American people as His chosen Nation to finally lead to the regeneration of the world. . . . We are trustees of the world's progress, guardians of its righteous peace." Secretary of State Richard Olney announced to the world in 1895 that the United States was supreme in the Western Hemisphere, where its will would be done.

Thus, by the end of the nineteenth century, government, religious, and business leaders alike spoke approvingly of expanding world markets and of a global foreign policy. Their talk soon led to action: U.S. overseas expansion into the Pacific and the Caribbean. Significantly that expansion began after the conquest of the frontier of the American West, after several decades of impressive industrial growth, and during the economic difficulties of the 1890s. Its chance came in 1898, when the United States intervened in Cuba's war for independence from Spain. The quick victory marked the debut of the United States as a world power embarked upon a new international course of extracontinental expansion, which one influential journalist of the day characterized admiringly as "the imperialism of liberty." Washington annexed Puerto Rico and made Cuba a protectorate, a state of dependency that virtually lasted for thirty-five years. Formal occupation ended only after United States insistence in 1901 that Cuba attach the Platt amendment to its constitution. Written by U.S. Senator Orville Platt, the amendment read, "Cuba consents that the United States may exercise the right to intervene for the protection of Cuban independence, the maintenance of a government adequate for the protection of life, property, and individual liberty."

U.S. officials doubted that Cubans could be trusted to manage their own affairs, a point of view that grew out of racism. In a speech about the status of the Philippines after the war, Senator Beveridge articulated common views about the people both freed and conquered by the Spanish–American War:

> We will not renounce our part in the mission of our race, trustee, under God, of the civilization of the world. . . . Mr. President, this question is deeper than

The United States became a world power and a threat to Latin America, with its intervention in Cuba's war of independence, right down to the renaming of the conflict as the Spanish–American War in 1898. In this engraving, Frederic Remington, special artist for *Harper's Weekly*, shows "The Storming of San Juan, The Head of the Charge." (Library of Congress)

any question of party politics, deeper than any question of the isolated policy of our country even; deeper even than any question of constitutional power. It is elemental. It is racial. God has not been preparing the English-speaking and Teutonic peoples for a thousand years for nothing but vain and idle self-contemplation and self-admiration. No! He has made us the master organizers of the world to establish system where chaos reigns.

Next, the United States turned to the issue of constructing an inter-oceanic canal, spurred by military and commercial considerations. The first step toward the realization of a canal was to abrogate the old Clayton-Bulwer Treaty. Under international pressure, London agreed in the Hay-Pauncefote Treaty in 1901 to permit the United States to build, operate, and fortify a canal across the isthmus. Washington then proceeded to negotiate with Colombia for rights across Panama, but the Senate in Bogotá balked at the terms suggested. At that point, the Panamanians seceded from Colombia and declared their independence on November 3, 1903. Panamanians, far from Bogotá, had long sought independence; but by rebelling at this time, they were guaranteed to have powerful outside support. They were helped by the presence of two U.S. gunboats, the Nashville and the Dixie, which prevented Colombian troops from countering the bloodless Panamanian insurrection. The commander of the Nashville had orders to take over the railroad, preventing the Colombian troops from boarding the railroad to travel from Colón to Panama City. Within a week of Panama's declaration of independence, the United States also sent the Atlanta, Maine, Mayflower, and Prairie to Colón and the Boston, Marblehead, Concord, and Wyoming to Panama City.

The Panamanians found their new sovereignty heavily compromised by the treaty signed fifteen days later by U.S. Secretary of State John Hay and the Frenchman Philippe Bunau-Varilla, an international adventurer who purported to represent Panama's interests. The treaty he signed in Panama's name granted the United States "in perpetuity" control of a ten-mile strip across the isthmus with power and jurisdiction "as if it were sovereign." It was negotiated without consulting the Panamanians. Work on the canal began in 1904 and terminated a decade later. Controversy over the canal and the treaty that made it possible raged until the canal was finally handed back to the Panamanians on December 31, 1999.

The trespassing of the North American giant on Latin American sovereignty evoked protest and aroused distrust. Many Latin American intellectuals of the period spoke out to denounce "the Yankee imperialism." Physically unable to prevent the interventions, Latin American governments sought recourse in international law. They labored long and determinedly to persuade Washington to renounce by treaty recourse to intervention.

But Theodore Roosevelt, who led his Rough Riders in Cuba before becoming U.S. president in 1904, expressed the new U.S. sentiment well in what became known as the Roosevelt Corollary to the Monroe Doctrine: "Chronic wrongdoing, or an impotence which results in a general loosening of the ties of civilized society, may in America, as elsewhere, ultimately require intervention by some civilized nation, and in the Western Hemisphere the adherence of the United States to the Monroe Doctrine may force the United States, however reluctantly, in flagrant cases of such wrongdoing or impotence, to the exercise of an international police power."

National rhetoric reflected that attitude. In his study of the relations between the United States and Latin America published in 1908, George W. Crichfield spoke pompously of the duty to impose "civilization" on the Latin Americans: "The United States is in honor bound to maintain law and order in South America, and we may just as well take complete control of several of the countries, and establish decent governments while we are about it." More than half the nations, he huffed, had "sinned away their day of grace. They are semibarbarous centers of rapine. . . . They are a reproach to the civilization of the twentieth century."

Diplomacy dictated that such ideas be expressed more subtly, but there can be no doubt that the same sentiments governed Washington's twentieth-century behavior in Latin America in the twin pursuits of trade and security.

President Theodore Roosevelt posed at the controls of a steam shovel at the Culebra Cut of the Panama Canal in 1906, three years after helping Panama secede from Colombia, which had turned down the U.S. offer for a canal route. (Library of Congress)

Theoretically, the United States was ready to put aside the gunboat diplomacy of the turn of the century for the more genteel "dollar diplomacy." But the United States did not hesitate to send troops in to protect those dollars. President William Howard Taft (1908–1912) left no doubt of where his government stood on those matters. Influenced by his experiences as the first civil governor (1901–1904) of the U.S.-controlled Philippine Islands and provisional governor of Cuba (1906), he announced that his foreign policy would "include active intervention to secure our merchandise and our capitalists opportunity for profitable investment."

The United States intervened militarily in Latin America twenty-three times between 1890 and 1913. While U.S. troops were sent to Argentina in 1890 and Chile in 1891, the countries that bore the brunt of U.S. domination were in the circum-Caribbean, an area the United States came to see as its backyard. Troops went to Nicaragua in 1894, 1896, 1898, 1899, 1907, 1910, and 1912, which was the beginning of a twenty-year occupation. Neighboring Honduras also had its share of interventions: 1903, 1907, 1911, and 1912. Haiti, Panama, Puerto Rico, the Dominican Republic and Mexico all felt the U.S. wrath.

The rationale for U.S. interventions varied. In the cases of the Dominican Republic and Haiti, the marines landed ostensibly to forestall threatened European intervention to collect debts; in Nicaragua, the country's alleged chaotic finances partially explained the U.S. presence, but probably more significant was the rumor that the Nicaraguan government might sell exclusive canal rights through its territory to either Japan or Great Britain. Threats, real or imagined, against U.S. citizens or property occasioned other U.S. interventions.

Of all these invasions, it was the intervention in the Cuban Independence War in 1898 that truly shook all of Latin America. The United States dubbed the conflict the Spanish–American War, an interesting act of naming that removes Cuba as an actor and arrogates the name of both continents to the United States alone. The United States had long been interested in Cuba, dating back to Thomas Jefferson's unsuccessful attempt to purchase it from the Spanish in 1808. Despite its colonial status, by the 1840s, half of Cuba's trade was with the United States. Cubans had tried to win independence from Spain in the Ten Years' War (1868–1878) and rose up again in 1895. By 1898, Cuba was close to winning its objective. The United States responded by sending the U.S. Maine to Havana, ostensibly to protect U.S. citizens. The ship was well received by the Spanish authorities—the captain of the Maine even went off to a bullfight with the Spanish commander. On February 15, 1898, the Maine exploded, killing 266 soldiers, most likely because of the gunpowder that it carried. The United States blamed the Spanish and entered the war in April. By December, it was over. Theodore Roosevelt labeled it a "splendid little war." The results for the United States were splendid indeed, gaining control of Guam, the Philippines, and Puerto Rico. Convinced that Cubans could not govern themselves, the United States marines occupied the country from 1899–1903. The condition for U.S. departure was that Cuba add to its constitution the Platt Amendment, which gave the United States the right to intervene in Cuba whenever it saw fit.

The reason for United States interest was clear. In 1900, the United States had $50 million in investments in Cuba. Economic interests drove U.S. policy, especially the desire to supplant Great Britain as the dominant trade partner. By 1914, the United States had $140 million in direct investment in Latin America, $79 million of that in Central America, and nearly $31 million in Latin American public debt. But these figures represented only 14 percent of the region's public debt and 18 percent of direct investment. In 1913, only 25 percent of Latin America's trade was with the United States. The United States was intent on supplanting Europe as the dominant economic force in the region. But U.S. economic interests collided with a new sense of nationalism in the region.

Latin Americans had admired the United States from its Declaration of Independence to its spectacular industrialization in the late nineteenth century. But by the end of the nineteenth century, some Latin Americans were beginning to doubt the relevance of foreign models in general and the intent of the United States in particular.

José Martí was one of the first prominent Latin Americans to voice these doubts. Martí's critiques had particular salience because he was a renowned poet and essayist throughout Latin America even before he became the "apostle" of Cuban independence. Furthermore, he lived in New York, as his words are usually translated, "in the belly of the beast," while organizing the Cuban independence movement and learning about the United States. (His literal phrase was, "I have lived in the monster and I know its entrails; my sling is David's.") Martí chastised the United States for its expansionist designs as well as the Cubans who were interested in annexing the island to the U.S. government. Martí died in battle in 1895, before the U.S. invasion and occupation of Cuba.

The U.S. role in turning the Cuban War of Independence into the Spanish–American War made many more Latin American elites see the Colossus of the North in a different light. In 1900, José Enrique Rodó of Uruguay published *Ariel*, an essay in which, after Shakespeare's *The Tempest*, he characterized the United States as Caliban, the evil spirit of materialism and positivism, in contrast to Latin America's Ariel, the lover of beauty and truth. He cautioned Latin Americans against mimicking the efficient but soulless United States and to appreciate the moral and spiritual superiority of Latin America.

Rodó's concerns were echoed in 1913 by Peruvian diplomat Francisco Garcia Calderón, who wrote, "Warnings, advice, distrust, invasion of capital, plans of financial hegemony all these justify the anxiety of the southern peoples. . . . Neither irony nor grace nor scepticism, gifts of the old civilizations, can make way against the plebeian brutality, the excessive optimism, the violent individualism of the [North American] people."

It was no wonder that Porfirio Díaz supposedly lamented, "Poor Mexico! So far from God, so close to the United States."

THE NEW MIDDLE CLASS

Latin American elites were challenged from within their countries as well as by foreign powers. In the cities there emerged a small middle class, which grew in size and influence over the course of the twentieth century. Members of the liberal professions, schoolteachers and professors, bureaucrats, military officers, businessmen, merchants, and those involved in the nascent industrialization composed the ranks of that group. The common denominator of the middle sectors rested on the fact that they were neither admitted to the ranks of the traditional elite nor associated with the lower and poorer ranks of society. The observant James Bryce noted during his tour of South America at the end of the first decade of the twentieth century, "In the cities there exists, between the wealthy and the workingmen, a considerable body of professional men, shopkeepers, and clerks, who are rather less of a defined middle class than they might be in European countries." They possessed a strong urge to improve their lot and tended to imitate, as far as it was possible, the elite.

Initially, the heirs of the creoles and mazombos tended to predominate in the middle sectors, but increasing numbers of mulattos and mestizos entered their ranks as well. Education and military service provided two of the surest paths of upward mobility, but initially the climb was too steep for any but the exceptional or the favored. In many of the Latin American nations, the mestizos or mulattos formed the largest part of the population. Mexico, Guatemala, Ecuador, Peru, Bolivia, and Paraguay, for example, had large mestizo populations, whereas the Dominican Republic, Venezuela, and Brazil had large mulatto populations. Representatives of the mestizos and mulattos entered the middle sectors in large numbers during the last decades of the nineteenth century and claimed their right to play a political and economic role in their nations' destinies. In some cases, the traditional social elites accommodated their ambitions; in others, their frustrations mounted as they were excluded from positions of control, prestige, or wealth.

Although few in number, the dominant presence of the middle sectors in the capital city of each nation allowed them to wield influence far out of proportion to their size. A high percentage of the intellectuals, authors, teachers, and journalists came from their ranks, and they had a powerful voice in expressing what passed for public opinion in the late nineteenth century. By the end of the century, they had enough direction to increasingly exert influence on the course of events in some nations, particularly in Argentina, Brazil, Chile, Mexico, Uruguay, and Costa Rica. Only later were they large and articulate enough to wield a similar influence in other countries.

Only an educated guess permits some approximation of the size of the middle sectors. At the end of the nineteenth century it is estimated that Mexico had an urban middle group numbering roughly three-quarters of a million, while another quarter of a million constituted a rural middle group. In contrast, there was an urban proletariat of more than one-third of a million and a huge peon class of eight million working on the haciendas. In Mexico, Chile, Brazil, Argentina, and Uruguay, the middle sectors may have included as many as 10 percent of the population by the turn of the century. In many of the other countries, it fell far short of that.

The swelling tide of foreign immigration contributed to the growth of the middle sectors. Many of the new arrivals were from the lower class, but still a high percentage represented Europe's middle class, and there was a high incidence of upward mobility among the immigrants in the lands of

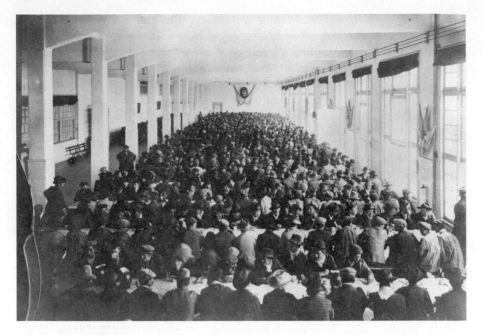

Thousands of immigrants flocked to Argentina, as illustrated by this crowd of men in the dining room of an immigrant hotel in Buenos Aires, photographed between 1890 and 1923. (Library of Congress)

their adoption. In Argentina in 1914, immigrants held 46 percent of the jobs associated with the middle sectors. Chile received only 100,000 European immigrants before World War I. They constituted at that time only 4 percent of the population, yet owned 32 percent of Chile's commercial establishments and 49 percent of the industries.

Certain characteristics of the middle sectors increasingly became evident. The majority lived in the cities and boasted an above-average education. Their income level placed them between the wealthy few and the impoverished many. Although the heterogeneous middle sector never unified, on occasion a majority might agree on specific goals, such as improved or expanded education, further industrialization, or more rapid modernization, and on certain methods to achieve them, such as the formation of political parties or the exaltation of nationalism. They consented to the use of the government to foment change, and with minimal dissension they welcomed the government's participation and even direction of the economy. Still, political preferences within their ranks varied from far right to far left.

Although the middle sectors expressed strong nationalistic sentiments, they also looked abroad for models, as did the elites. This contradiction was expressed most emphatically in their ambivalence toward the United States: on the one hand, a model of progress, and on the other a too-powerful neighbor with aggressive tendencies. Their nationalism prompted frequent outcries against "Yankee imperialism." Yet the middle sectors regarded the United States as the example of a New World nation that had "succeeded," an example of the "progress" preached but not always practiced in aristocratic Europe. True, the United States embraced impressive examples of poverty as well as wealth, but it seemed that large numbers, even a majority, lived somewhere between those extremes so characteristic of Latin American society. The aggressive strength of their counterparts in the United States inspired the Latin American middle sector.

They attributed part of the apparent success of the United States to industrialization and education, and so they prescribed industrialization as a panacea for their national ills. The high North American literacy rate seemed to provide the proper preparation for an industrial society, and the middle sectors appreciated the mobility that education afforded the citizens of that technological nation. The American educator Horace Mann became a revered figure to many Latin American leaders, and they eagerly imported not only his doctrines but also the Yankee books and schoolteachers to go with them. Domingo F. Sarmiento met Mann, imbibed his ideas, and as president of Argentina (1868–1874) hired New England teachers to direct the new normal schools he established. President Justo Rufino Barrios in Guatemala (1873–1885) encouraged the North American missionaries to set up Protestant schools. Finally, the comfortable life style of the U.S. middle class, with its increasing arsenal of consumer goods, impressed the Latin American candidates for middle-class status.

In the early twentieth century, middle-class women began to organize to demand suffrage. As in the United States, women in Cuba and Brazil were often drawn into the feminist movement through their roles in the struggle for abolition of slavery. The middle-class reformers who sought suffrage had no radical reforms in mind. In fact, many did not expect women to hold public office and merely wanted the right to vote for male candidates. Their position often was a moral one: Women could bring their superior morality to bear on the political world through voting, without actually having to participate in the rough and tumble of political contests. Not all feminists agreed with the goal of suffrage. Some argued that it gave too much credence to an ineffective political system in which votes were generally meaningless anyway. Many were more concerned about material needs.

The middle sectors favored reform over revolution. They sought entrance into the national institutions, not necessarily destruction of them. In fact, they demonstrated a preference for economic improvement and less concern with altering political structures. Although the elites at first distrusted the middle sectors, they eventually understood their potential as allies and not only incorporated them into their privileged institutions but also in due course let them administer them—a trust that the middle class did not betray.

Women's Suffrage in Latin America

Ecuador	1929
Brazil	1932
Uruguay	1932
Cuba	1934
El Salvador	1939
Dominican Republic	1942
Panama	1945
Guatemala	1945
Costa Rica	1945
Venezuela	1947
Argentina	1947
Chile	1949
Haiti	1950
Bolivia	1952
Mexico	1953
Honduras	1955
Nicaragua	1955
Peru	1955
Colombia	1957
Paraguay	1961

THE WORKING CLASS

The elites were less sure of the other significant element of the urban population: the working class. As urbanization and industrialization expanded, a larger, more cohesive, and militant proletariat appeared. Slowly becoming aware of their common problems and goals, these workers unionized despite relentless government opposition. The first unions appeared after 1850, evolving from mutual aid societies. They tended to be small, ephemeral, and local organizations.

The typographers, stevedores, railroad employees, artisans, miners, and textile workers were the first to organize, and most of the early union activity concentrated in Buenos Aires, Montevideo, Havana, Santiago-Valparaíso, and Mexico City as well as in the mining regions of northern Chile and central Mexico. By 1914, about half a dozen nations boasted well-organized unions, and at least some attempt had been made in the rest to institute them.

In Chile, union organizing was initiated by maritime, port, and rail workers, who quickly found support among the nitrate miners. Starting in 1900, the groups came together and formed the *mancomunal*, a regional organization designed to bring together skilled and unskilled workers. The mancomunal functioned as both mutual aid society and defender of the working class. Soon there was a mancomunal in every major port town and in the southern coal-mining region. In 1904, fifteen mancomunales with 20,000 members gathered for their first national convention. The newspaper *El Proletario* (The Proletariat) reported, "It is not just one mancomunal that is on strong footing today, but all of them; from Iquique to Valdivia one sees incredible movement of workers, a swelling of the ranks, a marvelous enthusiasm."

Labor conditions were generally poor throughout Latin America, but the situation of Chile's nitrate workers was among the worst. The deposits of sodium nitrate were located three to ten feet below the surface of the hot and hostile Atacama Desert. A worker called a *barretero* would locate the deposits, excavate holes, and place explosives in them. After the blast—which could well injure or kill the barretero—the other miners would break up the nitrate, load it into wheel barrows and take them to the mills, where the ore was crushed, dissolved in water, then dried. Heat, lack of water, and poisonous fumes were a routine part of the job.

In 1907, several nitrate companies denied stevedores and boatmen the right, won by railway workers, to have their salaries paid according to a stable exchange rate. They also wanted raises in salary, which was then barely enough to buy food. When the companies ignored them, they asked to be transported back to their hometowns in the south. When that demand was also denied, the workers organized a strike, which was quickly joined by the miners. They presented the nitrate companies with petitions, which were not accepted.

Within a few days, some 8,000 to 10,000 workers gathered in the town of Iquique, where they set up a makeshift camp in the Plaza Manuel Montt and the nearby Santa María School. Along with the workers were women and children. Worried as more workers marched toward Inquique, the government sent two regiments of troops to back up the two based in the area. While strike leaders met with government officials, six people were killed and others injured when they were shot to prevent them from joining the strike. Immediately after the funerals, civil liberties were suspended and the strikers were ordered to abandon the school and the plaza. When the strikers did not comply, the officials opened fire on the school; sources have estimated the number killed as anywhere from 130 to 1,000. The massacre had a chilling effect on the labor movement for several years, but poor conditions inevitably led to renewed organizing.

In Argentina, the elites faced a labor shortage as they tried to industrialize. Despite repeated attempts, there was no way to induce the gauchos of the pampas to accept work discipline. In search of an industrial labor force—and in the hope that Europeans who help whiten the population—the government encouraged foreign immigration. Officials hoped to attract northern Europeans, particularly Germans, who they saw as very industrious. To their chagrin, the call was answered by Italians and Spaniards, and they came in droves. In 1914, at least 50 percent of the Buenos Aires population was foreign born compared with 30 percent in New York at the same time.

By the turn of the century, 60 percent of the Buenos Aires population consisted of manual workers, many of them foreign-born. By 1914, immigrants constituted 60 percent of the urban proletariat. The Italian and Spanish immigrants brought with them ideas about socialism, anarchism, and anarcho-syndicalism. In 1895, the Socialist Party was formed, and the 1910 centennial celebration was marred by anarchist demonstrations and government repression.

Brazil also welcomed large numbers of Europeans, particularly Italians, Portuguese, and Spaniards. Between 1891 and 1900, approximately 112,500 immigrants arrived annually. The trend continued and reached record yearly averages just before World War I. From 1911 through 1913, half a million immigrants entered. However, the proportion of immigrants to the total population in Brazil never surpassed 6.4 percent, a figure reached in 1900. Nonetheless, because of their concentration in the south and the southeast, and particularly because of their importance in the cities of these two regions, they exerted an influence far greater than their numbers might indicate. The traditional elite soon grew wary of the immigrants and blamed them for many of the ills the burgeoning urban centers began to experience.

The labor agenda was increasingly important for women as they joined the workforce in ever greater numbers. In Colombia in 1870, some 70 percent of the artisans were women. In Mexico City in 1895, more than 275,000 women worked as domestic servants. Women led strikes in the tobacco and textile industries in Mexico as early as 1880, organized in such groups as the *Hijas de Anahuac* (Daughters of Anahuac). In Chile, working women were organizing around workplace issues long before middle-class women began to organize as feminists.

But women workers were not always welcomed as allies by men. Some anarchists urged women to stay home because they feared that by enlarging the labor pool, they depressed wages—especially because employers paid women less than men. However, women were usually relegated to the least technical and mechanized positions; in the Argentine textile industry of the turn of the century, they often still worked at home as weavers and seamstresses. As the industry slowly expanded, women's positions were limited because social reformers pushed for protective legislation. As late as 1914, as many women industrial workers were at work in their homes as in the factories.

Women in the cities who could not find work in industry found few options: domestic service, laundering, ironing, and prostitution. In Guatemala City starting in the 1880s, prostitution was legalized and state operated. Women over 15 years old who were found guilty of "bad conduct" could be sentenced to a house of prostitution. Both those forced into the brothels and those who went voluntarily signed contracts that amounted to debt servitude. Such bordellos existed until 1920. While Guatemala may have been alone in its sentencing of women to brothels, most Latin American countries tried to regulate the occupation, and often forced women into other kinds of employment. For example, in Mexico vagrancy laws were used to force

Women were widely employed in Latin America's factories, where they received lower wages than men. These women manufactured helmets in Santiago, Chile, circa 1929.

women to work in textile factories and bakeries, in which women were virtual prisoners.

In Argentina, poor women were often placed into domestic service under the theory that they would be protected by the family. Domestic service, however, has often offered the worst possible conditions of employment. Live-in servants were often given miserable lodging and food, expected to work day and night, and subjected to sexual abuse by men in the home. If they became pregnant, they were usually fired. Complaints were dismissed as signs of ungratefulness from "girls" who were supposedly regarded as members of the family.

When working women became politically active, they were more likely to join the socialist and anarchist movements than the new middle-class parties being formed. The Argentine Socialist party supported women's rights from its founding in 1896. Alfredo Palacios, the first Socialist elected to the Chamber of Deputies (1804–1808, 1912–1915), gave testimony before the chamber showing statistics on the deplorable conditions of women workers. He was a supporter of the Feminist Center, which demanded shorter working hours, daycare centers, and safer equipment, measures that were not enacted.

In the face of such worker unrest and anticapitalist sentiment, the elites found the middle class to be far less threatening.

THE MIDDLE CLASS IN POLITICS

As the heterogeneous middle class emerged, its members sought to play a political role. Inexperienced, they experimented. Their first goal focused on admission to power.

In Brazil, the middle sectors were strong enough to help overthrow the monarchy in 1889 and for a short time, in conjunction with the military, to rule the nation. The composition of Brazilian society had altered considerably in the nineteenth century. At the time of independence the new empire counted barely four million inhabitants, probably half of whom were slaves of African birth or descent. Sixty-five years later, there were fourteen million Brazilians, roughly 600,000 of them slaves. At the other end of the social scale stood 300,000 plantation owners and their families. Most of the population fell somewhere between the two extremes. The majority were impoverished, illiterate rural folk. But there was an important, growing body of urban dwellers, many of whom qualified for the ranks of the middle class.

The gulf between the countryside, with its many vestiges of the colonial past, and the city, with its increasingly progressive outlook, widened during the last decades of the nineteenth century. The urban dwellers were less favorably disposed to two basic institutions inherited from the past, slavery and monarchy, than was the rural population. They viewed those institutions as buttresses of the position of the elite and uncomplementary to their own best interests. Indeed, they perceived the two institutions as the means by which the traditional rural elite retained most of what was colonial in Brazilian society and in the economy while still rejecting, in the stricter legal sense, colonial status. The military, hostile to slavery, ignored by the emperor, and restless, shared the view of the urban middle sectors, to whom the officers were closely related both by family ties and philosophy. Together, they brought an end to both slavery and monarchy.

Not surprisingly the new republican government established by the military in 1889 reflected the goals and aspirations of Brazil's middle sector. The new chief of state, Deodoro da Fonseca, was the son of an army officer of modest means, and his cabinet consisted of two other military officers, an engineer, and four lawyers. They were sons of the city with university degrees, a contrast to the aristocratic scions who had formed previous governments. During its early years, the republic was identified with both the military and the urban middle groups much more than the monarchy had ever been. As one of their goals, they hoped to transform the nation through industrialization. The government raised the tariff on items that competed with national goods and lowered the duty on primary goods used in national manufacturing. To augment the number of technicians, four new engineering schools were opened in the 1890s. A high income from coffee exports, generous credit from the banks, and the government's issue of larger amounts of currency animated economic activity to a fever pitch. Speculation became the order of the day. Bogus companies abounded, but unfortunately for Brazil the speculation resulted in little real industrial progress. In 1893 a political crisis complicated the economic distress. The navy revolted and the southern state of Rio Grande do Sul rose in rebellion; together they threatened the existence of the republic.

The powerful coffee planters, with their wealth and control of the state governments of São Paulo, Minas Gerais, and Rio de Janeiro, held the balance of power between the government and the rebels. They promised aid to the government in return for a guarantee of an open presidential election in 1894. Both kept their sides of the bargain, and in the elections the coffee interests pushed their candidate into the presidential palace. The political victory of the coffee interests reflected the predominant role coffee had come to play in the Brazilian economy. Cheap suitable land, high profits, large numbers of immigrant workers, and a rising world demand made coffee a popular and lucrative crop. By the end of the nineteenth century it composed half of the nation's exports.

The alliance of the coffee planters and the federal government in 1894 superseded all previous political arrangements. Thereafter, the political dominance of the coffee interests characterized the First Republic (1889–1930). The new oligarchy, principally from São Paulo but secondarily from Minas Gerais and Rio de Janeiro, ruled Brazil for its own benefit for thirty-six years. The coffee interests arranged the elections of presidents friendly to their needs and dictated at will the policies of the governments. Sound finances, political stability, and decentralization were the goals pursued by the coffee presidents. The urban middle groups, whose unreliable ally, the military, was torn by disunion and bickering, lost the power they had exercised for so brief and unsettled a period.

At the same time that the middle sectors were maturing and tasting their first political power in gigantic Brazil, the small nation of Costa Rica felt the initial influences of its own middle group. Always remote from the activities of the Spanish empire, Costa Rica had been relatively isolated from the political turmoil of the rest of Central America. There was no privileged wealthy class from the colonial era, and this relative poverty had created a rough equality in a nation that contained only slightly more than one-quarter of a million inhabitants at the close of the century. Costa Rica engaged in minimal foreign trade until the midnineteenth century, when it became a leading coffee producer. Although there were indeed large landholdings, Costa Rica probably had a higher percentage of small and middle-range farmers than any other Latin American country at the end of the century. A society without the sharp edges of economic extremes offered good conditions for the growth of a middle class. The period from 1882 to 1917 boasted a remarkable record of constitutional government in which four-year presidential terms were honored and peacefully exchanged. Politicians and parties supported platforms substantively middle class in their goals. In the last half of the 1880s, Minister of Education Mauro Fernández laid the foundation for a system of free and compulsory public education that eventually would produce one of

Latin America's most literate populations. The government also began to pay greater attention to public health. The widespread medical and health care that the government provided its citizens made them the healthiest of Central America. The relatively equitable patterns of land ownership, the positive emphasis on education, and the comparatively widespread participation of the citizenry in politics marked Costa Rica as an essentially middle-class nation.

In Uruguay, the Latin American middle sector won their greatest victory in the early twentieth century. Uruguay changed dramatically under the government of the middle sectors, providing one of the best such examples of peaceful change in Latin America. Independent Uruguay emerged in 1828 as a result of the stalemate between Argentina and Brazil, which had continued the centuries-old Luso–Spanish rivalry over the left bank of the Río de la Plata. Uruguayans divided into two political camps, the Conservatives (Blancos) and the Liberals (Colorados). From independence until 1872 they fought each other almost incessantly for power. When the liberals got power in 1872, they managed to hang on to it until 1959, despite challenges from the conservatives and the military. During the last decades of the nineteenth century, relative peace settled over the small republic, by then in the process of an economic metamorphosis. Prosperity helped to pacify the nation. Exports of wool, mutton, hides, and beef rose. New methods of stock breeding, fencing, the refrigerated ship, and railroad construction (the mileage jumped five times from 200 to 1,000 miles between 1875 and 1895) modernized the economy.

During the same period, Uruguay constructed the foundation of its enviable educational system. New teacher-training institutes and public schools multiplied. Uruguay was on its way to becoming South America's most literate nation. Expanded and improved education was among the foremost concerns of the middle sectors, and the attention given to education in Uruguay reflected their increasing influence.

The outstanding political representative of the middle class at that time, not only in Uruguay but in all of Latin America, was José Batlle. He first exerted influence as the articulate editor of a prominent newspaper in Montevideo that spoke for the interests of the middle sectors and, by providing them with a voice, helped to organize that always amorphous group. By the end of the nineteenth century, he led the Colorado Party. He served twice as president (1903–1907, 1911–1915), and his influence over the government lasted until his death in 1929. During those decades, he sought to expand education, restrict foreign control, enact a broad welfare program, and unify the republic. He succeeded brilliantly in each instance, and through his strength and foresight he transformed Uruguay into a model bourgeois nation.

At the turn of the century, the conservatives controlled some of the departments (local territorial units) to the extent that they were virtually free of the control of the central government. Batlle extended the power of

LATIN AMERICA THROUGH ART

When Spaniards arrived in the New World, they found people who were already illustrating their lives through art. This art ranged from the images of hands found in a cave in Patagonia to the richly colored murals on the eighth-century Temple Bonampak. For the next five hundred years, the people of the Americas would continue to represent and decorate their worlds, drawing on the indigenous, African and European influences that have characterized Latin American society and culture.

In this section, we offer a small sample of Latin America's beautiful artwork, from the Conquest to the late twentieth century. The images show the ways in which Latin American culture has both changed and endured. They echo the historical realities of their time periods and offer a glimpse into Latin American society and culture.

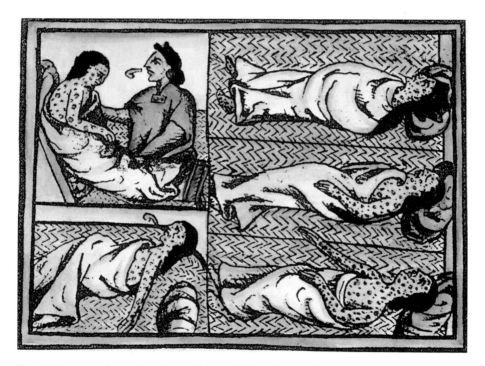

The Nahua people, under the guidance of Franciscan priest Bernardino de Sahagún, told the story of the preconquest Aztec empire and of the Conquest. Sahagún's sixteenth-century treatise, *General History of the Things of New Spain*, now known as the Florentine Codex, was a bilingual document that included this illustration of a Nahua healer attending to those suffering from smallpox. The illustration shows the devastating impact of European diseases that decimated indigenous populations. *The Granger Collection, New York.*

Latin American society was the product of miscegenation, but race mixture was a profoundly disturbing phenomenon for Spanish colonial elites. In this eighteenth-century painting, the artist depicts various racial groupings, each represented by a nuclear family with one child. *"Human Races (Las Castas),"* *18th century, oil on canvas, 1.04 × 1.48 m. Museo Nacional del Virreinato, Tepotzotlan, Mexico, Schalkwijk/Art Resource, NY.*

The details of everyday life in the colonies were captured in such paintings as this image of a Mexican market by an anonymous artist painting circa 1775. The European-style painting shows not just the typical wares on sale, but also indicates differences in class and race between the vendors and the customers. *Oil on canvas. Museo Nacional de Historia, Castillo de Chapultepec, Mexico City, D.F., Mexico © Schalkwijk/Art Resource, NY.*

The independence movements in Latin America typically were recorded by portraying leaders in heroic poses. Chilean painter Franco Gomez (1845–1880) provides an unlikely rendition of flawlessly regimented and uniformed troops flanking Simón Bolívar, celebrated as the father of the Latin American independence movements. Bolívar, resplendent upon a white steed, leads his troops across the Andes to liberate Peru. *SuperStock, Inc.*

A more prosaic image is provided by this anonymous artist's rendition of two women working in the kitchen of a house in Mexico circa 1850. The scene shows the classic high ceilings of Mexican architecture, and the details show clay jars, copper pots, and tiled walls. It is a seemingly peaceful domestic image, but it is also one that shows once again the race and class distinctions of nineteenth-century Latin America.

Xul Solar was one of the key figures of the South American avant garde movement of the 1920s, as well as the European modernist movement. Born Oscar Agustín Alejandro Schultz Solari (1887–1963), he changed his name to Xul Solar (Light of the Sun Reversed or Light from the Other Side), while living in Paris in 1916. He influenced writers such as Jorge Luis Borges as well as painters with his system of pictorial writing that he called "neocrillo" (Neo-Creole), which he intended to be understood throughout Latin America. A classic example of the neocrillo is this 1925 painting, "Patria B". *Christie's Images/SuperStock/ Museo Xul Solar Fundación Pan Klub.*

Cándido Portinari (1903–1962) has been credited with developing a distinctly Brazilian style of painting. His topic for this dynamic 1935 painting is certainly a distinctly Brazilian phenomenon: the slavery of the coffee plantation. Here he shows African male and female plantation laborers, dressed all in white, as they carry large bags across their shoulders and scoop piles of beans into sacks while other slaves pick the coffee beans from trees. *Cándido Portinari, "Café." The Art Archive/Museu Nacional de Belas Artes Rio de Janeiro Brazil/Dagli Orti.*

No survey of Latin American art, however brief, would be complete without an image by Mexico's Frida Kahlo (1907–1954). Kahlo has become a pop icon, but more importantly, she has become known as one of Latin America's most important artists of the twentieth century, perhaps even eclipsing the fame of her husband, muralist Diego Rivera. Her stormy marriages to Rivera made him a central motif in many of Kahlo's works, and this one is no exception. He is at the center of the surrealistic "Love Embrace of the Universe, the Earth (Mexico), Myself, Diego and Señor Xolotl," a 1949 painting marked by precolonial influences that explores the dichotomies of life and death, night and day, moon and sun, man and woman. *Oil on masonite, 70 × 60.5 cm, Vergel Foundation, New York. The Jacques and Natasha Gelman Collection, National Gallery of Australia. (c)2003 Banco de Mexico Diego Rivera & Frida Kahlo Museums Trust. Av. Cinco de Mayo No. 2, Col. Centro, Del. Cuauhtemoc 06059, Mexico, D.F. Reproduction authorized by the Instituto Nacional de Bellas Artes y Literatura.*

Juan O'Gorman (1905–1982) was best known as an architect whose most famous work is the library at the Universidad Nacional Autónima de Mexico (UNAM). In 1932, he took the helm of Mexico City's department of building and construction for Mexico City. His interests in architecture, art (he became a renowned muralist) and the development of Mexico City are all on display in his 1949 painting, "El Ciudad de Mexico." The painting, complete with angels heralding "Viva Mexico," shows the city and the country as a work in progress. *Temple sobre masonite, 66 × 122 cm, Col. Museo de Arte Moderno. Reproduction authorized by the Instituto Nacional de Bellas Artes y Literatura-CONACULTA.*

Rufino Tamayo (1899–1991) was a contemporary of Mexico's famous muralists—Diego Rivera, José Clemente Orozco, and David Alfaro Siquieros. Tamayo, however, rejected their emphasis on politics and muralism, choosing instead to focus on colors, textures, and abstract forms. This painting of abstract human shapes on a blue background is a fine example of the style that so earned the artist enmity that he chose to live in the United States for a decade. He later became one of Mexico's most famous painters. *Photography: Angel Hurtado, Art Museum of the Americas, OAS.*

Fernando Botero's images of inflated, rotund people have made his work instantly recognizable. The Colombian artist, born in 1932, says his work is deeply rooted in his country, showing the countryside, styles, and mores of his homeland. His paintings are frequently seen as being humorous, but even the most lighthearted have a sense of gentle mocking, while his more serious satirize the self-importance of the powerful. This 1968 oil painting, "El Patrón," is one of his more political canvases depicting the oversized employer next to his tiny, though still rounded, servant. *"El Patrón" 1968, oil on canvas, 186.7 × 114.3 cm. © Fernando Botero, courtesy, Marlborough Gallery, New York/The Bridgeman Art Library.*

In the 1980s, Central American artists drew acclaim for their folkloric paintings of village life. This 1989 painting by Pintor Ferman of Honduras is a classic example of the style: people in traditional garb stroll a cobbled street lined with lush foliage, the scenery marked by the church in the distance and the red-tiled roofs of homes. *Photography: Mireille Vautier, Woodfin Camp and Associates.*

The terror of military rule inspired many artists, including Carlos Alonso (1929–) of Argentina. Like many Argentines, Alonso went into exile to escape repressive military rule in the 1970s. He returned in 1981 and began to paint the series known collectively as "Manos Anónimas" to denounce the kidnappings, disappearances, and torture that were still being carried out by the government. This 1982 painting shows an older woman being silenced by hands disembodied from the perpetrator of the violence. *Manos Anónimas, 1982, acrylic on canvas.*

Some of the most beautiful contemporary art of Latin America can be found in the marketplaces, where indigenous motifs are as important a part of artistic expression as they were five hundred years ago. One beautiful example can be seen in the brightly colored patterned mola cloth produced by the Cuna Indians of the San Blas islands of Panama. *Photograph by Will and Deni McIntyre, Getty Images, Inc.*

Another lovely work of art is this Ecuadoran tapestry, featuring figures in hats and ponchos gazing upon distant, snowy mountain peaks. It may be tempting to read into these images the idea of an unchanging Latin America. But, of course, these textiles were created in a far different context than the works of the artists' ancestors. In art, as in history, there is both continuity and change.

his government over them by assuring the conservatives proportional representation in the central government. He managed to balance the budget, repay foreign creditors, and strengthen the national currency. National banks grew in confidence and were able to lend to Uruguayans so that they no longer had to look abroad for much of their capital. To protect national industry, congress raised the tariffs. The government began to enter business, taking over light, power, insurance, and many other formerly private enterprises and continued to do so on an ever increasing scale. The government entered the meat-packing business to offer competition to the foreign companies that had long been engaged in the industry, so vital to a nation dependent on stock raising. The enactment of advanced social-welfare legislation guaranteed workers their right to unionize, a minimum wage, an eight-hour day, pensions, accident insurance, and paid holidays. Batlle said the government should play a positive role in improving the living conditions of the less-favored citizens. On one occasion he announced, "There is great injustice in the enormous gap between the rich and the poor. The gap must be narrowed—and it is the duty of the state to attempt that task." These reforms, like others taking place in Latin America at the time, affected only the urban areas and never extended into the countryside.

Strong as Batlle was, he never directly challenged the landowners or the rural socioeconomic structures. In fact, he saw no reason to, as he stated in 1910: "There is no pressing agrarian problem requiring the attention of the government. The division of the landed estates will take place in response to natural forces operating in our rural industries." It was a point of view shared by the middle-sector leaders of the period. Thus they permitted the continuation of the oldest and most fundamental land and labor institutions. Obviously such a neglect restricted national reforms and circumscribed the limits of change. The neglect of rural reforms reflected the middle sectors' fear of the power of the landowners, their preoccupation with the city, their own intermarriage and connections with the landowning families, and a desire to acquire estates of their own.

The climax of the Batlle reforms came in the new constitution, written in 1917 but promulgated in 1919. It provided a model of the type of government the middle class of the period wanted, which was one, of course, that guaranteed them power. It authorized direct elections, reduced the powers of the president and created a National Council of Administration to share the presidential powers (with the hope of eliminating any future threat of dictatorship), established a bicameral legislature elected by means of a proportional representative system, reduced the military to a minor institution, separated the Church and State, and provided a comprehensive program of social welfare. In creating the first welfare state in the Western Hemisphere, the middle class acknowledged their political debt to the working classes and rewarded them for their support.

In Argentina, the middle class gained power largely because the elites feared the working class. The political leaders, the Generation of 1880, were members of or allied to the landowning class. They monopolized the instruments of state power—the army, the electoral system—and used fraud when necessary. They controlled the ruling Partido Autonomista Nacional (PAN), and made decisions by *acuerdo*, informal agreement. But by the beginning of the twentieth century, these elites faced challenges from newly prosperous landowners, the old aristocracy from the interior who didn't profit from the export boom, and from the rising middle class. The three groups joined forces to form the Radical Party.

An attempted armed revolt in 1890 ended with an acuerdo and recognition of the Radical Civil Union, formed in 1892. The 1910 demonstrations convinced the conservatives that they needed to ally with the middle classes against the masses. In 1912, President Roque Saenz Peña oversaw passage of the Saenz Peña law, giving universal male suffrage to all Argentine citizens, with compulsory voting in elections by secret ballot. The Radicals took the opportunity to seize power and retained control until the Great Depression.

Latin American elites generally found that the middle class was an important ally against the interests of the poorer masses. The middle classes advocated a wide variety of reforms, but in practice they proved to be essentially conservative, fearful that too much reform might harm rather than benefit them. If the elites doubted that the admission of the middle class to political power was a wise move, all they had to do was look at the violent results of exclusion in Mexico.

RECOMMENDED READINGS

Bergquist, Charles. *Labor in Latin America: Comparative Essays on Chile, Argentina, Venezuela, and Colombia*. Stanford, CA: Stanford University Press, 1986.

Coerver, Don M. and Linda B. Hall. *Tangled Destinies: Latin America and the United States*. Albuquerque: University of New Mexico Press, 1999.

Ehrick, Christine. *The Shield of the Weak : Feminism and the State in Uruguay, 1903–1933*. Albuquerque: University of New Mexico Press, 2005.

Langley, Lester D. *The Banana Wars: United States Intervention in the Caribbean, 1898–1934*. Wilmington, DE: Scholarly Resources Books, 2002.

McCreery, David J. *The Sweat of Their Brow: A History of Work in Latin America*. Armonk, NY: M.E. Sharpe Inc., 2000.

Pérez, Louis A. *The War of 1898: The United States and Cuba in History and Historiography*. Chapel Hill: University of North Carolina Press, 1998.

CHAPTER 7

THE MEXICAN EXPLOSION

The struggles for political voice and economic space that characterized Latin America at the turn of the century were not resolved at the electoral polls in Mexico. Mexico continued to represent the extremes of Latin American patterns, from its exceptional chaos in the early nineteenth century to the amazing endurance of its liberal, modernizing caudillo, Porfirio Díaz, at century's end. The dictator refused to open the political system to the new economic elites, and their desperation for a role in the system ignited long-simmering disputes with the masses. The result was the Mexican Revolution, or perhaps more accurately, revolutions (the "long" revolution ran from 1910–1940).

By revolution, we mean the sudden, forceful, and violent overturn of a previously relatively stable society and the substitution of other institutions for those discredited. Change by revolution thus denotes sweeping change, the destruction of old social, political, and economic patterns in favor of newer ones. Use of this definition divides genuine revolutions from the innumerable palace coups, military takeovers, civil wars, and the wars of independence, which were nothing more than shifts in the holding of power within the same or similar groups unaccompanied by fundamental economic, social, or political changes. These changes are also accompanied by new ideology and national mythologies reflecting a change in the balance of power.

Octavio Paz wrote one of the most famous and moving descriptions of the Mexican Revolution: "Like our popular fiestas, the Revolution was an excess and a squandering, a going to extremes, an explosion of joy and hopelessness, a shout of orphanhood and jubilation, of suicide and life, all of them mingled together." But in that explosion, much was unclear: Who won? Who lost? What were the goals, and were they achieved? And were the results worth the loss of more than one million lives?

Cracks in the Regime

By 1910, Porfirio Díaz and the "New Creoles" had ruled for thirty-four years, without a popular mandate, for the benefit of privileged native elites and foreign investors. The economy still depended upon foreign whims and direction, a neocolonialism clearly seen in the statistics: 75 percent of all dividend-paying mines in Mexico were owned by U.S. interests. Foreign capital represented 97 percent of investment in mining, 98 percent of rubber, and 90 percent of oil. Some Mexicans resented the high level of foreign investment. Others were concerned that the Porfirian prosperity was narrowly based, relying mostly on mining, utilities, commerce, and large-scale agriculture, with relatively little industry.

The majority of the population did not share the wealth. Real wealth actually declined for the majority: Hacienda peons earned an average daily wage of 35 cents, which remained almost steady throughout the nineteenth century, while corn and chile prices more than doubled, and beans cost six

The initial target of the revolution was Porfirio Diaz, who by the time of his overthrow in 1911 had ruled for thirty-six years. (Library of Congress)

times more than they had at the beginning of the century. Life was a little better for urban workers, who worked eleven- to twelve-hour days, seven days a week, and lived in squalid housing with one bathhouse per 15,000 residents.

Land, a principal source of wealth, remained in the hands of a few. Foreigners owned between 14 and 20 percent of it. Ninety-five percent of the rural population owned none. Not even 10 percent of the indigenous communities held land. Fewer than 1,000 families owned most of Mexico. In fact, fewer than 200 families owned one-quarter of the land. Private estates reached princely proportions. The De la Garza hacienda in the state of Coahuila totaled 11,115,000 acres; the Huller estate in Baja, California, sprawled over 13,325,650 acres. Productivity was low, and absentee landlords were common. The fact that a majority of Mexicans lived in the country and worked in agriculture made the inequity of land distribution all the more unjust.

At the same time, the growing mestizo urban classes were dissatisfied with the inequitable institutions inherited from the past. The mestizos had grown rapidly in number over the centuries. By the end of the nineteenth century they surpassed the indigenous in number and totally overshadowed the tiny "creole" class. It was obvious from their size, skill, and ambitions that the mestizos held the key to Mexico's future. The mestizo working and middle sectors of the cities voiced discontent with their inferior and static position in Porfirian Mexico. The inflexibility of Mexico's neocolonial institutions retarded their mobility and inhibited their progress.

As early as 1900, intense criticism of the Porfiriato was launched by the anarchists Jesus, Enrique and Ricardo Flores Magón in their weekly newspaper, *Regeneración*. The brothers were jailed in 1901 for criticizing the political chief of Oaxaca. From their subsequent exile in St. Louis, Missouri, they issued the Liberal Plan, calling for an eight-hour work day and a six-day week; abolition of the notorious plantation store (*tienda de raya*); abolition of payment in scrip, which could only be used at the tienda de raya; restoration of the ejidos; and redistribution of uncultivated land.

However, it was actions within Mexico that revealed the intensifying contradictions of the Porfiriato. In 1906, workers went on strike at Colonel William Greene's Cananea Consolidated Copper Company, one of the ten largest mines in the world. One of the workers' chief complaints was that Mexicans were paid less than U.S. workers, who held all the technical and managerial posts. Furthermore, the foreigners were paid in gold dollars, whereas the Mexicans received silver pesos, which were worth far less. When the 3,000 Mexican workers went on strike, Greene refused to negotiate. When unarmed workers tried to force their way through a locked gate at the company lumberyard, high-pressure water hoses were turned on them. The gate collapsed and workers streamed into the yard. Company guards fired into the crowd, killing dozens of workers. The chaos spilled into the town, where Greene's guards shot indiscriminately into crowds. When Díaz could not get his rurales to the scene quickly enough, Greene turned to the United States, and 275 Arizona Rangers were brought in, a direct challenge to Mexican sovereignty that angered Mexican elites.

Six months later, new violence broke out at the Rio Blanco textile mill in Orizaba, Veracruz, where the poorly paid workers put in twelve-hour days, and the workforce included children as young as eight years old. The 1907 conflict began when wives of the employees were denied credit to purchase food at the company store. What began with pushing ended with shots, as rurales fired into the crowd at point-blank range, killing women, children, and workers. When survivors returned later to claim the bodies, they were again assaulted.

Despite these harbingers of problems, it was not the oppressed workers who led the uprising. It was the upper classes, who had their own complaints about the regime. The theoretical justification for the Porfiriato was "Order & Progress"—but order had become rigidity, and progress had slowed. These dissatisfied elites wanted a share of political power, and they questioned the dictatorship. Northern elites in particular chafed under Mexico City's control, made possible by the telegraph, the railroad, and Díaz's grip on centralized power. Furthermore, his support of foreign commercial interests brought unwanted competition to the north, hurting their economic fortunes as well. It is not surprising, then, that it was a northern son who led the uprising.

Effective Suffrage and No Reelection

Francisco I. Madero was the son of a wealthy rancher from the border state of Coahuila, Evaristo Madero, who had been a supporter of Díaz in the early days of his leadership. Francisco was educated at the University of California, Berkeley, and the Sorbonne. The Madero family was among the elites: Among the family's vast holdings was the Compañía de Tierras de Sonora, comprising 1,450,000 acres of land, as well as iron and coal mines.

Despite their wealth, northern elites such as the Maderos were too far away from Mexico City to compete with the foreign interests that gathered around Díaz. His concessions to foreign companies translated into direct losses for Mexican businesses. For example, the Maderos were among cotton planters mired for years in lawsuits to reduce the unlimited water rights of the British-owned Tlahualilo Company. The Maderos were also the only serious competitor to the Rockefellers' Continental Rubber Company, which tried to eliminate the competition by merging with the U.S. Rubber Company and glutting the market, driving the price of rubber down from $1.00 to 25 cents per pound. In addition, the Maderos were among only a few Mexicans who owned smelters that could compete with foreign mining firms, and the only ones to survive after Díaz gave generous concessions to the Guggenheims' American Smelting and Refining Company.

In 1908, the elites were taken by surprise when Díaz announced in an interview with journalist James Creelman in Pearson's Magazine, a U.S. publication, that he would not seek reelection in 1910. "I have waited patiently for the day when the people of the Mexican Republic would be pre-pared to choose and change their government at every election without danger of armed revolutions and without injury to the national credit or in-terference with national progress. I believe that day has come. . . . No matter what my friends and supporters say, I retire when my present term of office ends, and I shall not serve again."

His opponents immediately began to express their views. In 1909, Andrés Molina Enriquez published *Las Grandes Problemas Nacionales* (The Great National Problems). Molina was no revolutionary. In fact, he was a positivist who hoped that reform, particularly agrarian reform, could avert revolution. The same year, Francisco I. Madero published *The Presidential Succession of 1910*, calling for political change. The challenges were felt on the local level as well: In Morelos, Patricio Leyva challenged Díaz candidate Pablo Escandón. Leyva's candidacy drew popular support from such local community leaders as Emiliano Zapata.

But despite his claims, Díaz chose to run again in 1910. Madero, under the banner of the Antireelectionist Party, ran as well. His platform called for political reform and free and open elections. His motto was the same one that Díaz himself had raised long ago in the Revolution of Tuxtepec: Effective suffrage and no reelection. When asked about economic issues, however, Madero replied that the Mexican people wanted liberty, not bread. Madero was more than willing to compromise with Díaz, even offering to run as his vice presidential candidate. But Díaz refused and instead threw Madero in jail the night before the election. To no one's surprise, Díaz declared his victory at the polls—with more than one million votes to less than two hundred for Madero—and took office for the eighth time.

Madero escaped to the United States. When he saw the popular response that his political opposition to the old dictator had aroused, he chose to launch a revolution. In San Antonio, Texas, he wrote his revolutionary plan, then crossed the border in October 1910, to announce the Plan de San Luis Potosí on Mexican soil. His plan showed the simple goals of his move-ment: the forced resignation of Díaz and electoral reforms. Repeatedly, his fol-lowers voiced the slogan "Effective suffrage and no reelection," a clue to the exclusively political, urban, and middle-sector origin of the revolution.

PATRIAS CHICAS

Mexico's vast territory was a country of regions, each with its own set of local traditions and problems. The reaction to Madero's call for revolution depended as much on local conditions as on resentment toward the Díaz regime. Indeed, the impact of Díaz policies differed by region. The two main geographic divisions were north and south. The north included the contiguous northwestern states of Chihuahua, Sonora, Sinaloa, Durango, and Coahuila. The south comprised the five adjoining central states of Guerrero, Morelos, Puebla, Tlaxcala, and Veracruz.

In general, the north was characterized by its distance from the political power center of Mexico City. There was no sedentary indigenous population, and settlers on the frontier had been united in their struggle against the Apaches. A border region, restless workers could cross to the United States in search of better jobs. It was a region where the Catholic Church had less impact, indeed, where Protestants and Mormons from the United States had made inroads. If there was any tradition to the northern states, it was one of independence and mobility. That independence was threatened during the Porfiriato by increasing state intrusion without a corresponding inclusion of local elites in the national power structure. Within this region, states had their own peculiarities. For example, residents of Chihuahua chafed against the monopoly over politics and economics exerted by the Terrazas-Creel family, whereas in Durango, Díaz had alienated the middle class by his generous support to foreign mining companies.

The south and central states, on the other hand, were places where the Catholic Church and the large hacienda had formed the main structures of society. Small villages of campesinos struggled to maintain their farms against the encroachment of modernizing and expanding haciendas, eager for their land and labor. Nowhere was this more apparent than in Morelos, where the sugar plantations threatened the continued existence of traditional haciendas, the small rural settlements known as ranchos, and of entire villages. In contrast, in Veracruz, industrial workers labored in foreign-owned textiles mills under miserable conditions.

In isolated areas of Mexico, the revolution initially would have little impact. It was not until 1913 and 1914, well after the Maderista phase had ended, that people in Chiapas and Tabasco were aware of the revolution. Isolation was only one factor keeping Yucatán removed from revolutionary upheaval: There was also the iron-fisted power of the henequen industry. As a result, the revolution would not come to the peninsula until 1915. Oaxaca, on the other hand, was quiet because most of the land was still in traditional indigenous villages, relatively untouched by the capitalist displacement and political intrusion of the Porfiriato.

THE MADERISTA REVOLT

Madero called for Mexicans to rise in revolution on November 20, 1910. The only response to his call came in Chihuahua, where Abraham Gonzalez, head of the state's Antireelectionist Party, called for an uprising. When the

Revolutionary leader Pancho Villa rides among his troops on a dusty trail in 1916 during raids in the United States and northern Mexico. (Library of Congress)

conspirators found that their plans for November 20 had been discovered by the authorities, they rose instead on November 14. They were led by Toribio Ortega, a campesino leader who had led his native village in a 1903 attempt to recover lost lands. Ortega began with sixty men, and they were soon joined by the residents of nearby villages who had also struggled over lost lands. In Parral, a mining town, it was a wealthy merchant, Guillermo Baca, who led forty men in an attack on the jefe politico and was soon joined by 300 men. The revolt spread quickly throughout Chihuahua's mining towns and old military colonies. While they were responding to Madero's call, the local rebellions were aimed primarily at unpopular local authorities and were fueled by local grievances. When the revolutionaries failed in attacks on local police, they retreated to the mountains to regroup for guerrilla warfare.

There were many local leaders like Ortega and Baca, but two men would emerge to coordinate the local uprisings in the north: Pascual Orozco and Pancho Villa. Orozco was a member of the new middle class, the minimally educated son of a store owner. He made his money as an enterprising muleteer leading convoys of precious metals through the mountains. His knowledge of the region and the danger of his occupation made him a natural revolutionary leader. He was at first much better known than Pancho Villa, who entered the revolution as the leader of only twenty-eight men.

Villa was born Doroteo Arango into a family of hacienda peons in the state of Durango. Legend has it that he shot the hacendado, or perhaps his son or an administrator, after the man attacked Villa's sister. He fled to Chihuahua and began a career as a small-time bandit; he was arrested for minor robberies and sent to the army, where he served one year before deserting. He fled to Chihuahua and changed his name to Francisco "Pancho" Villa. Much has been made of Villa's life as a bandit with several gangs, eventually switching from holdups and robberies to cattle rustling. But he also worked at a number of legal jobs, mostly for foreign companies; he was a muleteer for a silver mine and a contractor for a railway line, as well as the organizer of cock fights. In all of these legal activities, he proved to be honest and reliable, as well an effective leader of men. Perhaps it was for those reasons that Abraham Gonzalez recruited Villa to the revolution. As the first to defeat regular government troops, Villa's fame as a revolutionary drew hundreds of men to serve under him.

Initially, there was less action in the south. Would-be revolutionaries, including Zapata, met in Morelos in November, but they took no action until a delegation sent to Madero in mid-December returned in February with formal appointments to leadership positions. On March 11, the leaders marched to the Villa de Ayala and read Madero's Plan de San Luis Potosí, gathered seventy men, and headed for the mountains south of Puebla.

Despite his October call to action, Madero had remained out of the country until February, when he arrived in Chihuahua to assume control. He ordered an attack on Ciudad Juárez, a border city that would have given him control over customs duties. The attack failed, but Madero's presence in Mexico inspired more uprisings. By March 21 the federal army was in retreat, and on April 1, Díaz promised reforms, including land reform and an end to reelection. But the promises came too late and served only to show the revolutionaries the weakness of the regime.

By mid-April, the revolutionary guerrilla bands had become organized armies, and Madero again ordered them to march on Ciudad Juárez. Orozco and Villa each headed a column of 500 riders, and Madero led another 1,500. The Díaz government frantically proposed negotiations, and Madero implemented a ceasefire in order to carry out the talks. On April 22, Madero and government representatives agreed to a treaty that did not demand the resignation of Díaz, though Madero was told confidentially that the president would step down. Villa and other leaders were outraged, leading Madero to change his position and insist that Díaz resign. At that point, negotiations broke down, but Madero continued the ceasefire. He had been convinced by the government that an attack would provoke the Taft administration, which in March had sent 20,000 U.S. troops to the border and ships to patrol Mexico's coastline.

Orozco and Villa chose disobedience at this point and fired on the federal troops. They took the city easily, and on May 21 the Treaty of Ciudad Juárez

Map 7.1 The Overthrow of Diaz

Source: http://users.erols.com/mwhite28/mexico.htm.

ended the war. The revolutionaries had no more respect for the treaty than for the ceasefire, for it promised little change. Díaz and his vice president, Ramón Corral, would resign; foreign minister Francisco de León de la Barra would become provisional president until new elections were held in the coming months. Madero would approve the interim cabinet and name fourteen provisional governors, but nothing else would change: judges, mayors, state legislators, police—all would stay in office. The revolutionary army, however, was required to disband, a sure signal of Madero's limited goals.

On May 26, 1911, Porfirio Díaz boarded the ship *Ypiranga* and sailed to exile in Paris, where he died in 1915. As he left, Díaz commented, "Madero has unleashed a tiger; let us see if he can control him."

Madero in Power

On the same day that Díaz left the country, two other key events occurred. A victorious Emiliano Zapata rode into Cuernavaca at the head of 4,000 troops waving the image of the Virgin de Guadalupe. Zapata and his followers had been motivated by the third clause of Madero's Plan de San Luis Potosí, a vague plank calling for illegally obtained land to be returned to the rightful owners. But that same day, Madero issued his first manifesto since the end of the war. He noted "the aspirations contained in the third clause of the Plan of San Luis Potosí cannot be satisfied in all their amplitude."

In Morelos, land had been the reason for fighting. Zapata had given orders that village lands be restored, and haciendas were occupied during the struggle. The terms of the treaty, however, essentially restored the Díaz regime in Morelos as the governor, state legislature, jefes politicos and municipal presidents were all reinstated. Once subject to arrest for resisting the revolution, the old leadership now expected the revolutionaries to respect their authority.

On June 7, Madero arrived in Mexico City. Among those greeting him at the train station was Zapata. When they met the next day, Zapata tried to convince Madero of the importance of land reform. Madero dismissively told Zapata that it was a complicated issue, and that it was far more important for Zapata to disband his rebel troops. Stunned, Zapata wondered how Madero could trust the army to be loyal to an unarmed revolutionary government. The unspoken answer was that there was nothing revolutionary about Madero's aims.

Zapata convinced Madero to visit Morelos, but the visit backfired. Madero was influenced by the Mexico City press, which called Zapata "the Attila of the South," and by the Morelos "revolutionary" elites, who insisted that Zapata could not control his "barbaric" troops.

Madero stood by ineffectually as de la Barra, the interim president, ordered troops south to Morelos to disarm the Zapata forces. Zapata was at his wedding celebration on August 9 when he was informed that more than 1,000 troops were entering the state under the leadership of Brigadier General Victoriano Huerta. By August 29, Zapata had been declared an outlaw. Huerta's forces rampaged through Morelos, and the campesinos became Zapatistas.

During those summer months, there was little peace in Mexico. Despite conciliatory statements, Madero was criticized by both the right and the left. Madero turned his forces on the anarchist Partido Liberal Mexicano (PLM) in Tijuana, then began to demobilize his troops. In July, miners formed unions and began a series of strikes. In August, right-wing leader Bernardo Reyes began to campaign against Madero, but he fled to the United States in September after he was physically attacked by Maderistas and congress refused to postpone the election.

Madero won a massive victory at the polls in October and took office in November. But he was quite unprepared for the task he faced. His political platform contained some vague planks on political reform and almost nothing solid on social or economic change. He represented the traditional liberalism of the nineteenth century, which did not harmonize with the newer demands being made. Although he restored some ejidos, villagers bore the burden of proof to reclaim lands. He used troops to break up strikes,

Emiliano Zapata was the revolutionary leader who embodied the goals of the poor campesinos. He is shown in what forever became the image of the Mexican revolutionary: wearing a large sombrero, chest crossed with bandoleros, holding a Winchester single-action rifle and a sheathed saber. (Library of Congress)

and his education budget was a mere 7.8 percent, little more than Díaz's 7.2 percent. Instead of changing the old Porfirian regime, he worked with it to end the social instability that threatened elite wealth. Coahuila governor Venustiano Carranza complained that Madero was "delivering to the reactionaries a dead revolution which will have to be fought over again." His words were prophetic.

¡VIVA ZAPATA!

Emiliano Zapata was not a typical campesino. He had estate land to share-crop and apparently a personal relationship with hacendado and Díaz son-in-law Ignacio de la Torre y Mier, who had used his influence to help Zapata leave the army after a scrape with the law. Zapata was a renowned horse-man, had some education, and sometimes hired laborers, making him a patrón and a member of the rural middle class. He was well-respected and had been elected to head his village of Anenecuilco. In that role, he once had armed eighty men to retake the land that the government had allowed big landowners to take from the village.

Zapata went on to earn admiration during his fighting for Madero. But when Madero abandoned the cause of land reform, Zapata abandoned Madero. In his Plan of Ayala, issued in November 1911, Zapata called for the overthrow of Madero and the return of land to the people. Campesinos rallied to his cause. A new force had been unleashed and it represented what distinguished the Mexican Revolution from previous movements in Latin America: the stirring of the masses. It became clear that a social revolution had begun.

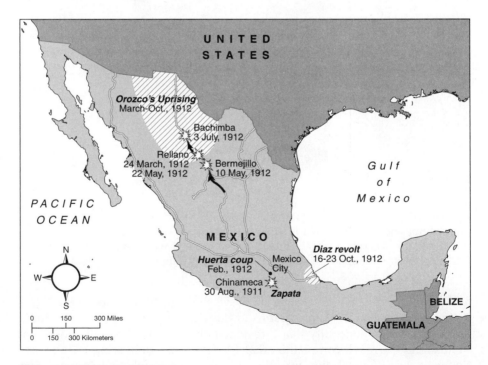

Map 7.2 The Madero Regime
Source: http://users.erols.com/mwhite28/mexico.htm.

By January 1912, the Zapatista example had inspired movements in Tlaxcala, Puebla, Mexico state, Michoacán, Guerrero, and Oaxaca, creating a crisis in the south just as Pascual Orozco was becoming increasingly estranged from Madero in the north. Zapata called on Orozco to lead the new revolution. At first, Orozco remained loyal to Madero, but by March, Orozco, too, had turned on the government, won over by the Terrazas-Creel clan. Despite the support from wealthy elites, his Plan Orozquista called for the end of the ten-hour day and child labor, higher wages, better working conditions, the end of the tienda de raya, and, like Zapata, agrarian reform. Villa, however, remained loyal to Madero, who asked Villa to merge his forces with Huerta's; together they defeated Orozco in May. The Huerta-Villa relationship was, naturally, conflictive, given that Huerta had originally defended the Díaz regime against Villa. On trumped up charges, Huerta had Villa arrested, and he spent seven months in jail before escaping to El Paso, Texas, in December 1912.

As before, the attacks on Madero came from the right as well as the left. Bernardo Reyes had returned to Mexico and was imprisoned after leading an unsuccessful revolt against Madero. In prison, he and Felix Díaz, Porfirio's nephew, bribed a general to release them and launched another coup in February 1913. In what became known as the *Decena Tragica*, the

The revolution was led by Francisco I. Madero, a northern rancher who wanted political democracy but worried less about economic change. (Library of Congress)

Tragic Ten Days, Mexico City became a maze of barricades and trenches. Cars burned in the streets, horses ran wild, and gunfire claimed thousands of civilian lives. Businesses closed and food shortages drove the desperate to live on rats, while bodies rotted in the streets.

Madero relied on Huerta to defend the government. Huerta promised Madero that he would bring peace, but it was a peace brokered by Felix Díaz and Huerta at the United States Embassy, with the blessing of Ambassador Henry Lane Wilson. On February 20, Huerta switched sides and arrested Madero, who was soon killed.

HUERTA AND THE COUNTER-REVOLUTION

Huerta became the symbol of reaction, of the counterrevolution. A native of Jalisco, Huerta was the son of a poor Huichol farmer who worked an unirrigated plot of land. He joined the military in order to receive schooling, and a general took him on as a personal secretary and aide. He was sent on to military college, and his career coincided with that of Porfirio Díaz; both fought the Yaqui and Maya peoples during their uprisings. His coup was supported by the upper classes, business interests, the Church, and the federal army. Although Orozco initially opposed Huerta, by March he had joined him.

Huerta's coup was deplored by both Villa and Zapata, but neither leader had national standing. Only one Madero government official called for resistance to Huerta, and that was Coahuila governor Venustiano Carranza. Carranza was an unlikely revolutionary. A rich hacendado from an old colonial family, he had held positions in the Díaz regime and been a supporter of Bernardo Reyes. When Díaz blocked Carranza from becoming governor, Carranza turned against the regime; but he only joined Madero after Reyes went into exile. Carranza was even more conservative than Madero on all but one issue: nationalism. As governor of Coahuila, he had supported strikers at foreign-owned companies.

Carranza tried to rally the other northern governors, but he soon found himself alone as the governors were murdered and imprisoned. He then tried to negotiate with Huerta, and when that failed, took up arms. Villa returned from the United States to organize resistance in Chihuahua, while in Sonora forces were led by Alvaro Obregón, the owner of a medium-sized ranch who had also worked as a mechanic, schoolteacher, and tenant farmer. Although he was not involved in the Madero revolution, Obregón had fought against the Orozco uprising. In the struggle against Huerta, Obregón quickly emerged as one of the most talented military leaders of the revolution. In March, Carranza issued the Plan de Guadalupe, in which he declared himself "First Chief of the Constitutionalist Army" and claimed to be Madero's rightful successor. Zapata, meanwhile,

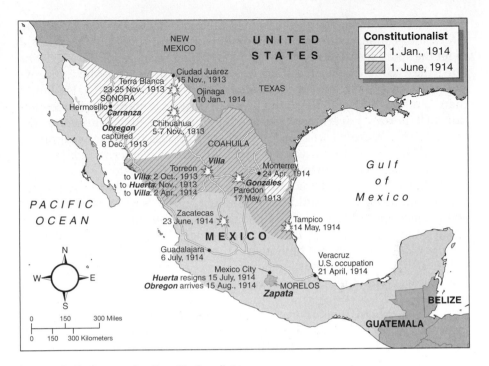

Map 7.3 Huerta vs. the Constitutionalists
Source: http://users.erols.com/mwhite28/mexico2.htm.

continued to fight on his own in the south, trusting neither Huerta nor the Constitutionalists to restore the ejidos.

From 1913 to 1914, Mexico devolved into a bloody civil war. At the same time, however, Huerta's government initiated some domestic reforms: The education budget rose to 9.9 percent of the national budget, and Education Minister Nemesio Garcia Naranjo overturned Gabino Barreda's positivism. One hundred thirty-one rural schools were built, and community projects were initiated in many indigenous villages, including the restoration of seventy-eight ejidos to Yaqui and Mayo Indians of Sonora.

However, any achievements were outweighed by his increasingly dictatorial measures. Huerta closed congress, ordered the assassination of his rivals, and dragged poor conscripts from the streets in the detested *leva* (military draft). But perhaps his biggest problem was U.S. President Woodrow Wilson's refusal to recognize the Huerta regime, despite the urging of the ambassador. And it was the United States that Huerta would eventually blame for his downfall.

In April 1914, the USS Dolphin was stationed off the shores of Tampico. The ship's captain sent a small group of sailors to get fuel, and they wandered into a restricted area. They were immediately arrested, but released within a few hours, along with an official apology. But the United States refused to let the small incident go so easily, instead demanding that the Mexicans hoist the U.S. flag and give a twenty-one gun salute. The Mexican government reluctantly agreed, but said the United States officials should then salute the Mexican flag, which Wilson saw as tantamount to recognition of Huerta's government. Before they could resolve the matter, the United States received word that a German ship was bringing weapons to Huerta. U.S. naval forces were ordered to occupy Veracruz, where they prevented the Germans from landing, controlled the custom's house, and killed hundreds of civilians. Villa was not particularly concerned about U.S. occupation, if it would help topple Huerta. Zapata said the U.S. actions made his "blood boil," but so did the idea of uniting with Huerta against the United States. The Constitutionalist forces raged against the insult of U.S. invasion, but obviously, Huerta could not ally with the Constitutionalists. Spontaneous demonstrations erupted in Mexico against U.S. actions, and Huerta concentrated his troops in the east to counter the occupation.

The northern revolutionaries capitalized on the U.S. distraction. In June, in the bloodiest battle of the war against Huerta, Villa captured Zacatecas, a railway junction essential to the route to Mexico City. The battle resulted in the deaths of 6,000 federal troops and 1,000 rebels, and the injured numbered 3,000 federales and 2,000 constitutionalists. On July 15, Huerta resigned; like Díaz, he fled to Europe on the *Ypiranga*.

But Huerta's fall was no more of a unifying force than the fall of Díaz had been. The revolutionaries had been able to agree when they focused on the overthrow of a particular leader. But their interests conflicted, and there was no peace to be gained. Instead, each revolutionary force tried to be the first to reach Mexico City and take control of the federal government. The northern forces had split into factions led by Carranza and Villa, with Obregón eventually swinging his support to Carranza. Villa's and Zapata's forces discussed a possible alliance, while the other revolutionaries tried to keep both of them from the capital.

On August 20, Carranza arrived in Mexico City and declared himself the new chief executive. He called a convention for October 1 and made sure that only Carrancistas would attend. To his dismay, the convention voted to move to Aguascalientes, where Villistas could join them. The delegates then declared their sovereignty and invited Zapata to attend. The convention was split, with the forces of Carranza and Obregón on one side, Villa and Zapata on the other. Carranza and Obregón represented the elites and middle class, those whose interests focused more on political than economic and social change. Zapata and Villa represented the lower classes, the Mexican masses that hungered for redistribution of land and economic opportunity. The convention tried to find a compromise in Eulalio Gutierrez, who was installed with the backing of Villa's troops. A furious Carranza fled and established his own government at Veracruz.

As 1914 drew to a close, Zapata and Villa met, trying to ally their more radical Conventionist forces against the elite Constitutionalists. Unfortunately, neither Zapata nor Villa was able to articulate a message that went beyond their regional and social bases. Neither had an overarching ideology, and some would argue that Zapata's concerns were anachronistic, envisioning a return to a past that was long gone.

Villa and Zapata fought on, but by late 1915, the tide had turned; Gutierrez abandoned Mexico City to rule from Nuevo León, and Carranza was able to return to Mexico City and consolidate his position. Zapata was driven out of Mexico City, although his forces kept pressure on the capitol. Villa controlled Chihuahua, but he struggled in the rest of the north against Obregón's forces.

The beginning of the end for Villa came with his defeat in April 1915 at the town of Celaya. Obregón, using the new tactics of the European war, dug trenches, enclosed his defensive positions with barbed wire, and used machine guns to mow down 14,000 of Villa's men. With a subsequent defeat at León, Villismo was destroyed as a national force. Villa's army disintegrated,

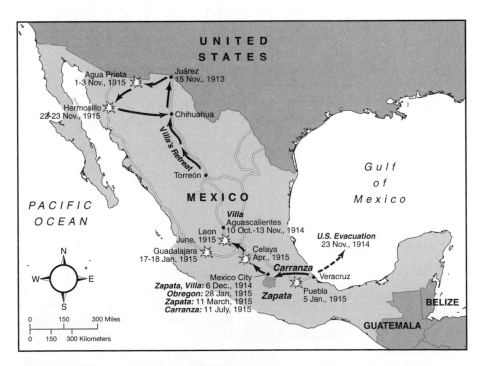

Map 7.4 Carranza vs. the Conventionists
Source: http://users.erols.com/mwhite28/mexico2.htm.

and even many of his closed collaborators turned against him. In his heyday, the Division of the North had boasted 50,000 men. By the time he headed to Sonora, he was down to 12,000 demoralized troops, short on food and supplies. The coup de grace came with an ambush at Agua Prieta on November 1, 1915, made possible by U.S. President Wilson giving permission for Carrancista troops to pass through the United States. Villa disbanded his army and disappeared into the mountains with a few hundred men. No one expected to hear from him again.

But Villa blamed Wilson for his defeat. He wanted revenge, and he hoped to provoke a United States invasion that would cause a backlash against the Carranza regime. First, Villista forces stopped a train carrying U.S. mining engineers and technicians from the Cusi Mining Company, hoping to reopen their mine. Instead, they were dragged from the train and fifteen were killed. Villa took his revenge again in March on the town of Columbus, New Mexico, where seventeen U.S. citizens were killed. Villa failed to get money, supplies, or arms and lost 100 men in the raid. But he succeeded in luring the United States into Mexico.

President Wilson sent General John J. Pershing and 5,000 U.S. troops on what was called the Punitive Expedition, which included cavalry, infantry, artillery, and eight planes. In April and May 1916, Villa was injured and in hiding, with 10,000 U.S. troops and 10,000 federales occupying Chihuahua. He seemed defeated. Yet, by the end of the year, his forces numbered 6,000 to 10,000, and they controlled a substantial part of Chihuahua, where he had the support of the majority of the people.

The year was not as successful for the Zapatistas. Carranza's forces invaded Morelos, wreaking such havoc that the campesinos adopted the word *carrancear*, meaning to loot. By the fall of 1916, Zapata had disbanded his 20,000-member regular army and reverted to guerrilla warfare with only 5,000 men.

A RADICAL CONSTITUTION

With the Zapatistas nearly defeated and U.S. forces chasing Villa, Carranza decided to institutionalize his position by calling a constitutional convention at Querétaro. This time he would not repeat the mistakes of Aguascalientes: Only Constitutionalists would be allowed to attend. Carranza envisioned minor changes to the 1857 constitution. But as he soon found out, the Constitutionalists were no more unified than the other revolutionary bands. The desire for more radical social changes dominated, and Carranza was presented with a document far from the one he had envisioned.

Ideological differences split the delegates. The radicals, supported by Obregón, gained control and imposed their views. The constitution that emerged after two months of bitter debate at Querétaro contained many of the traditional enlightened ideas characteristic of the former constitution. In the customary Latin American fashion, the constitution conferred strong authority on the president. However, it went on to alter significantly some fundamental and traditional concepts.

The new constitution exalted the state and society above the individual and conferred on the government the authority to reshape society. The key articles dealt with religion, labor, and land. Article 130 placed restrictions on the Church and clergy. Churches were denied juridical personalities and could not own property. States could limit the number of clerics by law, and priests were not allowed to vote, hold office, or criticize the government. The Church was barred from participating in primary education. These provisions would give the State the supremacy over the Church that Mexican liberals had sought since the midnineteenth century.

Article 123 protected the Mexican workers from exploitation by authorizing the passage of a labor code to set minimum salaries and maximum hours. Workers were to receive accident insurance, pensions, and social benefits. The right to unionize and to strike was guaranteed. Because foreign investment in Mexican industrialization was significant, this article

Map 7.5 Carranza in Charge
Source: http://users.erols.com/mwhite28/mexico2.htm.

could be potentially used as one means of bridling the operations of the foreign capitalist.

The most significant change was Article 27, which laid the foundation for land reform and for restrictions on foreign economic control. It declared government ownership of mineral and water resources, subordinated private property to public welfare, and gave the government the right to expropriate land. This clause annulled all alienations of ejidos since 1857 and recognized communal ownership of land.

Carranza was unhappy with the constitution and had little intention of following its tenets when he was sworn in as president in May 1917, after an election in which he was unopposed. Nonetheless, the constitutional reforms stole some of Zapata's thunder.

THE RADICALS LOSE

By the summer of 1917, Zapata was struggling to hold his revolution together. In March 1918, he issued new manifestos, for the first time recognizing the different needs of the different regions, but no new support was forthcoming. In November, Spanish flu swept Morelos, where the campesinos had already suffered the effects of typhus, malaria, and dysentery. The population dropped 25 percent in 1918 alone, and Zapata was left with only 2,000 soldiers, each armed with only 304 cartridges. The final blow came on April 10, 1919, when Zapata walked into an ambush. As he walked into a meeting with supposed Carrancista defectors, a bugle sounded three times and soldiers who appeared ready to shoot in his honor instead lowered their guns and fired twice at point-blank range.

In the north, it became clear that Villa himself would never be caught. Growing more concerned about events in Europe, the United States began withdrawing the Pershing Expedition in early February 1917. Villa continued to fight Carranza, but there seemed to be little justification. By the end of the year, Villa had lost popular support. With his limited forces, he failed in an attack on Parral in 1918 and in an ill-conceived plan to kidnap Carranza in 1919.

Confident that the wars were over, Carranza attempted to name his own successor to the presidency. His arrogance was greeted with another revolt, led by three Sonorans: Álvaro Obregón, Adolfo de la Huerta, and Plutarco Elias Calles. Carranza fled and was killed by his own guard. With Carranza dead, Villa was ready to negotiate. De la Huerta, as interim president, gave amnesty to Villa's men and gave Villa a ranch, Canutillo, where he could have security and a means to live in retirement. Nonetheless, Villa met the same end as Zapata when he was assassinated in 1923 after a newspaper article indicated that he might be planning a comeback.

FROM DESTRUCTION TO CONSTRUCTION

The periodization of the Mexican Revolution typically casts 1910–1920 as the violent phase and 1920–1940 as the constructive phase. In some ways, the periodization is a bit misleading. Full-scale war had largely ended by 1917, when Villa's and Zapata's movements were in disarray and the constitution promised a new political order. Violence, however, continued to plague the countryside and to play a role in politics well into the 1920s.

The period from 1920–1934 was dominated by two veterans of the revolution: Alvaro Obregón and Plutarco Elías Calles. Obregón was the undisputed leader of the revolution, having been the architect of Villa's military defeats and leader of the coup that prevented Carranza from maintaining control of the presidency. Both were from a lower middle-class background in Sonora. But Obregón had been the epitome of the successful middle-class entrepreneur; he raised chickpeas on a 150-acre farm and became an expert mechanic, even patenting a harvester. Calles was less fortunate. The illegitimate son of a prominent hacendado, he had little success in his business endeavors before the revolution. As a school teacher, he was fired because parents complained about him. He was fired from a position as city treasurer because funds were missing from his department. He tried hotel management—the hotel burned down; farming—the farm went bankrupt; and milling—business that failed. His true success came with the revolution: He was an early supporter of Madero, rose to be a divisional general and governor of Sonora. Calles served as Obregón's government secretary before becoming president himself.

These leaders from Sonora declared themselves to be the rightful heirs of Madero and proclaimed an era of peace and reconstruction. A practical man, Obregón tried to reach compromises among the various conflicting sectors in order to rebuild the country. The destruction of the war had indeed been considerable: The railroad was bankrupt and in ruins; more than a 1,000 miles of telegraph lines were destroyed, agricultural and mining production had fallen by half. The foreign debt topped $1 billion, interest payments were overdue, and foreign governments demanded compensation for destruction of the property of their citizens. And the military consumed 60 percent of the national budget.

At the same time, veterans of the wars expected their goals to be met. As Saturnino Cedillo of rural Morelos, told the new government: "I want land. I want ammunition so that I can protect my land after I get it in case somebody tries to take it away from me. And I want plows, and I want schools for my children, and I want teachers, and I want books and pencils and blackboards and roads. And I want moving pictures for my people, too. And I don't want any Church or any saloon."

Obregón wisely named Zapatistas to be minister of agriculture and to head the new agrarian reform commission. But it took campesinos five to

Land Distribution in the Mexican Revolution

	EJIDOS HECTARES	0.1–1,000 HECTARES	1,000 HECTARES
1910	1.6%	26.6	71.8
1923	2.6	19.6	77.9
1940	22.5	15.9	61.6

Source: Adolfo Gilly, *The Mexican Revolution* Copyright 1983. Reprinted by permission of Verso, an imprint of New Loft Books Ltd.

eight years to get their land grants. Obregón distributed three million acres of land benefiting 140,000 people. But Luis Terrazas, who Obregón allowed to return from exile to Chihuahua, owned as much as Obregón distributed. More than half of Mexican territory in 1923 was still owned by 2,700 wealthy families, and 25 percent of the land belonged to a mere 114 families. Furthermore, the majority of Mexico's rural population consisted of resident farmhands, and they were not eligible to get land. Calles went further than Obregón, distributing eight million acres of land, mostly in the form of ejidos from 1924 to 1928. He accompanied the land grants with credit and agricultural schools. But from 1928 until 1934, agrarian reform became a low priority and little land was distributed.

The record on labor reform was equally mixed. During the war, Obregón had cultivated the Mexico City workers' organization Casa del Obrero Mundial. He supported their strike against the Mexican Telegraph and Telephone Company, and in turn 5,000 union members joined his army, forming the Red Battalions. When he ran for president in 1919, Obregón again sought out the workers, forging an alliance with the *Confederación Regional Obrera Mexicana* (CROM; Regional Confederation of Mexico Workers). Nonetheless, real wages barely improved and remained well below the three peso a day minimum that, according to the national labor commission, was necessary for subsistence. Calles took the alliance even further, naming CROM boss Luis Morones to his cabinet as minister of industry, commerce and labor. A massive union organizing drive brought even Mexico City's prostitutes into unions.

One of the most significant aspects of building the new Mexico was the construction of a new culture. Obregón named as his education minister José Vasconcelos, one of Mexico's leading intellectuals. Vasconcelos was determined to bring education to the masses, partly through a commitment to rural education and partly by making art available to the masses by fostering the painting of murals in public places.

The beginning of the mural movement generally is attributed to the paintings in the *Escuela Nacional Preparatoria* (National Preparatory School), which prepared students to enter the National University. It was there that the great artists Diego Rivera, José Clemente Orozco, and David Alfaro Siquieros made their first contributions to the movement. In 1922, Rivera initiated the formation of the *Sindicato de Pintores, Escultores y Grabadores Revolucionarios de México* (Syndicate of Revolutionary Technical Workers, Painters, and Sculptors of Mexico), an organization that urged collective art creation that would play a significant role in the struggle for justice for the masses. The syndicate rejected easel painting and championed "monumental art in all its forms, because it is public property." However, the largely conservative art community denounced the murals, which were even attacked by the students, who threw mud and stones at the murals by Orozco and Siquieros.

All three went on to paint other murals, which reflected their radical political views. But it was Rivera's work that would become emblematic in its adulation of traditional folk elements of Mexican culture. Critics charged that he represented an idealized indigenous past, whereas the real Mexican masses would gladly trade their colorful pottery and woven clothing for modern, mass-produced goods. The veneration of the indigenous *campesino* went hand-in-hand with Vasconcelos's desire to bring education to the countryside. But while the revolution supposedly celebrated rather than denigrated the campesino, it shared the old liberal doctrine of wanting to assimilate the indigenous into a society that was largely not of their making. Vasconcelos set up an "Indian Department" focused on teaching Spanish to the indigenous so that they could enter the school system and be incorporated into mestizo society.

A tremendous effort was made to educate teachers and send them to the countryside, where more than 1,000 rural schools were established from 1920 to 1924. The curriculum was basic—reading, writing, arithmetic, geography, and history. The tone was secular, and teachers often encountered hostility from both the Church, which was losing its educational role, and from rural families themselves, who often viewed the teachers as atheist outsiders. Nonetheless, the government continued to emphasize education, adding another 2,000 rural schools from 1924 to 1928.

In the 1920s, education in Mexico took a socialist turn. Math lessons calculated excess profits of factory owners and geography classes examined imperialist exploitation. New history texts focused on the struggle of the oppressed masses against capitalists, imperialists, and importantly, the Church. A textbook published by the state of Tabasco's Redemption Press in 1929 cautioned, "The worker's ignorance is very dangerous, for it allows him to be victimized by the exploiters, priests, and alcohol."

The attitude towards the Church displayed in the schools was one of the factors leading to the Cristero Revolt, an armed conflict between militant Catholics and the government. The catalyst for the uprising was Calles's determination to enforce the anticlerical provisions of the 1917 constitution. The Church had been hostile to the revolution almost from its beginning. In 1911, the clergy formed *Partido Católico Nacional* (PCN; National Catholic

Party), whose candidates for the 1912 congressional elections swept Jalisco and Zacatecas, making it a major political party. The Maderistas annulled the results, turning the PCN against Madero and the revolution. Huerta courted the Church hierarchy, and both Zapata and Villa had cordial relations with the Church. The Zapatistas in particular tended to be religious, riding into battle with banners of the Virgin de Guadelupe. Carranza was hostile to the Church and welcomed the anticlerical aspects of the 1917 constitution, but he did not try to enforce them.

Obregón was committed to reconciling all elements of Mexico, so he did not enforce the constitution either. But during the heated days of the war, in 1914 and 1915, Obregón had been unsparing in his pursuit of anti-revolutionary clergy. Church leaders did not forgive him for having priests and nuns imprisoned, seizing churches and convents, and closing Catholic schools. During Obregón's presidency, Church leaders became more openly opposed to the revolution. The Church also challenged the State and its connection to labor in 1920 by creating the *Confederación Nacional Católica de Trabajadores* (CNCT; Catholic Labor Confederation); by 1922, the organization boasted 80,000 members, as many as the CROM, which responded to the competition by sending thugs to attack priests and churches.

Calles was determined to demonstrate the supremacy of the state and to end the Church's challenge. He took aim at the Church within weeks of taking office by reminding the state governments that they needed to control the activities of the clergy. The states immediately began to take action; for example, the state of Tabasco limited the number of priests to six, one for each 30,000 residents. In 1926, the archbishop of Mexico, José Mora y del Río, commented in a newspaper interview that, given such incidents in the various states, Roman Catholics could not accept the Constitution. His comments gave Calles an excuse to attack the Church by disbanding religious processions, deporting foreign-born priests and nuns, and closing monasteries, convents and Catholic schools. The Church, in turn, went on strike, refusing to conduct masses or administer the sacraments. The strike lasted three years, leaving babies unbaptized and sending the old to the grave without last rites.

Loyal Catholics were incensed and ready to fight. Most priests—some 3,390 out of 3,600—fled to the cities. Of those who remained, only about forty openly supported what became known as the Cristero Rebellion, named after their cry, ¡*Viva Cristo Rey*! (Long live Christ the King!). The rebellion was essentially a series of uncoordinated local protests. There was little activity in the generally secular northern states or in the south, where strong indigenous cultures in such states as Oaxaca and Chiapas competed with the Church. But the central states of Michoacan, Jalisco, Guanajuato, and Colima were in open revolt.

The violence was as severe as the darkest days of the revolution. Catholic militants murdered teachers and burned down government schools. Government troops retaliated by trying to kill one priest for every teacher. By the time the war was over, it had cost the lives of 90,000 combatants and thousands of people caught between the government and militant Catholics. The war was finally ended by Calles's successor, Emilio Portes Gil, who agreed to enforce the laws in a less provocative way.

Portes Gil came to the presidency after the Cristeros claimed their ultimate victim—Obregón had won another term of office, but before he could take office, he was assassinated by a Cristero militant. Portes Gil was appointed to serve from 1928 to 1930, and Calles protégé Pascual Ortiz Rubio won election to the 1930–1934 term. Ortiz ran as the first candidate of the new *Partido Nacional Revolucionario* (PNR; National Revolutionary Party) founded by Calles to consolidate the revolution. Ortiz Rubio lasted two years before resigning and being replaced by Abelardo Rodriguez.

It was clear to everyone, however, that none of the three presidents who served from 1928 to 1934 had any power. It was Calles who continued to rule as Jefe Maximo, lending the period the name Maximato. During these years, Calles moved revolutionary action to the right, while creating a public image and ideology that spouted leftwing rhetoric. For example, Zapata was hailed as an official national hero, conveniently overlooking the fact that the winners of the revolution actively fought Zapata and were responsible for his death. The cooptation of Zapata's image occurred as the actual distribution of agricultural land dwindled.

THE APEX OF THE REVOLUTION

Calles expected to continue ruling Mexico under the next president, Lázaro Cárdenas. Cárdenas, who joined the revolution when he was 15 years old, had been a protégé of Calles, who called him "the kid." He moved up along with his mentor. In 1930, he was named president of the PNR, and in 1934 he was tapped as the party's presidential candidate.

Although his victory was all but assured, Cárdenas campaigned across the country, building a network of supporters. He developed a reputation for modesty, largely by refusing to live in Chapultapec castle, the traditional presidential palace. His immediate goal in the presidency was to wrest control from Calles. He purged his cabinet of Callistas and gave generous retirement benefits to generals so that he could replace them with his own men. He favored the new labor organization, the *Confederación de Trabajadores de México* (CTM; Mexican Workers' Confederation), rather than the CROM. The final confrontation took place in 1936, when demonstrating workers demanded that Calles be removed from the political scene. Cárdenas ordered Calles into exile and emerged as his own man.

Cárdenas also reorganized the revolutionary party into the *Partido Revolucionario Mexicano* (PRM; Mexican Revolutionary Party), based on four pillars of society: the military, labor, agrarian, and popular sectors. Mexicans were mobilized into groups that communicated directly with the government, encouraging a vertical hierarchy of base and state, rather than a horizontal linking of mass organizations. This corporate structure minimized social conflict, and during the Cárdenas years, it largely worked in favor of the masses. For example, labor unions dealt directly with the government, rather than industry; the government intervened on labor's behalf. However, the corporatist organization also created the basis for future state domination of society.

The president also turned his attention to agrarian reform, intent upon rebuilding the traditional ejido. During his administration, which was Mexico's first sexenio, or six-year term, the Cárdenas government distributed nearly fifty million acres of land, representing 66 percent of the total land distributed from 1917 to 1940. In addition to land distribution, the government created the *Banco de Crédito Ejidal* (Ejido Credit Bank) to provide financing. The massive distribution of land dramatically changed society in some parts of Mexico, destroying the old hacendado class. But that class was replaced by a welter of new elites: agrarian reform officials and local political bosses. The process to receive land was often long and torturous, the amount received frequently insufficient. And in many parts of Mexico, no redistribution of land took place at all.

Although Cárdenas has been portrayed as a beloved figure among the campesinos, many rose up against him over his hostility toward the Church and a renewed socialist emphasis in school curriculum. Even in his home state of Michoacán, campesinos who were the very targets of his policies boycotted the schools and said they would prefer not to get land unless local churches were reopened.

The most dramatic event in the Cárdenas presidency was the expropriation of the foreign-owned oil companies. The conflict began in 1936, when workers went on strike to demand higher wages and improved working conditions. The dispute was sent to an industrial arbitration board, which ruled in favor of the workers. The oil companies appealed to the Mexican Supreme Court, which upheld the board's ruling. At that point, the companies simply refused to abide by the decision. Cárdenas insisted that foreign companies must follow national laws and ordered the nationalizing of seventeen oil companies. The president wrote of his decision in his diary: "I believe that there are few opportunities so special as this for Mexico to achieve independence from imperialist capital, and because of this my government will comply with the responsibility conferred by the revolution." The confiscated companies were organized into *Petroleos Mexicanos* (PEMEX) and became a symbol of economic sovereignty.

However, the outcry from the oil companies was matched by the U.S. and British governments. Cárdenas negotiated a settlement of $24 million to the companies—a far cry from the $200 million they claimed, and far above the $10 million he deemed to be fair. The United States and Great Britain responded by boycotting Mexican oil and silver, with oil output falling by nearly 60 percent and silver production falling 50 percent.

Nonetheless, the expropriation was wildly popular in Mexico. Even the Catholic Church supported the decision by raising the Mexican flag above the national cathedral. Throughout the country, people gathered to contribute their pesos to pay the indemnity to the companies.

U.S. Ambassador Josephus Daniels observed women lining up in the Zócalo, Mexico City's main plaza, to contribute: "They took off wedding rings, bracelets, earrings, and put them, as it seemed to them, on a national altar. All day long, until the receptacles were full and running over, these Mexican women gave and gave. When night came crowds still waited to deposit their offerings, which comprised everything from gold and silver to animals and corn."

A REVOLUTIONARY BALANCE SHEET

By 1940, Mexico was a far different country than it had been in 1910. There was progress in many areas, but the country was still beset with problems. Although nearly 23 percent of the nation's land had been redistributed into ejidos, 62 percent of the land remained in farms of 1,000 or more hectares (down from 72 percent in 1910). School attendance for children six to ten years old increased from 30 to 70 percent. But rural poverty was still endemic. In 1940, 27 percent of the population was too poor to afford shoes—a figure that rose to 75 percent in the mostly indigenous states of Chiapas and Tabasco. Eighty percent of the population outside Mexico City lived without indoor plumbing or sewage disposal.

By 1940, critics wondered whether the Mexican Revolution was dead or whether it had been a revolution at all. Some dismissed it as a bourgeois revolution, won by the middle classes, who now took the place of the former Porfirian elites. Others complained that the country was still run by caudillos and that the new political party was as corrupt as its predecessors.

Perhaps the best analysis is offered by Michael J. Gonzales: "The popular and agrarian character of the revolution makes it a social revolution. The conflict pitted landless peasants, elements of the working classes, and discontented provincial gentry against the dictator Díaz, his elite supporters, and the federal army. The revolution threw out the old guard, reinvented the state, and made possible historic social and economic reforms. The revolutionary state gave landless peasants hundreds of thousands of hectares of land, nationalized foreign-owned petroleum companies, and significantly expanded public education. If the final outcome failed to eradicate poverty, create democracy, or achieve economic independence, the event still remains revolutionary."

RECOMMENDED READINGS

Becker, Marjorie. *Setting the Virgin on Fire: Lázaro Cárdenas, Michoacán Peasants, and the Redemption of the Mexican Revolution*. Berkeley: University of California Press, 1995.

Brunk, Samuel. *¡Emiliano Zapata! Revolution and Betrayal in Mexico*. Albuquerque: University of New Mexico Press, 1995.

Gonzales, Michael J. *The Mexican Revolution, 1910–1940*. Albuquerque: University of New Mexico Press, 2002.

Hart, John Mason. *Revolutionary Mexico: The Coming and Process of the Mexican Revolution*. Berkeley: University of California Press, 1987.

Katz, Friedrich. *The Life and Times of Pancho Villa*. Stanford, CA: Stanford University Press, 1998.

Knight, Alan. *The Mexican Revolution, v. 1. Porfirians, Liberals and Peasants v. 2, Counter-revolution and Reconstruction*. Cambridge: Cambridge University Press, 1986.

Womack Jr., John. *Zapata and Mexican Revolution*. New York: Random House, 1968.

CHAPTER 8

FROM WORLD WARS TO COLD WAR

While Mexico dealt with its domestic divisions, the entire region was buffeted by a series of international shocks: World War I (1914–1918), the Great Depression (1929–1940), and World War II (1939–1945). The crises were particularly problematic because by the early twentieth century, the export economy was well entrenched throughout Latin America, making the region extremely dependent on the well-being of foreign economies. Latin American food sales depended on working-class buying power in Europe and in the United States. The expansion of tin, henequen, and other raw material production depended on technological advances abroad. National governments had become dependent on export revenues to balance their budgets, keep the armed forces paid and equipped, and to meet domestic demands for services.

The international crises disrupted Latin American foreign trade: Economic downturns led to political instability, and throughout the region dictators came to power. These strongmen increased government's role in the economy, and new institutions were created to help stem the crisis. Import substitution industrialization and agriculture made the Latin American region less dependent on the international economy and more interdependent.

In the aftermath of World War II, the United States replaced Europe as the model for Latin Americans. They looked north and considered two issues: democracy and development. The U.S. rhetoric of the war years in the fight against fascism inspired Latin Americans, who saw their dictators in a new light. And the unprecedented wealth of the United States in the postwar years prompted Latin Americans to reconsider how to modernize their economies. By the 1950s, however, Latin Americans would discover that their own attempts at democracy and development would become entangled with United States economic expansion and the new Cold War realities.

Old questions surfaced again: Why had Latin America not developed? How can development be achieved? Can democracy and development occur simultaneously?

ECONOMIC CRISES

From 1914–1945, Latin America was buffeted by international affairs, paying a price for its extensive openness to the world economy. As Europe became immersed in World War I, investment in Latin America plummeted. Public loans to Brazil fell from $19.1 million in 1913 to $4.2 million in 1914 and to zero in 1915. Commodity exports suffered from both shortages of shipping and a decline in European demand for goods. Because most Latin American governments relied on import tariffs, there was a precipitous decline in government revenue. Chile, for example, saw government revenues drop by two thirds from 1911 to 1915.

World War I also provided opportunities for a few Latin American countries. Venezuela began exporting oil, and Mexican oil imports increased. Peruvian copper, Bolivian tin, and Chilean nitrates were in demand. Despite the success of these products, economies suffered as import prices rose along with trade surpluses and budget deficits, fueling inflation. Inflation eroded urban real wages, leading to political upheavals.

The curtailment of trade with Europe benefited the United States, which became the main supplier not just of Mexico and Central America, but of the entire region. The United States proved to be a limited market, however, for those whose products competed with American products, such as grain and beef. At the end of the war, Great Britain's slow recovery led the United States to consolidate its new prominence in Latin America by becoming the dominant lender. U.S. capital, however, was usually tied to foreign-policy concerns. This was the era of dollar diplomacy, and the United States gave substantial loans—then took over customs houses to guarantee their repayment.

Europe's recovery in the 1920s did little to help Latin America. A drop in the birth rate in Europe led to a slowdown in the demand for Latin American primary products. European investors turned their attention to their own continent. And new synthetic substitutes dried up the market for Latin American cotton, rubber, forest dyes, timber, and nitrates. The instability of commodity prices led Latin Americans to increase production, which in turn led to a decline in prices. Furthermore, the increase in worldwide production of strategic war products, such as oil, copper, and tin, led to market gluts and a drop in prices.

To rebuild their economies, Latin Americans sought loans. The United States responded with so much money—$1 billion from 1926 to 1928—that it became known as the dance of the millions. Some of the

Exports as Share of Gross Domestic Product in Latin America, 1928 and 1938

COUNTRY	1928	1938
Argentina	29.8	15.7
Brazil	17.0	21.2
Chile	35.1[a]	32.7
Colombia	24.8	24.1
Costa Rica	56.5	47.3
El Salvador	48.7	45.9
Guatemala	22.7	17.5
Honduras	52.1	22.1
Mexico	31.4	13.9
Nicaragua	25.1	23.9
Peru	33.6[a]	28.3
Uruguay	18.0[b]	18.2
Venezuela	37.7	29.0

[a]Data are for 1929.
[b]Data are for 1930.
Source: Victor Bulmer-Thomas, *The Economic History of Latin America Since Independence*, 2 ed. New York, NY: Cambridge University Press, 2003, 190.

money went into the still-small industrial sector, which by 1914 was well-established in Argentina, Brazil, Chile, Mexico, Peru, and Uruguay. However, most expansion of industrial production involved a more intensive use of existing facilities. By the end of the 1930s, Argentina was the only country in the region where industry's share of gross domestic product exceeded 20 percent. Most of the region continued to rely on exports. By the end of the 1920s, almost all export earnings were still earned from production of primary products, and as few as three products accounted for at least half of all foreign exchange earnings. Seventy percent of foreign trade was conducted with the United States, Great Britain, France, and Germany.

When the Great Depression hit in 1929, Latin American governments saw the markets for their products shrivel. As industry contracted in the industrialized countries, they stopped importing minerals from the developing world. Demand and prices for primary products fell, with the unit value of exports dropping more than 50 percent from 1928 to 1932. In Argentina, export values dropped from $1,537 million in 1929 to $561 million in 1932. But while prices and volume of exports fell, the interest on the sizable foreign debts of the 1920s did not. Governments began to default on their loans, and new credits were not forthcoming.

The economic turmoil caused Latin American attention to shift to yet another form of nationalism: economic. The difficult years emphasized once again to the Latin Americans the dependency and vulnerability of their economies. Their monocultural export economies collapsed. Cuba's economy broke down: Foreign Trade in the early 1930s was 10 percent of the 1929 figure. Uruguay's exports dropped 80 percent in the early 1930s. Brazil's exports plummeted from $445.9 million in 1929 to $180.6 million in 1932. In short, by 1932, Latin America exported 65 percent less than it had in 1929,

Annual Average Rates of Growth by Sector, 1939–1945 (in Percentages)

COUNTRY	VALUE OF EXPORTS[a]	VOLUME OF EXPORTS[b]	GDP[c]	AGRICULTURE[d]	INDUSTRY[e]
Argentina	8.0	−2.9	2.1	0.2	3.6
Bolivia	15.7	+6.0			
Brazil	13.6	−2.0	2.4	0	5.3
Chile	7.1	+3.4	4.0[f]	0[f]	9.3[f]
Colombia	10.4	+3.4	2.6	2.2	5.1
Costa Rica	5.6	−2.2	−0.1	0	−3.5
Cuba	17.1	+2.0[g]	1.8	n/a	4.3
Dominican Republic	15.4	−1.4			
Ecuador	20.1	+2.5	4.2	2.7	5.2
El Salvador	9.8	−1.1	2.2	1.4	3.9
Guatemala	8.5	+3.7	0.9	−6.3	4.4
Haiti	15.2	+1.5			
Honduras	3.5	+2.1	3.5	2.4	4.7
Mexico	9.4	+1.3	6.2	2.3	9.4
Nicaragua	6.2	−4.9	3.9	−2.6	7.9
Panama	4.7	−9.3			
Paraguay	21.6	+8.0	0.4	−1.7	1.0
Peru	6.6	−1.8	4.8[f]	n/a	4.8
Uruguay	11.7	+1.8	1.7	−1.0	3.5
Venezuela	13.6	+8.9	5.3	0	9.2
Latin America	10.5	−0.5	3.4	0.8	5.7

[a]Based on dollar values at current prices.
[b]Based on constant (1963) prices.
[c]Based on 1970 prices.
[d]Net agricultural output (1970 prices).
[e]Net manufacturing output (1970 prices).
[f]Data are for 1940–1945.
[g]Based on volume of sugar exports only.
Source: Victor Bulmer-Thomas, *The Economic History of Latin America Since Independence*, 2nd ed. New York, NY: Cambridge University Press, 2003, 237.

proving once again that foreign trade contributed mightily to the cyclical fluctuations of the Latin American economy.

Nationalists demanded that steps be taken to increase the viability of the national economies and conversely to reduce their dependency on the fluctuations of the international market caused by the buying whims of a few highly industrialized nations. Plans were made to increase economic diversification and to promote industrialization. Industrialization appealed to both common sense and pride. For one thing, it promised to diversify the economy; for another, it kept foreign exchange from being spent to import what could be manufactured at home. At the same time, an acute shortage of foreign currencies meant that either the nations manufactured their own goods or they did without.

The economic crisis motivated the governments to play an increasingly active role in the national economies. They introduced long-range economic planning, exerted new controls, and offered incentives. Devalued currency, import controls, and higher tariffs stimulated national industry, and all these measures received the support of the nationalists. The wider participation of the governments in the economies and the mounting demands for faster development shifted the leadership of the nationalist movement from the intellectuals, who had long enjoyed a near monopoly, to the governments themselves, which began to understand the potential power of nationalist thought. At the same time the base of support for nationalism expanded to sometimes include the urban working classes.

Latin America responded to the Great Depression with domestic production of formerly imported goods, both manufactured products and food crops, which had often been imported by countries that had turned their fields over to commercial crops for export. The two strategies—import-substituting industrialization (ISI) and import-substituting agriculture (ISA)—coupled with export promotion helped foster domestic demand for goods. Some countries, such as Brazil, Mexico, Chile, Cuba, Peru, Venezuela, Costa Rica, and Guatemala, made fast recoveries as a result. Recovery came much slower for the rest of the region, and particularly lagged in Honduras, Nicaragua, Uruguay, Paraguay, and Panama. Some of the recovery can be attributed to new trade partners. From 1932 to 1938, Germany, Italy, and Japan became important importers of Latin American goods. The European market was purchasing 55 percent of exports and supplying 45 percent of imports by 1938.

Those new markets, however, were cut off with the outbreak of World War II. But the Second World War also presented new opportunities for Latin America, which became the only raw material producer in the world that was not a site of hostilities. Trade increased between Latin America and the United States, particularly for tin and oil, and trade increased among Latin American countries, with the larger, industrializing regions exporting to the rest. Argentina, Chile, Brazil, and Mexico even developed a limited capital goods industry. Brazil's President Getulio Vargas (1930–1945, 1951–1954) played Germany against the United States, convincing the U.S. to replace the German steel manufacturer Krupp's planned investment in a steel industry. As a result, the United States funded construction of the Volta Redonda steel mill.

Nationalism remained an amorphous sentiment, but passions could be brought to a boil over certain issues and none was more inflammable than oil. It symbolized economic nationalism and represented the longing many Latin Americans felt to control their own natural resources. Nationalists argued that the discovery and exploitation of their own petroleum was not only economically desirable but was also the guarantee of real national independence and, in the case of several of the larger countries, of world-power status. "Whoever hands over petroleum to foreigners threatens our own independence," one Latin American nationalist leader warned. No acts in recent memory received more popular acclaim than the nationalization of foreign oil industries in Bolivia in 1937 and in Mexico in 1938.

When the oil question is handled adroitly, it can serve as a strong prop buttressing a nationalist government. Brazil's Vargas ably used the oil issue to his advantage. Sensing the growing importance of oil, emotionally and economically, he created the National Petroleum Council in the 1930s to coordinate and intensify the search for oil. In 1939, the first successful well was drilled. The excited nationalists at once called for the creation of a national oil industry. In a bid for wider popular support, Vargas urged the creation of a state oil monopoly to oversee exploration and to promote the development of petroleum resources. Its creation in 1953 followed a passionate national campaign and marked a major victory for the nationalists. They had triumphed over those who argued that it would be more economical for experienced foreign companies to drill for oil and pay Brazil a royalty on whatever was pumped out. The nationalists denounced that argument. After all, the issue was an emotional, not an economic, one. They wanted Brazil to retain control over one of its most precious and important resources. Their arguments convinced the masses that a national oil industry represented sovereignty, power, independence, and well-being. The masses responded with enthusiastic support, a demonstration of the power that economic nationalism can muster.

DICTATORS AND POPULISTS

As the prosperity of the 1920s gave way to the depression of the 1930s, unrest rippled through Latin America, and governments fell in rapid succession. In 1930, the armed forces overthrew the governments in the Dominican Republic, Bolivia, Peru, Argentina, Brazil, and Guatemala. In 1931, the pattern continued in Panama, Chile, Ecuador, and El Salvador.

Anastasio Somoza García was one of the dictators to come to power in Latin America during the 1930s. Somoza's rule, however, endured far beyond that of most of his contemporaries. He was followed in office by his sons, Luis and Anastasio Somoza Debayle. (Library of Congress)

The men who came to power in the 1930s tended to be personalist dictators who put their own stamps on government. They were known for their brutality and corruption, and they amassed fortunes during their years of absolute control. Some came to power through the institutions founded during the years of United States occupation: Rafael Léonidas Trujillo, who dominated the Dominican Republic from 1930 to 1961, was the commander of the Army that formed out of the constabulary that the United States established before withdrawing its occupation forces in 1924. Anastasio Somoza García came to power as head of the National Guard, which the United States created in Nicaragua to guarantee order when U.S. troops withdrew in 1934. Somoza took power in 1936 and ruled until his assassination in 1956. His elder son, Luís, inherited the mantle until his death in 1967, when he was succeeded by his younger brother, Anastasio.

The new dictators served U.S. interests by guaranteeing order. Their authoritarianism was ignored under the guise of Franklin Delano Roosevelt's new policy of nonintervention in the region, known as the Good Neighbor

Establishment of Depression Dictatorships, 1930s

COUNTRY	REGIME
Argentina	Gen. José Uriburu, 1930–1932 Gen. Agustín P. Justo "elected" president (1932–1938)
Bolivia	Self-coup and "elections" with oversight by military junta, 1930; army "arrests" President Daniel Salamanca, 1934; Cols. David Toro, Germán Busch; "military socialism" (1936–1939)
Brazil	Military junta, then regime of Getúlio Vargas with army support (1930–1945)
Chile	"Socialist republic" (1932)
Cuba	Fulgencio Batista; "sergeants' coup" (1933)
Dominican Republic	Gen. Rafael Trujillo (1930–1938; 1942–1952)
Ecuador	Nineteen presidents from 1931 to 1948; none complete term; 1932, four-day civil war, Quito garrison drives congress from capital, provincial regiments restore congress; coup in 1935, army imposes Federico Páez (1935–1937); coup by Minister of Defense Gen. Alberto Enriquez (1937–1938)
El Salvador	Gen. Maximiliano Hernández Martínez (1931–1944)
Guatemala	Gen. Jorge Ubico (1931–1944)
Honduras	Gen. Tiburcio Carías Andino (1932–1947)
Nicaragua	Gen. Anastasio Somoza García (1936–1956)
Paraguay	Col. Rafael Franco (1936); Gen. José Félix Estigarribia (1937–1940)
Peru	Col. Luis Sánchez Cerro (1931–1933); Gen. Oscar Benavides (1933–1939)
Uruguay	President Gabriel Terra (self-coup) (1933–1938)
Venezuela	Gen. Eleazar López Contreras (1935–1941)

Source: Brian Loveman, *For la Patria: Politics and the Armed Forces in Latin America.* Copyright 1999. Reprinted by permission of SR Books, now an imprint of Rowman & Littlefield Publishers, Inc.

Policy. The brutality of the regimes was no secret to the United States, as evidenced by the oft-told, but apparently apocryphal tale, that FDR once said of Somoza, "He's a son of a bitch, but he's our son of a bitch." The words were likely uttered by FDR's Secretary of State Cordell Hull, but FDR certainly shared his sentiments. Interestingly, some Dominicans insist that the words were spoken in relation to Trujillo, not Somoza.

Both Trujillo and Somoza censored the press, suppressed or co-opted labor movements, and used the police force to punish enemies and dissenters. Trujillo was known for his megalomania; he held at least forty official titles, including "Genius of Peace" and "The First and Greatest of the Dominican Chiefs of State." His brutality was most clearly demonstrated in the 1937 military massacre of Haitian workers, killing as many as 25,000 people.

Somoza García was not shy about using the National Guard to intimidate or eliminate his enemies, as evidenced by the assassination of Augusto César Sandino, the Liberal general whose ragtag army fought against U.S. occupation from 1927–1933. But he also saw the need to make alliances. He wooed labor during the 1930s and made deals with the political opposition in the 1940s, guaranteeing them representation but preserving his own power. Somoza's regime was characterized by his greed, and he became perhaps the wealthiest man in Nicaragua, and by his lack of concern for the people. Reportedly, when it was suggested that Nicaragua might benefit from a more educated population, Somoza replied, "I don't want an educated population; I want oxen."

Somoza and Trujillo's brutality paled, however, next to Maximiliano Hernandez Martínez, who took power in El Salvador in 1932 after overthrowing the constitutionally elected president Alberto Araujo. Araujo had adopted as his campaign the ideas of Salvadoran intellectual Alberto Masferrer, who called for redistribution of wealth, providing the "vital minimum." Araujo named Hernandez Martínez as his vice president, and he watched the fledgling Communist organizations under Faribundo Martí conduct hunger strikes and protests, while the countryside grew restive as the coffee economy collapsed. (The average price of coffee had dropped from $15.75 per hundred weight in 1928 to $5.97 in 1932.) An easily defeated uprising in the province of Sonsonate led the Hernandez Martínez government to respond with that has become known as *la matanza* (the massacre), a brutal attack on the rural, mostly indigenous, population, leaving an estimated 30,000 dead. After the *matanza*, Hernandez Martínez became known as El Brujo, the warlock, because of his devotion to the occult. He held seances in the presidential palace, encouraged children to go barefoot so they could "better receive the beneficial effluvia of the planet, the vibrations of the earth," and hung colored lights across the streets in San Salvador to stem a smallpox epidemic.

In Cuba, the path to dictatorship was a bit different: a democratically elected president became a dictator. Gerardo Machado was elected in 1924 on the "Platform of Regeneration." His reform program included diversification of exports, encouragement of new industry, and tariff reform, and his efforts won him reelection in 1928. But his reforms depended on prosperity, which came to an end with the Great Depression. Sugar had sold for 22.5 cents per pound at the height of 1920s prosperity; but by 1930 it dropped to 2.5 cents. Sugar production dropped by 60 percent, sending shock waves through the economy. Machado greeted the inevitable social and political unrest with repression. By 1931 there was open warfare as moderate leaders were jailed. His brutal attempts to hold power, however, led the army to overthrow him in 1933 rather than face the possibility of U.S. intervention.

A longer lasting rule was demonstrated in Brazil by Getúlio Vargas, a defeated presidential candidate who took power in a military coup in 1930. Vargas suspended congress, the state legislatures and local governments and ruled by decrees. In 1934 he staged elections and instituted a new constitution, which nationalized banking and insurance. He also emphasized industrialization and oversaw the formation of the national oil industry, Petrobras, and the founding of the steel mill Volta Redonda. The resulting increase in the working class led to worker mobilizations and fears of social revolution. Vargas responded in 1937 with the Estado Nôvo, or New State, an idea he took from Mussolini's Italy. His government became increasingly authoritarian, and he relied on press censorship and secret police to prevent dissent.

Vargas discovered, however, that he could win the masses to his side via populism, a new political tool. Populism was the political movement that characterized much of Latin America from roughly 1930 to 1965. It was labeled as a people's movement because it was based on mass electoral participation and pledged to address popular concerns. But populism was also hierarchical and was directed from above by a charismatic leader. These urban movements relied largely on a coalition of the working class, labor unions, middle classes, and industrial elites. In the process, they coopted the more radical ideas of the masses and redirected them in a nonrevolutionary direction. Growing poverty, first because of the Depression and then because of the nature of industrial development and urban growth, led to fears of revolution. Populism was the answer, and it seemed to please most sectors of the increasingly diverse Latin American society—all except the oligarchic elites and their revolutionary opposition. The oligarchy objected to their loss of power and to the transfer of wealth to the working class. The revolutionary left complained that populism depended on the largesse of the populist leader rather than on structural changes won by organized masses.

But the charismatic populist leaders spoke an intoxicating nationalist vocabulary. Rhetorically convincing, ideologically weak, they offered immediate benefits—better salaries, health services, the nationalization of resources—rather than institutional reforms. With the notable exception of Mexico's Lázaro Cárdenas, they focused their attention on the cities.

Vargas clearly understood the importance of the growing proletariat in Brazil. Almost at once after taking power in 1930, he created the Ministry of Labor to serve as the means by which the government dealt with the workers. By careful maneuvering, he used the urban workers to help check the formerly overwhelming power of the traditional elite. The workers pledged their support to him in return for the benefits he granted them. With a highly paternalistic—and some say demagogic—flourish, Vargas conceded to the workers more benefits than they had previously obtained through their own organizations and strikes. A decree ordered the Ministry of Labor to organize the workers into new unions under governmental supervision. By 1944, there were about 800 unions, with membership exceeding one-half million. The government prohibited strikes but established special courts and codes to protect the workers and to provide redress for their grievances. Under the government's watchful eye, the unions could and did bargain with management. Further, Vargas promulgated a wide variety of social legislation favoring the workers. He decreed retirement and pension plans, a minimum wage, a work week limited to forty-eight hours, paid annual vacations, maternal benefits and child care, educational opportunities and literacy campaigns, safety and health standards for work, and job security. In short, Vargas offered to labor in less than one decade the advances and benefits that the proletariat of the industrialized nations had agitated for during the previous century. Little wonder, then, that the urban working class (for the benefits did not extend into the rural areas) rallied to support the president. In 1945, Vargas created the Brazilian Labor Party, which frankly and aggressively appealed to the urban worker. Small at its inception, the party grew in size and strength during the following two decades, while the other two major parties declined in strength.

One of the icons of Latin American populism was Juan Domingo Perón, who came to power in Argentina as part of the string of military governments that took power beginning with a coup in 1930. Previous Argentine governments had done little to favor the workers, despite the industrial surge and expansion of labor's ranks. Perón perceived the potential of the working class and utilized it after the military coup d'etat of 1943 to project himself into power. As secretary of labor in the new government, he lavished attention in the form of wage increases and social legislation on the hitherto neglected workers, who responded with enthusiastic endorsement of their patron. During the two years that Perón held the labor portfolio, the trade unions nearly quadrupled in size. Perón adroitly manipulated the labor movement so that only leaders and unions beholden to him were officially recognized. When military leaders, suspicious and resentful of Perón's growing power, imprisoned him in October of 1945, workers from around the country angrily descended on the center of Buenos Aires and paralyzed the capital. The military, devoid of any visible popular support, immediately backed down and freed Perón. With the full backing of labor, he easily won the presidential elections of 1946 with 56 percent of the vote, and his followers dominated the new congress. During his decade of government, Perón relied heavily on the approval and support of organized labor. Urban workers, many of whom were inadequately integrated into city life, constituted the basis for Perón's highly successful mass movement.

Perón's popularity with the working masses was rivaled only by that of his wife, Eva Duarte de Perón (1919–1952), known affectionately as Evita. A former radio actress, Evita's dramatic flare made her an effective speaker in support of her husband. Furthermore, she drew on her own impoverished background, making her a sympathetic figure for the masses. She established the Eva Perón Foundation to provide aid to Argentina's poor, with funding coming from the private sector, induced sometimes by such strong-arm tactics as threats of government inspections, fines, and company closures. It has been suggested that the Peróns divided their political work along gendered lines, with Evita serving the maternal role, nurturing the poor and the needy. Although she scorned feminists, Evita devoted much time to strengthening the Peronist Women's Party and was instrumental in achieving the enfranchisement of Argentine women in 1947. In the 1951 elections, more than two million women voted for the first time, and six female senators and twenty-four deputies, all Peronistas, were sent to Congress.

Critics have noted that these populist governments gave a great deal to workers, but the price was government control of the labor movements. It would be too simplistic, however, to lament the demise of labor's freedom under the Peróns. In truth, labor never had enjoyed much liberty—at best it was tolerated—under previous governments, and certainly prior to Perón the unions had gained few victories for their rank and file. Unions did compromise their liberty but they did so in return for undisputed advantages and for a greater feeling of participation in government than workers had ever felt under the elitist leaders who had governed Argentina, with the possible exception of the middle-class government of Irigoyen. Perón's nationalist rhetoric cheered the workers, who identified more closely with his

Argentine president Juan Domingo Perón and his wife, the adored Evita, greet a throng of supporters from the balcony of the Casa Rosada, the presidential mansion, in 1950. The Peróns claimed to represent "los descamisados," the shirtless ones. (Library of Congress)

programs than with those of any previous government. They rallied behind him to taunt the foreign and native capitalists who they believed had exploited them. Perón, like the other populist leaders of the time, exuded a charismatic charm. He never lost the support of the working class. His fall from power in 1955 resulted from economic problems, loss of Church approval, the firm and increasingly effective opposition of the traditional oligarchy, and—most importantly—the withdrawal by the military of its previous support. The middle class and the elite rejoiced in his fall; the event stunned great multitudes of the masses who had given their leader enthusiastic support in return for more benefits and dignity than they had received from all the previous governments combined.

Obviously such populist governments as the one Perón so well represented found little favor among Latin America's elite, both the traditional elite and those who, thanks to greater social fluidity in the twentieth century, had recently achieved that exalted status. They resented any erosion of their power from below. Increasingly the middle class seemed frightened by the prospects of populist government and consequently tended to align with the elite. Certainly the previous accords between urban labor and the middle class, noticeable in some instances during the first decades of the twentieth century, disintegrated as the middle class became apprehensive of a threat, real or imagined, to their status and ambitions from labor. By the mid-twentieth century, identifying more with the elite against whom they had once struggled but whose lifestyle they incessantly aped, the middle class when forced to choose between the masses advocating change and the elite-backed status quo tended to opt for the latter.

Latin America Turns Inward

As World War II ended, Latin America faced a new world order, dominated by the United States and dedicated to free trade. The new order was established by the allied powers meeting at Bretton Woods, where they determined how to rebuild the postwar economy. The United States guaranteed a more international economy by providing a market, through open borders and unilaterally reduced tariffs; a stable currency, by pegging the dollar to gold at $35 an ounce; and providing capital, by investing in the rest of the world. Institutionally, the new order rested on three pillars: The International Monetary Fund, which would stabilize monetary relations by lending money to governments; the International Bank for Reconstruction and Development (IBRD, World Bank), which was to lend money at long-term rates to developing countries to build the infrastructure that would attract private investment; and the International Treaty Organization, which led to formation of the General Agreement on Trade and Tariffs (GATT), designed to negotiate tariff reductions and to free world trade.

At the Eighth Inter-American Conference held in Chapúltepec, Mexico, in 1945, U.S. representatives announced their commitment to free trade, ending the wartime agreements that had provided guarantees to Latin America. The United States then turned its attention to rebuilding the destroyed European economies via the Marshall Plan. Now that the United States could once again access Asian raw material supplies that had been cut off by the war, Latin America became a low priority.

Latin America tried to turn back to its former European markets, but Europe was struggling to rebuild and could buy little of Latin America's products. Although export volume grew slowly, export prices increased dramatically. Foreign exchange reserves grew, but they were quickly depleted by repayment of debts and the high demand for imports that once again flooded the region. Pessimistic about exports and buoyed by economic nationalism, Latin American leaders chose to look inward.

Their view was bolstered by the theories of the United Nations Economic Commission for Latin America (ECLA), founded in 1948 and headed by Argentine economist Raúl Prebisch. ECLA and Prebisch contended that over time the terms of trade went against Latin America because it exchanged low-price primary products for higher valued manufactured goods. Furthermore, international markets were dangerously unreliable and commodity prices were subject to boom-and-bust cycles. ECLA's recommendation was to take the unofficial import substitution industrialization policy of the war and the Depression years and make it a conscious policy decision. The policy of ISI gained a number of adherents: nationalists who believed it was important to have local industries to meet national needs; urban industrialists and workers, who wanted to see an expansion in industry; the middle-class, who anticipated the growth of the service sector associated with industrialization.

Argentina, Brazil, Chile, and Uruguay enthusiastically adopted the ISI model, erecting tariff barriers to limit imports that would compete with fledgling industries. They subsidized the inputs needed for industrial production, provided low-rate credit to create and expand an industrial base, and passed legislation requiring particular levels of domestic content for goods on the market. Brazil amply illustrated the growing importance of industry within the economy. In 1939, the industrial sector provided 17.9 percent of the national income; by 1963, it furnished 35.3 percent.

All nations of Latin America did not participate equally in the industrial surge. Industrialization concentrated in a few favored geographic areas. At the end of the 1960s, three nations, Argentina, Brazil, and Mexico, accounted for 80 percent of Latin America's industrial production. In fact, more than 30 percent of the total factory production was squeezed into the metropolitan areas of Buenos Aires, Mexico City, and São Paulo. Five other nations—Chile, Colombia, Peru, Uruguay, and Venezuela—produced 17 percent of Latin America's industrial goods, leaving the remaining 3 percent of the manufacturing to the twelve other republics.

Industrialization sowed the seeds of new problems for Latin America. For one thing, it was creating a new type of dependency in which the region relied ever more heavily on foreign investment, technology, technicians, and markets. For another, it funneled wealth increasingly into the hands of a few industrial elites. Furthermore, the ties between industrialists and large landowners were closer than most people realized or cared to admit. While at times there were separate landowning and industrialist classes, in many instances the two groups overlapped. Thus, one could observe a growing industrial concentration in the hands of a few alongside a great concentration of land ownership, and very often the same persons played the dual role of landowner and industrialist. Such an interrelationship of interests complicated reform efforts.

One significant consequence of industrialization has been the growth of a better defined urban proletariat class conscious of its goals and powers. As the labor movement expanded in the decades between 1914 and 1933, its leadership spoke increasingly in terms of major social changes. The ideological content of the labor programs, the increasingly efficient organization of the unions, and the new power that labor wielded worried the elites and the middle class. Governments yielded to some basic labor demands to limit working hours, set minimum wages, provide vacations, ensure sick and maternal leave, and legislate other social-welfare laws. But at the same time they moved to dominate, control, and finally co opt the labor movement.

One of the things that labor demanded, especially when it could not secure higher wages, was cheap food. Yet, though agriculture still formed the basis for the area's economy, few nations tried to reform the centuries-old agrarian structure. Mexico was the sole exception until the 1950s. The landowning system in most of Latin America remained flagrantly unjust and was based, at least in part, on the accumulation of huge tracts of land often by means of force, deceit, and dubious measures approved by the passage of time and the connivance of bureaucrats.

In no other area of comparable size in the world did there exist a higher concentration of land owned by the few than in Latin America. In the 1950s, 80 percent of the land in the region was owned by 5 percent of the population. On the opposite end of the scale lay another problem: the minifundium, a property so small that it often failed to sustain its owner, much less to contribute to the regional or national economies. These small farms constituted 80 percent of all farm units but comprised only 5 percent of the land. Statistics for the early 1960s showed that 63 percent of the rural population, or 18 million adult farmers, owned no land; another 5.5 million owned insufficient amounts of land; 1.9 million possessed sufficient land; and 100,000 owned too much land for the social and economic good of the area.

In very general terms, and with notable exceptions, a lack of efficiency characterized the large estates. They included much land their owners either did not cultivate or undercultivated. Experts estimated that Latin Americans in the midtwentieth century farmed only about 10 percent of their agricultural holdings. In Brazil, Venezuela, and Colombia, approximately 80 percent of the farmland was unused or unproductively used for cattle raising at the end of the 1950s. A 1960 study of Colombia revealed that the largest farmers, in control of 70 percent of the agricultural lands, cultivated only 6 percent of it. Farmers of fewer than thirteen acres, on the other hand, cultivated 66 percent of it.

The landowners continued to hold their property, not to farm but for purposes of prestige, investment, and speculation. As in the past, control of the land ensured control of the work force as well because the resulting land-lessness forced people to work on the great estates. With such large supplies of cheap labor, estate owners saw no need to modernize their farming tech-niques. The slash-and-burn method remained the most popular means of clearing the land. The farmers rarely spread fertilizer or did so sparingly. Consequently, the land eroded, became easily exhausted, and depleted quickly. Productivity, always low, fell. The farmer used the hoe, unmodified for centuries. The plow was rare, the tractor even rarer.

Increasingly Latin America needed to import food. Chile, for example, shifted in the 1940s from being a net agricultural exporter to becoming a net importer. By the mid-1950s, agricultural products accounted for 25 percent of Chile's total imports. In short, that nation was spending about 18 percent of its hard-earned foreign currency on food that Chile could grow itself, a tragedy by no means unique to Chile. By 1965, foodstuffs constituted 20 per-cent of Latin America's purchases abroad. Even with imports supplementing careless local production, the poor masses could not afford import prices. Starvation was not unknown, and malnutrition was common in wide regions of Latin America.

Agriculture in the twentieth century lost none of the speculative, reflexive nature so characteristic of the mercantilist past. For its prosperity, agriculture continued to rely heavily on a few export commodities, which were always very vulnerable on the international market. Prices depended on the demands of a few industrialized nations. Further, new producers and substitutes appeared to challenge and undersell them, thus increasing Latin America's economic vulnerability. Africa, in particular, emerged as a for-midable competitor for international markets. After World War II, the prices of agricultural products gradually declined to the dismay of the Latin Americans (while at the same time the prices of imported capital goods spiraled upward). Still, the latifundia by and large followed their usual practice of offering one crop for sale. For example, the well-being of an alarming number of Latin Americans at the end of the 1950s depended on a fair price for coffee; coffee composed 67 percent of Colombia's exports, 42 percent of El Salvador's, 41 percent of Brazil's, 38 percent of Haiti's, 34 percent of Guatemala's, and 31 percent of Costa Rica's. Other Latin American economies depended on the export of sugar, bananas, cacao, wheat, beef, wool, and mutton.

A Flirtation With Democracy

The economy was not the only aspect of Latin America to change in the post-war years. The rhetoric that accompanied the United States as it marched into World War II was heard throughout the hemisphere. The Allies' victory marked democracy's triumph over dictatorship, and the consequences shook Latin America. Questioning why they should support the struggle for democracy in Europe and yet suffer the constraints of dictatorship at home, many Latin Americans rallied to democratize their own political structures. A group of prominent middle-class Brazilians opposed to the continuation of the Vargas dictatorship mused publicly, "If we fight against fascism at the side of the United Nations so that liberty and democracy may be restored to all people, certainly we are not asking too much in demanding for ourselves such rights and guarantees."

In the surge toward democratic goals, the ideals of the nineteenth-century liberals revived. The times favored the democratic concepts professed by the middle class. Governments out of step with them toppled. A wave of freedom of speech, press, and assembly engulfed much of Latin America and bathed the middle class with satisfaction. New political parties emerged to represent broader segments of the population. Democracy, always a fragile plant anywhere, seemed ready to blossom throughout Latin America.

Nowhere was this change more amply illustrated than in Guatemala, where Jorge Ubico ruled as dictator from 1931 until 1944. Ubico, a former minister of war, carried out unprecedented centralization of the state and repression of his opponents. Although he technically ended debt peonage, the 1934 vagrancy law required the carrying of identification cards and improved the landlords' position in disputes with workers. The landlords, in turn, supported his regime because he prohibited independent labor organizing. He massacred the indigenous who rebelled, killed labor leaders and intellectuals, and made his friends rich.

In May and June of 1944 there were a series of anti-Ubico protests, led primarily by schoolteachers, shopkeepers, skilled workers, and students. They were influenced by Franklin Delano Roosevelt's four freedoms: freedom of speech and religion, freedom from want and fear. They were also influenced by Mexican President Lázaro Cárdenas's nationalization of the oil industry and agrarian reform program.

As he faced his opponents, Ubico could not count on the support of the United States, who viewed him as unreliable. He was openly pro-Nazi until the United States pressured him to support the Allies, and he was so untrustworthy that FBI agents were sent to oversee his confiscation of German property. The establishment of a U.S. air base near Guatemala City was as much to keep an eye on Ubico as to watch over the Panama Canal.

The series of nonviolent protests that led to Ubico's overthrow began when teachers refused to march in the annual Teachers' Day Parade. During one of the protests, the Guatemalan cavalry charged, killing and injuring some 200 people. Ubico then declared a state of siege. As the crisis mounted, a group of prominent teachers, lawyers, doctors, and businessmen, who supported the protesters, drew up the Petition of the 311, calling on Ubico to step down. The petition was presented to Ubico by several prominent citizens who he considered to be friends. Defeated, he resigned on July 1, 1944, and turned power over to General Federico Ponce. Ponce stood for election that fall, and the opposition recruited as their candidate Dr. Juan José Arévalo, a prominent educator, author of several textbooks on history, geography and civics, who was in exile in Argentina.

Arévalo considered himself a "spiritual socialist," an inspiration he credited to F.D.R. In his inaugural address, Arévalo said of the U.S. president: "He taught us that there is no need to cancel the concept of freedom in the democratic system in order to breathe into it a socialist spirit." Arévalo dissolved the secret police, removed all generals from their positions, dissolved the National Assembly, and repealed the constitution. An elected constitutional assembly wrote a new constitution and elected a new national assembly. The four priorities of the new government were to carry out agrarian reform, protect labor, improve education, and consolidate political democracy.

The challenge was formidable: An experienced bank clerk in Guatemala earned about $90 a month. A farmworker earned about five to twenty cents a day. Only 2 percent of all landowners owned 72 percent of the land. Ninety percent of all landowners only held 15 percent of productive acreage. Indigenous workers were still held by debt labor for 150 days of the year. Illiteracy was 75 percent in the general population and 95 percent among the indigenous, who constituted more than half of the population. Life expectancy for ladinos was 50 years and only 40 for the indigenous.

Coffee production was dominated by Guatemalan elites, and banana production was dominated by the U.S. giant, the United Fruit Company (UFCO). Arévalo addressed these problems by adopting a labor code, setting a minimum wage, and creating a National Production Institute to distribute credit, expertise, and supplies to small farmers. He distributed the confiscated German landholdings, ensured that smallholder titles were registered, and passed the Law of Forced Rental to guarantee that land would be rented to anyone with less than one hectare (2.5 acres). He also established a national bank and national planning office.

In 1950, after historic free elections, Jacobo Arbenz took office, having won 65 percent of the vote in an election that all observers agreed was fair and honest. Although democracy had been consolidated by Arévalo, it fell to Arbenz to work for economic change. In 1950, the annual per capita income of agricultural workers was $87. Of four million acres in plantations, less than 25 percent of the land was cultivated. In his inaugural address, Arbenz pledged to convert the country from a dependent nation to economic independence, to convert from a "feudal" to a modern, capitalist economy, and to raise the standard of living for the masses.

His blueprint was a report issued in 1950 by the International Bank for Reconstruction and Development. The report recommended government regulation of the energy companies and autonomous National Power Authority, setting wages to take prices into account, regulation of foreign business, industrialization to decrease reliance on foreign trade, and institution of a capital gains tax. The report criticized Guatemalan elites for raking in exorbitant profits and then investing them abroad.

Arbenz knew that the place to begin was the countryside, which he claimed was feudal and needed to be restructured for successful capitalism. The tool was to be the Agrarian Reform Law of 1952. The law declared that the uncultivated land on estates over 220 acres where less than two-thirds of the estate was under cultivation was subject to expropriation and redistribution. It left untouched farms smaller than 220 acres, and there was no upper limit on farm size as long as the land was fully cultivated. Confiscated land was to be compensated in 25-year bonds at 3 percent interest, based on the value of the property as declared by the owners for tax purposes as of May 1952. Land was redistributed in maximum parcels of 42.5 acres, and 100,000 people were given 1.5 million acres of land. Among the property confiscated was 1,700 acres taken from Arbenz himself. Arbenz had a firm legal base for the reform he intended. The Constitution of 1945 declared large estates to be illegal and conferred on the government the power to expropriate and redistribute land. Nonetheless, the landowning elite immediately and vociferously charged that the reform was communistic.

The charge of communism was guaranteed to get the attention of U.S. officials. The United States had never been friendly to socialism and communism and had been wary since the beginning of the Soviet Union, with whom the United States reluctantly allied in World War II. But after the "hot" war of fighting the Axis powers was over, the United States became immersed in a new war: the Cold War. This time there would be no fighting—at least not directly between the United States and the U.S.S.R. But the United States was determined to stop the spread of communism—or anything perceived as communism—around the world. Communism is based on a planned rather than a market economy, and the United States was committed to markets, now more than ever.

Guatemala's agrarian reform was far less severe than the one carried out in neighboring Mexico. But it came at the wrong time and in the wrong place. In another decade, the United States would encourage programs such as these. But in the 1950s, the attack on the UFCO was seen as an attack on U.S. capital. And in the zero-sum game of the Cold War, anything that limited capitalist development must be socialist. And socialism equaled the supposedly monolithic communism of the Soviet Union.

In Washington, the State Department watched apprehensively but said nothing until 1953, when the Guatemalan government seized 233,973 acres of unused land claimed by the UFCO, a figure later raised to 413,573 acres. The company exercised formidable economic powers. Not only was it the largest single agricultural enterprise in the country, but it also owned and controlled the principal railroad and the facilities in the major port, Puerto Barrios. It was extremely unpopular among the nationalists and vulnerable because it was foreign and exercised too powerful an influence over an economy being challenged as semifeudal and exploitative. As a matter of record, the company paid the Guatemalan government in duties and taxes about 10 percent of its annual profits, a sum regarded by indignant nationalists as far too low.

The U.S. State Department rushed to support the claims of the UFCO against the Guatemalan government on the basis that the compensation offered was insufficient. Yet, the sum offered equaled the value of the lands declared by the company for tax purposes. At that point, the State Department began to charge that the Guatemalan government was infiltrated with, if not controlled by, Communists. The UFCO enjoyed unusually close connections to the U.S. government, which led some critics of U.S. foreign policy to wonder about the government's motivations. The law office of Secretary of State John Foster Dulles had written the drafts of the UFCO's 1930 and 1936 agreements with the Guatemalan government. CIA director Allen Dulles, brother of the secretary of state, had served as president of the UFCO. For that matter, the family of John Moors Cabot, then assistant secretary of state for inter-American affairs, owned stock in the banana company.

Although UFCO may have had unusually close links to the U.S. government, it was certainly not unusual for the government to intervene on behalf of U.S. corporations. That intervention had, in fact, been U.S. policy for many years. Furthermore, U.S. corporations were not the only ones deeply opposed to Arbenz's economic policies. Guatemalan businesses, particularly the coffee industry, were equally incensed. They applauded U.S. opposition to Arbenz and would have asked for such help had it not already been forthcoming.

Despite the mounting pressure, Arbenz pushed ahead with his program to decrease Guatemala's dependency. He announced the government's intention to build a highway from Guatemala City to the Atlantic coast and thereby end the transportation monopoly of the International Railways of Central America, owned and operated by the UFCO. Further, he decided to construct a national hydroelectric plant. Until that time, foreigners produced Guatemala's electrical power, and the rates charged were among the highest in Latin America.

By late 1953, the Arbenz government feared intervention. Arbenz repeatedly requested arms, arguing that his more conservative neighbors in Honduras and El Salvador were encouraging exiles to prepare an attack on his country. The State Department responded with an embargo on arms sales to Guatemala. Unable to equip the army with materiel from the United States, the president turned to another source. On May 17, 1954, a shipment of arms arrived from Czechoslovakia. To the State Department, its arrival served as final proof that Guatemala had fallen under communist control.

The U.S. Air Force at once ferried military supplies to Tegucigalpa in order to equip a small army under the command of a Guatemalan army exile, Colonel Carlos Castillo Armas. On June 18, 1954, Castillo Armas and approximately 150 men crossed the border into Guatemala. They penetrated about twenty-five miles but engaged in no significant action. They did not need to. The Arbenz government fell because the army refused to act and the workers were not armed. A series of air attacks on the unarmed capital terrorized the population and broke the morale of the people. The attacks caused more psychological than physical damage. The planes were furnished by the CIA and flown by U.S. pilots, as former President Dwight D. Eisenhower revealed in a publicly recorded interview. U.S. Ambassador John Peurifoy handled the changing of the government and, with the enthusiastic endorsement of Washington, installed Castillo Armas in the

A small plane drops leaflets in Guatemala City during the 1954 U.S.-sponsored coup that overthrew President Jacobo Arbenz. (Library of Congress)

presidency. In violation of United Nations and Organization of American States treaties and international law, the United States blatantly intervened in the small country. In a radio address on June 30, 1954, John Foster Dulles informed the American people of the changes in the Guatemalan government, which prompted him to declare, "The events of recent months and days add a new and glorious chapter to the already great tradition of the American states."

A year after the United States placed Castillo Armas in power, Vice President Richard Nixon wrote, "President Castillo Armas' objective, 'to do more for the people in two years than the Communists were able to do in ten years,' is important. This is the first instance in history where a communist government has been replaced by a free one. The whole world is watching to see which does the better job."

In a plebiscite echoing the Ubico practice of the 1931–1944 period, Castillo Armas confirmed himself in power. Deriving his major support from local elites, the UFCO and the U.S. State Department, he ruled for three years without ever offering to hold elections, free or otherwise. Nonetheless, he took the precaution of abolishing all political parties that did not please him and disenfranchising all illiterates, thus canceling the voting rights of more than half the adult population. The police jailed, tortured, exiled, and executed political opponents, excusing their crimes with the accusation that the victims were Communists. Castillo Armas eradicated whatever traces of communism might be found or fabricated, but in the process he also eliminated democracy and reform.

Guatemala after 1954 offered the first Latin American example of the reversal of a land reform. Castillo Armas returned to the UFCO the lands his predecessor had nationalized. What is more, he signed a new contract that facilitated the company's exploitation of Guatemala until 1981, limiting its taxes to a maximum of 30 percent of the profits. (That figure contrasted with the 69 percent oil companies had to pay Venezuela.) Approximately 1.5 million acres, which under the 1952 Agrarian Reform Law had been confiscated as idle and distributed to 100,000 landless rural families, reverted back to the original owners. The newly created campesino class suffered severely. Much of the land returned to the original owners lay fallow, while Guatemala imported food that the country was perfectly capable of growing.

Castillo Armas was assassinated by one of his own presidential guards in 1957, but that did not put an end to the country's political repression. A series of military governments during the second half of the twentieth century, always under the banner of anticommunism, ignited the fires of a holocaust for the indigenous population. Reflecting on the brutality and arrogance of military rule in Guatemala, the *Los Angeles Times* (July 5, 1984) termed the CIA intervention in 1954 and its dismal aftermath "one of the most shortsighted 'successes' in the history of U.S.–Latin American relations."

RECOMMENDED READINGS

Bulmer-Thomas, Victor. *The Economic History of Latin America Since Independence.* 2nd ed. Cambridge: Cambridge University Press, 2003.

Fraser, Nicholas, and Marysa Navarro. *Evita.* New York: W.W. Norton & Co., 1996.

Gleijeses, Piero. *Shattered Hope: The Guatemalan Revolution and the United States, 1944–1954.* Princeton: Princeton University Press, 1991.

Plotkin, Mariano Ben. *Mañana es San Perón: A Cultural History of Perón's Argentina.* Wilmington, DE: Scholarly Resources Books, 2003.

Rock, David, ed. *Latin America in the 1940s: War and Postwar Transitions.* Berkeley: University of California Press, 1994.

Schlesinger, Stephen, and Stephen Kinzer. *Bitter Fruit: The Story of the American Coup in Guatemala.* Cambridge, MA: Harvard University Press, 1999.

CHAPTER 9

THE REVOLUTIONARY OPTION

By the late 1950s, much of the promise of development and democracy seemed hollow. In most nations and for major segments of the populations, reforms came too slowly and too ineffectively, if, indeed, they came at all. On five occasions in the twentieth century, Latin Americans despairing of evolutionary change and reform opted for revolution as a quicker and surer path to change. The Mexican Revolution marked the first half of the twentieth century. Four more countries would erupt in revolution during the second half of the century: Bolivia, Cuba, Chile, and Nicaragua.

All four revolutions had some common patterns: They were led mainly by young men and women who were the children of the middle class and sometimes even the elites, but who had opted to reject their class privileges and work for social change. The leaders created a coalition of middle-class, urban working-class, and poor rural groups, joined by disaffected sectors of the elites. They wanted revolution—a sweeping change of economic, political, social, and cultural structures—not just reform. And they wanted to create programs that would benefit the poor masses. But the specific circumstances of each country, and the international circumstances at the time of each revolution, led to differences in the paths taken and in the outcomes.

Revolution is an extreme option that people choose when legal and peaceful paths to change fail. By revolution, we mean the sudden, forceful, and usually violent overturn of a previously stable society and the substitution of other institutions for those discredited. This is sweeping and fundamental change, not just in political organization but in social and economic structures and the predominant ideology. These are not just personnel changes, like the numerous coups d'etat (or *golpes de estado*) that changed the individual in the presidential palace but changed none of the social structures.

Bolshevik leader Leon Trotsky famously opined that if all one needed to make revolution was poverty and oppression, then there would be revolutions everyday all around the world. The causes of revolution do not develop overnight but are the result of long-term problems. Foreign control of the economy or political processes can cause local resentments. Another cause of revolution is the public's perception of economic conditions, which can include rising expectations because of economic growth and development programs, or the social dislocations caused by rapid changes in the economy, as well as the hardship of economic crises.

Political disputes can also lead to revolution, particularly when new economic leaders want political power. Political openings can create increased hopes for democratization and a violent reaction when expected freedoms are not granted. A government's inability to meet the needs or desires of various constituencies can weaken its bases of support. When the government becomes the target of protest, threatened officials often respond with brutality, which turns more people against the government.

For revolutions to occur, there must be both leaders and followers. Eloquent leaders focus the discontent of the masses and plan actions, frequently violent ones, to ignite the revolution. But they also need the support of the masses, or their exhortations to action will fall on deaf ears; no leaders can make a revolution by themselves. Importantly, the leadership offers guidance and justification for revolution, shattering old myths and creating new ones. They articulate the goals of the revolution, which frequently have focused on nationalism and some form of socialism or redistribution of wealth.

Although Bolivia led the new wave of revolutions, it would turn out to be the least influential of the four. The Bolivian revolution fell apart because of internal problems. Furthermore, it was atypical because it was not actively opposed by the United States, which became the nemesis of the revolutions in Cuba, Chile, and Nicaragua.

Like Guatemala, Bolivia is a mostly indigenous country, and in the 1950s its population was characterized by illiteracy, undernourishment, sickness, low per capita income, and short life expectancy. Bolivia depended primarily on exports of tin, and the mines were owned by three Bolivian families: Patiño, Hochschild, and Aramayo. Patiño's annual income exceeded the national government's, and the annual allowance of one of his sons was greater than the government's education budget.

In 1941, urban intellectuals under the leadership of Victor Paz Estenssoro organized the *Movimiento Nacional Revolucionario* (MNR; National Revolutionary Movement). Its two primary goals were to nationalize the tin mines and to combat international imperialism. In the presidential election of 1951, as was customary, the government controlled the electoral machinery and suffrage was restricted to literate males, about 7 percent of the population. Despite these handicaps, the MNR won a resounding victory. The government and army refused to let Paz Estenssoro take office, leading to a bloody struggle in April 1952 in which the MNR seized power by force. The revolution represented a broad-based alliance of the progressive elements of the middle class, intellectuals and students, organized labor, and the rural landless. The urban and rural workers' militias provided the backbone of armed strength and emerged as a key power group.

President Paz Estenssoro nationalized the tin mines without compensating the owners, a move nearly the entire population supported. More controversial was the unexpected rural agitation that forced the urban movement to undertake agrarian reform. The indigenous rose up and took land, and Paz responded to the reality: He formalized the reforms in a decree-law of August 2, 1953.

After serving his four-year term, Paz Estenssoro turned over the presidency to MNR stalwart Hernán Siles, who won the 1956 elections. A term out of office permitted Paz Estenssoro to run again for the presidency in 1960, and the voters enthusiastically endorsed his new bid for office. But when Paz tampered with the constitution in 1964 to allow himself another term, the army took the reins of power. Revolutionary activity declined, then disappeared.

The United States had few investments in Bolivia and did not consider the isolated country to be strategically important. Instead of aggressive opposition, Washington lavished funds, technical aid, and support on the MNR governments of Bolivia as a way to support the moderate, middle-class leaders of the revolution, Paz Estenssoro and Siles, against the radical, working-class factions. George Jackson Eder, who the Bolivian government was required to accept in 1956–1957 as the director of its stabilization program, reminisced in his book *Inflation and Development in Latin America* (1968) that he helped to break the power of the radical labor unions over the government. His stabilization program "meant the repudiation, at least tacitly, of virtually everything that the Revolutionary Government had done over the previous four years."

For the rest of Latin America, Bolivia was an example of a revolution that had imploded. It was co-opted by the middle classes and destroyed by its leadership's greater concern for power than for the goals of the revolution. As a result, its impact was minimal. It did little to inspire other revolutionary movements. In fact, by 1967, Bolivia's situation was so dismal that Cuban revolutionary hero Ernesto "Che" Guevara tried to start a new revolutionary movement there, ending in his death. The Cuban, Chilean, and Nicaraguan revolutions would have a much greater impact on the region, and the role of the United States would become crucial in all three.

As historians, we need to ask three main questions: What did these revolutionaries want to achieve and why? How did they go about it? And why has the United States so vigorously opposed them?

CUBA

Perhaps no other event in Latin American history has had the impact of the Cuban Revolution of 1959. It became the model for revolutionary change throughout Latin America and beyond. It also became a model for U.S. Cold War policy. The Cuban Revolution particularly rankled Washington leaders, partly because of the historically close relationship between the two countries and partly because it occurred a mere ninety miles from our shores.

At first glance, Cuba in the 1950s seemed an unlikely place for revolution. By Latin American standards, Cubans enjoyed a high literacy rate and high per capita income. It was an urbanized nation with a relatively large middle class. However, aggregate statistics can be misleading. Much of the population lived in the countryside, and the story there was quite different: 43 percent of adults were illiterate, 60 percent lived in homes with dirt floors and palm roofs, 66 percent had no toilets or latrines, and only one in fourteen families had electricity. The largest group in Cuba was the rural wage workers, who were 600,000 strong. They were mostly sugarcane cutters, and they were fully employed only during the harvest. Agricultural wage workers averaged only 123 days of work a year. Cuba was dependent on one crop, sugar, which brought in 75–85 percent of all export earnings. And it was further dependent primarily on one market, the United States.

The United States has loomed overly large in Cuba's history, ever since stepping in just as Cubans were about to win their independence from Spain in 1898. Afterward, U.S. military occupation deprived Cubans of the opportunity to reorganize their economy. In the process, the United States consolidated its hold on the Cuban economy: As early as 1890–1895, U.S.-owned mills produced 10 percent of Cuba's sugar. In 1953, U.S. owners produced 40 percent of the sugar and owned 50 percent of the railways and 90 percent of the utilities. In 1958, U.S. investment totaled over $1 billion, more than in any other Latin American country except Venezuela, and in per capita terms, more than three times U.S. investment in any other Latin American country. Furthermore, the large-scale and attendant capital requirements of sugar production kept Cubans from expanding their share of ownership, and the development of secondary industries occurred in the United States rather than in Cuba.

The United States was Cuba's most important market, and the amount of sugar that Cuba could sell depended on quotas set by the U.S. Congress, with an eye toward the needs of American sugar growers and refiners in the United States. This dependence on congressional action goes well beyond the disadvantageous position in which most agricultural-exporting peripheral countries find themselves in a world market controlled by the industrialized countries. In addition, in exchange for the quota, Cuba gave preference to more than 400 U.S. products, in essence trading away the island's industrialization opportunities.

All that was left to the Cubans was real estate speculation and the government, which became synonymous with theft and corruption—clearly the practice of the dictator Gerardo Machado (1924–1933). The resistance to Machado mobilized masses of Cuban workers and students, although his removal finally came via an army coup led by Sargeant Fulgencio Batista. The new president was Ramón Grau San Martín, a doctor and professor who proclaimed a socialist revolution. Washington officials immediately became worried and urged Batista to step in again. This time, Batista took power himself, and he dominated Cuba for the next twenty-five years. Many Cubans felt that yet another chance at democracy and sovereignty had been taken from them by U.S. intervention.

From 1934 to 1940, puppets held the presidency while Batista held the real power. He ruled directly from 1940 to 1944, then retired to Miami an estimated $20 million richer. In his absence, a now conservative Grau finally won his turn in the presidency. Batista returned in 1948 and served in the Cuban Senate during the presidency of Carlos Prio Socorrás, which reached new lows of political corruption. Batista responded with a coup in 1952 and ruled with dictatorial powers until the 1959 revolution. It seemed there had been no change from 1924, when Machado took power, until 1959, when Batista was toppled. Indeed, some would argue that there really had been no change since independence. The system was corrupt, elections were fraudulent, and the island was dominated by the United States. It was this long and tortured history that set the stage for the Cuban Revolution.

Batista was toppled in a popular revolution led by Fidel Castro, a brash young representative of middle-class students and intellectuals. Castro, the illegitimate son of a Spanish-born landowner and his maid, was an attorney who represented the poor. He was an Orthodox Party candidate for Congress, but elections were aborted by Batista's coup. Fidel used the creative approach of filing a lawsuit charging Batista with violating the 1940 constitution, but, of course, Batista's courts would not hear the suit. At that point Fidel followed Cuba's long historical tradition of armed uprising. In 1953, he and a ragtag band of 162 men set out to attack the Moncada Barracks, and they failed miserably. After Fidel's release from prison, he escaped to Mexico, where he organized an invasion force.

Among the trainees in Mexico was the young Argentine medical doctor Ernest "Che" Guevara. Guevara had traveled the length of Latin America and come to the conclusion that many of the medical problems he had hoped to solve were related to poverty and could only be solved by systemic change. He arrived in Guatemala in 1954 and was impressed by Arbenz's attempted reforms, only to see the government toppled by the U.S. coup. He gladly joined Fidel's invasion force of eighty-two men who sailed to Cuba on a fifty-eight-foot yacht, the Granma, in 1956. Most of the men were lost at sea or killed in the landing, but twelve survived, and they drew support from the poor farmers of the Sierra Maestra. The guerrilla forces attacked Rural

Guard posts, prompting Batista to send army units to the mountains. At the same time, in the cities, the 26 of July Civic Resistance, named for the attack on Moncada, carried out a sustained campaign of sabotage and subversion; they set bombs, cut power lines, and derailed trains. Finally, the United States withdrew its support of the government, and Batista fell. Triumphant revolutionary forces marched into Havana in January 1959.

Castro visualized a reformed Cuba. He said his struggle was to end the latifundia, limit foreign ownership, establish cooperatives, nationalize public services, enact social legislation, spread education, and industrialize the nation. Those programs appealed to broad segments of the Cuban population and stirred the island's nationalism. They echoed the basis upon which Grau San Martín had founded his middle-class party in 1935: "nationalism, socialism, antiimperialism."

The changes that Castro advocated rested on a strong historical precedent, dating back to Cuba's struggle against Spain. The hated Platt Amendment, repeated U.S. intervention, support for Batista, and dominance of Cuba's economy left a bitter legacy. Cubans resented Washington's hegemony, and succeeding generations of patriots challenged it. Castro also looked to Cuba's 1940 constitution, which banned latifundia, discouraged foreign ownership of the land, and permitted the expropriation of property "for reason of public utility or social interest." The constitution authorized the state to provide full employment, claimed the subsoil for the nation, empowered the government to "direct the course of the national economy for the benefit of the people," and conferred on the state control of the sugar industry. The succeeding middle-class governments turned their backs on the new constitution and governed as though it never existed. But in the writings of Cuban independence hero José Martí, in the rhetoric of the forces that overthrew Machado, and in the Constitution of 1940, Fidel found much of the inspiration for the changes he proposed.

Despite Castro's intense nationalism, he tried to initiate good relations with the United States. In April 1959, he was invited to Washington by the National Press Club. In meetings with Vice President Richard Nixon and Secretary of State Christian Herter, Fidel sought an increase in Cuba's sugar quota, but the officials refused. Fidel assured them that Cuba would remain a member of the Organization of American States, that it would not abrogate the treaty giving the United States rights to its base at Guantánamo, and that the island would continue to welcome U.S. investment and protect U.S. strategic interests. Nonetheless, the officials offered no U.S. or World Bank aid, although there had been a great deal of financial support for Batista.

Fidel's attempts to reform the economy, however, brought him into conflict with Cuban elites and the United States. One of the revolution's first acts was to cut the exorbitant utility rates charged by U.S. companies, providing compensation via state bonds. The next step was the agrarian reform law. Sugar companies owned 70–75 percent of the arable land, and 3 percent of the sugar producers controlled more than 50 percent of production. At the same time, although most of the arable land stood uncultivated, 70,000 Cubans had no jobs and the country imported fully 50 percent of the food its people ate.

In June 1959, the Castro government issued the Agrarian Reform Law. The law was relatively modest: It limited farms to 1,000 acres, but there were exceptions, including highly productive sugar and rice plantations, which were limited to 3,333 acres. Even larger farms owned by foreigners would be permitted if the government decided they served the national interest. In fact, only 10 percent of the farms were affected by the 1,000-acre limit; they represented, however, 40 percent of farmland. The confiscated estates were worked as cooperatives under the management of the *Instituto Nacional de Reforma Agraria* (INRA; National Institute of Agrarian Reform). Eisenhower responded in September 1959 by recalling the U.S. ambassador, citing the utility cuts and agricultural expropriation, even though no property had been nationalized without compensation.

In February 1960, Cuba negotiated an agreement with the Soviet Union for $200 million in trade over four years, which was less than Soviet trade had been with the Batista government. The United States, however, interpreted the agreement as a sign of the Cuban government's allegiance. In June, tension between the United States and Cuba intensified when Texaco, Royal Dutch Shell, and Standard Oil demanded payment for oil imports rather than extending credit. Fidel canceled the exclusive contract held by the three and established a national petroleum institute to find other supplies. When no one in the West would sell to him, Fidel turned to the Soviets, who traded crude oil for sugar. The next day, Eisenhower cut Cuba's sugar quota. In retaliation, on October 12, 1960, Cuba expropriated the oil companies. On October 14, the United States announced a trade embargo on all goods except medicine. On January 4, 1961, Washington broke diplomatic relations.

By then the United States had labeled the Cuban Revolution a communist one and saw Cuba as a tool of the Soviet Union. This judgment showed a profound misunderstanding of the domestic roots of the Cuban Revolution. Further, U.S. isolation of the revolutionary government gave Fidel only two options: turn to the Soviet Union or capitulate to U.S. demands. But the legacy of the Platt Amendment and the long involvement of the United States with the Batista regime made the latter an impossible choice. The break in relations was probably inevitable given the genuine desire of the Cuban masses for egalitarian programs, which forced confrontations with international capital. Cuban social welfare and U.S. investment as constituted were not compatible.

Ironically, Fidel at that point did not consider himself or the revolution to be socialist or communist. He distrusted the *Partido Socialista Popular* (PSP; Cuban Socialist Party, a traditional Communist party), which had allied with

Batista in exchange for privileges. The Communists, in turn, had believed that a socialist revolution could not be made until the country had gone through the stages predicted by Karl Marx; therefore, no revolution could happen in Cuba until it became fully capitalist and industrialized. They dismissed Fidel as a bourgeois adventurer.

Fidel turned to the Cuban Communists because he needed administrative help. First the Batista property fell into state hands, followed by the expropriated property. The new state enterprises had to be managed, and much of the bourgeoisie with administrative skills had fled the island. Furthermore, the well-organized masses called for more and more social programs to meet their needs. The masses pushed the revolution to establish more sweeping programs, and the Communists provided organizing know-how. When the United States refused aid and pressured its allies to isolate Cuba, the Soviets became the only alternative for aid. In part to facilitate relations with the Soviets, the Cubans formed the Partido Comunista de Cuba (PCC; Communist Party of Cuba), though no party congress met until 1975.

Castro did not declare Cuba's revolution to be socialist until the U.S. invasion in 1961. Washington was not content to break ties with the revolution—in Cold War mentality, the revolution had to be defeated and rolled back. The United States launched an invasion at the Bay of Pigs, using anti-Castro exiles trained by the CIA. The planners expected another Guatemala, a quick and easy government overthrow.

To prepare for the landing, CIA operatives strafed several airfields, killing seven. At the funeral the next day, Castro declared for the first time that the Cuban Revolution was a socialist one—"This is the Socialist and Democratic Revolution of the humble, with the humble, for the humble"—a cry for help to the Soviet Union, which had promised to aid socialist revolution anywhere in the world. Although Soviet help would be crucial in the future, however, it was Cubans who defeated the Bay of Pigs forces. Fidel himself was at Playa Girón, the beach at the Bay of Pigs, to lead the forces. His popularity soared.

Fidel became a heroic symbol of antiimperialism throughout the Third World. But his domestic popularity also came from the programs that the new government carried out. He regarded education as one key to the new future. Teacher-training institutes sprang up; in a decade, the number of teachers tripled; the number of schools quintupled; young, eager volunteers fanned out into the remotest corners of the island to teach reading and writing. Within a few years illiteracy virtually disappeared. By 1971, nearly one-quarter of the country's 8 million inhabitants were in school. Education was free from nursery school through the university. Reading became a national pastime. In 1958, Cuba published 100 different titles and a total of 900,000 books; in 1973, it published 800 titles and a total of 28 million books. Cuba has the highest per capita book production in Latin America, and the highest literacy rate in the hemisphere.

Exultant Cuban revolutionaries pose with rifles on a monument in Matanzas in February 1959. The sculptures are of Cuban independence hero José Martí and a female allegorical figure of liberty brandishing broken chains. (Library of Congress)

Health care also became a revolutionary priority. Hospitals were built in remote cities and doctors became available in the countryside for the first time. All medical services were free. By 1965, Cuba spent $19.15 per person per year for medical care, a figure that contrasted sharply with the $1.98 Mexico spent or the $.63 Ecuador spent. As a consequence, the health of the nation improved dramatically and life expectancy lengthened. Cuban medical care became the envy of the hemisphere, and Latin Americans from throughout the region traveled to the island to seek medical help.

The government dealt with Havana's housing problem by guaranteeing everyone housing at no more than 10 percent of their income. No one was allowed to own more than one dwelling, which could be passed on to family but could not be sold. Buildings abandoned by Batista supporters who fled were converted into housing units. Volunteer work crews were enlisted to build more housing, and a great deal of the focus was put on the Cuban countryside. By building housing and economic ventures in rural areas, the government kept more people from flooding into the capital.

The government also encouraged the arts, and painting, literature, and music flourished. The National Ballet of Cuba emerged as one of the principal dance companies of the world and frequently toured to critical and popular acclaim. The *nuevo trova* movement, led by such singer/songwriters as Silvio Rodriguez, brought revolutionary themes to 1960s music, combining rock and Latin sounds, leading a musical movement that swept Latin America.

It was probably in film, however, that the Cuban Revolution reached its maximum cultural achievement. The first law of the revolutionary government in the field of culture created the *Instituto Cubano del Arte e Industria Cinematográficos* (ICIC; Cuban Film Institute) in March 1959. It has produced documentaries, newsreels, and feature-length films in addition to publishing the most serious Latin American journal on film, *Cine Cubano*. Cuban film retrospectives have been organized in New York, San Francisco, and Los Angeles, and Cuban films have become regular features of film festivals, where they consistently win international awards.

Much of the Cuban filmmakers' attention focused on reinterpreting their country's past. In his alternatingly lyric and realistic *Lucia*, Humberto Solas studied the woman's role in three Cuban struggles that have shaped the history of modern Cuba: the war for independence in 1895, the fight to overthrow the Machado regime in 1933, and the literacy campaign of the 1960s. The final segment's focus on continuing *machismo* in Cuban society shows a fascinating element of Cuban cinema—its capacity for criticism of the revolution. Double standards penalizing women were again criticized in *Portrait of Teresa*, the story of a woman trying to balance a job, union activism, cultural work, and a family. Her husband, widely recognized as a good worker and staunch revolutionary, does nothing to help in the home and indulges in extramarital affairs. It was a theme that struck a chord with Cuban women.

Che talked about the selfless virtues of the Cuban "new man" that the revolution was creating. But women found that all too often the new man was much like the old man, despite some of the efforts made by the new government. Fidel targeted women as a group from the beginnings of the revolution, encouraging the formation of the *Federación de Mujeres Cubanas* (FMC; Federation of Cuban Women) just three months after the triumph of the revolution. Their first goal was to mobilize women to support the revolution through work, participation in the literacy campaign, and in neighborhood projects. The government responded to women's increased activity outside the home by providing day care centers. Their health needs were particularly targeted through perinatal care and the legalization and availability of abortions. Female participation in education soared, and women entered professions in record numbers. To balance work and home, legislation guaranteed women eighteen weeks of paid maternity leave.

But in the home, the double standard prevailed. The revolution responded with the 1975 Family Code, which required a revolutionary couple to be equal partners. Article 26 required both parents to participate in child rearing and housework. Of course, there were no revolutionary police knocking on doors to make sure that men did their part, but at least the moral weight of the revolution was behind the idea of equality.

The change in women's roles was just one of the many social changes that discomfited the old oligarchy, most of whom fled within the first two years of the revolution. As changes were instituted, the traditional power of the old oligarchy, military, and Church vanished; the state and new mass organizations, like the FMC, filled the vacuum. Castro claimed his government to be one of the people, and to prove his confidence in popular support, he distributed arms to the peasants and workers to defend their new government. He frequently convoked the people to mass meetings in which he spoke extemporaneously for hours to enthusiastic crowds. The old electoral system, which Cubans disdained for its corruption, was abandoned. New systems of power were formalized starting in 1976 with the formation of *Poder Popular* (People's Power). Neighborhoods elect representatives to municipal assemblies, which in turn elect provincial assemblies, deputies to the National Assembly, and judges for municipal courts. The National Assembly elects the council of state, and Fidel serves as president of both the council and the Council of Ministers, his cabinet.

By the early 1970s, Cuba's successes were irrefutable and recognized even by the revolution's critics. Pat M. Holt, chief of staff of the Senate Foreign Relations Committee, made a brief visit to Cuba and then wrote *A Staff Report Prepared for the Use of the Committee on Foreign Relations, United States Senate* in which he concluded that all Cubans enjoyed the necessities of life and indeed as a group had an impressive standard of living.

Cuba was able to make these changes in part because the Soviet bloc paid above-market prices for sugar, on the theory that the market price did not reflect adequate compensation for Cuban labor and profit. At first, Cuba vilified sugar and strove to diversify the economy and to industrialize via food processing and manufacture of fertilizers, sugarcane derivatives, agricultural supplies, pharmaceuticals, textiles, apparel, machinery, steel, and construction materials. By 1961, there was a renewed emphasis on sugar production to pay for the industrialization; nonetheless, sugar dropped from 90 percent of exports in 1975 to 65 percent in 1985. Domestically, the government allowed private peasant markets to function until

1986, when fears of exploitation by middle men led to their closure. Other private businesses were discouraged, however, and in 1968 they were confiscated, sending a second wave of Cuban exiles to Miami.

Cuba's growth rate has generally been better than Latin America as a whole, averaging 6 percent in the 1970s and 5 percent in the 1980s. But the world economic crises eventually were felt on the island as well, leading to shortages. As growth rates fell, the revolution alienated the most marginal elements of the labor force, people who had sacrificed for the revolution and who could accept no more discipline in the name of socialism. They, too, wanted out. Castro opened the doors in mid-1980, and over 100,000 Cubans migrated to the United States from the port of Mariel.

The 1990s presented Cuba with new challenges. With the fall of the Soviet Union, Cuba began the "special period," a time of both austerity and market incentives. Private businesses were allowed to open, and Fidel agreed to allow foreign investment, particularly in tourism. "Not only do [foreign companies] have an opportunity to do business with Cuba, but they will find in Cuba the only market in the world where they don't have to compete with United States companies," noted Carlos Lage, vice president of Cuba's Council of State. The government still refused to let the market, however, determine the distribution of housing, health care, education, and basic necessities.

After the initial downturn, the economy began to revive, albeit along with some of the problems that come with greater openness; for example, the new tourism also brought a resurgence of prostitution. The influx of foreign investment helped Cuba recover, and by 2005 the government was increasing salaries and pensions. The government also decided to address the inequalities that had arisen from the new market mechanisms; for example, people involved in tourism earned dollars in tips, which gave them more money than government employees. In 2004, the government eliminated forty of the 150 categories of self-employment, and in 2005, 2,000 licenses of private businesses were revoked.

Cuba also faced criticism, even from supporters, over two key issues: handling of the AIDS crisis and ongoing censorship. Although Cuba provided extensive health care services for people with AIDS, biases against homosexuals also stigmatized the population. The price of health care was quarantine, albeit in facilities that were the envy of AIDS activists in other parts of the world. Internal criticism of the system was muted, however, by the continuing censorship. Writers who disagreed with the government found they could not get their work published, and they were denied jobs and travel opportunities.

In 2003, the Cuban government arrested seventy-five dissidents, who received jail sentences of six to twenty-eight years for conspiring with the United States to overthrow the Cuban government. The dissidents had met with the head of the U.S. interest section—the United States does not have an embassy in Cuba—who had openly called for Castro's overthrow. The arrests and detentions drew international criticism, but the Cuban government continued to see the revolution as embattled, in no small part due to the United States.

Beginning with the Bay of Pigs, U.S. hostility has been unremitting. Successive U.S. governments employed the CIA to finance and influence myriad Cuban exile organizations in support of U.S. policies toward the Castro government. The machinations of the CIA included commando raids on the island, false news reports, assassination attempts, the overthrow of Latin American governments that refused to break relations with Cuba (e.g., the government of President J. M. Velasco Ibarra of Ecuador in 1961). The government has also turned a blind eye to ongoing efforts to overthrow the Cuban government, including bombings of Cuban hotels and tourist sites, by Miami-based Cuban exiles.

Although the U.S. government continues to wait for Fidel Castro to die—he has outlasted ten U.S. presidents—Cubans have their own plans for the future. These plans will likely include a mixture of social programs and greater political freedoms. The examples of the former Soviet Union and Eastern bloc countries, where social safety nets were destroyed after the fall of Communist government, served as a warning. Cubans are unlikely to advocate the return of confiscated property and a full rollback of the revolution to the old days for which so many exiles long.

Despite criticisms of Cuba's restrictions on free speech and travel, Fidel has become a respected elder statesman in Latin America. He is welcomed at Latin American government conferences, where he still preaches the gospel of equality and independence.

Cuba's Impact

The Cuban revolution forced the United States to acknowledge that there were, indeed, many deep-rooted causes for revolution in Latin America. When the attempt to return to the Guatemala-style coup failed, the United States realized that new tactics were needed. If the United States could not overthrow the Cuban Revolution, perhaps it could prevent similar revolutions throughout the region. As President John F. Kennedy declared, "Those who make peaceful revolution impossible make violent revolution inevitable."

In 1961, President Kennedy launched the Alliance for Progress, a small-scale Marshall plan for Latin America designed to encourage economic development, which presumably would promote the growth of democracy. The Alliance charter, drawn up at the 1961 Inter-American Conference at Punta del Este, Uruguay, called for an annual increase of 2.5 percent in per capita income, the establishment of democratic governments, more equitable income distribution, land reform, and economic and social planning. Latin American countries (with the exception of Cuba) were to invest $80 billion during the next 10 years. The United States pledged $20 billion.

The Alliance struggled along for ten years. The desired outcomes were often contradictory; for example, simultaneous goals were to raise agricultural productivity and to redistribute land in the countryside. Large landowners were loath to reduce their landholdings so that property could be redistributed. In fact, the aim of increased productivity was often achieved through further concentration of landholdings, with greater mechanization, leading to more rural unemployment and unrest. Alliance funds too often ended up paying for infrastructure that benefited large landowners and did nothing for the rural poor. The Alliance eventually failed because the traditional oligarchy had no intention of freely volunteering to give away or sell a portion of its lands, to tax itself more heavily, or to share power with a broader base of the population.

Throughout the 1960s, intellectuals and political activists debated the merits of reform versus revolution. Some political leaders genuinely believed that meaningful change in social and economic structures could be enacted within existing political systems. The solution was to be found in developmentalism, a focus on economic growth that would bring prosperity and the growth of a stabilizing middle class. But such changes entailed costs that many elites were not willing to pay. The Brazilian case was instructive.

President Juscelino Kubitschek (1956–1960) promised to give Brazil "fifty years of progress in five." He focused on creating a modern infrastructure, building highways, dams, and hydroelectric power plants. He even tried to open Brazil's interior by moving the capital to a new city, Brasilia, in the state of Goiás. Kubitschek encouraged the development of domestic industry, but he also encouraged foreign investment to enlarge the industrial sector. The result was, for example, a Brazilian automobile industry—the seventh-largest producer in the world—but 69 percent of it was owned by foreigners. They created jobs, but they sent their profits out of the country.

Meanwhile, Brazil remained dependent on coffee as its main generator of income, and agriculture remained unchanged. Thousands of desperate Brazilians left the countryside for the cities, but they found limited opportunities there. Capital-intensive industrialization was highly mechanized and created a limited number of new jobs. The unskilled and unemployed rural folk constructed *favelas*, shanty towns with cardboard houses that crawled up the hillsides ringing Rio de Janeiro and São Paulo, a testament to the limits of the developmentalist plans. Slum dweller Carolina Maria de Jesus summed up the contradictions well: "What our President Senhor Juscelino has in his favor is his voice. He sings like a bird and his voice is pleasant to the ears. And now the bird is living in a golden cage called Catete Palace. Be careful, little bird, that you don't lose this cage, because cats when they are hungry think of birds in cages. The *favelados* are the cats, and they are hungry."

By the time that Kubitschek left office in 1961, inflation and corruption were rampant. His successor, Janio Quadros, the quirky governor of São Paulo, campaigned with a broom, promising to sweep away corruption. Quadros tried to establish a foreign policy that was more independent of the United States, but, on domestic issues, he had no qualms about accepting help from the International Monetary Fund and the Alliance for Progress to keep the economy afloat. Impatient, he resigned after a scant seven months in office.

His vice president was João Goulart, who had served as secretary of labor in populist leader Getúlio Vargas's second administration. Goulart tried to carry out reforms to rectify Brazil's vast economic inequality: He urged land reform, a limit on foreign profit remittances, tax reform, wage raises for labor, and the granting of the vote to illiterates. The rural and urban masses supported Goulart's proposals and responded with mobilizations and strikes. But his policies, and the mass mobilizations they encouraged, drew the wrath of the elites and frightened the middle class. Front-page editorials in middle-class newspapers called for his ouster. Rio de Janeiro's *Correio da Manhã* trumpeted the headlines "Enough" and "Out." The military hierarchy, which had been criticized by Goulart, was happy to oblige.

Military coups certainly were not new phenomena in Latin America. There were 99 successful coups from 1920 to 1960, occurring in every country except Mexico and Uruguay. But it is striking that there were ten coups in the

Latin American Military Coups, 1961–1964*

COUNTRY	DATE
El Salvador	January 24, 1961
Ecuador	November 8, 1961
Argentina	March 29, 1962
Peru	July 18, 1962
Guatemala	March 31, 1963
Ecuador	July 11, 1963
Dominican Republic	September 25, 1963
Honduras	October 8, 1963
Brazil	March 31, 1964
Bolivia	November 4, 1964

*The proclaimed motivation for these coups varied greatly, but the threat of "more Cubas" was a backdrop to each of them.

Source: Brian Loveman, *For la Patria: Politics and the Armed Forces in Latin America.* Copyright 1999. Reprinted by permission of SR Books, now an imprint of Rowman & Littlefield Publishers, Inc.

sliver of time from 1960 to 1964. The rationale was usually the threat of Communism, but even the reform efforts sanctioned by the United States and the Alliance for Progress smacked of Communism for many in the Latin American military.

Brazil, torn between the demands of the impoverished masses and the intransigence of the elites, was but an extreme example of Latin America in the 1960s. Hopes that the middle class would be a moderate voice for change disintegrated in the fear of Communism, which strengthened the military. As the Alliance for Progress sputtered along, the fears of U.S. officials were realized—revolutionary movements proliferated throughout Latin America.

U.S. officials blamed revolutionary movements on Soviet and Cuban provocateurs. But Latin Americans did not need foreign agents to foment revolution—they were well aware of their own problems of poverty and oppression. What Cuba provided was an example and an inspiration. Latin Americans were inspired by Cubas success in throwing off a brutal dictator and flouting U.S. domination. But they were also inspired by the ultimate revolutionary, Che Guevara.

In 1960, Cuban photographer Alberto Korda snapped the most famous image ever taken of Che Guevara. Titled "Guerrillero Heróico," the photograph seemed to capture Guevara's idealistic quest for revolutionary change.

Here was a middle-class Argentine medical doctor who had turned his back on personal economic opportunity to adopt the cause of another country as his own. Furthermore, Che turned the July 26 Movement's accidental tactics of warfare in the Sierra Maestra into a formal strategy in his manual, *Guerrilla Warfare*, published in 1960. He argued that revolutionaries did not have to wait for ideal conditions to emerge, as traditional Communist parties argued. According to his theory, revolutionaries by their very actions could draw others to the cause and topple an entrenched dictatorship.

Che also lived up to his word, choosing to leave Cuba to try to bring revolution to Bolivia, where he was killed in 1967. Two famous photographic images appeared that year: one was of Che's dead body, in an almost Christ-like pose. The other was the famous Alberto Korda photograph of a hopeful-looking Che in his dashing beret, a photograph snapped in 1960 but unpublished until Giangiacomo Feltrinelli, an Italian publisher, acquired it. The romantic image of the young, handsome revolutionary, eyes gazing upward, turned up on walls of young would-be rebels around the world, along with Che's idealistic pronouncement: "Let me say, at the risk of seeming ridiculous, that the true revolutionary is guided by great feelings of love."

His message did not fall on deaf ears.

Starting in the 1960s, guerrilla movements developed throughout Latin America. Although there had been only three armed uprisings in the region in the 1950s, including the Cuban revolution, there were twenty-five armed groups founded in the 1960s. By the 1980s, armed groups had appeared in seventeen of the nineteen countries in Latin America. Some of the groups were ephemeral, disappearing in a year or less after they formed. Others continued struggling for a decade or more, sometimes going underground only to appear again when conditions seemed more propitious. They were generally met by the arm of the Alliance for Progress that the Kennedy administration did not publicize—government counterinsurgency forces armed and trained by the United States and designed to combat armed revolutionary groups.

Revolutionary groups even appeared in Mexico, where the government still claimed to be revolutionary. The official party changed its name in 1946 from the Mexican Revolutionary Party to the Institutional Revolutionary Party (*Partido Revolucionario Institucional*, PRI). By the 1950s, as railroad workers were repressed and arrested, the emphasis seemed to be far more on the institution than the revolution. In 1968, students organized a series of peaceful protests demanding democratic reforms, including autonomy for the country's universities, the freeing of political prisoners and social justice. The protests culminated in a rally on October 2 at Mexico City's *Plaza de las Tres Culturas* that included students and workers. They were attacked by government troops, killing hundreds and imprisoning dozens.

But in 1970, one country offered an alternative—a peaceful revolution.

Latin American Guerrilla Groups

COUNTRY	GROUP	YEARS
Argentina	Tiger-Men	1959–1960
	Uturuncos	
	Guerrilla Army of the People	
	Ejército Guerrillero del Pueblo (EGP)	1963–1964
	Peronist Armed Forces	1967–1974
	Fuerzas Armadas Peronistas (FAP)	
	Revolutionary Armed Forces	1967–1973
	Fuerzas Armadas Revolucionarias (FAR)	
	Montonero Peronist Movement	1969–1977
	Movimiento Peronista Montonero (Montoneros)	
	Armed Forces of Liberation	1969–1974
	Fuerzas Armadas de Liberación (FAL)	
	People's Revolutionary Army	1970–1977
	Ejército Revolucionario del Pueblo (ERP)	
Bolivia	Army of National Liberation	1966–1970
	Ejército de Liberación Nacional (ELN)	
	EBN/Commando Nestor Paz Zamora	1989–1990
	EBN/Nestor Paz Zamora Commando	
Brazil	October 8th Revolutionary Movement	1960s–1970s
	Movimiento Revolucionario de Outubre 8 (MR-8)	
	National Liberating Action	1968–1971
	Acao Libertadora Nacional (ALN)	
	Popular Revolutionary Vanguard	1968–1970s
	Vanguardia Popular Revolucionaria (VPR)	
Chile	Movement of the Revolutionary Left	1965–
	Movimiento de Izquierda Revolucionaria (MIR)	
	Manuel Rodríguez Patriotic Front/Communist Party of Chile	
	Frente Patriótico Manuel Rodriguez/	1980–
	Partido Comunista de Chile (FPMR/PCC)	
Colombia	Movement of Workers, Students and Peasants	1959–1961
	Movimiento de Obreros, Estudiantes y Campesinos (MOEC)	
	Army of National Liberation	1964–
	Ejército de Liberación Nacional (ELN)	
	Revolutionary Armed Forces of Colombia	1966–
	Fuerzas Armadas Revolucionarias de Colombia (FARC)	
	Popular Army of Liberation	1967–1984
	Ejército Popular de Liberación (EPL)	
	April 19th Movement	1974–1990
	Movimiento 19 de Abril (M-19)	
Costa Rica	The Family	1981–1983
	La Familia	
	Santamaria Patriotic Organization/Army of Democracy and Sovereignty	1985–1988
	Organización Patriótica Santamaria/Ejercito de la Democracía y la Soberanía (OPS)	

Latin American Guerrilla Groups (*continued*)

COUNTRY	GROUP	YEARS
Cuba	July 26th Movement *Movimiento 26 de Julio* (M-26)	1953–1959
Dominican Republic	June 14th Movement *Movimiento 14 de Junio* (M-14)	1963, 1970
Ecuador	Alfaro Lives, Damn It! *¡Alfaro Vive, Carajo!* (AVC)	1981–1992
El Salvador	People's Revolutionary Army *Ejército Revolucionario del Pueblo* (ERP)	1970–1992
	Popular Forces of Liberation–Farabundo Martí (FPL) *Fuerzas Populares de Liberación–Farabundo Martí*	1970–1992
	Armed Forces of National Resistance *Fuerzas Armadas de Resistencia National* (FARN)	1975–1992
	Revolutionary Armed Party of the Workers of Central America/Armed Revolutionary Forces of Popular Liberation *Partido Revolucionario de Trabajadores de Centroamerica/ Fuerzas Armadas Revolucionarias de Liberación Popular* (PRTC/FARLP)	1976–1992
	Armed Forces of Liberation *Fuerzas Armadas de Liberación* (FAL)	1977–1992
	Farabundo Martí National Liberation Front *Frente Farabundo Martí de Liberación National* (FMLN) (Union of FPL, ERP, FARN, PRTC, FAL)	1980–
Guatemala	Rebel Armed Forces *Fuerzas Armadas Rebeldes* (FAR)	1960–1996
	Revolutionary Organization of the People in Arms (ORPA) *Organización Revolucionaria del Pueblo en Armas*	1971–1996
	Guerrilla Army of the Poor *Ejército Guerrillero de los Pobres* (EGP)	1972–1996
	Guatemalan Labor Party/Revolutionary Armed Forces *Partido Guatemalteco del Trabajo/Fuerzas Armadas Revolucionarias* (PGT-FAR)	1968–1996
	Guatemalan National Revolutionary Unity *Unidad Revolucionaria Nacional Guatemalteca* (URNG) (Union of EGP, FAR, ORPA, PGT/FAR)	1982–
Honduras	Morazanist Front of Honduran National Liberation (FMLNH) *Frente Morazanista de Liberación National Hondureña*	1967–1991
	Revolutionary Party of Central American Workers-Honduras *Partido Revolucionario de Trabajadores Centroamericanos-Honduras* (PRTCH)	1977

COUNTRY	GROUP	YEARS
	Popular Revolutionary Forces Lorenzo Zelaya (FPR-LZ)	1981–1991
	Fuerzas Populares Revolucionarias Lorenzo Zelaya	
	Popular Movement of Liberation "Chinchoneros" *Movimiento Popular de Liberación "Chinchoneros"* (MPL-Chinchoneros)	1980–1990
Mexico	Revolutionary Party of Workers and Peasants/ Party of the Poor *Partido Revolucionario de Obreros y Campesinos/ Partido de los Pobres*	1969–1974
	Communist League September 23rd *Liga Comunista 23 de Septiembre* (L-23)	1973–1976
	Zapatista Army of National Liberation *Ejército Zapatista de Liberación National* (EZLN)	1994–
Nicaragua	Sandinista National Liberation Front *Frente Sandinista de Liberación National* (FSLN)	1961–
Paraguay	United Front of National Liberation *Frente Unido de Liberación National*	1960
Peru	Revolutionary Leftist Front *Frente Izquierdista Revolucionario* (FIR)	1961–1963
	Army of National Liberation *Ejército de Liberación National* (ELN)	1962–1965
	Movement of the Revolutionary Left *Movimiento de Izquierda Revolucionaria* (MIR)	1962–1965
	Tupac Amaru Revolutionary Movement *Movimiento Revolucionario Tupac Amaru* (MRTA)	1975–1993
	Communist Party of Peru Through the Shining Path of the Thought of José Carlos Mariátegui *Partido Comunista del Peru por el Sendero Luminoso del Pensamiento de José Carlos Mariátegui* (*Sendero Luminoso*)	1980–
Uruguay	Movement of National Liberation–Tupamaros *Movimiento de Liberación National Tupamaros*	1962–1972
Venezuela	Movement of the Revolutionary Left/ Armed Forces of National Liberation (MIR-FALN) *Movimiento de Izquierda Revolucionaria/Fuerzas Armadas de Liberación National*	1960s
	Communist Party of Venezuela/Armed Forces of National Liberation *Partido Comunista de Venezuela/Fuerzas Armadas de Liberación Nacional* (PCV-FALN)	1961–68

Source: Handbook of Leftist Guerrilla Groups in Latin America and the Caribbean by Liza Gross. Copyright 1985. Reprinted by permission of Westview Press, a member of Perseus Books, LLC.

Chile

Chile has always been a little different from its neighbors. From its earliest independence days, the country enjoyed greater stability than the rest of the region. It also enjoyed a long democratic tradition: From 1833 to 1973, Chile had only two constitutions. They provided for a strong presidency but also a strong voice from Congress. Chile's constitution gave political parties proportional representation, fostering an active political process.

Chile first became a regional power after the War of the Pacific (1879–1883), in which it fought Bolivia and Peru over the nitrate-rich region of the Atacama Desert. At the end of the nineteenth century, Chile was positioned as a serious aspirant to world power. It had a stronger navy than the United States and tremendous wealth from the export of nitrates, which were used for fertilizer and for making explosives. During World War I, Germany developed synthetic nitrates, and Chile lost its position in the market. During World War II, Chile accelerated development of its copper industry to take the place of nitrates. But by the twentieth century, Chilean entrepreneurs had exhausted the easily accessible copper deposits and needed foreign capital and technology to access the rest. Two United States companies came to dominate the industry: Anaconda and Kennecott.

By 1960, some 30–35 percent of the Chilean population had reached the upper or middle class. This sector was even larger in Santiago and Valparaíso, where almost half of Chile's population lived. Seventy percent of the country's population was urban, and 90 percent of them were literate. Nationwide, literacy was 84 percent. Yet the image of Chile as urbane, educated, and well-to-do hid gross inequality: While the per capita income of the top 5 percent was $2,300, the lower 50 percent only earned $140. Copper earnings paid for limited industrialization, whereas the countryside was little changed from the nineteenth century. Change was clearly needed.

Chile in the 1960s became a showcase for the Alliance for Progress, which invested heavily in the government of President Eduardo Frei (1964–1970). Frei represented a new political trend of the era, the Christian Democrats, who stressed the moral responsibility of government to mitigate societal ills, but stopped short of advocating revolutionary change. The Frei government promised "a revolution in liberty," and it did make some substantial changes. By 1970, the state had acquired ownership of most of Chile's copper mines. An agrarian reform gave land to 30,000 families. Farm laborers were unionized and given a minimum wage. Much of the change was funded by U.S. aid and high prices for copper fueled by the Vietnam War.

Frei's reforms had two political results: Some felt that he did not go far enough, and ended up joining the left; others felt he had gone too far, and joined the right. The center lost its strength, and in 1970 the presidency was won by Salvador Allende, a medical doctor and committed Marxist who had been one of the founders of the Socialist Party in 1931. He was the candidate of six parties that had joined in *Unidad Popular* (Popular Unity). Allende was a dedicated democrat: he had served as president of the Chilean Senate, served in Congress for thirty years, and ran for president four times. He had won a plurality of the vote, but not a majority, which was typical in Chilean elections because of the large number of parties participating.

Allende's election redefined revolution. Chileans in 1970 believed they had shown the world that a socialist revolution could be made without resorting to violence and force of arms. Chile had acted within its 140-year democratic tradition. But the experiment was doomed to failure. Three years later, the presidential palace was in flames, Allende was dead, the military controlled the streets, and General Augusto Pinochet established a brutal dictatorship that would rule Chile until 1989. Allende's defeat came at the hands of a familiar alliance: Chilean rightwing forces and the United States, who objected to the new government's policies.

Allende's program was a radical one, calling for the abolition "of the power of foreign and national monopoly capital and of large units of agricultural property, in order to initiate the construction of socialism." His economic advisors were influenced by Marxist theory but also by the structuralist theories popular in Latin America after World War II and propounded by Raúl Prebisch and ECLA, which was based in Santiago. The structuralist analysis contended that the economy could not grow because the market was limited by lack of buying power. The answer was to redistribute income, thereby increasing consumer demand. Income was to be redistributed by increasing wages while holding prices down and by expropriating large businesses, especially those that were foreign owned, so that the government could rechannel profits into social spending. Finally, a more widespread agrarian reform would make agriculture more efficient, producing enough low-cost food to feed the workforce without expensive imports. The government increased wages, gave low-interest housing loans to the poor, and created new social programs, including daycare centers, health and welfare programs, and school lunches.

For the first year, Allende's policies were effective, fueled by a foreign-reserve surplus from the high prices of copper. The government also simply printed more money and borrowed money to pay for imports of food and consumer goods. But in 1971, the economy took a sharp decline. First, copper prices dropped precipitously, then world food prices rose, and Chile had hit the limits of industrial expansion possible without increased investment. Then the United States stepped in.

The United States was wary of Allende from the start. Secretary of State Henry Kissinger commented tartly, "I don't see why we must sit with our arms folded when a country is slipping toward Communism because of the irresponsibility of its own people." President Richard Nixon gave orders to "make the economy scream." Some $8 million of CIA funds were used to support Allende's opponents, including support for a truckers' strike that paralyzed the country and infiltration of the newspaper, *El Mercurio*, which kept up a drumbeat of denunciations, blaming the Allende government for limits imposed by the world market and the United States. The United States cut off loans and influenced other western sources to do so as well.

By 1973, middle-class housewives were marching in the streets, banging pots and pans, complaining that they could not buy enough food for their families. At the other extreme, radical workers were taking over factories and urging Allende to take even more drastic action. The right wing, the elites, and the middle-class clamored for a change. The military became restive, convinced that civilian rule was ruining Chile and that only military control could restore order. General Carlos Prats, chief of the army, was loyal to Chilean constitutional structures, but he resigned when it became clear that he had lost military support. The next in command was Pinochet, who coordinated with the navy and ordered the occupation of the cities of Valparaíso, Concepción, and Santiago. On September 11, the presidential palace, La Moneda, was bombed. Allende, who was inside, committed suicide rather than be taken by the Pinochet forces.

Chileans were shocked. Theirs had been a peaceful, democratic country. Suddenly, it was a country of brutal military rule. Santiago's two stadiums were filled with prisoners, many of whom were brutally murdered. Between 3,000 and 10,000 people were killed during and after the coup. Left wing political parties were outlawed, and Pinochet systematically eliminated rivals in the military and removed both the leftwing and the moderates in unions, universities, and other institutions. Chile descended into a state of siege.

For the rest of Latin America, the lesson was clear: Revolutions were not won at the ballot box. As Augusto César Sandino said, "Liberty is not won with flowers but with gunshots."

NICARAGUA

The dominant reality of twentieth-century Nicaraguan history was the lack of opportunity the Nicaraguan people had to govern themselves. The United States intervened in 1909 to overthrow President José Santos Zelaya and occupied the country, with some brief interruptions, until early 1933, a period characterized by the disintegration of both the state and the economy. During its final years of occupation, the United States created the Guardia Nacional and appointed as its commander Anastasio Somoza García. The maintenance of order and stability were the primary duties of the Guardia, and it received U.S. training, financing, and equipment to fulfill them. The Somoza dynasty, a father and two sons, ruled from the mid-1930s until 1979. One political scientist termed the Somoza rule as "government by kleptocracy." The family stole everything it could put its hands on. By 1979, the Somozas owned 20 percent of the arable land (the best lands with good soil and ready access to roads, railroads, and ports), the national airline, the national maritime fleet, and a lion's share of the nation's businesses and industries. One of the great symbols of Somoza rapacity was Plasmaferesia, a blood plasma factory where the poor sold their blood for as little as $1 per liter; Somoza then sold the blood to the United States for ten times that amount.

The Somozas were loyal to only the Guardia, a small coterie of relatives and members of the old elite who supported the regime, and the United States. Nicaragua's voting record in both the Organization of the American States and the United Nations, for example, conformed 100 percent with the United States. The senior Somoza provided airstrips in support of the overthrow of Arbenz in Guatemala. The Bay of Pigs invasion was launched from Nicaragua's Atlantic coast; indeed, Luís Somoza was on hand to send them off and asked that they bring him back a hair from Fidel's beard.

During the long Somoza decades, the Nicaraguan people exercised neither political power nor influence, and the Guardia dealt swiftly and brutally with anyone courageous or foolish enough to try. The voice of the Nicaraguans remained muted from 1909 to 1979.

In 1961, an opposition group emerged to oppose the third member of the dynasty, Anastasio Somoza Debayle. It was inspired, like so many others, by the Cuban Revolution. But they also looked to their own history and particularly to the struggle of Augusto César Sandino, who fought against U.S. Marine occupation from 1927 to 1933, when he was killed on Somoza García's orders. The *Frente Sandinista de Liberación Nacional* (FSLN; Sandinista Front for National Liberation) advocated entrusting political and economic power to the people, agrarian reform, national unity, emancipation of women, the establishment of social justice, and an independent foreign policy.

The struggle of the Sandinistas against the well-armed and trained Guardia Nacional proved to be long and bloody, but the greed and brutality of the last Somoza were their most effective allies. One example is Somoza's handling of the massive 1972 earthquake, which destroyed much of Managua. Some $250 million in aid was rushed to Nicaragua, only to be stolen by Somoza and his cronies. Opposition was met by brutal torture in Somoza's prisons. By the late 1970s, even the small but potent middle class and members of the tiny elite joined the opposition, and Somoza's military arsenal could no longer repel popular wrath.

As in Cuba, the United States withdrew its support when it was clear that the dictator could not win. The Guardia, and thus the government, collapsed, and the victorious rebels led by the FSLN entered Managua triumphantly on July 19, 1979.

The challenge of reconstruction surpassed even the task of overthrowing the regime. The Sandinistas inherited an economy in shambles. Somoza

Thousands of Sandinista supporters crowd the Plaza de la Revolucion to commemorate the anniversary of Augusto César Sandino, the anti-imperialist hero from whom the revolutionaries took their name. (Photo by Julie A. Charlip)

had bombed the cities and industries. War damages amounted to approximately $2 billion; 40,000 were dead (1.5 percent of the population), 100,000 were wounded, 40,000 children were orphaned and 200,000 families were without homes. The national treasury was empty, and the foreign debt exceeded $1.6 billion. Add to these woes the reality of an underdeveloped country: Fifty-two percent of the population was illiterate, life expectancy was slightly more than 53 years, infant mortality was 123 per 1,000 live births, and malnourishment plagued 75 percent of the children.

During the early months after the victory, a wide variety of political groups supported and participated in the revolution. However, Sandinista emphasis on redistribution of wealth via agrarian reform and support for labor was not the goal of many middle- and upper-class Nicaraguans. They withdrew their cooperation and became critical, some even hostile. Such behavior followed the classic model of revolutions: United to overthrow a common enemy, a heterogeneous group brings about the final victory. Later, the temporary alliance disintegrates as some realize that their own interests will not be served by revolutionary change. As a last resort, the disaffected try to stop the revolution by force, more often than not by allying themselves with some sympathetic foreign power in order to enhance their strength. Events in Nicaragua followed this predictable pattern.

The Catholic Church was divided over the revolution. The hierarchy had always been allied with Somoza, but the brutality of the final years led the Church to split from the regime. Thus, the religious hierarchy gave its blessings to the overthrow of Somoza, an extremely unusual position for the Church in Latin America. But though the hierarchy opposed Somoza, they did not support many of the changes proposed by the Sandinistas. They, like the middle class and elite opposition, wanted what the Sandinistas called "Somocismo without Somoza."

Although the church hierarchy feared the revolution, many lower ranking priests and nuns embraced it. The religious represented a new wave of Catholicism, liberation theology, which had its roots in the Second Vatican Council (1962–1965), convoked by Pope John XXIII and continued under Pope Paul VI. The result of Vatican II was the issuing of the Pastoral Constitution on the Church in the Modern World, which urged Catholics not to shirk their responsibility to the poor and oppressed. Priests and nuns around the world responded by becoming involved in social organizing.

The greatest impact of Vatican II was felt in Latin America, where economic and social inequalities were extreme. Latin American theologians developed a new doctrine, called liberation theology, which drew on Jesus's first sermon in Luke (4:18–4:21), in which the gospel says Jesus had come "to liberate those who are oppressed." Liberation theology was given impetus in the region by the Second Latin American Bishops Conference in Medellín, Colombia, in 1968. Pope Paul spoke at the conference, the first pope to visit Latin America. He told the bishops, "We wish to personify the Christ of a poor and hungry people." The bishops accepted the "preferential option for the poor," that is, they prioritized social justice. They also chose to deal with the shortage of trained religious by giving their blessing to the organization of Christian-based communities (*comunidades de base*), which were lay Bible groups. Many Sandinistas came to the revolution through these communities and through other Christian youth groups, and several priests held positions in the government. The religious component of the revolution was one of the characteristics that set the Nicaraguan revolution apart from the revolutions in Mexico and Cuba.

The Sandinista government embarked on an ambitious program to improve the quality of life of the majority. A 1980 literacy campaign reduced illiteracy from 52 to 12 percent. The government followed up by doubling the number of schools in four years and making education free from pre-school through graduate studies. In 1988, more than one million Nicaraguans (40 percent of the population) were studying.

Attention was also focused on expanded health care. Nicaragua eliminated measles, diphtheria, and polio, diseases that once took a heavy toll among children. Clinics and hospitals sprang up in the countryside and in small towns. The number of health centers multiplied from twenty-six to ninety-nine, and Cuban physicians and nurses volunteered to staff them.

Infant mortality fell 50 percent. Despite the shortage of medicine, medical equipment, and physicians, health-care delivery was so impressive that the World Health Organization cited Nicaragua in 1983 as a model nation. A proper diet further explained the improving health of Nicaraguans. Caloric intake rose because more basic foods were now available to larger numbers of people.

One of the three founders of the FSLN, Carlos Fonseca, had vowed, "In Nicaragua, no peasant will be without land, nor land without people to work it." A far-reaching agrarian reform law based on Sandino's hopes, Fonseca's promise, and global experiences with rural restructuring was promulgated in 1981. It provided land for anyone who wanted it and would work it. As the largest nation in Central America, Nicaragua (54,864 square miles) had more than enough land for its relatively small population (3.2 million). The principal goal of the reform was to put the land into use so that Nicaragua could both feed itself and export crops for needed foreign exchange. For six years, the government distributed only land that once belonged to the Somozas or their closest allies, abandoned lands, and unused lands. On January 11, 1986, after successfully distributing nearly 5 million acres of land to 83,000 families, the government made significant changes in the Agrarian Reform Law, permitting the expropriation of any unused land without compensation and, indeed, of any land needed for the goal of assuring land to anyone who wanted to farm. For the first time, the government began to distribute lands that were already in production in areas where rural workers demanded land. Despite these changes, the government continued to guarantee the right to private property, and the majority of the land remained in private hands.

In the redistribution of land, the government gave preference to those willing to organize themselves into cooperatives. Cooperative organization facilitated governmental services—clinics, schools, child care centers, credit, machinery, and technical aid. Further, cooperatives enjoyed a reputation for efficiency. Nonetheless, the government also conferred individual land titles as well. Title holders received the land gratis but could not sell or alienate it, a safeguard to prevent future land concentration. Although land titles could be inherited, the land could not be divided among heirs, thus averting the problems of minifundia.

There was also an important cultural component of the revolution. Popular culture centers offered classes in folk dance. The Ministry of Culture supported the primitivist art movement, which began at Father Ernesto Cardenal's community on the island of Solentiname. Popular Poetry Workshops sprang up in barracks, factories, cooperatives, and neighborhoods, encouraging Nicaraguans to emulate the national hero Rubén Darío, the father of Spanish modernism. Musicians such as the brothers Luis Enrique and Carlos Mejía Godoy wrote music dedicated to the revolution, joining similar *nuevo canción* movements in Cuba and Chile.

Women played an important role in the Sandinista revolution, starting from the days of armed conflict, when they made up 30 percent of the people bearing arms. The revolution targeted women as a group to mobilize, opened day care centers, and broadened employment opportunities. Although no women served on the Sandinista directorate until the 1990s, there were several women in high positions, including Dora Maria Telles, the secretary of health, who had been the second in command in the daring takeover of the National Palace in 1978 and who headed the column that took León in 1979. However, many women chafed against the continuing double standard and the tendency to prioritize the armed conflict over all domestic needs. For example, the Sandinistas refused to legalize abortion to avoid further conflict with the Church; but the leading cause of death among women of child-bearing age was self-induced abortions. Despite these conflicts, many women felt that the Sandinista revolution provided more opportunities for them and benefits for society than any previous system.

Nationalism, socialism, and Christianity converged in Nicaragua to offer a different model for change than other revolutions had presented. The revolution drew international attention, including the wary gaze of the U.S. government. President Jimmy Carter had tried to prevent the Sandinistas from taking power in the waning days of the war. But under President Ronald Reagan, Nicaragua was labeled a Communist threat.

Washington allied itself with the remnants of the discredited National Guard, the dispossessed elite, and members of the frightened middle class to terminate the revolution and drive the Sandinistas from power. The CIA financed, trained, and armed counterrevolutionaries, known as the *contras*, short for the Spanish term *contrarevolucionario*, who invaded Nicaragua as early as November 1979 from Honduras and later from Costa Rica. The contras became known for their brutality; they particularly took aim at schools and clinics, the symbols of Sandinista change. As the war intensified, the Sandinistas lacked the money to rebuild these targets, and teachers and doctors were afraid to enter the war zone. In 1984, the CIA mined the harbors of Nicaragua in violation of international law, drawing the outrage and condemnation of the international community. In 1985, President Reagan imposed a trade embargo on Nicaragua, which plunged the economy into crisis.

In 1984, Nicaragua held its first free elections, with the participation of eight political parties. The Sandinistas won with 67 percent of the vote. In early 1990, the revolution celebrated its second presidential election; and, like the earlier election, it was open and democratic. However, much had occurred during the intervening years. In 1984, Nicaraguans were buoyant, hopeful, and proud of the achievements of the revolution; by 1990, they were anxious about the prolonged war and its destruction. The powerful pressure of Washington weighed ever more heavily on the small and impoverished

Daniel Ortega, one of nine comandantes in the leadership of the Sandinista National Liberation Front, became Nicaragua's first democratically elected president. (Photograph by Julie A. Charlip)

nation. The FSLN lost the 1990 presidential elections to a heterogeneous political coalition, the National Opposition Union (Unión Nacional Opositora, UNO), financed, advised, and otherwise encouraged by Washington. It took twenty-one parties united in UNO and backed by the United States to defeat the Sandinistas, who still garnered 41 percent of the vote. The new president, Violeta Chamorro, had promised that her close ties to the United States would benefit Nicaragua by bringing in aid and investment. But once the United States had achieved the goal of unseating the Sandinistas, Nicaragua receded from the U.S. agenda. Subsequent Nicaraguan governments steadily rolled back the Sandinista achievements.

The revolutions in Cuba, Chile, and Nicaragua were landmark events in Latin American history. Cuba showed what was possible, but also showed the limits of being a small country torn between superpowers. Chile tried to show that a peaceful path was possible, but as the revolution died in flames, Latin American revolutionaries contended that it could have survived had Allende dismantled the armed forces and armed the workers and farmers. Nicaragua tried to show a new way via political pluralism and a mixed economy, but it met the usual intransigence from Washington, which was unwilling to let Latin Americans decide their own fate. By 1990, many wondered whether the era of revolutions had indeed come to an end. And if indeed there was no revolutionary option, what chance was there for political, economic, and social change?

RECOMMENDED READINGS

Black, George. *Triumph of the People: The Sandinista Revolution in Nicaragua*. London: Zed Press, 1981.

Grindle, Merilee, and Pilar Domingo, eds. *Proclaiming Revolution: Bolivia in Comparative Perspective*. Cambridge, Mass.: David Rockefeller Center for Latin American Studies, Harvard University, 2003.

Jesus, Carolina Maria de. *Child of the Dark: The Diary of Carolina Maria de Jesus*. David St. Clair, trans. New York: New American Library, 1962.

Pérez, Louis A., Jr., *Cuba: Between Reform and Revolution*. 3rd ed. New York: Oxford University Press, 2005.

Rabe, Stephen G. *The Most Dangerous Area in the World: John F. Kennedy Confronts Communist Revolution in Latin America*. Chapel Hill: University of North Carolina Press, 1999.

Wright, Thomas C. *Latin America in the Era of the Cuban Revolution*. Rev. ed. Westport, CN: Praeger, 2001.

CHAPTER 10

DEBT AND DICTATORSHIP

The central dynamic of Latin American history in the late twentieth century was the tension between equity and efficiency, democracy and dictatorship. Leaders searched for ways to make their economies grow and sometimes for ways to redistribute some of the wealth. Reformers tried to appease the masses to forestall revolution, but all too often their failures led to unrest, reaction, and repression. Throughout the 1970s and 1980s, Latin American economies careened from boom to bust, democratic openings alternated with brutal military regimes, and the specter of revolution continued to haunt and inspire.

In many ways, the 1970s and 1980s reenacted the problems of the 1920s and 1930s. Extensive loans fueled economic growth, but the debt became a trap when an international recession made repayment impossible. Economic distress fueled popular mobilization, which was crushed by military dictatorship. But the late twentieth century brought a new kind of military dictatorship that focused on economic development and carried repression to new levels. The military eventually were defeated, not so much by a new political movement as by their ultimate economic failures.

CHANGING ECONOMIC PATTERNS

As early as 1965, some countries in Latin America were experiencing the limits of the strategy of import-substitution industrialization (ISI) that had dominated the region either by default or as a conscious policy for much of the twentieth century. Import substitution was blamed for chronic inflation because tariffs and overvalued exchange rates artificially raised prices of foreign goods, while local producers had no incentive to produce more efficiently. Although many countries produced more consumer goods, they still needed to import capital goods, the sophisticated machinery needed in manufacturing. Capital-intensive industry, which relied more on machines than on people, did little to increase urban employment. But increased mechanization and production of export crops drove more people to the cities. The shantytowns that had started to circle Latin America's capitals in the 1950s became massive centers of poverty in the 1970s. Even the middle class was in straitened circumstances as policies meant to foster industrialization tended to concentrate income among the upper sectors. The result was a limited market for the new consumer goods. But the goods, inefficiently and at times shoddily produced behind tariff barriers, could not be exported.

One theory held that Latin America needed more money to invest in improved infrastructure and to improve and expand industrialization for export. The multilateral and official lending organizations, such as the World Bank, did not offer the large amounts needed or carried too many restrictions on the use of the funds. Latin American leaders looked elsewhere and found that their interest in borrowing large sums of money fortuitously coincided with an increase in international banking and investment.

In the 1970s, the money poured in. The lending was fueled in part by the oil crisis of 1973, when the Organization of Petroleum Exporting Countries (OPEC) raised prices and restricted exports after the Arab–Israeli War in 1973. The OPEC countries deposited the enormous sums of money they earned (petrodollars) in U.S. and European banks (Eurobanks), which eagerly sought investment opportunities. Latin America seemed to be an ideal place for such ventures, leading to a new dance of the millions, echoing the boom of the 1920s. According to Mexico's Minister of Finance David Ibarra, "I had many bankers chasing me trying to lend me more money." The interest rates were lower than inflation, meaning the loans would be paid back, in real terms, at less than they had cost.

In the late 1960s, Latin America was borrowing around $300 million a year from private lenders; by the early 1970s, the region's debt was $34 billion. As long as the money yielded productive investments, then debts could be paid. World trade was growing, commodity prices were at an all-time high, and Latin America was prospering.

The prosperity depended on several key factors: a supply of foreign funds to invest, healthy international trade to generate repayment income, and, perhaps most importantly, a docile, low-cost workforce. Wage limits would enable Latin American governments and capitalists to increase corporate profits, which would make the region more attractive to foreign companies. The concentration of wealth would, in theory, increase money for investment; however, in Latin America, elites pocketed their increased income—often sending it out of the country to safer foreign banks—and depended instead on borrowing to fuel investment.

The constraint of the labor movement was most easily accomplished by authoritarian governments, who contended that labor organizers were part of an international Communist movement that threatened western democracy. Given the Cold War fears of the 1960s, these authoritarian contentions easily won the support of Latin American elites and middle classes, and the backing of the United States.

The success of these policies was measured in the spectacular growth rates of Latin American economies. The "Brazilian miracle," as it was dubbed, produced average annual growth rates of 11 percent in gross domestic product. Although less spectacular, Mexico boasted growth of 6–8 percent a year. Such rates are staggering, considering that a 3 percent growth in gross domestic product had been considered healthy.

Most of the debt was taken on by governments, which passed the money on to private ventures, funded state-run business, or created a combination of the two. Much of the money went to industrial investment, particularly in Brazil, where there were significant increases in the production of steel, automobiles, and machinery. Even more went to the creation of new infrastructure: Brazil's Itaipu hydroelectric power plant, Venezuela's Guri Dam, the Yacyretá Hydroelectric Dam on the Argentina–Paraguay border. Even Guatemala built the Chixoy Dam. The huge development projects required enormous investment, but they would take many years to complete before they would produce income.

The problem came with the second oil crisis of 1979, which followed the fall of the Shah of Iran. In an attempt to reign in galloping inflation, the U.S. Federal Reserve raised interest rates above 20 percent. The increase in U.S. interest rates echoed in the European financial markets, where interest rates were set by the London inter-bank offer rate (LIBOR). LIBOR rose to 17 percent in 1981 and 14 percent in 1982. The loans that had been made to Latin America had floating, not fixed, interest rates, generally set as a percentage above LIBOR. Suddenly, the Latin American governments found their interest rates soaring from 9 percent to 19 percent.

Then came the final blow: Because of the worldwide recession, buyers in other countries stopped or drastically reduced their purchases of Latin American goods. Without sales, there were no earnings to repay the spiraling debt. In 1981 and 1982, Latin American governments borrowed frantically, often at high short-term rates, in order to simply meet the debt service on the existing loans. According to the Bank for International Settlements, the region was borrowing $4 billion a month during the latter half of 1981.

Even oil-rich Mexico, which discovered more oil reserves in the 1970s, had dipped into the international lending pool. Rather than rely on its own income from new oil discoveries, the Mexican government borrowed, using the money to fund petrochemical development, steel production, and upgrading of infrastructure. Much of the spending was nonproductive, including subsidies to private industry and lavish lifestyles among the elites.

On August 12, 1982, Mexican Finance Minister Jesús Silva Herzog reported to the United States and the International Monetary Fund (IMF) that Mexico had no money to repay its loans. The next day, debt negotiations began. In November, Brazil was in the same boat, and the crisis spread thoughout the Third World in the next year. The specter of nonpayment on loans threatened the entire international banking system. Banks depended on interest income from loans to pay interest on depositors' capital and to repay other banks from which they borrowed. This was particularly true of U.S. banks that had borrowed petrodollars from Eurobanks. The key was to keep interest income flowing into the banking system.

Negotiations led to debt refinancing rather than to forgiveness. A key player in the negotiations between Latin American governments and international banks was the IMF. The IMF promised to provide funds to help the Latin American companies meet their obligations. But there was a catch: The borrowing countries needed to cut government spending. The final effect was to increase debt even further, with new loans to repay interest on the old loans. The cost of repaying those loans was then transferred to the Latin American masses because the IMF imposed austerity programs, which cut social spending.

Mexico's foreign debt jumped from $14.5 billion in 1975 to $85 billion in early 1984, surpassing $110 billion by 1989. The price was paid by the masses. In 1983, President Miguel de la Madrid, following IMF recommendations, cut government spending in half, eliminating subsidies for some basic foods and for transportation. While inflation continued in the 75 to 100 percent range, the president held wage increases between 15 and 25 percent. From 1981 to 1987, consumer prices increased fourteen times and unemployment and underemployment rose to approximately 45 percent. The IMF-imposed austerity program created no jobs, even though Mexico needed 700,000 new jobs a year to absorb the new entrants into the work force.

Throughout the 1980s, per capita income fell an average of 1.1 percent a year, leading the Economic Commission on Latin America and the Caribbean (ECLAC) to dub those years "the lost decade." By 1990, the region's foreign debt exceeded a staggering $420 billion, several times Latin America's annual income. Payment of interest alone came to absorb more than 40 percent of all export earnings. A significant percentage also went to fund the military.

The leadership that adopted the disastrous economic strategies of the 1970s and 1980s were mostly military regimes. Their initial success, along with their willingness to use brutality, kept them in power. The failure of their economic policies led to their downfall.

Antipolitical Military Regimes, 1964–1990*

COUNTRY	YEARS
Ecuador	1963–1966; 1972–1978
Guatemala	1963–1985
Brazil	1964–1985
Bolivia	1964–1970; 1971–1982
Argentina	1966–1973; 1976–1983
Peru	1968–1980
Panama	1968–1981
Honduras	1972–1982
Chile	1973–1984
Uruguay	1973–1984
El Salvador	1948–1984[†]

*In some cases, dating the beginning of these regimes is difficult inasmuch as military governments succeeded one another with changes in policies and personalities but maintained, overall, an antipolitical outlook and national security rationale for direct military rule. Sometimes brief civilian interludes seemed to interrupt military domination (for example, in Guatemala from 1966 to 1969, and Panama after General Omar Torrijos's death in 1981).

[†]El Salvador was dominated by military regimes from 1948 onward. It may be more appropriate to date the last episode from 1979, although the developmental focus and antipolitical themes of the junta headed by Major Oscar Osorio in 1948 anticipated a "Peruvianist" (or populist) version of antipolitics.

Source: Brian Loveman, *For la Patria: Politics and the Armed Forces in Latin America.* Copyright 1999. Reprinted by permission of SR Books, now an imprint of Rowman & Littlefield Publishers, Inc.

MILITARY MODELS FOR CHANGE

The shadow of the military has loomed large over Latin America. First it was the caudillos of the early independence era who ruled by force. Professionalization of the armed forces in the late nineteenth century, generally with training provided by Great Britain or Germany, seemed to successfully subordinate the institution to its proper role as defender of national interests, led by civilian governments. Then the unrest of the Depression era brought a new military figure, a caudillo-like dictator who rose from the professional armed forces.

Yet another military model emerged in the 1960s–1980s—a bureaucratized military that believed it could rule better than civilians. Military leaders believed they could restore order and bring development. These new military regimes tended to rule as an institution, rather than under the leadership of a caudillo-like personalistic dictator, with the notable exception of Chile's Augusto Pinochet. It was a military that distrusted civilians, and it was fully willing to use force to enforce its agenda.

The traditional concern of armed forces is to defend the country against foreign attack. Though some Latin American countries resorted to arms to settle border disputes, in general the region did not face any foreign attacks in the late twentieth century. But the military believed that it faced an internal threat from the forces of the political left. They were encouraged in this view by the United States, which poured money into the coffers of Latin American armed forces. The Cold War between the Soviet Union and the United States that began in the years after World War II came to be fought not in their own countries but in developing nations that were seen as vulnerable to Communist propaganda. The Cuban Revolution became the proof that there was a clear and present danger.

These Latin American generals, however, went even further in developing a doctrine of national security and development. According to this doctrine, a strong economy was essential for a country's security, making economic development as important an issue as military protection. Furthermore, it was impossible for a country to create a strong economy, especially by attracting foreign investment, if there was domestic unrest and subversion. By linking these two ideas, the suppression of supposed subversion gave the military a role that linked national defense to the economy.

Brazil was the first country in the region to fall under the rule of the new military model, after the overthrow of the government of João Goulart in 1964. The new regime was different than any the region had seen before. It was not led by one charismatic or all-powerful military caudillo; there was no Perón, no Somoza, not even a Vargas. The officers agreed from the beginning that there would not be one figure as dictator; instead, Brazil had a succession of military presidents, all generals (Humberto de Alencar Castello Branco, 1964–1967; Artur da Costa e Silva, 1967–1969; Emílio Garrastazu Médici, 1969–1974; Ernesto Geisel, 1974–1979; João Baptista Figueiredo, 1979–1985).

Using extensive foreign loans, the generals oversaw the transformation of Brazil's economy. In 1960 industrial goods constituted a mere 3 percent of the country's exports, whereas the industrial share of exports jumped to 30 percent by 1974. Brazil's factories turned out steel, automobiles, military equipment–including tanks and submarines–and computers. The results, measured in terms of gross national product, were stunning: growth rates of 10 percent a year. *The Economist* dubbed the impressive growth the "Brazilian miracle."

Because a strong economy was essential to Brazil's national security, anyone who disagreed with the agenda was viewed as a threat to the nation's security. And disagreement was not long in coming. The generals did indeed produce a Brazilian miracle, but it was achieved by shifting income from lower to upper sectors, concentrating wealth at the top to create investors and a market, and by contracting large foreign loans to make up for the lack of investment by elites, who largely chose to pocket their newfound wealth. The loans were also necessary because Brazil's low rate of taxation limited government funds available for investment.

As the *Los Angeles Times* pointed out in an editorial on July 21, 1974, "Despite Brazil's impressive growth rate, the gap between the rich and the poor is wider than ever." Grim statistics supported that conclusion. Of the total gain in Brazilian income during the 1964–1974 period, the richest 10 percent of the population absorbed 75 percent, whereas the poorest 50 percent got less than 10 percent. Compounding that inequity was a regressive tax system that put the heaviest burden on the working class.

The military government, determined not to let union organizers stand in the way of the miracle, formed secret police and death squads to torture and eliminate the people they saw as threats. The government solicited the help of the major U.S. and European corporations with subsidiaries in Brazil, which routinely provided lists of suspected union activists. As a result, there were no strikes against major companies in Brazil from 1969 to 1978. The military governments continued in power until 1985.

Sadly, Brazil was not alone in its turn to brutal military dictatorship. In South America, military dictatorships also came to power in Argentina, Bolivia, Chile, Ecuador, and Uruguay. Paraguay had already been under the iron hand of General Alfredo Stroessner since 1954.

As in Brazil, military leaders in Argentina came to believe that civilian control was irresponsible and left the country in chaos. At first, the military would step in to restore order, then turn the government back to civilians. In 1955, the armed forces ousted Juan Domingo Perón, who fled to exile in Paraguay. The Peronist party was outlawed as the military ruled from 1955 to 1958. The military then allowed elections, won by Radical Civic Union candidate Arturo Frondizi, who concentrated during his 1958–1962 term in office on building the steel and oil industries. Following the common pattern, economic restructuring led to economic difficulties, which in turn led to unrest and the intervention of the military. A new election in 1962 brought Radical Arturo Illia to power, but in 1966 he was ousted. This time the military kept power until 1973, when Juan Perón returned from exile to reclaim his mantle as leader of the workers. His vice president was his new wife, Isabel, a former nightclub dancer who had been his secretary while in exile.

In July 1974 Perón died, and Isabel found herself trying to solve problems that would have challenged an experienced politician. Economic chaos reigned, armed guerrillas challenged the government, and finally the 1973 oil crisis crippled the economy. This time the military stepped in with a vengeance. From 1976 to 1983, a series of generals ruled the country (Jorge Rafael Videla, 1976–1981; Roberto Eduardo Viola, March–December, 1981; Carlos Alberto Lacoste, December 1981; Leopoldo Galtieri, December 1981– June 1982; Alfredo Oscar Saint-Jean, June–July 1982; Reynaldo Bignone, July 1982–December 1983).

Like the Brazilian generals, they worried about national security. And like the middle classes of Brazil who had urged the 1964 coup against Goulart, the Argentine business sector turned to the military. The business community was concerned about guerrilla kidnapping of foreign businessmen (170 kidnappings in 1973), violence at factories, and inflation rising to 30 percent despite price controls. The result was a meeting in September 1975 between the leading business organization, the Argentine Industrial Union, and Army Chief of Staff General Jorge Rafael Videla, in which the two groups agreed on a coup that took place six months later. "The 1976 coup was either silently accepted or overtly supported, since virtually no political party tried to mobilize society in defense of the democratic system," according to Luis Moreno Ocampo, who later prosecuted the generals. "The coup was not simply a case of the military imposing its will upon a reluctant civil society but the result of a civic–military alliance, which found support in the international community."

The generals disbanded Congress and the Supreme Court and launched a campaign of murder and torture that killed perhaps 30,000 people. However, the generals were concerned about their international image, especially as the brutal regime of General Augusto Pinochet across the Andes in Chile was drawing international outrage. The Argentine generals wanted to keep their targeting of dissidents clandestine. In Argentina, supposed subversives were kidnapped and tortured in some 340 secret detention centers. The bodies of more than 10,000 who were killed were dropped from planes or buried in mass graves. Because civilian government had been destroyed, and all means of communication were censored, the government was simply able to deny that anything had happened. A new noun entered the Argentine vocabulary—*desaparacido* (disappeared).

The military–business alliance supported economic liberalization, which consisted largely of dropping the tariff barriers established under ISI and forcing local industry to compete with lower-priced imports. Government would do its part by cutting back on the public sector, which had become bloated through years of populism and ISI. The government sold public enterprises, cut wages and increased taxes. Some domestic manufacturers collapsed in the face of competition, and their laid-off workers swelled the ranks of the unemployed, allowing the surviving firms to pay lower wages. New investments were funded by massive foreign borrowing.

Finally, the generals were brought down in 1983 by their failure in the one legitimate role they could claim—defenders of the nation. In an attempt to divert domestic attention from the crumbling economy and increasing repression, the generals launched a war to reclaim the Malvinas Islands from the British, who had de facto control of the island since the 1830s. The Falklands, as the British called it, were populated by fewer than 2,000 English-speaking residents and 600,000 sheep. The generals assumed that Great Britain would not fight over the insignificant and distant possession and successfully rallied the population around the flag. But British Prime

A 1977 poster from a New York protest against the Chilean dictatorship is an example of the solidarity movements that arose in the United States in the 1970s. (Library of Congress)

Minister Margaret Thatcher chose to meet the Argentine challenge as a way of rousing British patriotism and deflecting attention from Britain's economic crisis. The much stronger British forces easily defeated the Argentines, killing thousands of young, ill-trained troops. It was the last straw for the Argentine military government.

Though Argentina had suffered more than its share of military coups throughout the twentieth century, Chile had a long history of rule by democratic institutions. Even Chile's path to revolution had taken a democratic, electoral route. Because of that history, the military coup that toppled Allende in 1973 was particularly shocking. Like the other military dictatorships, Chile under Pinochet was characterized by repression and brutality. Unlike Argentina and Brazil, however, the Pinochet government sought to limit governmental involvement in the economy.

The Pinochet government subscribed to monetarist economic policies. Popularized by the conservative economists of the University of Chicago, nicknamed "the Chicago boys," monetarism advocated minimizing governmental control over the economy, extensive budget cuts, reduction of tariffs, and incentives for foreign investments. The dictatorship reduced government involvement in the economy by divesting the state of more than 550 businesses. The budget was cut by virtually dismantling social security and pension plans. Between 1977 and 1980, Pinochet balanced the budget, reduced inflation, and witnessed substantial economic growth. In 1982, Milton Friedman, Chicago's theoretician of monetarism, wrote, "Chile is an economic miracle." Friedman conveniently confused growth with development: Chilean economic growth certainly did not improve the living standards of the majority.

Chile's indisputable economic growth depended largely on a substantial inflow of foreign credit, which financed the import of luxury goods for the elites. Pinochet did not expand Chile's limited manufacturing sector, focusing instead on the export of primary products. Much of Chile's growth depended on high prices for copper, which alone accounted for 95 percent of export earnings. But after 1975, the world price of copper plummeted from $1.70 to $0.52 per pound in 1982. Chile also promoted export of grapes and wine. But Chile's export model was no more successful in the long run than was Brazil's industrialization model. The recession of the 1980s sunk all boats.

For many, Chile's miracle was a myth. Rising foreign debt accompanied by falling export earnings revealed the fragility of Chile's economic growth. In 1982, the gross national product fell 14 percent; in 1983, it dropped another 3 percent. Chile holds a record for the steepest drop in gross national product in Latin America. By the mid-1980s, the economy lay in ruins. A foreign debt, by 1988 in excess of $20 billion, gave Chile the dubious distinction of having one of the highest per capita debts in the world. Servicing that debt consumed fully 80 percent of the nation's export earnings. Bankruptcies multiplied; unemployment soared. The *Los Angeles Times* (February 22, 1983) reported, "Businesses are going bankrupt at a record pace, the banking industry has all but collapsed, and the country is dangerously near default on its foreign debt."

The poor and the middle class felt the brunt of the economic deterioration. Chile's Cardinal Raul Silva Enriquez observed, "I could be wrong, but never in my life have I seen such a disastrous economic situation." One Chilean wryly observed, "The free-market policies of the Chicago Boys destroyed more private enterprises in the past year than the most radical sectors of Allende's coalition dreamed of nationalizing in three years; they have turned more middle-class people into proletarians or unemployed than any Marxist textbook ever described." British economist Philip O'Brien labeled the Chilean economy in 1984 as a "spectacular example of private greed masquerading as a model of economic development."

The military dictatorship's economic experiments left seven million out of twelve million Chileans impoverished. Observers estimated a seven-fold increase in the number of people living in substandard conditions. They concluded that 10 percent of the population benefited from the "miracle" at the expense of the other 90 percent.

The military rulers of these countries did not restrict their authoritarian policies to their own national territories. In 1976, Argentina, Bolivia, Brazil, Chile, Paraguay, and Uruguay joined in what became known as Operation Condor, organized by the Pinochet government. The purpose was to help like-minded governments track down dissident refugees and assassinate them in other countries. Chile provided the leadership of Secret Police Director Manuel Contreras as well as computers and centralized services. The United States facilitated communications among the South American intelligence chiefs. Victims of Operation Condor included Chilean General Carlos Prats and his wife, Sofia Cuthbert, who were killed in Buenos Aires in 1974, and the car-bombing assassination of former Allende government diplomat Orlando Letelier and Ronni Moffitt, U.S. research associate, in Washington, D.C., in 1976.

WAR IN CENTRAL AMERICA

In fundamental ways, Central America serves as both an exaggerated and instructive example of the crises of underdevelopment besetting late twentieth-century Latin America. The region can be described by the classic dependent growth model, an emphasis on exports rather than internal production and on profits rather than on wages. The economies grew but could not develop. Growth depended on highly cyclical external demand for its primary products: coffee, bananas, cotton, sugar, and beef. Any benefits from periodic growth accrued to a small portion of the population; the majority remained marginalized and voiceless in a society that was run neither by nor for them. Conservative estimates place 60 percent of the population in the impoverished category. No amount of economic growth could help—or had helped—the masses achieve a satisfactory standard of living. In late 1986, in a homily during Mass at the cathedral in San Salvador, Archbishop Arturo

Rivera y Damas stated, "The real cause of underdevelopment is the ideological, economic, and political dependence of our countries."

Most of Central America afforded its citizens few democratic rights. Occasionally the elite and, much later the middle class, exercised the formalities of democracy for their own enhancement, but the military always kept a sharp eye on such rare experiences and readily intervened if the ballot box suggested even a hint of social, economic, or political change in the offing. The electoral farces in Guatemala, El Salvador, Honduras, and Nicaragua in the 1960s and 1970s confirmed the traditional forces in power or served as excuses for further military intervention. To those who wanted to challenge underdevelopment, poverty, dependency, authoritarian rule, and a long catalog of social inequities, the ballot box offered no opportunity, a realization that gave form to the guerrilla movements in Guatemala and the formation of the Sandinistas in Nicaragua in the 1960s.

Like the rest of the region, Central America made its own attempt at economic change in the 1960s. The five nations agreed to create the Central American Common Market (CACM) in 1960–1963 with the hopes that a regional market could sustain some import-substitution industries that no single Central American nation could support. But the CACM had problems and weaknesses from the start. Industrialization proved to be capital intensive, therefore creating few jobs. Heavy expenditures for machinery and technology drained hard currencies. Many of the plants assembled rather than manufactured—importing component parts, putting them together; and then exporting the finished product. Such assembly plants did little for the local economy except employ a few workers at modest salaries. And the profits from those few industries left the region because 62 percent of all industries were in foreign hands.

The CACM also was characterized by unequal industrial growth, which ignited regional rivalries and jealousies. Guatemala and El Salvador boasted the lion's share of the industrialization, to the annoyance and economic disadvantage of Honduras, Nicaragua, and Costa Rica. Even though El Salvador was the site of much of the manufacturing, the assembly plants provided little employment. Tiny El Salvador had insufficient land for its population, with more than 6.5 million people inhabiting 8,260 square miles. Thus, El Salvador had twice the population of Nicaragua packed into less than one-sixth of the area. Most of that land was controlled by a group of elites so small that they were referred to as "the 14 families," although their numbers were certainly far greater. Roughly 2 percent of the population owned 60 percent of the arable land. The Salvadoran escape valve had been the Honduran border; by 1968, there were some 300,000 Salvadorans living illegally in Honduras.

Honduras, in contrast to El Salvador, has a relatively low population density. For many years, there was little competition for land in the Pacific zone of the country because the economy centered on the banana enclave of the Atlantic region. Hondurans tended to have access to land, though not all was of good quality and landholdings tended to be small. Subsistence farming came under pressure in the 1950s, however, as the government encouraged agricultural modernization and export diversification. For the first time, beef, cotton, and coffee became significant export products, pushing Honduran subsistence farmers off their land. By 1965, landlessness had become a problem. As Honduran campesinos began to organize, politicians sought to deflect their anger by using Salvadoran immigrants as a scapegoat. Salvadorans were targeted as squatters in the Pacific zone and as low-wage workers in the Atlantic. Salvadorans began to leave Honduras in droves, some expelled by the government and others escaping the new antipathy of Hondurans. El Salvador, which could ill afford the immigrants' return, claimed that Honduras was brutalizing the immigrants.

Conflict between the two countries came to a head in June 1969 when riots broke out during the soccer matches leading up to the World Cup games. In July, El Salvador invaded Honduras; the "soccer war" lasted only four days before the Organization of American States succeeded in ending the violence, but it took ten years to heal the diplomatic wounds, and the CACM never recovered. Limited industrialization clearly was not going to be the answer to Central America's problems.

Like the rest of the region, Central American governments availed themselves of foreign loans during the 1970s, though they funded little in the way of productive investment. Much of the borrowing paid for increased fuel costs because none of the countries produced their own oil. In 1975, prices for Central America's exports plummeted, while the price of imports steadily rose. Economic reverses sparked political unrest, particularly among rural populations hungry for agrarian reform. A nervous alliance of landowners, commercial bourgeoisie, and the military forcefully repressed the protest when and where it occurred. To do so, they turned increasingly to the United States for military support to thwart rebellion.

The United States had always had a particular interest in the Central American region, viewed as the U.S. sphere of influence. Interest increased when Central American elites claimed the unrest was caused by Communists. It was in this context that the Sandinistas came to power in Nicaragua in 1979, and bloody wars raged through El Salvador and Guatemala, spilling over into Honduras and Costa Rica.

El Salvador had a bleak history of violent repression dating back to the 1932 *matanza* carried out by General Maximiliano Hernandez Martinez. The military ruled thereafter, in close alliance with Salvadoran elites, but cracks in the system began to appear in the 1960s. The Christian Democratic Party was founded in 1960, and by 1964 it had won significant legislative and regional representation. Further, the war with Honduras opened the debate on agrarian reform, culminating in a national conference on the issue in January 1970. This was followed by urban strikes, particularly on the part of teachers, and a new militancy among Salvadoran university students.

The oligarchy responded by using the ferocious National Guard to form violent paramilitary forces, which were focused on terrifying peasant leaders, and by stealing the presidential election from Christian Democrat candidate José Napoleon Duarte in 1972. As even the moderate Christian Democrats were targeted for repression, more radical Salvadorans turned to armed struggle. By the end of 1975, there were three guerrilla organizations in the countryside. When years of frustration came to a head over the military's rigging of the 1977 presidential elections, the nation disintegrated into civil war. A military coup staged by junior officers on October 15, 1979, turned the government over to a civilian–military junta.

In early 1980, the junta, even though it had become more conservative in its composition, made some serious efforts to institute reforms. It nationalized the banking system and the sale of coffee. Most significantly, on March 8, 1980, the junta promulgated Decree 153, a land reform. In the first phase of the reform, the government nationalized estates exceeding 1,250 acres and turned them into cooperatives run by the workers themselves. The government promised payment in bonds to former owners. Those estates grew mainly cotton and sugar cane, although some produced coffee and raised cattle. A second phase was to have nationalized estates exceeding 375 acres, later raised to 612 acres. A third phase, called "Land to the Tiller," was intended to benefit the campesinos directly by transforming renters of small plots into owners. Over 80 percent of such plots measured fewer than five acres each. The land reform looked good on paper, and efforts were made to implement it, but unfortunately they did not succeed. Jorge Villacorta, a former undersecretary of the Ministry of Agriculture, observed, "In reality, from the first moment that the implementation of the agrarian reform began, what we saw was a sharp increase in official violence against the very peasants who were the supposed 'beneficiaries' of the process."

Later in 1980, after the junta of reformers had been pushed aside by more traditional figures, the advocates of change formed a political alliance, the FDR (*Frente Democratico Revolucionario*; the Revolutionary Democratic Front), and a united military front, the FMLN (*Frente Farabundo Marti para la Liberación Nacional*, the Farabundo Martí Front for National Liberation). Together, they created a viable infrastructure for revolution. The FDR issued a broad program of its objectives. It called for

1. national independence, priority to Salvadoran needs, and subservience to no foreign country;
2. profound political, economic, and social reforms to guarantee human dignity, welfare, liberty, and progress;

A U.S. advisor instructs a Salvadoran air force cadet in the use of an M-60 mortar. The United States funded the Salvadoran government's war against the Farabondo Martí National Liberation Front and the repression carried out against the civilian population.

3. nonalignment in international affairs;
4. democratic government;
5. a new national army;
6. support for private enterprise; and
7. religious freedom.

Obviously the implementation of this program would revolutionize El Salvador. In the process it would eliminate the army and reduce the influence of the agrarian-industrial elite. The lines were clearly drawn between the beneficiaries of the traditional society and the advocates of change. A smoldering struggle between the army and the guerrillas erupted into a full-scale civil war as the rebel ranks expanded.

Until 1979, the military and the elites had been capable of dealing effectively with any challenge to their authority. The events of 1979–1980 demonstrated they could no longer frighten their opponents, regardless of how violent their death squads became. For the first time, they had to reach out to the United States for direct support. Their tactic was a simple one that had already proven effective in many parts of the hemisphere. The Latin American elites identified any longing for change, no matter how modest, with Communism. They fully appreciated the Pavlovian response of U.S. officials to any charge that Communism was afoot in the Western Hemisphere. Once the alert to a "Communist threat" in El Salvador had been sounded, military aid from Washington cascaded over the nation.

U.S. intervention exacerbated the civil war, which intensified during the decade. By 1989, the FMLN forces, estimated to number 10,000, occupied one-third of the country as liberated territory. They collected their own taxes along the national highways and their attacks and sabotage nearly destroyed the national economy. Successful in penetrating the largest cities, they were attacking military and other targets in San Salvador by early 1989. Pentagon officials concluded that the demoralized army could not fight without U.S. support. With more than 60,000 people killed in eight years—many of them civilian victims of right-wing death squads—El Salvador suffered one of the bloodiest civil wars in Latin American history. The tragic history of modern El Salvador illustrates the lengths to which those who hold power will go to keep it and to prevent change.

Although the revolutionaries proved themselves capable of dispatching the Salvadoran army, they could not defeat the United States. In response to the lengthening, bloody stalemate, the FMLN signed peace accords with the U.S.-sponsored government on January 16, 1992. They were influenced in no small part by the defeat of the Sandinistas at the polls in 1990. The Sandinistas had won their revolution in 1979, but the counterrevolution launched by the Nicaraguan right wing and its U.S. allies had cost 30,000 lives and had destroyed the economy. Under threat of continued war, the exhausted Nicaraguans voted the Sandinistas out. By 1990, the days of Soviet or Cuban support for Latin American revolution—to the limited extent that they had ever existed—were long gone.

Guatemala was the other scene of brutal warfare in Central America in the 1980s. The roots of the struggle were in the overthrow of Jacobo Arbenz in 1954 and the string of military governments that ruled thereafter. The wars began with an unsuccessful 1961 revolt by nationalist Guatemalan military officers, angered that the government allowed the CIA to use national territory to train Cuban exiles for the unsuccessful invasion of Cuba at the Bay of Pigs. Two of the officers, Marco Antonio Yon Sosa and Luis Turcios Lima, became radicalized by their experiences in the countryside and ended up heading revolutionary guerrilla groups. In 1966, the military allowed the election of the civilian government of Julio Cesar Mendez Montenegro (1966–1970), prompting the guerrillas to suspend action. The military then took advantage of the unofficial truce to launch a brutal counterinsurgency campaign.

Although the military had a free hand during the Mendez government—indeed, he was forced to sign an agreement with the military before taking office—the military decided that it needed direct control over the government, so it retained military officers in the presidency from 1970 to 1986. At the same time, peasant leagues formed to organize for social change, and guerrilla forces regrouped and worked to recruit the mobilized campesinos, especially the indigenous majority.

In 1982, several guerrilla groups united under the umbrella organization *Unidad Revolucionaria Nacional Guatemalteca* (URNG; Guatemalan National Revolutionary Unity). In response, the military pursued a scorched earth policy, burning the villages of suspected guerrilla sympathizers, torturing and killing thousands. In 1982 alone, the government's counterinsurgency campaign claimed 75,000 lives and razed 440 villages. But that same year, the military rethought its strategy, moving from blind brute force to a more selective targeting. The military then shifted to a more strategic plan of killing 30 percent of the population and pacifying 70 percent with government programs. The political–military project was designed to bring government, through the military, to formerly isolated villages.

Some 200,000 Guatemalans were killed in the struggles after the fall of Arbenz, most of them by death squads, while another 250,000, mainly indigenous, fled across the border into Mexico to escape the holocaust. By the time the military allowed a civilian president to take power, Vinicio Cerezo in 1986, the state bureaucracy had been reconfigured to create a seamless alliance between military and government. The military remains as the architect of national stability and arbiter of democratic limits.

Finally, Guatemalan peace talks began in 1990, and accords were signed in 1996. The limits to peace, however, were clearly shown two years later, when Auxiliary Bishop Juan Gerardi Conedera was beaten to death two days after presenting a scathing report on human rights violations that blamed the Guatemalan army and civilian paramilitary groups for nearly 80 percent of rights abuses in the civil war.

The neighboring Central American countries were unable to avoid the struggles in El Salvador, Guatemala, and Nicaragua. Costa Rica became involved against its will when one group of counterrevolutionaries set up base along the uninhabited Costa Rican side of the border with Nicaragua. The United States also exerted considerable pressure on Costa Rica both to support the counterrevolutionaries and to oppose the Sandinistas. Confronting a faltering economy that could not be addressed, let alone solved, in a war-ravaged Central America, President Oscar Arias seized the diplomatic initiative after his inauguration in 1986, calling for a broad, peaceful settlement among Central Americans of their region's political problems. He won the Nobel Peace prize in 1987 for his imagination and energy. But carrying out his broad proposals for peace challenged him and the Central Americans, partially because the United States gave only lip service to the plans.

More than Costa Rica, Honduras became completely involved in the crises. It has the uncomfortable geographic distinction of being bordered by the three nations in the throes of change or challenge, characterized by simmering guerrilla warfare in Guatemala, civil war in El Salvador, and a revolutionary government in Nicaragua. At the same time, monumental economic problems challenged Honduras, which was the poorest of the Central American states and the second most impoverished nation of Latin America, after Haiti. Its population of 5.1 million grew at an annual rate of 3.5 percent, one of the highest in the world. All of its economic statistics indicated widespread social injustice. Approximately 53 percent of the population was illiterate; infant mortality was 118 per 1,000 live births. Nearly 90 percent of the rural population and 66 percent of the urban population lived below the poverty level. The economy rode a roller coaster of rising fiscal deficits and foreign debts and falling export income and foreign reserves.

Honduras exemplified the classic enclave economy. In the first half of the twentieth century, three companies—United Fruit, Standard Fruit, and Rosario Mining—dominated the economy. The first two grew and exported bananas, and the third extracted gold and silver. Foreigners owned those companies; they shipped their products abroad from specific locales, leaving only an insignificant residue of the wealth in Honduras, in the form of low wages. They did not contribute to the creation of support industries or related businesses. Those companies owned and operated the railroads as well as several of the principal ports. The banana companies controlled the oil, beer, and tobacco industries. In 1950, the three companies earned sums equal to the entire Honduran budget. Occasionally Hondurans made efforts to regulate the companies. A major strike against the banana companies in 1954 strengthened the unions and increased salaries and benefits for the workers. The victory instilled a better sense of nationalism among the Hondurans and made the unions a new social and economic force. President Ramón Villeda Morales (1958–1964) tried to further curb the fruit companies as well as to institute a modest land reform and social security program.

The victorious strike and the reforms of Villeda Morales unnerved the landowners and the military. The generals overthrew him during his final days in office and, with a brief exception in 1971–1972, ruled Honduras directly until 1982. Corruption and ever greater conservatism characterized the military governments. When the military turned the government over to an elected civilian in early 1982, the economy was in a shambles.

At that moment, the administration of President Ronald Reagan discovered the strategic location of Honduras and resolved to use it in order to destabilize Nicaragua and contain the Salvadoran rebels. Consequently, U.S. military aid to Honduras jumped impressively. The United States held joint military exercises with Honduras throughout the 1980s. Honduras provided ample opportunity for the United States to construct air bases and strips, a sea port, radar sites, military encampments, and tank traps. After

1983, Honduras was for all intents and purposes an occupied country. When the war finally ended in 1990, Honduras was left with hundreds of land-mines in the border area and a significant problem with HIV/AIDS as a result of prostitution linked to U.S. military installations and contra camps.

The Church Under Attack

The Catholic Church became a significant adversary of right wing govern-ments in Latin America in the 1970s and 1980s. Nicaragua was not the only country that felt the impact of liberation theology and the option for the poor that the Latin American bishops adopted at Medellín in 1968. Throughout Central America, Christian base communities formed.

In 1972, Salvadoran Jesuit Retulio Grande was one of several priests sent to the countryside to train lay leaders, delegates of the word, to help organize for labor rights and agrarian reform. Local landowners were out-raged, and priests were targeted by death squads, who distributed flyers exhorting, "Be a patriot! Kill a priest!" In a 1977 wave of repression, Grande was assassinated. His death came just three weeks after Oscar Arnulfo Romero was selected as a compromise choice to serve as San Salvador's new archbishop. Romero had been seen as a scholarly, conservative figure likely to steer clear of politics. Grande's death and the continuing repression led Romero to take a stand.

The archbishop traveled El Salvador, visiting parishes and seeing the conditions of poverty and repression first hand. He addressed these realities in his weekly sermons, which were broadcast on Church radio. He even resorted in 1980 to writing to U.S. President Jimmy Carter, begging him to stop sending aid to the Salvadoran government, which by then amounted to $1.5 million a day, because "it is being used to repress my people."

Two months later, Romero took his most daring step and spoke directly to the army in his Sunday homily. "Brothers, you are from the same peo-ple . . . ," Romero preached. "No soldier is obliged to obey an order that is contrary to the will of God. . . . In the name of God then, in the name of this suffering people I ask you, I beg you, I command you in the name of God: stop the repression." The next day, Romero was assassinated while saying Mass. The crowds of mourners at his funeral were greeted by gunfire.

Salvadoran religious were not the only targets of the Salvadoran mili-tary. In December 1980, a shallow grave on an isolated road revealed the tor-tured bodies of Maryknoll Sisters Maura Clarke and Ita Ford, Ursuline Sister Dorothy Kazel, and lay missioner Jean Donovan. The women, all from the United States, had been working with the archdiocese of San Salvador to help refugees fleeing rural violence.

Brazil was also a site of significant participation in the liberation theol-ogy movement, and the religious paid a high price. From 1968 to 1978, the worst years of the dictatorship, more than 120 bishops, priests, and nuns were arrested, along with nearly 300 Catholic lay workers. Seven were killed, most were tortured. Churches were raided, and Church-run media were censored or closed.

But liberation theology was never accepted by all of the Church hierarchy; indeed, many fought actively against it. Some supported the dictatorships, whereas many more simply believed that the Church should not be actively involved in the struggle. The latter were given support in 1978, when Cardinal Karol Wojtyla became Pope John Paul II. One of his first acts in 1979 was to attend the third Latin American Bishops Conference, which met in Puebla, Mexico. He endorsed the option for the poor, and he critiqued the poverty created by unrestrained capitalism. But he also made clear that he had two important concerns. One was the maintenance of theological orthodoxy, which was interpreted as a defense against the influence of Marxism and liberation theology. His distrust of the socialist implications of liberation theology had their roots in his youth in Soviet-dominated Poland. The second concern was to conserve traditional institutional authority patterns, which translated to lack of support for delegates of the word and Christian base communities.

Lest there be any doubts about John Paul's views, he made them clear on an official visit to Nicaragua in 1983. The pope refused to allow Father Ernesto Cardenal, the Minister of Culture, to kiss his ring and advised Nicaraguan priests to leave the Sandinista government. As he lectured about the importance of traditional Church hierarchy, he ignored the chants of *Madres de Mártires y Heroes* (Mothers of Martyrs and Heroes), who begged him to say a prayer for their children who had been killed in the contra war.

By 1985, the Vatican attack on liberation theology had reached new levels. The Vatican's Congregation for the Doctrine of the Faith, headed by Cardinal Joseph Ratzinger, silenced Brazilian priest Leonardo Boff, one of the founders of liberation theology. When he was silenced again in 1992, Boff left the Franciscan order and became a lay worker. In 2005, Ratzinger succeeded John Paul II as Pope Benedict XVI.

As liberation theology began to decline, the Catholic Church braced for another struggle—competition from evangelical Protestantism. In 1986, the Vatican published a study titled "Sects or New Religious Movements: Pastoral Challenges." The Vatican agreed that there were powerful U.S. economic and political institutions backing Protestant proselytizing in Latin America, but the study also reflected on the genuine appeal of evangelicals, who were filling "needs and aspirations which are seemingly not being met in the mainline churches. The [Catholic] church is often seen simply as an institution, perhaps because it gives too much importance to structures and not enough to drawing people to God in Christ."

In 1988, Catholic Church surveys claimed that four hundred Latin Americans converted to evangelical churches every hour. Among the reasons for conversion was the scarcity of Catholic priests, as well as a view that the Church does not speak to people's real spiritual needs. Evangelical theology, which demands personal responsibility, also has succeeded in transforming husbands who had been drinkers and womanizers, to the delight of many women in Latin America.

The Catholic Church has borrowed a page from the evangelicals in a movement known as Catholic Charismatic Renewal (CCR). Like the Pentecostals, CCR uses baptism of the Holy Spirit, speaking in tongues, and faith healing. The CCR also invokes the image of the Virgin Mary, which the evangelicals eschew in favor of a focus only on Jesus. The Virgin already has a strong appeal in Latin America, particularly for women, who have always made up the majority of church congregations.

By 2005, an estimated 20 to 30 percent of Latin Americans identified as evangelical Protestants, most frequently as Pentecostals. Their numbers are strongest in Guatemala, Brazil, and Colombia, but the phenomenon includes all countries in the region. Some social activists fear that the movement is conservative, focusing on personal salvation rather than community action. They also fear the evangelicals' links to right-wing movements in the United States because many of the conversions in Latin America have been the result of U.S. evangelical missions.

THE NEW SOCIAL MOVEMENTS

During the long years of repression, Latin Americans watched as the traditional twentieth-century means of opposition were systematically closed off. Political parties were outlawed and their leaders assassinated. Labor unions and student groups were targeted by death squads and torturers. The news media were censored.

But the repression did not stop people from organizing. Instead, it resulted in a change of actors and kinds of organizations. Frequently, the organizers were women, who were already outside the traditional forms of organization because they had been ignored or marginalized by unions and political parties. They tended to organize around specific issues, such as the need for water in a community, the establishment of neighborhood kitchens to feed the hungry during the worst years of the recession, and the struggle to protect environments endangered by reckless economic policy. Most importantly, they organized around the issue of human rights.

In Santiago, Chile, according to one survey, 20 percent of the urban poor were involved in popular organizations in the 1980s. Among the groups were 201 soup kitchens, 20 community kitchens, 223 cooperative buying organizations, 67 family garden organizations, 25 community bakeries, and 137 health groups, claiming 12,956 active members.

Many of these organizations were formed under the protective arms of the Catholic Church, which also criticized the Pinochet regime's human rights violations and economic policies. One of the ways that the Church helped to organize was by providing a space where women could gather to seek help. At one parish, the women were encouraged to document what had happened to their families by making *arpilleras*, patchwork tapestries telling their stories. Eventually there were some 230 churches where secret workshops were conducted, making thousands of arpilleras, which were smuggled out of the country to expose the Pinochet dictatorship.

The most famous of the groups to emerge among the new social movements was Argentina's *Madres de la Plaza de Mayo* (Mothers of May Plaza), who marched in front of the Casa Rosada on the Plaza de Mayo once a week for many years to demand the return of their disappeared loved ones. The women came together as they crossed paths while relentlessly questioning police and military officials about the whereabouts of missing relatives, especially their children. The mothers were mostly traditional housewives who had never considered entering politics. It was that very maternal role that led them into the streets to search for missing loved ones, to keep their families intact. The traditional maternal role at first protected the Madres from military repression. First, they were not seen as a threat. Later,

The mothers of the Plaza de Mayo formed when Argentine women discovered that there were many of them searching for their missing relatives, who were "disappeared" during Argentina's Dirty War. Here they display kerchiefs with the names of their missing relatives while demonstrating in Buenos Aires in 1982.

the military hesitated in its use of repression because it would be hard to justify attacks on apparently harmless older women. Eventually, several of the Madres had disappeared, and one general said it had been a mistake to leave them alive.

The Madres have not weathered the transition to electoral government well. First the group split on the issue of whether to support Raúl Alfonsín, the first civilian president after the fall of the military. Some were satisfied with the return of electoral politics and the trials for the Dirty War. Others still demanded a full accounting of the disappearances, that their children be brought back alive or their deaths be fully explained. Some childless women resented the group's emphasis on motherhood, although the Madres argue that they represent a radicalized and socialized maternity that defines the entire population of the nation as children who must be fed, housed, educated, and protected. In this way, they struggle to make maternal values society's dominant paradigm, in place of the traditional patriarchal values that have exalted economic competition and authoritarianism.

New social movements also emerged in countries with civilian governments that were no more responsive to community needs than were the military dictatorships. For example, in Mexico City people organized self-help groups in the aftermath of the September 19, 1985, earthquake that killed at least 8,000 people. The government response was so ineffectual that several organizations formed, including *Coordinadora Única de Damnificados* (CUD; Victims' Coordinating Council). Leslie Serna described how the CUD began: "We didn't have much of an idea of what to do, and we didn't have any great plan; we did one thing at a time, and things had their own dynamic. Suddenly we were an organization and we had named commissions and a board of directors." The groups helped to clear rubble and look for people trapped in the wreckage. For the homeless, they helped construct squatter settlements, collected clothing, furniture and blankets, and created nurseries. They also organized demonstrations and lobbied the government for assistance.

The largest social movement to emerge in the 1980s was Brazil's *Movimento dos Trabalhadores Rurais Sem Terra* (MST; Landless Workers Movement). The MST is still the largest social movement in Latin America, representing hundreds of thousands of landless workers. According to the MST, 60 percent of Brazil's agricultural land is idle, while 25 million people lack year-round agricultural work and access to land. Since the MST organized in 1985, with the help of the Catholic Church, more than 250,000 families have occupied 15 million acres of idle land under MST auspices and won land titles from the government. These victories were hard fought. Land occupations have been greeted with violence, both from landowners and from the police. From 1989 to 1999, more than 1,000 people were killed in land conflicts, but as of August 1999, only 53 suspects had been brought to trial.

The MST adopted the kinds of strategies carried out by revolutionary governments—creation of food cooperatives, small agricultural industries, and a literacy program—and their efforts have been supported by such international organizations as UNESCO (United Nations Educational, Scientific, and Cultural Organization). Within Brazil, the group also enjoyed widespread support. A 1997 public opinion poll showed that 77 percent approved of the MST and 85 percent supported their nonviolent occupation of idle farmland.

The MST made a point of linking with international movements to fight globalization and its effects on local economies, as well as with Brazil's *Partido dos Trabalhadores* (PT; Workers' Party). In January 2001, the PT sponsored the World Social Forum, which attracted an estimated 5,000 scholars, politicians, labor union leaders, and representatives of grassroots organizations from around the world to challenge the business elite who were meeting at the same time at the World Economic Forum in Switzerland.

A highlight of the gathering came when 1,300 members of the MST, joined by forum participants, invaded the grounds of the U.S. biotechnology firm Monsanto. The protesters were led by Joao Pedro Stedile, head of the MST, and French trade unionist Jose Bove, a French sheep farmer who became famous when his Farmers Confederation stormed a McDonald's restaurant in rural France to draw attention to the risks of genetically modified crops to farmers, consumers, and the environment. The forum showed the possibilities of linking social movements with progressive political parties to work for change. Such links were clearly important, even with the return to electoral politics in Latin America.

Do Elections Make Democracies?

One by one, from the mid-1980s to 1990, the countries of Latin America returned to electing civilians to run their governments. Officials in Washington applauded the new but fragile "democracy" in the region. But the mere existence of electoral politics is not all that is required for a country to be democratic. A true democracy requires a change in the power balance among the various groups in society and institutions that are responsive to the majority. For Latin America, true democracy has been elusive.

In Brazil, the transition to civilian government was ushered in during the government of Ernesto Geisel (1974–1979), when opposition to the military in power mounted. The Catholic Church raised its voice against social injustice and demanded economic opportunities for the masses and freedom for all. Labor showed a renewed independence. In May of 1978, a strike in São Paulo involving some 50,000 workers was the first in a decade. The students, too, became vocal again. In 1977 they organized a number of important demonstrations.

More significantly, the business community began to voice criticism. In November of that year, some 2,000 businesspeople gathered in Rio de Janeiro and called for democratic liberties, and in July of 1978 a document signed by eight wealthy industrialists advocated a more just socioeconomic system. It can be argued that it was the elite criticism that mattered most because they could not be repressed with impunity. They were a key part of the power structure that the military upheld. Finally, within the ranks of the military, reform sentiment was growing, and it became increasingly difficult for the governing generals to disguise the cracks in the facade of unity they wanted to project.

Unlike his military predecessors, Geisel did not consult his colleagues in selecting a consensus candidate to replace himself in the presidency. Arbitrarily he picked General João Baptista Figueiredo, a relatively unknown figure who formerly had directed the National Intelligence Service. Assuming a six-year presidency on March 15, 1979, Figueiredo expressed his hope to preside over the political transition from dictatorship to democracy. In 1985, the government enfranchised illiterates (perhaps as many as 40 percent of the adult population) and an electoral college selected a civilian president, Tancredo Neves, who died shortly after his election and was succeeded by José Sarney. In 1989, the first direct presidential election was held since the election of Goulart. But the transition to electoral politics was not an easy one: The winner, Fernando Collor de Mello, was impeached after a scandal in 1992.

In Argentina, the generals had been discredited by their defeat in the Malvinas war and the downward spiral of the economy. They agreed to allow elections in 1983, and the winner was Radical Party candidate Raúl Alfonsín. In an historic decision, Alfonsín vowed to prosecute the generals who carried out the Dirty War. In 1985, after detailed testimony about disappearances and torture, five men were convicted: General Jorge Rafael Videla and Admiral Emilio Eduardo Massera were sentenced to life imprisonment. General Roberto Viola was sentenced to seventeen years in prison, whereas Brigadier Ramón Agosti was sentenced to only four and half years. Brigadier Omar Graffigna, air force commander of the second junta, was acquitted, along with three members of the third junta, General Leopoldo Galtieri, Admiral Jorge Anaya, and Brigadier Basilio Lami Dozo. But Argentina remained a deeply divided country. During the first term of Peronist Carlos Saúl Meném (elected in 1989 and in 1995), he responded to a military uprising by pardoning Videla, Viola, Massera, and top commanders of the Buenos Aires police force who had been convicted.

The demise of the Pinochet regime was even more startling than the fall of the other South American regimes. Unrest began in 1982; by then Chile had accumulated the highest debt in Latin America, $16 billion, and one-third of the workforce was unemployed. In 1983, labor leaders organized mass protests, and even sectors of the right began to fear an uprising that might be avoided by removing Pinochet as a rallying point. Pinochet declared a state of siege in 1984, but in 1985 he was presented with the National Accord for Transition to Full Democracy, an agreement brokered by Cardinal Juan

Francisco Fresno among eleven political groups, ranging from center right to socialist. The call for legalization of political activity was signed by enough groups to indicate that Pinochet could no longer claim that he enjoyed majority support. But the general refused to acknowledge the accord or meet with the groups it represented.

By 1987, the economy improved and Pinochet had survived an assassination attempt. Feeling that his popularity was assured, he agreed to a plebiscite on his continued rule. The election was announced only five weeks in advance, but a coalition of fourteen parties and many social movements organized, finally even gaining access to television. In a stunning defeat, 57 percent voted against Pinochet. Perhaps more frightening for the future, however, was that 43 percent voted for him to continue.

The dictator agreed to step down, although he retained his military rank and a position as a senator for life. In 1989, Christian Democrat Patricio Aylwin was elected. In his campaign, Aylwin assured the business community that there would be no change in the basic structure of the economy. He also campaigned on a human rights platform, and the National Commission on Truth and Reconciliation was formed. But the emphasis was on reconciliation, not on justice. Although the report presented a great deal of information, the conclusions called for apologies and forgiveness, not for legal action.

The civilian regimes simultaneously increased and narrowed the spaces for political participation and the development of an involved, politicized civilian society. Clearly, there was more freedom of speech and freedom to organize groups to work for social change. But there was little support from these governments for the kinds of social movements that appeared in the 1970s and 1980s. The new governments saw such groups as the Madres as necessary only during the struggle against dictatorship. The civilian leaders presented themselves as the logical successors of the aspirations of the new social movements. But though the new leaders were opposed to repression and dedicated to electoral democracy, they were not interested in changing the economic and social programs of the dictatorships.

Demands for economic and social democratization fell on deaf ears, especially as the new governments represented the same economic interests as did the old. This was seen most clearly in Chile during the Aylwin government. Six months before the election, Aylwin and colleague Alejandro Foxley met with Eduardo Matte, president of Cape Horn Methanol, one of the largest transnational corporations in Chile. Matte later told an interviewer,

> "[T]hey gave us all sorts of guarantees that economic policy would continue to be the same as what we had known before: an open market, favorable investment terms, in sum, all the good things that we inherited from the military government. And a year later, there is no doubt in my mind that the warranty that this country has, in fact, is precisely Alejandro Foxley as Minister of Finance."

Another businessman observed that Foxley, a Christian Democrat, and economics minister Carlos Ominami, a member of the Socialist Party, "could perfectly well have been members of Pinochet's cabinet."

Quite simply, the new governments were still run by members of the economic elites. Their interest in pushing social change from the top was minimal, and the pressures for change from the bottom came from a weakened, disorganized mass whose political parties and representative groups were destroyed during the dictatorships. The social movements that arose in their place, as they tended to be specific to issues of the dictatorship, frequently were not in a position to take up the struggle.

Meanwhile, the institutions of governance—and even many of the individuals within them—remained unchanged. Military officers, Supreme Court justices, and bureaucratic appointees were frequently holdovers from the dictatorships. In most of the transitions to elected government, guarantees were given to the outgoing governments about just such continuity. The strength of such institutions was made clear with the military uprising in Argentina that prompted Meném's pardons. Clearly, the military still had a key role to play. Furthermore, history has shown that human rights violations are not restricted to military regimes. Thousands of Latin Americans have been killed by death squads during the rule of civilian regimes in the Dominican Republic, Guatemala, Peru, El Salvador, Brazil, and Mexico.

Much of the open violence to which people were subjected during the dictatorships had disappeared. But the violence of everyday life that comes from unequal economic structures, that causes malnutrition and high infant mortality, had not changed. In Brazil, under the Sarney and Collor governments, agrarian reform proposals were blocked, a program to provide low-income housing was first retargeted to the middle class and then dropped, and emergency distribution of food to the poor became an opportunity for corruption and political patronage.

As the 1990s began, Latin American elites continued to confuse their own well-being with that of the nation.

RECOMMENDED READINGS

Chesnut, R. Andrew. *Competitive Spirits: Latin America's New Religious Economy*. New York: Oxford University Press, 2003.

Dinges, John. *The Condor Years: How Pinochet and His Allies Brought Terrorism to Three Continents*. New York: New Press, 2004.

Lernoux, Penny. *Cry of the People: The Struggle for Human Rights in Latin America— The Catholic Church in Conflict With U.S. Policy*. New York: Penguin Books, 1982.

Loveman, Brian. *For la Patria: Politics and the Armed Forces in Latin America*. Wilmington, DE: Scholarly Resources, 1999.

Menjívar, Cecilia, and Nestor Rodriguez, eds. *When States Kill: Latin America, the U.S., and Technologies of Terror.* Austin: University of Texas Press, 2005.

Partnoy, Alicia. *The Little School: Tales of Disappearance and Survival in Argentina.* Pittsburgh, PA: Cleis Press, 1986.

Petras, James, with Todd Cavaluzzi, Morris Morley, and Steve Vieux. *The Left Strikes Back: Class Conflict in Latin America in the Age of Neoliberalism.* Boulder, CO: Westview Press, 1999.

Walker, Thomas W., and Ariel C. Armony, eds. *Repression, Resistance, and Democratic Transition in Central America.* Wilmington, DE: Scholarly Resources, 2000.

CHAPTER 11

FORWARD INTO THE PAST

In December 2000, the volcano Popocatépetl erupted in Mexico. It was the worst eruption in 500 years. "In Mexican culture, Popo's activity represents a premonition of historic events," said poet Homero Aridjis. "It is full of omens." Historians are wary of predictions. The significance of historic events can be seen much more clearly when they are well past. But some important trends appear to be emerging.

At the turn of the twentieth century, there was an eerie return to old patterns: Neoliberalism and its love affair with the world market reprised the free-trade liberalism of the late nineteenth century. A new revolutionary movement in Mexico resurrected an historic name and claim—Zapata and the land—while waging its struggle largely on the Internet. An old revolutionary movement in Colombia transitioned in the language of U.S. foreign policy from Communists to narcotraffickers to terrorists. Renewed economic crisis swept politicians out of office and put in their place left-leaning leaders who tried to find yet another new path for Latin America.

Yet, the same questions remained: Who will rule Latin America? Who will benefit? How does a region create prosperity and equality? Why do so many poor people inhabit rich lands?

NEOLIBERALISM AND ITS DISCONTENTS

The original liberals were Adam Smith and David Ricardo, who touted free markets and comparative advantage as the routes to prosperity. Neoliberalism is a return to that unfettered capitalism, and in Latin America, its achievement meant undoing years of state involvement in the economy. The tenets of neoliberalism in Latin America are cuts in social spending, privatization of public activity, encouragement of market solutions to social problems, deregulation of private activity, and, of course, free trade. Neoliberalism is backed by the United States, in what is known in development circles as the "Washington consensus," and the basic ideas are embedded in the development strategy advocated by the IMF, the World Bank, and the IDB. Liberalism returned to Latin America in the form of structural adjustment policies demanded by the IMF and the World Bank so that the region could repay its debts and pull out of the tailspin of the "lost decade" of the 1980s. Throughout the 1990s, the region's leaders were busy lowering and eliminating tariff barriers, welcoming foreign investment, and selling off state-owned industries.

Globalization was initially greeted in Latin America with great euphoria. Latin American governments opened their economies wide, dropping tariff barriers and inviting foreign investment, which flowed into the region for the first time since the wave of defaults that began with Mexico in 1982. But by the end of the 1990s, many Latin Americans were disappointed and pessimistic. Free markets were supposed to bring economic growth, but growth levels were far lower than expected. Whereas the world's developing economies grew on average 4.7 percent a year, Latin America mustered only 3.3 percent, with less than 2 percent growth in Ecuador and Venezuela. Growth in per capita income lagged even further, growing only 1.3 percent.

From 1990 to 1997, the Latin American economies grew, and poverty fell, although it was still higher than it was in 1980. But starting in 1997, growth rates plummeted and poverty increased. By 2002, economists were talking about a "lost half decade," much like the lost decade of the 1980s. ECLAC warned that to meet United Nations goals of halving poverty by 2015, Latin America would have to grow by unrealistically high percentages. It was time, the agency recommended, for the region to rely not just on growth but to also carry out government-led redistribution of wealth. But government intervention in the economy was anathema in the 1990s as governments adhered to neoliberal precepts with an almost religious fervor.

Globalization also had a profound impact on the structure of Latin American economies. For much of the twentieth century, government leaders focused on industrialization as the way to modernize their economies. But during the 1990s, productivity in manufacturing either declined or remained stagnant. In fact, most of Latin America deindustrialized, according to the United Nations Commission on Trade and Development (UNCTAD). Although Mexico and several Central American nations increased manufacturing, it was only through the addition of assembly plants using imported components. South America, with the exception of Brazil, returned to the export of natural resources. And the prices of those products declined during the decade, just as the terms of trade on commodities had declined for much of Latin America's history.

Although the neoliberal policies were instituted largely because of the debt crisis, Latin American debt grew precipitously. By 2005, the region's debt totaled $720 billion, equivalent to 38 percent of its gross domestic product. Although net foreign direct investment in 2004 was a sizable $44 billion, this was more than offset by the $49.6 billion that left the country. The outflow included debt payments and capital flight.

The new policies were shocking not just because of the economic changes but because of what that implied about nationalism, one of Latin America's most important philosophies of the twentieth century. While Mexicans in 1938 had rallied around their government in support of a nationalized PEMEX as a symbol of Mexican sovereignty, in 1998 they rallied to make sure that the state would not sell PEMEX off to the highest bidder. Their fears were justified, as the government went from owning 1,050 enterprises in 1983 to 210 in 2003, with many of the companies purchased by foreigners.

Economists insisted that privatization would eliminate problems of inefficiency and corruption in state-run corporations. Officials were so enthusiastic that Latin America led the world in privatization in the 1990s, representing nearly half of the value of sales worldwide. The value of these privatizations was more than 10 percent of the nation's gross domestic product in Bolivia, Peru, and Brazil, and greater than 5 percent in Argentina, El Salvador, Guatemala, Mexico, Venezuela, and Colombia.

The effects of privatization, however, were problematic. The sales concentrated wealth in the hands of even fewer people and corporations because few had the resources to buy these companies. The sales also increased foreign ownership of the economy because foreign corporations had more resources to buy the state assets. Between 1990 and 2002, multinational corporations acquired 4,000 banks, telecommunications, transport, petroleum, and mining interests in Latin America. Furthermore, privatization directly affected the services provided to Latin Americans, who saw utility rates rise and the quality of services deteriorate.

By the end of the decade, nearly two-thirds of Latin Americans polled were opposed to privatization. The reasons were exemplified by the case of Aguas Argentinas. In 1993, the Argentine government sold the Buenos Aires water company to a consortium comprising the Suez group from France, the largest private water company in the world; Spain's Aguas de Barcelona; the World Bank, which bought a small stake in the consortium; and several small Argentine banks that included relatives and business partners of government officials. The consortium slashed its workforce in half and raised water rates by 88 percent from 1993 to 2002, earning profits of 20 percent—compared with typical water company profits of 6 percent in Europe and 6 to 12 percent in the United States. By 1997, the company had failed to honor 45 percent of its commitments to improve and expand services and it stood accused of dumping sewage into the Río de la Plata.

The reduction of the size of government was not carried out solely through the sale of state companies. It was also managed through cutbacks in public spending, which meant that many of the rights that were won through years of struggle—such as labor rights, public maintenance of water and sewage, and education—were eroded or abandoned. One example is Nicaragua's health budget, which was slashed in half from 1990 to 1991 to meet demands from multilateral lenders.

The result of globalization by early in the new millennium was an increase in poverty. In 2002, 44 percent of Latin America's people—221 million—were living in poverty. Of them 97 million—19.4 percent of the population—lived in extreme poverty or indigence. Poverty in Latin America is considered an income of $2 a day, whereas extreme poverty is $1 a day or less. Part of the reason for the increased poverty was an increase in unemployment. Joblessness rose 10 percent across the region from 1990 to 2000.

There also was a corresponding increase in child labor. In Argentina, one of the region's most developed economies, an estimated 1.5 million children under the age of 15 were forced to go to work in 2004, an increase of 600 percent since 1998. The most common forms of child labor were street performers (14 percent); *cartoneros*, who help their parents scavenge through trash for recyclables (11 percent); and children selling things in bars, mass transit, or the streets (4 percent). In Colombia, a staggering 2.5 million children were found to be working, approximately 20 percent of children from 5 to 17 years old. Close to half of them received no pay, whereas the rest earned only 25 percent of Colombia's minimum wage ($41 a month).

Such results of the neoliberal agenda were predicted in 1994 by the *Ejercito Zapatista de Liberación Nacional* (EZLN; Zapatista Nacional Liberation Army), which emerged along with the North American Free Trade Agreement (NAFTA).

NAFTA AND THE ZAPATISTAS

One of the hallmarks of the new liberalism was pressure from the United States to form free-trade areas. U.S. officials saw these agreements as an interim step to the freeing of trade worldwide. The negotiations regarding trade and tariffs had been carried out since 1948 under the auspices of the General Agreement on Tariffs and Trade (GATT), one of the agencies created at Bretton Woods. The GATT was superseded in 1995 by the World Trade Organization (WTO), which provides the institutional framework for multilateral trade.

According to the Congressional Budget Office, "One reason for the recent U.S. pursuit of [free-trade areas] is that progress in multilateral trade negotiations has become more difficult. The increasingly large membership of the GATT/WTO over time means that more countries must reach agreement in each subsequent round of negotiations. The newer members are generally developing countries that see their interests as being different from those of the United States and other industrialized countries that were more dominant in the earlier rounds."

The first free-trade area to emerge in Latin America was NAFTA, which encompassed the United States, Canada, and Mexico. NAFTA was supposed to boost trade between the regions and create more prosperity on both sides of the border. The Mexican elites saw it as their salvation. Others saw it as "a death sentence."

On January 1, 1994, the day that NAFTA took effect, a group of armed guerrillas rose up and occupied government buildings in the town of San Cristobal in Chiapas, the poorest and most indigenous state in Mexico. They stated, "This is our response to the implementation of the North American Free Trade Agreement, because this represents a death sentence for all of the indigenous ethnicities in Mexico." They called themselves the EZLN, or Zapatistas, harkening back to the Mexican Revolution. The choice was no accident—Emiliano Zapata's cry of Land and Liberty resonated even more after 1992, when congress amended Article 27 of the Mexican constitution, which essentially ended land reform by allowing the privatization of ejido plots.

It was also no accident that the movement began in Chiapas. In the nineteenth century, Chiapas was a timber and coffee region where Maya lived as virtual debt slaves. The region was split between the relatively prosperous west, which was fertile and characterized by commercial development, and the poor, subsistence-oriented east. The struggle between ranchers, landowners, and subsistence farmers was intensified at the turn of the century by competition with Guatemala.

Many say that Mexico's 1910 revolution never reached Chiapas. Large estates were left intact, while the rest competed for the remaining land. As the Mexican economy industrialized in the 1950s, state economists advocated the production of cheap food for urban workers. Low food prices meant low prices for small farmers and low wages on large farms. Then commercial farmers in western Chiapas expanded, encroaching on subsistence farming in the east. Desperate indigenous farmers colonized the Lacandón jungle. In the 1970s, the government built two hydroelectric plants in Chiapas on the Grijalva River, and in the 1980s large landowners converted the land they had once rented to small farmers into cattle grazing areas. More land was lost to subsistence production as territory was marked off by the government for bioreserves.

Meanwhile, Chiapas could be characterized overall as the poorest and most indigenous state in Mexico. In 1994, only 11 percent of the population earned a moderate income, compared with 24 percent nationwide. Less than 50 percent had running water, compared with 67 percent nationwide. While Chiapas had only 3 percent of Mexico's population, it produced 54 percent of the nation's hydroelectric power, 13 percent of its gas, and 4 percent of its oil—yet nearly one-half of Chiapas was without electricity.

The Zapatistas began organizing in Chiapas in 1983, biding their time until just the right moment. Tying the uprising to NAFTA focused world attention on the tiny group and their remote region. The armed battle lasted only twelve days, but the EZLN had not expected to win a military victory and take state power. They intended to capture world attention and build a movement.

The Zapatistas are different from other revolutionary groups in Latin American history. They reject vanguardism, the idea that only a tiny revolutionary elite knows the way to effect change. Although the media have focused on their charismatic leader, Subcomandante Marcos, the organization runs on communal decision making. And while the majority is indigenous, the EZLN is not just an ethnically based movement. The Zapatistas have urged all Mexicans to join them, not by also taking up arms but by calling on the Mexican government to create true democracy, to develop the country rather than just grow the economy, and to give regions such as Chiapas their autonomy.

The Mexican government responded by keeping some 40,000 troops, one-quarter of the nation's armed forces, stationed in Chiapas. The army launched an assault against the guerrillas in February 1995, but then agreed to enter peace negotiations. Throughout the negotiations, however, guerrillas and campesinos were attacked by paramilitary groups linked to landowners and ignored or supported by the government. By 2000, there were at least ten such groups, and more than 20,000 people were displaced by paramilitary terror from 1995 to 2000. The worst episode was a massacre in the town of Acteal in December 1997, when forty-five people, mostly women and children, were driven from the town church and killed. Negotiations from 1995 to 1996 resulted in the San Andres Accords, but they were never implemented, although in a March 1999 referendum, three million Mexicans went to 15,000 Zapatista polling places and voted their support for the agreement.

During the 1990s, Mexico's National Migration Institute kept close tabs on foreigners traveling to Chiapas, fearful that negative international publicity would affect NAFTA. Hundreds of observers were deported, and in 1998, Interior Minister Francisco Labastida claimed there was an "international movement to intervene in the internal affairs of our country." Labastida was later tapped as PRI's presidential candidate in the historic 2000 elections, in which PRI allowed an opposing candidate to win the elections for the first time since the party took power 71 years earlier. New president Vicente Fox prioritized a resolution of the Chiapas crisis, and began withdrawing troops from the region.

But foreigners do not have to travel to Chiapas to find out about the Zapatistas. One of the most striking elements of the EZLN has been their use of new technology. The Zapatista website shares the organization's declarations with the world. This is an enormous shift from just a decade earlier, when internationalists in solidarity with the Nicaraguan revolution carefully carried Sandinista brochures and posters back to their home countries.

The Web site features the witty writings of Subcomandante Marcos, who has been identified by the Mexican government as Rafael Guillén, a mestizo who grew up in Tamaulipas, the son of a furniture salesman, and

The intriguing Zapatista military leader Subcomandante Marcos became a media darling, but he insisted that he was but one of many leaders in the struggle in Chiapas, Mexico.

graduate of the Universdidad Autónima de México (UNAM). Marcos does not confirm or deny his identity, but his writing is worldly, with references ranging from Shakespeare and Cervantes to Jane Fonda and "Barbarella," Bolívar, Zapata, and Guevara. It is the Web site that has prompted pundits to call the Zapatistas the first postmodern revolutionaries.

In 2001, the Zapatistas marched from Chiapas to Mexico City, gathering huge crowds along their trek, and culminating with an historic speech before the Mexican congress. In response, congress finally approved an autonomy plan, but it was so weak that the states with the largest indigenous populations voted against it. "The March for Indigenous Dignity" showed that the Zapatistas continued to enjoy massive support among Mexicans, but still they could not achieve change on a national level.

Meanwhile, NAFTA's performance has been as dire as the Zapatistas predicted. The promised growth in Mexican trade was sluggish: a mere 1 percent per capita during the decade (compared with 3.2 percent per capita from 1948 to 1973). At the same time, Korea grew 4.3 percent per capita, even with the East Asian financial crisis, and China grew 7 percent. Instead of curbing illegal immigration, the number of Mexicans crossing the border rose from 200,000 to more than 300,000 a year.

Part of the reason for the exodus was the loss of Mexican jobs as businesses collapsed under the onslaught of less expensive U.S. goods. More than one million jobs were lost in Mexico during the first year alone. When jobs did begin to appear, they were in the *maquiladoras*, the assembly plants that proliferated along the border. By 2001, there were 2,000 border plants that employed more than 1.3 million workers. But the health of the assembly plants was tied to a U.S. market, and sales plummeted in the 2001 recession. More than 400,000 workers lost their jobs. Most of the people who managed to keep their jobs earned the minimum wage for border work, $4.20 a day, which had not changed since 1994. The income disparity between the two sides of the border grew by nearly 11 percent, and real wages in Mexico actually fell by one-half.

The situation was even more precarious in the Mexican countryside because NAFTA ended farm subsidies in Mexico but not in the United States. In 2002 alone, the United States paid $10 billion in subsidies to agricultural giants Cargill and Archer Daniels Midland, which tripled their corn exports to Mexico. By 2004, corn prices in Mexico dropped more than 70 percent, destroying the livelihood of the 15 million Mexicans who had depended on corn production.

Jorge Castañeda, who served briefly as Mexico's foreign minister, commented that NAFTA was "an accord among magnates and potentates: an agreement for the rich and powerful...effectively excluding ordinary people in all three societies."

But the ordinary people refused to be excluded.

LATIN AMERICA SWINGS LEFT

Throughout Latin America, people took to the streets. They formed organizations based on their very marginalization—women, indigenous, landless, unemployed. They protested in the streets and at the polls, where they swept out the parties and leaders who had overseen the neoliberal agenda. In their place, they brought to power candidates who promised a more radical platform: Hugo Chávez in Venezuela in 1999, Ricardo Lagos in Chile in 2000, Luis Inácio "Lula" da Silva in Brazil, Néstor Kirchner in Argentina in 2003, and Tabaré Vázquez in Uruguay in 2005.

Even more remarkable was the December 2005 election of Evo Morales in Bolivia, the first indigenous president of a country where the indigenous make up some 70 percent of the population. Morales spent ten years as head of Bolivia's indigenous coca growers union before becoming a leader of the *Movimiento a Socialismo* (Movement to Socialism), the multi-party coalition that brought him to the presidency. The day before his inauguration in January 2006, more than 50,000 indigenous people—not just from Bolivia but from around the Americas—gathered at the ruins of the ancient Indian city of Tiwanaku to confer the "Power of the Original Mandate" on Morales. The new president comes to power in a country where the two previous presidents were toppled amid hundreds of demonstrations. Bolivians also have protested foreign control over their resources, most dramatically in 2000 when a popular uprising forced out Bechtel Corporation, which had taken over control of Cochabamba's water system and drastically increased prices. Bolivia has the region's second largest (after Venezuela) proved reserves of natural gas, and Morales supporters expected that he would stand strong against international interests. He could look to the examples set by the region's other "new left" leaders.

Kirchner set a particularly exciting example for the region when he succeeded in restructuring Argentina's debt. In December 2001, Argentina defaulted on more than $100 billion in foreign debt. In the ensuing crisis, the country went through five presidents in two weeks as desperate Argentines rioted. Kirchner had his hands full when he took office, but he pulled off a major coup: He convinced bankers to restructure some 70 percent of Argentina's debt at 35 cents on the dollar, lowering the nation's debt payments and creating some breathing room to rebuild the economy. The IMF, however, objected to the debt arrangement and tried to pressure Kirchner to reopen negotiations with the banks, while also trying to force another austerity program on Argentina. Kirchner refused to follow the IMF plan and prioritized domestic spending to stimulate the economy over payment to creditors. "We want to pay off our debt; we don't want to owe anything anymore to the IMF," Kirchner explained. "Because of the debt, the Fund wants to impose domestic and foreign policies on us, but Argentina is a sovereign country." In another interview, Kirchner quipped, "There is life after the IMF, and it's a very good life....[B]eing in the embrace of the IMF isn't exactly like being in heaven."

The real celebrity of the new group of Latin American leaders is Venezuela's Hugo Chávez. A former army paratrooper, Chávez came on the scene in 1992 when he led an unsuccessful attempt to overthrow the government of President Carlos Andres Perez. When the coup had clearly failed, Chávez went on television and took responsibility, apologized, and urged his compatriots to avoid a bloodbath by abandoning the cause "*por ahora*" (for the moment). Venezuelans, who were sick of politicians lying and blaming others for their failures, were captivated by Chávez, and "por ahora" became a rallying cry, showing up as graffiti during the two years while Chávez was in prison.

Seven years later, Chávez won a landslide electoral victory, ending the dominance of *Acción Democratica* (Democratic Action) and *Partido Social Cristiano de Venezuela* (COPEI, Christian Party of Venezuela), the parties that had alternated in power since 1958, when Gen. Marcos Pérez Jiménez was overthrown by a popular uprising. Chávez tapped into popular discontent that had been brewing for years in a country where 3 percent of the population owned 77 percent of the land and nearly 60 percent of the population lived in poverty, despite Venezuela's substantial petroleum reserves and annual oil executive salaries of $100,000 to $4 million. That discontent was expressed in the Caracazo, a series of protests and rioting in February 1989 in response to an IMF austerity program that raised bus fares.

One of Chávez's first actions was to convene a National Constituent Assembly to rewrite Venezuela's constitution. Various sectors of society, including Venezuela's twenty-eight indigenous groups, elected representatives to the assembly, which produced a constitution that protects minority rights, permits people to claim title to their farms and homes, and expands political participation at the grassroots level.

Chávez then set out to reassert government control over the semi-autonomous oil industry, putting a halt to privatization, reinvigorating OPEC to improve oil prices, and charging foreign producers output royalties. By raising and taking control of oil industry revenues, Chávez was able to fund an ambitious social agenda: a literacy campaign, job training, land reform, food subsidies, and small business loans. He also expanded health care, partly by providing Cuba with low-cost oil in exchange for the services of 13,000 Cuban doctors.

The new policies, part of what Chávez calls his Bolivarian agenda, drew the wrath of local elites, particularly oil executives, and their U.S. allies. In April 2002, Chávez was ousted for forty-eight hours in a coup attempt that was quickly endorsed by the U.S. government and condemned by Latin American leaders. He was returned to power in a surge of support by a majority of Venezuelans. His opponents failed again in a 2004 recall election that gave Chávez 59 percent of the vote.

Chávez's influence extends well beyond Venezuela's borders. He was instrumental in derailing the Free Trade Area of the Americas (FTAA) agreement, joined in his opposition by the governments of Brazil, Argentina,

Bolivia, and Uruguay. Chávez was working to unite the region in *Alternativa Bolivariana para las Américas* (ALBA; Bolivarian Alternative for the Americas), fostering economic cooperation and integration of Latin American nations as a bloc without the United States. By the summer of 2005 he had already launched Petrosur, a Latin American-wide petroleum company with participation from Argentina and Brazil, and Telesur, a TV channel to provide news from a Latin American perspective as a counter to CNN in Spanish, the only continent-wide channel. Co-owners in Telesur are the governments of Venezuela (51 percent), Argentina (20 percent), Cuba (19 percent), and Uruguay (10 percent).

In a 2005 poll, Latin Americans named Chávez the second most important leader in the region. The first was Fidel Castro. With Castro then 79 years old to Chávez's 51, the new leader stood poised to take over his mantel. The greatest challenge to Chávez's ambitions for Latin American integration was located across Venezuela's border, where the region's oldest guerrilla war still raged.

The leftward swing of Latin American politics is represented by Venezuela's Hugo Chavez, who has oil wealth to help fund his social programs, and Evo Morales, the first indigenous president of Bolivia. In January 2006, Chavez joined Morales in Bolivia to sign accords promising aid with energy, education, agriculture, and social development. (The *Economist*)

COLOMBIA'S WAR WITHOUT END

While the Zapatistas waged a war of words and the rest of Latin America wielded ballots, in Colombia the war of bullets escalated from 1990 to 2005. The war pitted the Colombian military, with the aid of the United States, against the *Fuerzas Armadas Revolucionarias de Colombia* (FARC; Revolutionary Armed Forces of Colombia), and the much smaller *Ejército de Liberación Nacional* (ELN; National Liberation Army). Both groups were founded in 1964, and in 2004 they were stronger than ever.

Colombia's history has been characterized by lack of control over its territory—the loss of Panama in 1903 being the most extreme example—and resort to violence to resolve political disputes. As in much of the region, the nineteenth century was characterized by conflict between the Liberal and Conservative parties. Colombia's struggle was unusually long and bitter, culminating in the War of a Thousand Days (1899–1902), in which 100,000 people died before the Conservatives won control.

Even when the Liberals regained power in 1930, elites of both parties agreed on an economy based on exports of coffee and bananas grown primarily on large landholdings. From 1931 to 1945, elites privatized about 150,000 acres of public land each year, leading to the increasing impoverishment of most Colombians. It was during this period that dissident Liberal leader Jorge Eliécer Gaitán rose to prominence in the national assembly, where he investigated and condemned a military massacre that put an end to a 1928 banana workers' strike against the United Fruit Company, an incident later immortalized by Gabriel García Márquez in *One Hundred Years of Solitude*. Gaitán became a popular champion of the lower classes and served successively as representative, senator, minister of education, and mayor of Bogotá. He was expected to win the next presidential election when he was assassinated in 1948, sparking a series of riots known as the Bogotazo, the beginning of a ten-year period of armed struggle between Liberals and Conservatives so bloody that it came to be known simply as *La Violencia*. Some 200,000 people were killed from 1948 to 1958, when the parties finally agreed to share power. The FARC was an outgrowth of Liberal guerrillas that emerged during this period.

Land concentration worsened as privatization of public land continued throughout the 1950s, and workers and tenants were evicted from traditional haciendas as they mechanized during the 1960s. In the 1970s, production of cocaine began to edge out traditional farmers; coca growth expanded in the 1980s, as drug cartels invested 45 percent of their earnings in land, acquiring an estimated 7.5 to 11 million acres. In 1960, farms of more than 500 hectares constituted 29 percent of cultivated land; by 1996, they accounted for 61 percent. At the same time, the share of the smallest proprietors went from 6 percent to 3 percent of cultivated land.

From 1964 to 1980, FARC fought in the countryside, allied with the campesinos and demanding land reform. The failure of the government to carry out a serious agrarian reform produced more guerrillas: From 1970 to 1982, FARC's numbers rose from 500 to 3,000. The government responded with a state of siege, beginning in 1978, and human rights abuses escalated. By the 1980s, the guerrillas agreed to peace talks. Although they did not give up their weapons, they put them down and opted to form a political party, *Union Patriótica* (UP; Patriotic Union). In the 1986 congressional election, UP won a surprising fourteen seats. The response was a series of assassinations by paramilitary groups, and FARC took up its weapons again.

In the 1980s, FARC took advantage of increasing drug production as a way to finance its guerrilla struggle. FARC provided law and order in drug areas, and in exchange for protection of coca cultivation and production, they charged a 10 percent tax. With these profits, FARC was able to train and equip a professionalized army, with some 17,000 troops by the 1990s. By the end of the decade, FARC had a presence in 622 of Colombia's 1,071 munici- palities. In 1998 they were powerful enough to convince the government to cede control over an area the size of Switzerland. In areas under FARC control, the guerrillas essentially are the state, providing education, courts, health, road construction, and even loans to small farmers.

While the FARC has remained fairly strong throughout its history, the ELN made a dramatic comeback in the 1980s after almost being eliminated. The group had considerable appeal in the 1960s, when they were joined by rad- ical priest Camilo Torres, who died in battle in 1966. The ELN was supported by middle-class students and intellectuals, but the organization never held na- tional territory and frequently suffered from internal divisions. In 1972, 100 of its members were jailed, and in 1978 the organization almost disappeared. In the 1980s, the ELN developed a new strategy focused on controlling the regions that produced oil, coal, and bananas. The ELN raised funds by taxing multina- tional corporations and kidnapping executives, and by the 1990s the group was economically self-sufficient. By 2000, the ELN had 4,500 troops.

The guerrillas have been countered not just by the Colombian army but by nineteen right-wing paramilitary groups, united since 1997 in the *Autodefensas Unidas de Colombia* (AUC; United Self-Defense Forces of Colom- bia). According to Amnesty International, the paramilitaries, numbering 8,000 to 11,000, are responsible for 75 percent of the rampant human rights violations in Colombia.

The drug industry now pervades all aspects of the Colombian struggle. Drug production began in the late 1970s; by 2000, more than 300,000 acres of land was cultivated in coca. Colombia produces 80 percent of the world's coca, as well as significant amounts of opium poppies. Many of the produc- ers are small farmers who have turned to coca because they can make a 49 percent profit, whereas with traditional crops they actually lose money. Coca is easy to produce, grows in poor soil, and gives a high return. The coca grower, however, makes only a tiny percentage of the profit in the illegal in- dustry; most of the profit is made during distribution in the United States.

Poverty, drug dealing and war have combined to make Colombia the most violent country in the hemisphere. More than 50,000 people were killed in political violence between 1985 and 2000, and two million fled their homes. Union leaders and human rights workers have been targeted, especially by the paramilitaries. But only 9 percent of homicides in the country are politically motivated, and some 26,000 people are killed each year in criminal violence. Although many campesinos support the guerrillas, they have also earned tremendous enmity through kidnappings. In addition, FARC has been criticized for its use of gas-cylinder bombs, domestic gas containers that are loaded with fuel and shrapnel, then packed in a tube with dynamite. Because they are inaccurate, the bombs have caused civilian casualties. There also has been criticism of FARC for using children as young as ten as soldiers. In 2001, FARC promised to demobilize all children under fifteen, but guerrilla leaders said children still came to them because they had no where else to go.

The United States has had a long military relationship with Colombia: 10 percent of the Latin American soldiers trained by the United States from 1950 to 1979 were Colombian. From 1950 to 1966, Colombia was the fifth largest recipient of U.S. military aid in Latin America. In the late 1960s, it moved up to fourth place, and in the 1970s and 1980s to third. In the 1990s, Colombia recieved more military aid than the rest of Latin America put together. Aid has risen from $6.5 million in 1987 to $800 million in 2000. The next year, the U.S. began Plan Colombia, and aid leaped to $1.5 billion a year.

When the United States first funded the Colombian military, the rationale was that the government was fighting a Communist threat. The threat was no longer credible after the fall of the Soviet Union in 1991, and the U.S. rhetoric changed: the new term was narco-guerilla. The war against drugs became the rationale for continued U.S. military presence. In 1996, U.S. Navy Rear Admiral James B. Perkins told the Senate Armed Services Committee: "The guerrilla forces that plagued Colombia for 30 years are today motivated by economic gain, not ideology. They render protection to narcotraffickers and extort money from legitimate businessmen."

There is no evidence, however, that the guerrillas have changed their reasons for fighting. Narcotics have become a means, not an end, to the war. And aside from the Colombian government, Latin Americans do not share U.S. concerns about the drug trade. The presidents of Mexico, Brazil, Uruguay, and Argentina have all suggested that legalization of drugs would do more to solve the problem than the U.S. drug war. The U.S. approach has meant the use of deadly chemicals to clear thousands of acres of land, in the process poisoning crops and people, only to have a balloon effect—when one area is squeezed, production reappears in another. Further, Latin Americans note that the market for drugs is in the United States, but efforts are focused on supply, not demand. There is a particular irony in efforts to control drug trafficking in an era of free trade and market sovereignty. Some of the very processes that facilitate trade across borders also make it harder to stop drugs from following market demand.

After the bombing of the World Trade Center on September 11, 2001, the United States began to recast the guerrillas yet again, this time as terrorists. "While Latin America has not been the focal point in the war on terrorism, countries in the region have struggled with domestic terrorism for decades," the Congressional Research Service reported in 2005. The Secretary of State designated FARC and the ELN as Foreign Terrorist Organizations (FTOs), along with the AUC. Through the newly created program of Anti-Terrorism Assistance, the United States allocated $27.5 million to Latin America in 2002, with $25 million of it going to Colombia.

In addition, the 2005 Defense Authorization Act doubled the size of the United States military contingent permanently deployed in Colombia from 400 to 800 and raised the ceiling on the number of U.S.-supplied military contractors from 400 to 600. These contractors were involved in fumigating coca fields, operating airplanes and helicopters that provide information on guerrilla activity for the Colombian military, and evaluating intelligence information. The use of private contractors was indicative of one more aspect of Latin American life that had become subject to privatization and the market. A disproportionate number of the U.S. military contingent was based not where the coca is grown but where a more important item in international trade is located—oil.

General Charles E. Wilhelm, Marine Corps commander of the U.S. Southern Command (Southcom), told the Senate in 1998: "No one questions the strategic importance of the Middle East, but Venezuela alone provides the same amount of oil to the U.S. as do all the Persian Gulf states combined. The discovery of major oil reserves in Colombia, and existing oil supplies in Trinidad-Tobago and Ecuador, further increase the strategic importance of this region's energy resources."

As U.S. relations with Venezuela have soured, the importance of other oil-rich regions in Latin America has loomed larger. One of those regions is Arauca, Colombia, just across the Río Arauca from Venezuela's Orinoco basin. Arauca is home to the Caño-Limon oil field, run by California-based Occidental Petroleum. Many of the U.S. military advisers in Colombia have been assigned to Arauca, overseeing a new Colombian antiguerilla army unit especially created to police Caño-Limon and its pipeline.

Citizens and Consumers

As Latin America moved into the twenty-first century, there were tremendous changes but also remarkable continuities. Unfortunately, what seemed to continue was the maldistribution of wealth, leaving many Latin Americans impoverished. Hunger, disease, malnutrition, and illiteracy still plague the region.

That such deplorable conditions can still exist in the midst of plenty, of growth, of structural changes in the economy, indicates the continued limitations of the development models used in the region. Subcomandante Marcos described the current program as the "destruction of Mexico as a nation and its transformation into a department store, something like a mega 'little shop' which sells human beings and natural resources at prices dictated by the world market."

Some Latin American intellectuals have wondered whether the core of the problem is not just Latin America's position in the international economy but the idea of development itself and the way development programs have been carried out since the end of World War II. At that time, officials in the United States were concerned about conditions in what became known as the Third World—everyone outside of the industrialized First World and the Soviet bloc's Second World. U.S. officials and businessmen had multiple concerns: Poor people make poor markets, and U.S. post-war strategy for rebuilding the world economy depended on trade. Furthermore, poor people are likely to rise up to protest their conditions, and that instability is bad for business. Unrest might also result in a successful revolution. At its worst, the revolution could result in the elimination of a market and source of cheap labor and primary goods—the Communist threat. At best, it might result in a government trying to mitigate the ills of the marketplace by insisting on higher prices for products, higher wages for labor, and the freedom to choose from multiple trade partners instead of being locked into exclusive relationships.

There were also many sincere people in the industrialized world who wanted to improve the standard of living for the masses in Latin America. Many of these people, with the best of intentions, went to work for the Agency for International Development and the Alliance for Progress in the United States, or for the many new development-oriented committees and agencies of the United Nations, such as the World Health Organization, the International Labor Organization, and the Food and Agriculture Organization.

Meanwhile, in Latin America, there was also a concern about development. Some elites, in an echo of nineteenth-century patterns, wanted to "modernize" their countries to be like the United States in the classic combination of wanting to make money and wanting to appear "modern" (no one said "civilized" anymore). At the same time, there were many Latin Americans who sincerely wanted to improve the lives of the majority. The question was how to do it.

The practical implementation of aid and investment programs designed to modernize Latin America was underpinned by a theoretical discussion that began with the ideas laid out by U.S. economic historian W. W. Rostow in his *The Stages of Growth: A Noncommunist Manifesto*, published in 1960. Rostow argued that modernization followed a set of stages from traditional to advanced societies, and that all of the world could develop by simply following the lead of their predecessors. The problem, in his argument, was that traditional societies needed to become more capitalist. His book launched entire schools of thought about modernization and served as the basis for many modernization programs.

The reaction in Latin America, however, was a bit different. Starting from the analyses by Raúl Prebisch and ECLA, Latin Americans concluded that the problem was not a lack of capitalism but the way that capitalism unfolded in Latin America. Because the United States and Europe already had highly industrialized economies, Latin America could not compete; limited, then, to production of primary products, the region was trapped into low growth, low wages, and declining terms of trade.

Out of this analysis came the dependency school, which turned modernization on its head. The problem was not too little capitalism but too much and in too unequal a form. *Dependentistas* described Latin America as the periphery, trapped by the desires of the metropolis, usually the United States. Instead of prescribing more capitalism, the theorists frequently advocated either disconnecting from the international market or turning toward some form of socialism.

Dependency challenged traditional paradigms that the so-called Third World could, through proper programs and economic policies, become like the First World. The theories took the focus off the countries at the center, and turned the spotlight on the periphery. The theory was articulated by Latin Americans themselves: Fernando Henrique Cardoso, Enzo Faletto, Theotonio Dos Santos (joined by U.S. and European scholars, most notably Andre Gunder Frank.)

From the 1950s to the 1990s, people concerned about Latin America focused on the issue of development. For some, it was just another word for progress or modernization. As we have pointed out in this text, development was often used to describe mere growth in gross national product. Others defined it as structural change in the economy, especially via industrialization. We have focused on development as providing the most good for the most people.

But half a century after the focus on development began, some argue, Latin America is in worse shape than it was before. Development programs frequently displaced people and disrupted traditional subsistence cultures that met people's basic needs and provided them with cultural well-being. Before 1960, when the majority of people still lived in the countryside, there were indeed subsistence cultures that provided a lifestyle that to North Americans might look impoverished but that might really be a more simple way of life that amply met community needs. These communities were frequently displaced by the spread of agro-industry and the so-called green revolution, which used many chemical inputs to increase yield and bring underutilized land into production. To the extent that development aid was aimed at modernizing Latin America, it facilitated the further expansion of commercial activity on the theory that subsistence equals poverty. The end result was often the production of a greater absolute poverty, both rural and urban, as well as the poverty that comes from destruction of community.

If, as Burns has argued elsewhere, the modernization of the nineteenth century brought with it the "poverty of progress," than the modernization of the twentieth century might be seen as the "devastation of development." How else can one view a situation in which the cure has often been worse than the supposed disease? For example, many countries that were not only self-sufficient in food but were actually food exporters ended up as food importers after the implementation of development programs that focused on exports, resulting in the creation and spread of hunger rather than its prevention.

Once again, Latin American scholars have challenged the dominant paradigm. In *Encountering Development: The Making and Unmaking of the Third World*, Colombian Arturo Escobar shows how development programs created a discourse of problematic categories, such as peasants who needed to be modernized and mothers whose fertility needed to be controlled. The process of development created the problems, then failed to solve them. Yet, the discourse has not changed.

> The rural development discourse repeats the same relation that has defined development discourse since its emergence: the fact that development is about growth, about capital, about technology, about becoming modern. Nothing else. "Traditional peasants need to be modernized; they need to be given access to capital, technology, and adequate assistance. Only in this way can production and productivity be increased." These statements were uttered pretty much in the same way in 1949 as in 1960 and in 1973, and today [1995] they are still repeated ad nauseam in many quarters. Such a poverty of imagination, one may think.

Escobar encourages us to a richer imagination, asking us to imagine a postdevelopment era, in a postmodern world. The debates about modernity and postmodernity are long and complex. To oversimplify, the modern was the project of the Enlightenment and industrialization, the optimistic belief in progress and universal truths. Postmodernity is the twentieth- and twenty-first-century condition of having seen the modern project fail so profoundly in so many ways—wars, pollution, oppression, destruction. In postmodernity, there is no one truth, but many truths, many ways of interacting with and viewing the world. It is a decentered, fragmented world.

Some argue that postmodernity is irrelevant for Latin America, a region that is still not modern—or at least not modernized—in so many ways. Others quip that Latin America is the original land of the postmodern because it has always been fragmented, always been a mixture of past, present, and future. Chilean Martín Hopenhayn suggests that Latin Americans are "becoming post-moderns by osmosis in the midst of a still-pending modernization."

Argentine Néstor García Canclini offers the concept of *hybridity*—not the syncretism usually connected with religion, nor the mestizaje usually connected to race, but elements of the traditional and the modern, creating new forms, with a new hybrid emerging. This hybridity is the product of Latin America's distinctive interaction with the modern. "The pluralist perspective, which accepts fragmentation and multiple combinations among tradition, modernity, and postmodernity, is indispensable for considering the Latin American conjuncture at the end of the century," García Canclini writes.

What does that hybrid, postmodern, postdevelopment world look like? Perhaps it is exemplified by the Kayapo Indians of Brazil, who use video cameras in their fight to preserve a traditional way of life. Or by the Zapatistas, who evoke the figure of Emiliano Zapata from the Revolution of 1910 to preserve elements of an older indigenous culture—albeit modified by colonialism and neocolonialism—in a new project of sustainable economics that seeks autonomy within rather than conquest and control of the nation–state.

The importance of the nation and its government is increasingly being challenged. The focus of mass protests against governments and the electoral victories of center-left leaders would seem to give renewed vigor to the

Unsatisfied With Privatization of Public Services	
COUNTRY	PERCENTAGE
Guatemala	98
Panama	88
Dominican Republic	87
Honduras	80
Nicaragua	79
El Salvador	78
Argentina	75
Bolivia	75
Ecuador	74
Colombia	74
Peru	71
Chile	70
Brazil	65
Mexico	63
Venezuela	59

Source: Latinamerica Press, October 28, 2004, using data from Latinobarómetro 2004.

importance of state control. But the power of globalization simultaneously minimizes state control, both because of the impact of international organizations such as the IMF and the WTO, and because of the power of corporations. In 2000, fifty-one of the world's largest one hundred economic entities were corporations. Mexico, Brazil, and Argentina all had gross domestic products that are larger than any single corporation's sales. But General Motors, Wal-Mart, Exxon Mobil, Ford Motor, and Daimler–Chrysler each had annual sales larger than any of the rest of Latin America's countries.

Another challenge to the nation–state comes from the nature of the groups that have challenged governmental policy. Prominent among the protestors are indigenous groups. In Bolivia, where indigenous groups helped bring down the neoliberal government of Gonzalo Sánchez de Lozada in 2003, Aymara leader Felipe Quispe spoke of a strategy "that seeks to replace all state authorities with our own traditional authorities." He has called for building an Aymara nation, a form of self-government that would include "making our own laws, exchanging the political constitution of the state with our own constitution, replacing the capitalist system with a communal one and changing the tri-colored flag with our seven-colored flag." Thus, a nation of self-governed communities would replace the current nation–state, a proposition even more radical than the Zapatistas' autonomy within the Mexican nation–state. Another radical plan emanates from Ecuador, where indigenous movements are demanding plurinationality, a state that would encompass many self-regulating nations.

Although such grassroots groups are based on community organizing, they are also increasingly linking at the international level, which has come to be represented by the annual World Social Forum. The forum was originally envisioned as a counterweight to the World Economic Forum, the gathering of those leading the neoliberal economic and political model, in 2001. All but one of the meetings has been held in Porto Alegre, Brazil. At the time of the first meeting, Porto Alegre was the municipal stronghold of the *Partido dos Trabalhadores* (PT; Workers' Party), which was experimenting with participatory government; one example was the use of public assemblies to decide on how to spend the municipal budget. The forum has provided a way for the many grassroots movements to come together to find global strategies.

The contradictions of grassroots, national, and international politics seemed to be embodied in 2003 in the election of "Lula" da Silva as Brazil's president. Lula, as he is affectionately called, was a former metal worker who became head of the metal workers union and helped found the workers' party. He ran for president unsuccessfully three times before his 2003 victory, and he became a fixture at the World Social Forum.

In 2003, Lula flew directly from the WSF to the World Economic Forum. Many in the crowd in Porto Alegre begged him not to go, but he assured them that he would bring the WSF message: "Another world is possible." Lula did bring that message to Davos, Switzerland—along with assurances that Brazil still wanted international trade and investment. The businessmen applauded. They continued to applaud during the next two years as his government outdid the IMF in its target for a budget surplus and pushed up interest rates to help attract finance capital.

At Porto Alegre in 2005, Lula still drew a crowd, but his popularity had declined. A larger and more enthusiastic crowd was on hand to greet Hugo Chávez. The fact that crowds gathered to see both leaders spoke to the continuing importance of the nation–state and national politics. The fact that both leaders came to the forum spoke to the importance of both grassroots movements and international connections.

Are these the portentious events that Popo's eruption predicted? On one hand, Latin American history has always been about the conflicts and consensus between individuals and groups, leaders and followers, the local and the international. What makes the twenty-first century different, perhaps, is the way in which these groups can come together now that technology is collapsing time and space. How are we to understand a world in which even elderly indigenous women in the highlands of Guatemala, who still dress in traditional woven *traje*, now use cell phones?

Again it is García Canclini who offers a new paradigm for looking at the region—the confluence of citizenship and consumerism. He argues that the right of citizenship should be to decide how goods are produced, distributed and used. "… [W]hen we recognize that when we consume we also think, select, and reelaborate social meaning, it becomes necessary to analyze how this mode of appropriation of goods and signs conditions more active forms of participation than those that are grouped under the label of consumption. In other words, we should ask ourselves if consumption does not entail doing something that sustains, nourishes, and to a certain extent, constitutes a new mode of being citizens."

It is disconcerting to move from citizen to consumer. But the idea of citizenship, he argues, must be reimagined under globalization. Latin Americans now feel rooted in a local culture—which is generally urban and encompasses the many nationalities and ethnicities of national migrants and international immigration. People travel with multiple passports or with no documents at all. "How can they believe themselves to be the citizens of only one country?" asks García Canclini.

If we now live in a world dominated by the market, why not reclaim what the market and the consumer mean? García Canclini points out that consumption is not just the elite preference to manifest class distinctions and live in luxury. Consumption is also at the heart of demands for wages, food, housing, health care, and education. Consumption is about meeting basic needs.

Oswaldo de Rivero, a former Peruvian diplomat, argues in *The Myth of Development* that basic needs and survivability must be the focus for Latin America in the future. He contends that Latin American countries are not really developing countries, as economists sometimes euphemistically label them. Nor are they likely to become NICs, newly industrialized countries. De Rivero offers two other potential categories: NNEs, nonviable national economies, which may describe current conditions, or UCEs, ungovernable chaotic entities, which could describe the future. "This reality is an invitation to discard the myth of development, abandon the search for El Dorado, and replace the elusive agenda of the wealth of nations with an agenda for the survival of nations."

The search for El Dorado is, indeed, where Latin America's complicated history began. The struggle for the majority of Latin Americans to meet their basic needs is not a new one. It has, in fact, shaped Latin American history for hundreds of years. It is a history characterized by international pressures and national responses; by diversity and complexity within each nation; by conflict and consensus between and among classes, races, ethnicities, and genders; and by wealth in the midst of plenty, with poor people inhabiting rich lands.

RECOMMENDED READINGS

Chilcote, Ronald H., ed. *Development in Theory and Practice: Latin American Perspectives in the Classroom*. Lanham, MD: Rowman & Littlefield, 2003.

De Rivero, Oswaldo. *The Myth of Development: Non-Viable Economies of the 21st Century*. London: Zed Books, 2003.

García Canclini, Néstor. *Consumers and Citizens: Globalization and Multicultural Conflicts*. Minneapolis: University of Minnesota Press, 2001.

———. *Hybrid Cultures: Strategies for Entering and Leaving Modernity*. Minneapolis: University of Minnesota Press, 1995.

Gott, Richard. *In the Shadow of the Liberator: Hugo Chávez and the Transformation of Venezuela*. London: Verso, 2000.

Livingstone, Grace. *Inside Colombia: Drugs, Democracy and War*. New Brunswick, NJ: Rutgers University Press, 2004.

Safford, Frank, and Marco Palacios. *Colombia: Fragmented Land, Divided Society*. New York: Oxford University Press, 2002.

Sawyer, Suzana. *Crude Chronicles: Indigenous Politics, Multinational Oil and Neoliberalism in Ecuador*. Durham, NC: Duke University Press, 2004.

Thorp, Rosemary. *Progress, Poverty and Exclusion: Economic History of Latin America in the 20th Century*. Washington, DC: Johns Hopkins University Press for the Inter-American Development Bank and the European Union, 1998.

A Chronology of Significant Dates in Latin American History

1492	Columbus reaches the New World.
1494	The Treaty of Tordesillas divides the world between Spain and Portugal.
1500	Cabral discovers Brazil.
1503	Spain legalizes the encomienda in the New World; Casa de Contratación created.
1512	The Laws of Burgos regulate the treatment of the Indians.
1513	Balboa discovers the Pacific Ocean.
1521	Hernándo Cortés completes the conquest of the Aztec empire.
1524	Creation of the Council of the Indies.
1532	First permanent settlements in Brazil.
1535	Francisco Pizzaro completes the conquest of the Incan empire; the first viceroy arrives in Mexico.
1542	The New Laws call for an end of the encomiendas.
1543	The first viceroy arrives in Peru.
1545	The Spaniards discover silver at Potosí.
1630–1654	The Dutch control as much as one-third of Brazil.

1695	The Luso-Brazilians discover gold in the Brazilian interior.
1763	The capital of the Viceroyalty of Brazil is moved to Rio de Janeiro.
1776	Creation of the Viceroyalty of La Plata.
1804	Haiti declares its independence.
1808	The royal family of Portugal arrives in Brazil.
1810	Padre Miguel Hidalgo initiates Mexico's struggle for independence.
1811	Paraguay and Venezuela declare their independence.
1816	Argentina declares its independence.
1818–1843	Jean-Pierre Boyer, a populist caudillo, rules Haiti.
1819	Brazil puts a steamship into service, the first in South America.
1821	Mexico, Peru, and Central America declare their independence.
1822–1823	Emperor Agustín I rules the Mexican empire.
1822	Prince Pedro declares Brazil's independence and receives the title of emperor.
1823	President James Monroe promulgates the Monroe Doctrine.
1824	The Battle of Ayacucho marks the final defeat of the Spaniards in South America.
1824–1838	The United Provinces of Central America in existence.
1825	Bolivia declares its independence.
1825–1828	The Cisplatine War between Brazil and Argentina to possess Uruguay results in a stalemate and Uruguayan independence.
1829–1852	The populist caudillo Juan Manuel de Rosas rules Argentina.
1830	The political union of Gran Colombia dissolves, leaving Colombia, Venezuela, and Ecuador to go their independent ways.
1838	The first railroad in Latin America is inaugurated in Cuba.
1839–1865	The populist caudillo Rafael Carrera governs Guatemala.
1846–1848	War of North American Invasion (Mexican-American War). The United States gains California, New Mexico, and Arizona from its victory.
1847–1903	The Cruzob rebellion in Yucatan and Mayan self-government.
1848–1855	The popular caudillo Manuel Belzú governs Bolivia.
1850	The United States and Great Britain sign the Clayton-Bulwer Treaty to check the expansion of each in Central America. Unionization of workers slowly begins in the largest Latin American nations.
1852	Chile inaugurates the first railroad in South America. Chile and Brazil initiate telegraphic systems.

1864–1867	Archduke Maximilian of Austria rules Mexico under French protection.
1865–1870	In the War of the Triple Alliance, Argentina, Brazil, and Uruguay fight and eventually defeat Paraguay.
1876	The first refrigerator ship carries beef from Buenos Aires to Europe.
1876–1911	Porfirio Díaz governs Mexico.
1879–1884	The War of the Pacific pits Chile against Peru and Bolivia.
1886	The University of Chile awards the first medical degree to a woman in Latin America.
1888	Brazil abolishes slavery.
1889	The military dethrones Emperor Pedro II of Brazil; Brazil becomes a republic.
1889–1890	The first Inter-American Conference meets in Washington, D.C.
1898	As a result of the Spanish–American War, Cuba gains its independence from Spain and the United States takes possession of Puerto Rico.
1901	In the Hay-Pauncefote Treaty, Great Britain acknowledges U.S. supremacy in Central America.
1903	Panama gains its independence and signs a treaty with the United States for the construction of an interoceanic canal.
1903–1929	José Batlle dominates Uruguayan politics, bringing stability and economic growth as well as the middle class to power.
1909–1933	U.S. intervention and occupation of Nicaragua.
1910–1940	The Mexican Revolution.
1911	Emiliano Zapata advocates agrarian reform in his Plan of Ayala.
1912	Argentina adopts the Saenz Peña law, giving all male citizens the right to vote, without property or literacy requirements.
1914	The Panama Canal opens.
1915–1934	The United States occupies Haiti.
1916–1922	Hipólito Irigoyen governs Argentina as its first middle-class president.
1916–1924	The United States occupies the Dominican Republic.
1917	Promulgation of the Mexican constitution, the blueprint for the Revolution.
1919	Promulgation of the Uruguayan constitution, the blueprint for middle-class democracy.
1920–1924	Arturo Alessandri, a representative of middle-class interests, governs Chile.

1927–1933   Augusto César Sandino leads the guerrilla struggle in Nicaragua to expel the U.S. Marines.

1929   The world financial collapse reduces Latin American exports but encourages import-substitution industrialization. Ecuador grants the vote to women, the first in Latin America.

1932–1935   Bolivia and Paraguay fight the Chaco War.

1934–1940   The Mexican Revolution reaches its apogee under President Lázaro Cárdenas.

1937   Bolivia cancels foreign oil contracts and takes control of oil industry.

1938   Mexico nationalizes foreign oil companies.

1940   Promulgation of the Cuban constitution, a middle-class and nationalist blueprint for change.

1944–1954   The era of Guatemalan democracy.

1945   Gabriela Mistral, Chilean poet, is the first Latin American to receive the Nobel Prize in literature.

1952   Guatemala promulgates its land reform.

1952–1964   The Bolivian revolution.

1953   Bolivia puts into effect its land reform.

1954   The CIA overthrows President Jacobo Arbenz of Guatemala.

1959   Triumph of the Cuban revolution and the advent of Fidel Castro to power. Cuba issues its Agrarian Reform Law.

1960   For the first time, urban Latin Americans equal in number their rural counterparts.

1961   Washington breaks diplomatic relations with Cuba. The CIA sponsors the Bay of Pigs invasion in an attempt to overthrow Castro. President John F. Kennedy announces the Alliance for Progress.

1964   The Brazilian military deposes President João Goulart and establishes a dictatorship.

1965   The United States invades and occupies the Dominican Republic.

1967   Che Guevara is killed in Bolivia while attempting to spark a revolutionary uprising.

1968   The Mexican government squelches a significant student movement by firing on peaceful protestors at the Plaza of Tlatelolco in Mexico City. Hundreds are killed.

1970–1973   President Salvador Allende sets in motion profound reforms to peacefully and democratically change Chile.

1973   The Chilean military overthrows President Allende, who dies in the attack on the presidential palace. The Uruguayan military terminates their nation's twentieth-century experiment with democracy.

1974–1976 Isabel Perón serves as president of Argentina, the first female chief of state in the Western Hemisphere.

1976–1983 Thousands are "disappeared" in the Dirty War in Argentina.

1977 Panama and the United States sign a treaty returning the Canal Zone to Panamanian control and putting the canal under Panamanian direction by 1999.

1979 Triumph of the Nicaraguan revolution. Young military reformers stage a coup d'etat in El Salvador.

1980 Sendero Luminoso initiates its armed struggle in Peru.

1981 Nicaragua promulgates its agrarian reform law. Latin America enters a severe economic crisis. President Ronald Reagan begins the contra war against Nicaragua.

1982 Argentina invades the Falkland Islands and is defeated by Great Britain.

1983 The United States invades Grenada and overthrows government. Economic reverses highlight Latin America's increasing difficulty in making international debt payments.

1984 Latin America's foreign debt reaches an unmanageable $350 billion.

1985 Brazil returns to civilian rule. Latin American population surpasses the 400 million mark.

1987 President Oscar Arias of Costa Rica wins the Nobel Peace prize.

1988 PRI (Partido Revolucionario Institucional) candidate Carlos Salinas de Gortari's defeat of Cuauhtemoc Cárdenas is decried as open fraud.

Augusto Pinochet is ousted by plebiscite.

1989–1990 U.S. invades and occupies Panama.

1990 Sandinistas lose presidential election to Violeta Chamorro, widow of the late newspaper editor Pedro Joaquin Chamorro, effectively ending the Sandinista Revolution.

1992 Quincentennial of European-American encounter. Sendero Luminoso controls much of rural Peru. Mexico's Carlos Salinas de Gortari amends the constitution to allow ejidos to be sold, rented and mortgaged. Privatization of state firms begins.

1994 The North American Free Trade Agreement (NAFTA) links the markets of the United States, Mexico and Canada. The day it takes effect, a rebellion breaks out in Chiapas, Mexico, led by the Zapatista Army of National Liberation.

1996 A peace agreement is signed in Guatemala.

1998   Former Chilean dictator Augusto Pinochet is arrested in England, on a Spanish warrant, on charges of human rights violations.

1999   The Panama Canal zone is returned to Panamanian control.

Hugo Chávez is elected president of Venezuela, the first of a new wave of Latin American leaders who challenge neoliberalism.

2000   For the first time in 71 years, PRI allows a free election in Mexico, and the voters elect Vicente Fox of the National Action Party (*Partido de Acción Nacional*). Augusto Pinochet is indicted in Chile.

Ricardo Lagos is elected president of Chile.

The Confederation of Indigenous Nationalities of Ecuador leads a national uprising that brings down Ecuador's government over plans to "dollarize" the economy.

2001   The U.S. launches Plan Colombia, a three-year agreement to provide $1.5 billion a year to Colombia to fight guerrilla groups.

2002   A coup ousts Chávez from the Venezuelan presidency for forty-eight hours. He is restored to office, and the rapid U.S. approval of his removal is widely decried by Latin American leaders.

2003   Luis Inácio "Lula" da Silva, former head of the metal workers union, is elected president in Brazil.

Néstor Kirchner is elected president in Argentina in 2003.

2004   Kirchner succeeds in renegotiating Argentina's debt and defying the International Monetary Fund.

2005   Petrosur, a petroleum company, and Telesur, a TV channel, are launched with the participation of several Latin American governments to provide oil and news to the region on Latin American terms.

Tabaré Vázguez is elected president of Uruguay.

Evo Morales is elected president of Bolivia, the first indigenous to head the country.

2006   Michelle Bachelet is elected President of Chile, becoming Spanish South America's first elected female president. Women were elected president in Nicaragua in 1990 (Violeta Barrios de Chamorro) and Panama in 1999 (Mireya Moscoso).

A Glossary of Spanish and Portuguese Terms

Adelantado   An individual in colonial Spanish America authorized by the crown to explore, conquer, and hold new territory. He pushed back the frontier and extended Spanish claims and control of the New World.

Alcaldes mayores   In colonial Spanish America, appointed officials who held administrative and judicial responsibility on local or district level.

Aldeia   An indigenous village or settlement in Portuguese America administered by the religious orders until the mid-eighteenth century and then by secular officials thereafter.

Arpilleras   Patchwork tapestries created in Chile to tell stories of the repression during the dictatorship of Augusto Pinochet, 1973–1989.

Audiencia   The highest royal court and consultative council in colonial Spanish America.

Ayllu   A communal unit in the Incan empire that worked the land in common, part for themselves and part for the Incan ruler and priestly elite.

Bandeirante   Particularly active during the 1650–1750 period, these individuals penetrated the interior of Brazil to explore, to capture indigenous slaves, or to search for gold.

Cabildo   The municipal government in Spanish America.

Cabildo abierto   The municipal council in Spanish America, which expanded under special circumstances to include most of the principal citizens of the municipality.

Calidad Literally quality.   The nineteenth-century view of elites regarding respectability, earned by family background, the organization and location of one's household, formal training and education, occupation, economic resources, and perceived color.

Campesino   Literally, a person from the country. It is frequently translated as peasant, a problematic English term that evokes medieval institutions of servile relationships, such as serfdom, and that implies a particular culture built around subsistence farming.

Capitão-mor (plural, *capitães-mor*)   A military rank given to commanders of the local militia in colonial Portuguese America.

Capitulación   A contract between monarch and *adelantado* stating the duties and rewards of the latter.

Casa da Suplicação   The highest court in the Portuguese empire and therefore the supreme court for judicial disputes in colonial Brazil.

Casa de Contratación   The Board of Trade established in Spain in 1503 to organize, regulate, and develop trade with the New World.

Caudillo (Portuguese, *caudilho*)   A strong leader who wields complete power over subordinates.

Cédula   A royal edict from the Spanish monarch.

Científico   A high administrator in the government of President Porfirio Díaz of Mexico (1876–1911), infused with Positivist ideas, who believed national problems could be solved by scientific solutions. Such men were prominent during the last two decades of his administration.

Compadrio   A godparent relationship.

Composición   A Spanish legal device for claiming land through surveys.

Comunero   A participant in the Comunero Revolt that occurred in New Granada in 1781.

Congregación   The Spanish policy of concentrating indigenous people into villages.

Consejo de las Indias   The Council of the Indies established in Spain in 1524 to advise the monarch on American affairs.

Conseiho geral   In Portuguese America, a municipal council expanded under special circumstances to include most of the principal citizens of the municipality.

Conselho Ultramarino   The Overseas Council established in Lisbon in 1642 to advise the crown on matters relating to the empire and its administration.

Consulado   In colonial Spanish America, a guild of merchants acting as a sort of chamber of commerce.

Contra.   Short for *contrarevolucionario*, counterrevolutionary. The term was used to refer to U.S.-trained forces fighting to overthrow the Sandinista government in Nicaragua in the 1980s.

Coronel (plural, *coroneis*)   A civilian political boss of a Brazilian municipality. The system of political control founded on the local bosses came to be known as *coronelismo*.

Corregidor   An official in colonial Spanish America who was assigned to Spanish as well as indigenous communities as tax collector, police officer, magistrate, and administrator.

Creole   A white born in the Spanish American empire.

Cumbe   A settlement of runaway slaves in Spanish America.

Denuncia   Under Spanish law, the process of claiming land that does not have legally recognized owners.

Desaparacido   Disappeared person.   A term coined to refer to people kidnapped by the military regime during Argentina's Dirty War, 1976–1983.

Ejido   The common land held by communities and used for agriculture in Mexico. Also the municipal lands available for common use in most regions of Latin America during the nineteenth and early twentieth centuries.

Encomendero   The person who received an *encomienda*.

Encomienda   A tribute institution used in Spanish America in the sixteenth century. The Spaniard received indigenous workers as an entrustment, *encomienda*, to protect and to Christianize, but in return he could demand tribute including labor.

Fazenda   A large estate or plantation in Brazil.

Fazendeiro   The owner of a large estate or plantation in Brazil.

Finca   A large estate in Spanish America.

Fuero militar   A special military privilege in Spanish America that exempted officers from civil legal jurisdiction.

Gaucho   The cowboy of the Pampas.

Gente alta   Elites.

Gente baja   Lower classes.

Gente decente.   Literally, decent people. Refers to the elites, or *gente alta*.

Gente de pueblo   Common people, or lower classes. Also *gente baja*.

Hacendado   A large estate in Spanish America.

Homens bons   In Portuguese, literally the "good men," those who belonged to the upper echelon of Brazilian colonial society. They voted for members of the municipal council.

Inquilino   A Chilean peasant.

Jefe   Chief or leader; boss. In Spanish America, it is often used as synonymous with *caudillo*.

Ladino   A person of mixed European and indigenous ancestry, or an indigenous person who adopts an Hispanic lifestyle. Used in place of mestizo in much of Central America.

Latifundia   The system of large landholdings in Latin America.

Mandamiento   A forced labor system.

Mazombo   In Portuguese America, a white born in the New World.

Mestizo   A person of mixed parentage. Usually it refers to a European-indigenous mixture.

Mita   A forced labor system in which the indigenous were required to labor for Spanish settlers, taken from the Quechua and Aymara tradition.

Oidor   A judge on the *audiencias* of Spanish America.

Palenque   A settlement of runaway slaves in Spanish America.

Patria chica   Literally, the small country, it refers to the immediate region with which people identify rather than the nation.

Patrón   In Spanish America, the owner or boss or one in a superior position.

Peninsular   In Spanish America, a white born in Europe who later came to the New World.

Pleybeyos   Plebeians.   The lower classes, considered coarse and common by elites.

Porfiristas   Those in Mexico who supported Porfirio Díaz or his policies.

Porteño   An inhabitant of the city of Buenos Aires.

Presidencia   A subdivision of the viceroyalties of Spanish America, having a president as the chief executive officer.

Pueblo   A town, but it can also mean "people."

Quilombo   A settlement of runaway slaves in Portuguese America.

Regidor   Municipal councilman in Spanish America.

Reinol (plural, *reinóis*)   In Portuguese America, a white born in Europe who later came to the New World.

Relaçao   The high court in Portuguese America.

Repartimiento   A labor institution in colonial Spanish America in which a royal judge made a temporary allotment of indigenous workers for a given task.

Residencia   In both the Spanish and Portuguese American empires, a formal inquiry into the conduct of a public official at the end of his term of office.

Senado da Câmara   In Brazil, the municipal government, in particular the town council.

Sertão   The interior, backlands, or hinterlands of Brazil. The term refers particularly to the hinterland region of northeastern Brazil.

Sesmaria   A land grant in colonial Brazil.

Soldadera   During the Mexican Revolution, a woman who was attached to a soldier. The *soldaderas* cooked for the soldiers, tended the ill and wounded, and fought.

Tenente   In Brazil, an army lieutenant. The word is often used to denote those junior army officers during the 1920s and early 1930s who favored social, economic, and political reforms.

Tienda de raya   The store on an hacienda that sold resident workers their supplies, frequently at inflated prices.

Vecindad   Literally "neighborhood" in Spanish, but in Mexico City it can refer to a "tenement" dwelling.

Visita   In both the Spanish and Portuguese American empires, an on-the-spot administrative investigation of a public employee ordered by the monarch.

Visitador   In colonial Spanish and Portuguese America, an official in charge of making a special investigation for the monarch in the New World.

Zambo   A person of mixed indigenous and African parentage.

A Glossary
of Concepts
and Terms

Scattered throughout this text are a series of concepts and terms, some of which are defined—"reform" and "revolution," for example—and some of which are not—"capitalism," "socialism," and "Enlightenment," for example. The purpose of this glossary is to provide brief working definitions for the concepts and terms frequently encountered in the text. Definitions vary widely. They can be slippery. We have attempted to define the words in accordance with their use in the text, but we realize these definitions will neither satisfy everyone nor be universally applicable.

Capitalism   An economic system characterized by private ownership and investment, economic competition, wage labor and profit incentive.
Centralism   A high concentration of political power in the capital city.
Communism   Communism really denotes a future society, one yet to be achieved. Societies often termed Communist are really at best in a transitional phase whose goal is a form of community living free from hierarchical controls and enjoying common property. This book uses the term within a contemporary context to mean a government ruling in the name of the workers and peasants to best serve their ends and an economic system controlled by that government. The government

owns the means of production in the name of the workers and peasants. This text distinguishes socialism from communism by the degree of state ownership, by the degree of democracy, and the existence of a plurality of political parties.

Conservatism   The term is generally associated with nineteenth-century political parties whose disposition was to preserve things much as they were, exercising caution in the acceptance of change.

Democracy   A system of government in which all or most of the citizenry participate in the decision-making process. Western democracy stresses equality of all citizens before the law, a government responsive to the majority, regular elections, civil liberties, and plural political parties.

Dependency   Dependency describes a situation in which the economic well-being, or lack of it, of one nation, colony, or area results from the consequences of decisions made elsewhere. Latin America was first dependent on the Iberian motherlands, then in the nineteenth century on England, and in the twentieth on the United States, whose decisions and policies directly influenced, or influence, its economic prosperity or poverty. Obviously to the degree a nation is dependent, it will lack "independence" of action.

Development   The maximum use of a nation's potential for the greatest benefit of the largest number of inhabitants.

Developmentalism   The belief that adoption of programs aimed at economic growth would bring prosperity and the growth of a stabilizing middle class.

Elites   Those persons who occupy the highest or most eminent positions in society.

Enclave economy.   An economic activity that depends on little from the host country other than low-wage labor, rather than depending on local material imports or interactions with local businesses. A class example is the banana industry, in which local workers cut bunches of bananas that were immediately loaded onto foreign-owned ships and sent out of the country.

Enlightenment   Broadly identified with eighteenth-century Europe, the Enlightenment introduced a series of ideas associated with the forms of democracy and capitalism of the nineteenth century. The Enlightenment thinkers believed in human social evolution and thus a kind of philosophy of progress and perfectability. The ideas of the Enlightenment exerted a profound influence on the writing of the U.S. Constitution and on the ideology of the Latin American elites.

Federalism   In a federal political system, political power is divided and/or shared between a central government and regional or local governments.

Feudalism   Strictly speaking, this term refers to a form of social organization prevalent in Europe from the time of the dissolution of Charlemagne's empire until the rise of the absolute monarchies, roughly from the ninth to the fifteenth centuries. Its general characteristics were strict class division, private jurisdiction based on local custom, and a landowning system in which the owner, the lord, allowed the serf to work land in return for services and/or payments. By extension, the term is used in Latin America to designate a system in which a few own the land and control the lives of the many who work the land for them. Those few enjoy comfortable lives, while the workers live in misery largely dependent on the whims of the landowners. The term today has connotations much more emotional than legal.

Globalization   The increased interconnectedness of communications, economics and cultural exchange of the late twentieth and early twentieth centuries. The term frequently refers to economic changes interlinked with neoliberal trade policies.

Growth   Growth indicates numerical accumulation in a country or region's economy and generally does not reveal who, if anyone, benefits from it.

Hegemony   Refers both to dominance, as in the United States is the hegemonic power in the hemisphere, as well as an acceptance by the majority of the role of the dominant power. A government has hegemony when the majority of the citizens recognize the government's rights to rule.

Hybridity   A mixture of premodern, modern and postmodern ways of life characteristic of Latin America in the late twentieth and early twenty-first centuries. The term was coined by Argentine writer Néstor García Canclini.

Institutions   This book's most frequently used term and its most difficult to define, "institutions" represent the recognized usages governing relations between people, an entire complex of such usages and the principles governing it, and the formal organizations supporting such a complex. Perhaps Webster's unabridged dictionary offers a more satisfactory and comprehensive definition: "A significant and persistent element (as a practice, a relationship, an organization) in the life of a culture that centers on a fundamental human need, activity, or value, occupies an enduring and cardinal position within a society, and is usually maintained and stabilized through social regulatory agencies." Examples range from patriarchal families to the military, from village social structure to land division.

Liberalism   This term is generally associated with nineteenth-century political parties whose disposition was to relax governmental control, to expand individual freedom, and to innovate.

Liberation theology.   An interpretation of Christianity, based primarily in the Gospel of Luke, that cast Jesus as a liberator of the people. The term was coined by Peruvian theologian Gustavo Gutierrez in 1973, and the ideas were further elaborated by Brazilian priest Leonardo Boff.

Luso-Brazilian   This term encompasses both Portugal and Brazil. In Roman times, the area we now associate with Portugal bore the name Lusitania, the adjective being Luso.

Mercantilism   A term coined in the eighteenth century, it is a belief that the nation's economic welfare can best be ensured by governmental regulation of a nationalist character. The policy as imposed by the Iberian nations meant that the welfare of the motherlands received preferential treatment to those of the Latin American colonies, generally considered to exist for the enrichment of Spain and Portugal.

Metropolis   This term refers to that country exerting direct or indirect control over another. For Spanish America, the metropolis in the colonial period was Spain; for Brazil, Portugal. During the nineteenth century, the metropolis for Latin America was England; in the twentieth century it has been the United States.

Modernization   In Latin America, modernization consisted largely of copying and adopting, rarely adapting, the styles, ideas, technology, and patterns of Northern Europe in the nineteenth century and the United States in the twentieth.

Nationalism   This term refers to a group consciousness that attributes great value to the nation–state, to which total loyalty is pledged. Members of the group agree to maintain the unity, independence, and sovereignty of the nation–state as well as to pursue certain broad and mutually acceptable goals.

Nation–state   This term, implying more than the area encompassed by the geographic boundaries of a country, signifies that a central authority effectively exercises political power over that entire area.

Neofeudalism   *Neo*, from the Greek, signifies "new" or "recent." See the entry "feudalism."

Neoliberalism.   Market-oriented reforms begun in the 1990s that echoed the liberalism of the nineteenth century. Such reforms included privatization of state businesses and public services along with elimination of tariff barriers.

Oligarchy   These privileged few rule for their own benefit, demonstrating little or no responsibility toward the many.

Patriarchal, Patriarchy   This term refers to a type of family arrangement, or government, in which the father or an elderly male rules.

Patrimonialism   A system in which the landowner exerts authority over his followers as one aspect of property ownership. Those living on his land fall under his control. He rules the estate at will and controls all contact with the outside world. The term describes the hacienda system.

Postmodernism   A set of theories that posit postmodernity as the twentieth- and twenty-first-century condition of failed "modern" projects based on Enlightenment ideals and the belief in progress. Postmodern theorists argue against the overarching narrative of modern theories and instead see many truths and views in a decentered, fragmented world.

Physiocrat Doctrine   This concept originating in the eighteenth century urges society to survey scientifically its resources and, once knowing them, to exploit them. Maximum profit results from the exploitation and international sale of those resources.

Populist   Political movements or governments that seem at least outwardly opposed to the status quo are in some cases termed "populist." They advocate a system appealing to and supported by large numbers of the ordinary citizens, generally the urban working class. In practice, they often provide temporary relief or benefits without actually reforming basic social structures.

Positivism   This nineteenth-century ideology originated in France. Its principal philosopher was Auguste Comte. Positivism affirmed the inevitability of social innovation and progress. According to Comte, that progress was attainable through the acceptance of scientific social laws codified by Positivism.

Reform   To reform is to gradually change or modify established economic, political, or social institutions.

Revolution   Revolution denotes the sudden, forceful, and violent overturn of a previously stable society and the substitution of other institutions for those discredited.

Socialism   As used in this text, socialism denotes a democratic society in which the community owns or controls the major means of production, administering them for the benefit of all.

The Novel
as History:
A Reading Guide

It sometimes strikes students as odd to read literature in a history class. After all, history is supposedly nonfiction, "the truth," whereas fiction is a work of imagination. But the line between the two is not that clear cut—historians use their imaginations to envision and order the past into narratives on the basis of careful reading of documents. Novelists use their imaginations to envision and order reality into narratives as well, but they do so with passion, excitement, and lyricism that few historians or social scientists can ever match. If, for example, one wanted to understand how capitalism worked in England during the Industrial Revolution, one could read the works of many fine historians, one could read the analyses of Karl Marx, and one could read Charles Dickens.

Novels can be read as a primary source giving insight into the concerns and perceptions of people living in a particular place and time. The actual characters may indeed be fictional, but their feelings and experiences reflect the reality of the era in which the novelist lived. Novelists make extremely important observations about their own societies, transcending simple description and supposedly objective analysis to reveal feeling and emotion. On one level, the novel reflects the writer's world view on a topic. On another level, it is a document of and a mirror on a period. Further and very importantly, novels expose and sensitize their readers to Latin American viewpoints.

The historian and the novelist share much in common. Time, space, people, factual exposition, causation, and interpretation are the ingredients compounded by historians. They are also the essential components of the successful novels written by Latin Americans. A concern with "raw facts" and interpretation as well as the use of imagination link historians with novelists, certainly with the novelists recommended in this bibliographic essay.

Ignacio Manuel Altamirano, *Christmas in the Mountains* (Gainesville: University of Florida Press, 1961). *La Navidad en las Montañas* first appeared serially in Mexico in 1871. Altamirano, of indigenous descent and from a rural folk community, lamented the chaos and bloodshed of the first half-century of Mexico's independent life. His vision of an ideal society, combining the best qualities of the traditional rural folk community with some of the best qualities of Spanish-imposed institutions, illuminates *Christmas in the Mountains*. He provides a unique, articulate, and romanticized view of the folk community and the contributions it could make to national society and the nation–state. He idealizes patriarchal folk society in this novel of political solutions—or of utopia—one of the extremely rare favorable nineteenth-century discussions of that prevalent and much maligned society. The novel relates the experiences of a young army officer who spends a Christmas in a small, isolated Mexican mountain village. The idealized military and Church combine with the noble characteristics of a patriarchal folk community to create a seemingly perfect society. The symbolism of Christmas and a snow fall hangs heavily over this sometimes irritating but always fascinating novel, unquestionably one of the most important windows for a view of nineteenth-century Latin America.

Clorinda Matto de Turner, *Torn from the Nest* (New York: Oxford University Press, 1999). Matto de Turner ranks as one of the foremost female writers of nineteenth-century Latin America. This novel, *Aves sin Nido*, published in 1889, represents the first "Indianist" novel. It also was one of the first to note the consequences of the changes that modernization imposed. Born near Cuzco, Peru, where she lived much of her life, Matto de Turner discusses the plight of Peru's indigenous majority, abused, in her opinion, by the Church, the State, and large landowners. Matto de Turner saw change occurring through two media: education and the cities. The novel invests great faith in both to rescue the indigenous and to develop Peru. Fittingly, a train transports the villagers from the rural past to the urban future.

Aluisio Azevedo, *The Slum* (New York: Oxford University Press, 2000). On the opposite side of the South American continent from Matto de Turner, Azevedo was in the process of writing and publishing one of the first major novels of urbanization, *0 Cortiço* (1890), a study of Rio de Janeiro at a moment of agitated change. The novel deserves attention partly because of Azevedo's concern with social problems but mainly because of the insight he provides, a wealth of details about the routines of daily life of ordinary people. One aspect of Rio de Janeiro was its pervasive poverty; another was the social mobility it permitted. The novel also discusses lifestyles, nationalism, social conflict, the roles of women, and race relations.

Carlos Gagini, *Redemptions: A Costa Rican Novel* (San Diego: San Diego State University Press, 1985). The meanings derived from the symbolism saturating this short novel, originally published under the title of *El Arbol Enfermo* (1918), far outweigh in importance the rather insipid story. Gagini emphasizes the new social, economic, and political forces at work in Latin America. By 1918, Costa Rica, the locale of the novel, clearly had surrendered its economic independence and mortgaged its future to foreigners, realities that greatly disturbed nationalists like Gagini and provided a bitter backdrop for *Redemptions*. Also present in the novel is a significant new social reality: the emergence of very small urban working and middle classes. The author rather idealistically suggests the potential and benefits of their political alliance. Nationalistic apprehensions over foreign influences dominate the novel. Much of the novel directly or indirectly centers on the differences between Anglo and Latin cultures, and Gagini captures the ambivalence of Latin American elites toward the United States in the early twentieth century.

Mariano Azuela, *The Underdogs* (New York: A Signet Classic, 1996). *Los de Abajo* initially appeared as weekly installments in Mexico City's *El Universal Ilustrado* in 1924 and was published as a novel four years later. The first novel of the Mexican Revolution, it reflects the deep cynicism and disillusionment felt by Azuela, who served as a doctor in the army of Pancho Villa. The protagonist of the novel, Demetrio Martínez, joins the revolution because of his hatred of the local political boss, but by the end he no longer knows why he is fighting. He is surrounded by pillaging and raping soldiers, and a variety of opportunists, who articulate the ethical ideals that all too often were not realized.

Ricardo Güiraldes, *Don Segundo Sombra* (Pittsburgh: University of Pittsburgh Press, 1995). Bearing the same title when first published in Argentina in 1926, this novel marks a significant passage in the national life of Argentina: the end of folk culture and the triumph of the city and "civilization." Specifically, for Argentina it marked the passing of the *gaucho*, the cowboy of the Pampas, and the domination of one city, burgeoning Buenos Aires. The young protagonist grows up under the care of Don Segundo Sombra, the consummate gaucho. Upon the death of his father, the youth must abandon his cherished life as a gaucho to assume the responsibilities of a landowner, distancing himself from the everyday activities of the estate to link himself with the markets and businesses in Buenos Aires and abroad. His moving farewell to Don Segundo Sombra is, in fact, Argentina's farewell to its rural past and entrance into modernity, a highly complex break in Latin America, which arouses deeply contradictory feelings. The concluding chapters, with their profound emotions, expose an ambivalence within Latin America about modernization. *Don Segundo Sombra* exudes poetry. It suggests the major Latin American epic.

Gregorio Lopez y Fuentes, *El Indio* (New York: Frederick Ungar, 1961). The English translation bears the same title as the Spanish–language edition of 1935. In a few pages, this popular and highly symbolic Mexican novel relates the sweeping dynamic of Mexican history. The symbolic characters and events develop an allegory of race relations—and cultural clash—since the conquest. "Civilization" constantly encroaches on the indigenous, and the novel raises the question of what benefits, if any, they receive from it. In the final, provocative part of the novel, Lopez y Fuentes seems to see the Mexican Revolution as a further enactment of the conquest. The changes it wrought benefit the "whites," not the indigenous, who seem destined by the changes to eventual extinction. By extension, the observations of López y Fuentes can be applied to other peoples across time throughout Latin America, giving the novel a universality in its meaning.

Graciliano Ramos, *Barren Lives* (Austin: University of Texas Press, 1992). In 1938, the Brazilian published *Vidas Sêcas,* a penetrating insight into the lives of the impoverished rural masses, the so-called rural proletariat, which possesses no land of its own. Fabiano, his wife Vitoria, their two small sons, and their dog Baleia, flagellated by the drought in the dry interior of Northeastern Brazil, take refuge in an abandoned hut. The rains save them. Later, another drought and oppressive conditions start them on another journey, a cycle of migration common throughout Latin America. Fatalism, the sinew of tradition, permeates Fabiano. This novel highlights at least two significant themes: the relationship of the ordinary people to the land and the common people as victim of institutions they did not create, cannot influence, and apparently cannot change.

Rachel de Queiroz, *The Three Marias* (Austin: University of Texas Press, 1991). The first woman admitted to the Brazilian Academy of Letters, Queiroz wrote the mainly autobiographical *As Três Marías* in 1939. The novel details the lives of three young Marias reaching womanhood in a provincial Brazilian city, Fortazela, during the 1920s and 1930s. The three feel the frustrations of women facing inequality, educational and career restrictions, and the definition of their own sexual feelings. Through the eyes of Queiroz, the reader sees Brazil at a given moment as the women of that time did.

Ciro Alegría, *Broad and Alien Is the World* (New York: Dufour, 1987). The Peruvian novelist Alegría depicts the life and disintegration of an Andean indigenous community in his *El Mundo Es Ancho y Ajeno* (1941). Harmonious with their environment, rooted in their soil, the members of the community are contented and well provided for until outsiders apply the "law" to deprive them of their lands, a story as old as the conquest in Latin America but one that continues through the twentieth century. Alegría contrasts the folk community with advancing capitalism and chronicles the effects of the changes on the Andean indigenous communities. This meaty novel thus operates on the levels of a given reality and a powerful allegory.

Jorge Amado, *The Violent Land* (New York: Avon Books, 1988). The first Portuguese-language edition, *Terras do sem Fim*, appeared in 1943. Amado writes about the acquisition, use, abuse, maintenance, and loss of land. In particular, the novel focuses on the struggle of Horácio Silveira and Juca and Sinho Badaro over land whose rich soil produces the cacao tree, source of chocolate. It details the acquisition and ownership of land and all the institutions related to the struggle and possession. While it concerns only cacao lands, it could just as accurately depict sugar or coffee estates—or any other, for that matter. The story includes, among other topics, the grandeur and force of nature, the institutions surrounding the rural workers, the conflict of cultures, the roles of women, and the significance of frontiers.

Amado's *The Tent of Miracles* (New York: Avon, 1988), *A Tenda dos Milagres* (1969), is a tour de force, based loosely but unmistakably on the life of the remarkable Manuel Raimundo Querino (1851–1923), the first African-Brazilian historian. Taking as its locale the state of Bahia, once a focal point of African slavery, the novel wittily discusses the rich topic of race relations, the hypocrisies and the realities. The mature Amado amuses while he instructs his readers.

Miguel Angel Asturias, *El Señor Presidente* (Prospect Heights, Illinois: Waveland Press, 1997). The roots for this Guatemalan masterpiece lie in the repressive dictatorship of Manuel Estrada Cabrera, who terrorized that nation between 1898 and 1920. Asturias began it in 1922 but the completed novel (it carries the same name in the English translation as in Spanish) only appeared in 1946. It remains the author's best novel and a major Latin American classic. Asturias won the Nobel prize for literature in 1967. *El Señor Presidente* details Latin American authoritarianism and illuminates the phenomenon of the *caudillo*. The reader not only receives an understanding of how a dictatorship gains and retains power but, thanks to the powerful prose of Asturias, a "feeling" of its omnipotence and omniscience and its effects upon the population.

Mario Vargas Llosa, *The Time of the Hero* (London: Faber and Faber, 1995). Vargas Llosas's first novel, *La Ciudad y los Perros* (1962), drew on his own experience at the Leoncio Prado Academy to explore the brutal ways in which boys are made men in a society dominated by the military. The novel was considered to be such an accurate portrayal of the military school in Peru that the academy burned 1,000 copies of the book. Vargas Llosa continued to explore the themes of dictatorship and repression in 1969 with *Conversación en la Catedral* (*Conversation in the Cathedral*; New York: Rayo, 2005), a story told as multilayered conversation set in the 1950s.

Carlos Fuentes, *The Death of Artemio Cruz* (New York: Farrar, Strauss and Giroux, 1991). In *La Muerte de Artemio Cruz* (1962), the eminent Mexican intellectual Carlos Fuentes confronted a question increasingly on the mind of Mexicans: "Was the Mexican Revolution dead?" Through the novel's central character, Artemio Cruz, Fuentes sweeps across the twentieth century in an effort to address that challenging question. Cruz fought in the Revolution but later becomes a business tycoon who gets rich via land reform and foreign capital, betraying and reversing the Revolution.

Another Fuentes novel that looks with a jaundiced eye on Mexico's reality is *Christopher Unborn* (Normal, IL: Dalkey Archive Press, 2005). *Cristóbal Nonato*, originally published in 1987, is narrated by the unborn Christopher who will be born on the 500th anniversary of Columbus's discovery of the New World. The world Christopher will be born into is described by Fuentes as "Makesicko City," a victim of rapacious politicians, international capitalism, ecological disaster, and violence. The work was controversial in Mexico in part for Fuentes's use of Spanglish, a mixture of Spanish and English detested by Spanish-language purists but that Fuentes viewed as reflective of the cultural pastiche of the late twentieth century.

Gabriel García Márquez, *One Hundred Years of Solitude* (New York: Harper-Trade, 1998). Originally published in 1967 as *Cien Años de Soledad*, this classic is perhaps the best known Latin American novel and is the prototype of the genre of literature that García Márquez dubbed the magic of the real and that has come to be known as magical realism. The novel follows the fortunes and failures of the Buendía family in the small town of Macondo, and through their lives tells the story of all Latin America, from discovery through the modern era. Particularly powerful are his renditions of the endless wars between Liberals and Conservatives, the impact of the North American-owned banana enclave, and the bloody repression of a labor strike that the government denies ever happened. When he accepted the Nobel Prize for Literature in 1982, García Márquez explained that Latin America's incredible reality left a novelist nowhere to go but to the fantastic; nonetheless, he maintains that every sentence has its beginning in truth.

Manlio Argueta, *One Day of Life* (New York: Vintage, 1991). The Salvadoran edition of *Un Día de la Vida* was published in 1980. Repression and rebellion permeate this novel of rural life in El Salvador during civil war. Men are absent. They fled military recruitment or the vicious death squads. Women populate this powerful novel, expressing their viewpoint of the institutions being attacked and defended and maintaining their households and communities. The novel carefully documents the brutal intrusions of official institutions into rural community life, an old but still ubiquitous Latin American reality.

Isabel Allende. *The House of the Spirits* (New York: Knopf, 1985). Allende's first novel, *La Casa de los Espiritus* (1984), became an overnight sensation as she gave a distinctly female voice to magical realism. The novel tells the story of the Trueba family through much of the twentieth century. We see the large estate of the countryside juxtaposed with the wealth and poverty that stand side by side as the city grows. The tensions between rich and poor become manifested in the political struggle between right and left that divides the family as much as society. Though not as celebrated, Allende's *Of Love and Shadows* (New York: Knopf, 1987) is in many ways a more masterful novel than *House of the Spirits*. In some ways, *De Amor y de Sombra* (1985) can be seen as a sequel. The wealthy Irene Beltrán falls in love with the photographer, Francisco Leal, and as they follow the story of a girl whose fits are taken for miraculous powers, they uncover the horror of the wars waged by the government against their own people in South America.

Diamela Eltit, *The Fourth World* (Lincoln: University of Nebraska Press, 1995). The appearance of *El Cuarto Mundo* in 1988 established Diamela Eltit as one of the most provocative voices of the new postmodern fiction of Latin America. Eltit uses the dysfunctional family as a metaphor for dysfunctional society and the fragmentation of modern reality. The book itself is told in fragments, the first narrated by a young man, and the second by his twin sister. There are echoes of García Márquez, especially in the symbolism of incest, but refracted through a distorted lens, or perhaps a clear lens viewing a distorted reality.

Alberto Fuguet, *Bad Vibes* (New York: St. Martin's Press, 1997). There is much literary debate about whether *Mala Onda* is a good novel. It is certainly a controversial one. Fuguet was born in Chile but lived in California until he was twelve, when the family returned to Chile. He has vehemently rejected the Latin American literary style of magical realism as overly folkloric. He is frequently considered the leader of the McOndo movement, a play on the town of Macondo from the ultimate magical realist novel, García Márquez's *One Hundred Years of Solitude*. McOndo is also, of course, a play on McDonald's and the use of the "Mc" as a prefix to indicate the primacy of the market and globalization (McUniversity, McWorld, etc.). The novel is about drug-using, disaffected youth who seem to look inward more than at the Pinochet dictatorship under which they are living. Dismissed by some as nihilistic, it offers the voice of a new generation that is more transnational in outlook and more interested in the individual than the collective.

Roberto Bolaño, *By Night in Chile* (New York: New Directions Publishing Corporation, 2003). Bolaño is widely regarded as the most important Latin American novelist of his generation. His elegant novels focus on individuals at the margins who are swept into larger historic events, frequently the brutal Chilean Pinochet dictatorship, of which Bolaño himself was a victim. In *Chile Nocturno,* originally published in 2000, Bolaño writes a novel in the form of a monolog by a priest who confesses his role in the Pinochet regime. In the 1996 *Estrella Distante* (*Distant Star;* New York: New Directions Publishing Corp., 2004), his mysterious protagonist uses a vintage German warplane to skywrite poetry above a Pinochet concentration camp.

These novels barely scratch the surface of the lengthy list of those available in English translation. For readers of Spanish and/or Portuguese, new literary worlds await discovery. Those who want to pursue further the ways in which literature and history can be linked might begin with Frederick M. Nunn, *Collisions With History: Latin American Fiction and Social Science From "El Boom" to "the New World Order"* (Athens: Ohio University Center for International Studies, 2001); David T. Haberly, *Three Sad Races: Racial Identity and National Consciousness in Brazilian Literature* (New York: Cambridge University Press, 1983); John S. Brushwood, *Genteel Barbarism. New Readings of Nineteenth-Century Spanish-American Novels* (Lincoln: University of Nebraska Press, 1981).

For more on the novel, try Raymond L. Williams, *The Postmodern Novel in Latin America: Politics, Culture and the Crisis of Truth* (New York: St. Martin's Press, 1996); Philip Swanson, *The New Novel in Latin America: Politics and Popular Culture After the Boom* (New York: St. Martin's Press, 1995); Santiago Juan-Navarro and Theodore Robert Young , eds., *A Twice-Told Tale: Reinventing the Encounter in Iberian/Iberian American Literature and Film* (Newark: University of Delaware Press, 2001).

And for more on the fine line between fiction and history, see Nina Gerassi-Navarro, *Pirate Novels: Fictions of Nation Building in Spanish America* (Durham, NC: Duke University Press, 1999) and Sara Castro-Klarén and John Charles Chasteen, editors, *Beyond Imagined Communities: Reading and Writing the Nation in Nineteenth-Century Latin America* (Washington, DC: Woodrow Wilson Center Press, 2003).

Testimonio:
A Rich and
Complex Source

In the 1980s, a new genre from Latin American captivated readers who were eager to hear the voices of the voiceless, those without the power and education to write histories and novels. *Testimonio* is the testimony of the most disenfranchised people of Latin America about how they live their lives and, most importantly, about how they struggle against the dominant powers that try to victimize them. The genre arrived in academic and activist circles at the height of the movements in solidarity with the revolutions in Central America.

The voices of the voiceless are transmitted by interviewers and translators, generally referred to as interlocutors. The interviewer gathers the testimony and edits it into a coherent narrative to be transcribed, published, and translated. Questions immediately arose about the role of the interlocutor in shaping the narrative, much as historians shape the stories they tell from the raw material of documents. The readers, of course, do not exactly hear the voices of the voiceless; they hear the voices provided by editors and translators.

Testimonio has been defined by its most prominent scholar, John Beverley, as "a novel or novella-length narrative in book or pamphlet (that is, printed as opposed to acoustic) form, told in the first person by a narrator who is also the real protagonist or witness of the events he or she recounts, and whose unit of narration is usually a 'life' or a significant life experience. *Testimonio* may include, but is not subsumed under, any of the following textual categories, some of which are conventionally considered literature, others not: autobiography, autobiographical novel, oral history, memoir, confession, diary, interview, eyewitness report, life history, *novela-testimonio*, nonfiction novel, or 'factographic' literature."

The genre came to be exemplified by *I, Rigoberta Menchú: An Indian Woman in Guatemala* (London: Verso, 1984), which first appeared in Spanish in 1983 as *Me llamo Rigoberta Menchú y así me nació la conciencia* (My name is Rigoberta Menchú and this is how my consciousness was born). The book won the prize for best testimonial narrative for 1983 from the prestigious Casa de las Americas, and was translated into German, Italian, Dutch, Japanese, Danish, Norwegian, Russian, and Arabic. It became a central text in many Latin American history classrooms. The book's iconic status was solidified when Menchú was awarded the 1992 Nobel Peace Prize for her struggles in support of Guatemala's indigenous communities that were targeted under dictatorial rule.

But in 1999, the work of anthropologist David Stoll temporarily dislodged *I, Rigoberta* from the curriculum. Stoll, in his book *Rigoberta Menchú and the Story of All Poor Guatemalans* (Boulder, CO: Westview Press, 1999) found errors in Menchú's account that he used to attack the overall veracity of her story. Stoll's book generated a storm of controversy and a reappraisal of testimony as a reliable source.

Most academics concluded that the inaccuracies were minor in comparison to the general truth of her story: Perhaps not everything happened to Rigoberta exactly as described by Rigoberta via her interlocutor, Elisabeth Burgos-Debray. But everything did indeed happen to indigenous people in Guatemala, hence the portion of the testimony's title "The Story of All Poor Guatemalans."

Despite its problems, testimonio is an excellent source to provide yet another strand in the complex tapestry of Latin American history. Unfortunately, the number of academic studies of testimonio, often highly specialized and densely written, is much larger than the number of available testimonies themselves.

There are four classics of the genre:

Let Me Speak: Testimony of Domitila, A Woman of the Bolivian Mines. By Domitila Barrios de Chungara with Moema Viezzer. Translated by Victoria Ortiz. (New York: Monthly Review Press, 1978.) Barrios de Chungara tells the story of life in the tin mines of Bolivia as well as within the patriarchal society at large.

Miguel Mármol, interviewed by Roque Dalton. (Willimantic, CT: Curbstone Press, 1987.) Mármol, a founding member of the Communist Party of

El Salvador and a survivor of the 1932 *matanza,* is interviewed by
Dalton, the poet/revolutionary who was later killed by a rival faction
in El Salvador's guerrilla wars.

Don't Be Afraid, Gringo: A Honduran Woman Speaks From the Heart: The Story of
Elvia Alvarado. Translated and edited by Medea Benjamin. (San Francisco, CA: Institute for Food and Development Policy, 1987). Most
activists and academics in the 1980s focused on Nicaragua, El Salvador
and Guatemala. Alvarado gives testimony to the similar conditions of
hardship in this neighboring country.

I, Rigoberta Menchú: An Indian Woman in Guatemala (London: Verso, 1984).
Menchú provides a view into the indigenous cultures of Guatemala, as
well as the struggle for land and the genocidal war waged against the
indigenous and the revolutionary movements of the 1980s.

A book sometimes considered a part of the testimonio genre, although
it predates the categorization, is *Child of the Dark: The Diary of Carolina Maria*
de Jesus, translated from the Portuguese by David St. Clair (New York: New
American Library, 1962; republished in 2003). A Brazilian newspaper re-
porter met de Jesus when, on an assignment in a São Paulo favela, he heard
her threaten her neighbors, saying that she would write about them in her
book. The book turned out to be a remarkable diary written by a woman
with only two years of formal education. Excerpts were printed in the newspaper before the diary appeared in Portuguese as *Quarto de Despejo* (The
Trash Room) and eventually in translation around the world.

De Jesus and her work were revisited in the 1990s by historian Robert
M. Levine: *The Life and Death of Carolina Maria de Jesus,* by Levine and José
Carlos Sebe Bom Meihy (Albuquerque: University of New Mexico Press,
1995); *I'm Going to Have a Little House: The Second Diary of Carolina Maria de*
Jesus, translated by Melvin S. Arrington Jr. and Levine, afterword by Levine
(Lincoln: University of Nebraska Press, 1997); *Bitita's Diary: The Childhood*
Memoirs of Carolina Maria de Jesus, edited by Levine, translated by Emanuelle
Oliveira and Beth Joan Vinkler (Armonk, NY: M.E. Sharpe, 1998); and, par-
adoxically, *The Unedited Diaries of Carolina Maria de Jesus,* edited by Levine
and Bom Meihy, translated by Nancy P. S. Naro and Cristina Mehrtens (New
Brunswick, NJ: Rutgers University Press, 1999).

The many books by United States poet Margaret Randall are often cat-
egorized as testimonio, although some of the people whom she interviews
could certainly write their own accounts of their lives and therefore do not
represent the people whose voices we would not hear if not for these interlocutors. Among Randall's works are *Cuban Women Now: Interviews With*
Cuban Women (Toronto: Women's Press, Dumont Press Graphix, 1974);
Women in Cuba, Twenty Years Later, with photographs by Judy Janda (N.Y.:
Smyrna Press, 1981); *Sandino's Daughters: Testimonies of Nicaraguan Women in*
Struggle (New Brunswick, NJ: Rutgers University Press, 1995), originally

published in 1981; *Sandino's Daughters Revisited: Feminism in Nicaragua* (New Brunswick, NJ: Rutgers University Press, 1994); *Our Voices, Our Lives: Stories of Women From Central America and the Caribbean* (Monroe, ME: Common Courage Press, 1995).

Other collections of interviews with Latin American women include: *Brazilian Women Speak: Contemporary Life Stories*, edited and translated by Daphne Patai (New Brunswick, NJ: Rutgers University Press, 1988); *The Hour of the Poor, the Hour of Women: Salvadoran Women Speak*, edited and translated by Renny Golden (New York: Crossroad, 1991), and *Guatemalan Women Speak*, edited and translated by Margaret Hooks, with an introduction by Rigoberta Menchú (Washington, DC: Ecumenical Program on Central America and the Caribbean, 1993).

More recent entries in the genre are *Reyita: The Life of a Black Cuban Woman in the Twentieth Century*, by María de los Reyes Castillo Bueno, as told to her daughter, Daisy Rubiera Castillo (Durham, NC: Duke University Press, 2000), and *Doña María's Story: Life, History, Memory, and Political Identity* (Durham, NC: Duke University Press, 2000), in which James presents the testimony of María Roldán, a meatpacker, union activist, and Peronista, along with interpretive essays providing both a broader historical narrative and a critical assessment of the use of oral sources.

There are myriad books about the genre of testimonio. A good place to start would be with *On the Politics of Truth*, by John Beverley (Minneapolis: University of Minnesota Press, 2004); *The Real Thing: Testimonial Discourse and Latin America*, edited by Georg M. Gugelberger (Durham, NC: Duke University Press, 1996); and *Testimonio: Woman as Witness: Essays on Testimonial Literature by Latin American Women*, edited by Linda S. Maier and Isabel Dulfano (New York: Peter Lang, 2004). For the controversy on Rigoberta Menchú, see *The Rigoberta Menchú Controversy*, edited by Arturo Arias, with a response by David Stoll (Minneapolis : University of Minnesota Press, 2001).

INDEX